COMPARATIVE POLITICS

Citizens, Democracy, and Markets Around the Pacific Rim

COMPARATIVE POLITICS

Comparative Politics is a series for students and teachers of political science that deals with contemporary issues in comparative government and politics. As Comparative European Politics it has produced a series of high quality books since its foundation in 1990, but now takes on a new form and new title for the new millennium—Comparative Politics. As the process of globalization proceeds, and as Europe becomes ever more enmeshed in world trends and events, so it is necessary to broaden the scope of the series. The General Editors are Professor Alfio Mastropaolo, University of Turin and Kenneth Newton, University of Southampton and Wissenschaftszentrum Berlin. The series is published in association with the European Consortium for Political Research.

OTHER TITLES IN THIS SERIES

Democratic Challenges, Democratic Choices
Russell J. Dalton

Democracy Transformed?
Edited by Bruce E. Cain, Russell J. Dalton, and Susan E. Scarrow

Environmental Protest in Western Europe
Edited by Christopher Rootes

Social Movements and Networks
Edited by Mario Diani and Doug McAdam

Delegation and Accountability in Parliamentary Democracies
Edited by Kaare Strøm, Wolfgang C. Müller, and Torbjörn Bergman

The Presidentialization of Politics
Edited by Thomas Poguntke and Paul Webb

Losers' Consent
Christopher J. Anderson, André Blais, Shaun Bowler, Todd Donovan, and Ola Listhaug

Elections, Parties, Democracy
Michael D. McDonald and Ian Budge

Citizens, Democracy, and Markets Around the Pacific Rim

Congruence Theory and Political Culture

Edited by

RUSSELL J. DALTON

AND

DOH CHULL SHIN

ecpr

OXFORD

UNIVERSITY PRESS

This book has been printed digitally and produced in a standard specification in order to ensure its continuing availability

OXFORD
UNIVERSITY PRESS

Great Clarendon Street, Oxford OX2 6DP

Oxford University Press is a department of the University of Oxford.
It furthers the University's objective of excellence in research, scholarship,
and education by publishing worldwide in

Oxford New York

Auckland Cape Town Dar es Salaam Hong Kong Karachi
Kuala Lumpur Madrid Melbourne Mexico City Nairobi
New Delhi Shanghai Taipei Toronto

With offices in

Argentina Austria Brazil Chile Czech Republic France Greece
Guatemala Hungary Italy Japan South Korea Poland Portugal
Singapore Switzerland Thailand Turkey Ukraine Vietnam

Published in the United States
by Oxford University Press Inc., New York

Reprinted 2008

ISBN 978-0-19-929725-2

Preface

East Asia is in the midst of a process of fundamental political and economic change—such periods are typically fraught with perils and opportunities. This volume is one of the first attempts to gauge public opinions toward democracy and markets across the region, and thus evaluate the current conditions in East Asia and the prospects for the future from the standpoint of the citizenry.

Indeed, one example of these fundamental changes is this project. Until recently, systematic survey evidence on public opinion across East Asia was not available. Surveys were conducted mostly in individual nations, but even these were typically limited to the consolidated democracies in the region. As a result, there was little comparative empirical evidence on public opinion, and a comparative study like this was unimaginable.

The 1999–2002 World Values Survey (WVS) (www.worldvaluessurvey.org) is the first major cross-national study of public opinion in East Asia, and that is linked to a larger study of public opinion on global scale. This book is based on national public opinion surveys in eight East Asian nations: China, Indonesia, Japan, the Philippines, Singapore, South Korea, Taiwan, and Vietnam. In addition, we compare opinions in Asia to those of four established Western democracies of the Pacific Rim: Australia, Canada, New Zealand, and the United States. Thus, this project illustrates the changes occurring in East Asia.

In addition, we would like to especially thank Ng Chun Hung for providing additional data from the 2005 'Hong Kong Values Survey', which is part of a larger project on 'Hong Kong Creativity Index' commissioned and funded by the government of the Hong Kong Special Administrative Region. This survey replicated large portions of the WVS. Even though this survey was conducted in 2005, we were able to include some of the basic findings on aggregate support for democracy in Chapter 4.

The contributors to this volume use these national surveys to examine the rich theorizing from prior ethnographic studies of East Asian public opinion and political culture, and the insights of single nation surveys, with the methodology of empirical survey research. Scholarship had depended on expert descriptions of the political cultures of East Asia—now we can consult the public themselves. This new empirical evidence is challenging the previous literature on several fronts. Claims about 'Asia values' for instance, seem overstated when one examines the actual opinions and values of publics in East Asia. Presumptions about the potential for further democratization in the region also change when one sees the breadth of democratic aspirations expressed by Asian publics. Similarly, despite the critiques of globalization and marketization by some Asian elites, we find that public opinion appears more supportive than previously presumed. In short, we believe that the insights provided by the WVS will challenge many of the prevailing scholarly views about political and economic values of East Asian publics.

In addition, this project is also significant in illustrating changes in the study of East Asian publics and political culture. Asia has been a traditional field of area studies, and most research still focuses on single nations. Most research also is based on the insights and research resources of individual scholars. There is tremendous value from this research in generating theory and in providing a detailed knowledge of each nation in East Asia, but the public opinion field is changing. The WVS is an example of a new wave of cross-national studies of the region, often embedded in even larger studies of global publics. In this new paradigm, teams of researchers from individual nations collaborate to collect comparable survey evidence—and then the research focus shifts to the study of nations in a comparative context. Survey data on Japan is valuable in understanding Japanese public opinion, but it is even more valuable if Japanese opinions can be studied in reference to other nations. Rudyard Kipling described the logic of comparative politics when he said: ‘And what should they know of England, who only England knows?’ The same applies to research on Japan, or China, or other single nation projects. Comparative politics must compare.

The WVS was the first large-scale project to survey East Asian public opinion. It was quickly followed by the East Asian Barometer project, and the Asia Barometer project.[1] Other surveys have been done by the Pew Center for People and the Press, and other international teams.[2] There is so much to learn, to compare, and to investigate in this new field of comparative public opinion research in East Asia that this should be a rich field for all these projects. Indeed, we hope our colleagues in these other projects critically test and challenge our findings, since this is how we can develop a more systematic understanding of public opinion in the region.

We also hope that these surveys mark a new age of comparative public opinion research in East Asia. Part of this development requires the sharing of data among scholars. The WVS is available from the Inter-university Consortium for Political and Social Research at the University of Michigan and other national social science archives. The data are also included on a CD-ROM in the data handbook from the project (Inglehart et al. 2004). The Asia Barometer data are also distributed on a CD-Rom in the projects data handbook (Inogouchi 2005). The East Asian Barometer is distributed through the project website (http://eacsurvey.law.ntu.edu.tw/). In addition, as part of this project we assembled a list of survey data sources across East Asia (www.democ.uci.edu/resources/asia.php). The development of an Asian Consortium for Political Research is another step in facilitating comparative studies across the region. Mao did not have survey research in mind, but his admonition to 'let a hundred flowers bloom' certainly fits the current blossoming of comparative public opinion research in East Asia.

Finally, we want to acknowledge the support of the many people who contributed to the 1999–2002 WVS and this volume. Ronald Inglehart has directed the WVS, and without his efforts, this project would not be possible. Thorleif Petersson has been instrumental in the 1999–2002 wave, and especially in obtaining funding for several of the Asian surveys. We also owe a debt of thanks to the national teams that collected the surveys in each nation, and they are listed in Appendix A to this volume.

Dr Choong Nam Kim of the East West Center in Hawaii also provided essential support for this project. Both Dalton and Shin were POSCO Fellows at the East West Center; the EWC provided partial funding for the conference where these analyses were first presented. It has been our great pleasure to work with Kim and the other excellent people at the East West Center. Funding for the EWC conference was provided by the Center for the Study of Democracy at the University of California, Irvine, the Research Board at University of Missouri, and the POSCO program.

Throughout the project, a large number of colleagues read chapters, commented on our findings, or offered fresh perspectives on this evidence. We would like to thank Robert Albritton, Tom Bernstein, Yun-han Chu, Larry Diamond, Wang Feng, Takaski Inogouchi, Hans-Dieter Klingemann, Chong-Min Park, Kamal Sadiq, Tianjin Shi, Dorie Solinger, Yang Su, Arun Swamy, Jack Van Der Slik, and William Zimmerman for their critical advice. All the contributors to this volume also exchanged comments and engaged in a dialogue about our joint findings. This was one of the main advantages of the EWC conference, and we think that has greatly improved the final volume. We also appreciated and benefited from the comments from the anonymous Oxford University Press reviewers.

We want to express our appreciation to Dominic Byatt at Oxford University Press. Dominic has supported this volume and offered the encouragement and advice throughout the production process. Working with Oxford University Press has been the rewarding and enjoyable experience that authors hope for. And Willy Jou provided valuable assistance in developing the index for this volume.

Finally, for generations, scholars have written about the opinions and values of the people of East Asia—but seldom have the people had their own voice in such a direct manner as a representative opinion survey. Through our interviews with tens of thousands of individual citizens, the WVS gives these people the opportunity to express their views about their society, economy, and political system, not just in the consolidated democracies where opinion polls are common, but also in the nations where the public's voice is less often heard. We hope this project gives all these citizens a new voice.

Russell J. Dalton, Irvine, CA
Doh Chull Shin, Columbia, Mo

ENDNOTES

1 The East Asia Barometer website is: http://eacsurvey.law.ntu.edu.tw The AsiaBarometer website is: http://avatoli.ioc.u-tokyo.ac. jp/~asiabarometer/

2 The Pew Center website is: http://pewglobal.org/

Contents

List of Figures

List of Tables

List of Contributors

Ahn Chung-Si is professor in the Department of Political Science, Seoul National University. Ahn is currently the president of the Korean Association of International Studies; he is also the president of the International Political Science Associations's (IPSA) Research Committee on the Politics of Local-Global Relations. Ahn has published over 100 articles and book chapters in both Korean and English and authored/coauthored/edited 25 books (including six in English) on South Korea's national and local politics, ASEAN and Southeast Asia, and East Asian international affairs. His recent English publications include *Koreans and Korean Business Interests in Central Europe and CIS Countries* (1998) and *Politics and Economy of Regime Transformations: Case Studies of South Korea and Central European Countries* (1999). He is currently developing two books on South Korea and Asian politics: *New Developments of Local Democracy in Asia* and *Korea in Changing Regional and Global World* (with Choong Nam Kim and Lee-Jay Cho, East-West Center, Hawaii)

Russell J. Dalton is professor of Political Science and former director of the Center for the Study of Democracy at the University of California, Irvine. He has been a Fulbright Professor at the University of Mannheim, a German Marshall Research Fellow and a POSCO Fellow. His scholarly interests include comparative political behavior, political parties, social movements, and empirical democratic theory. His recent publications include *Democratic Challenges, Democratic Choices* (2004), *Citizen Politics* (2006), *and The Green Rainbow: Environmental Interest Groups in Western Europe* (1994); he coauthored *Critical Masses: Citizens, Environmental Destruction, and Nuclear Weapons Production in Russia and the United States* (1999); and is editor of *Democracy Transformed?* (2003) and *Parties without Partisans* (2001).

Ken'ichi Ikeda received his Ph.D. in social psychology from the University of Tokyo. Currently he works as the Chair and Professor for the Department of Social Psychology, the University of Tokyo. He was the president of Japanese Association of Election Studies (2004–5). His research area covers political behavior, social networks, and the effects of mass communication as well as computer-mediated communication from the viewpoint of social reality construction. He is the author of several books: *Changing Reality of Politics* (1997), *Networking Community* (1997), and *Communication* (2000). He also publishes his papers in *Political Behavior*, *Political Psychology*, *Japanese Journal of Political Science*, and *The Japanese Journal of Electoral Studies*. Now as the principal investigator, he is directing Japanese Election Study 3 (2001–6 National Panel survey) comparable to the ANES study.

Ronald Inglehart is a professor of Political Science and Program Director at the Institute of Social Research, University of Michigan. Since 1988, he has directed the World Values Surveys. Author of more than 170 publications, his recent books include *Modernization and Postmodernization: Cultural, Economic and Political Change in 43 Societies* (1997); (with Chris Welzel) *Modernization, Cultural and Democracy: The Human Development Sequence* (2005); and (with Pippa Norris) *Gender Equality and Cultural Change* (2003). Recent articles include (with Wayne Baker) 'Modernization, Cultural Change and the Persistence of Traditional Values', in *American Sociological Review*. (2000); 'How Solid is Mass Support for Democracy—And How Do We Measure It ?', in *PS: Political Science and Politics* (2003).

Jiho Jang is an assistant professor in the Department of Public Administration, Han Kook University of Foreign Studies. He received his Ph.D. in Political Science from the University of Missouri at Columbia. His research interests include industrial policy, institutionalism, and the relationship between government and business.

Nhu-Ngoc Thuy Ong is a Ph.D. candidate in Political Science and a Peltason Democracy Fellow at University of California, Irvine. She helped conduct the first Vietnamese World Values Survey in 2001. Her research interests include Asian-American politics and the democratization process in Asia. Among her publications are 'Civil Society and Social Capital in Vietnam', in *Social Modernization in Vietnam*, and 'Social Capital and Social Relations in Vietnam', in *Comparative Sociology*.

Pham Minh Hac is professor of Psychology and Director of Institute for Human Studies,Vietnamese Academy of Social Sciences. His scholarly interests include the education, personality psychology, and human studies. His recent publications include *Vietnam's Education at Threshold of XXI Century* (1998, 2002), *Human Studies and Human Resourse Studies* (2001), *Psychological Research* (2003), and *Behavior and Activity* (2003).

Pham Thanh Nghi is associate professor of Psychology and Deputy Director of the Institute of Human Studies at the Vietnamese Academy of Social

Sciences. He has been a Fulbright Scholar at the State University of New York, Buffalo, and a Japan Foundation Research Fellow at the University of Nagoya. His scholarly interests include higher education management, psychology applied in higher education, social and cultural change in traditioanl contexts and human resource management. His recent publications include *Quality Management in Higher Education* (2000), *Strategic Management in Colleges and Universities* (2000), and *Policy and Planning in Higher Education* (1999).

Doh Chull Shin is professor of Political Science at the University of Missouri at Columbia, and holds the Korea Foundation and Middlebush chairs. He has been a Fulbright Professor at Seoul National University, a visiting scholar at the Nordic Institute of Asian Studies in Denmark and the University of Cape Town in South Africa, a Social Science Research Council fellow, and an East-West Center fellow. Since 1988, he has directed the Korean Democracy Barometer program monitoring the cultural and institutional dynamics of democratization in Korea, and he is one of the founding members of the East Asia Barometer program. His scholarly interests include cultural values, democratic regime change, market reform, and the quality of life. His recent publications include *Mass Politics and Culture in Democratizing Korea* (1999), *Institutional Reform and Democratic Consolidation in Korea* (2000), *The Quality of Life in Korea* (2003), and *Economic Crisis and Dual Transition in Korea* (2004).

Tan Ern-Ser is associate professor, Department of Sociology, and Academic Convener, Singapore Studies Program, Faculty of Arts and Social Sciences, at the National University of Singapore. He received his Ph.D. in Sociology from Cornell University. He is principal investigator of the World Values Survey, Singapore Chapter. He has written on industrial relations, welfare policy, ethnic relations, social stratification, and political values. He is author of *Does Class Matter? Social Stratification and Orientations in Singapore* (2004), and coeditor of *Understanding Singapore Society* (1997) and *Tourism Management and Policy: Perspectives from Singapore* (2001).

Zhengxu Wang recently received his Ph.D. from the University of Michigan. His research focuses on the impact of citizens' values and behaviors on democratization. He also studies political changes in China. A recent work of his on political trust in China was published by *International Review of Sociology*, other articles and book chapters are to be published. He is currently a visiting research fellow at the East Asian Institute of the National University of Singapore.

Christian Welzel is Professor of Political Science at the International University Bremen (IUB). He is a member of the Executive Committee of the World Values Surveys Association. Author of more than 60 publications, his recent article is "Democratization as an Emancipative Process" (2006). His recent book (with Ronald Inglehart) is *Modernization, Cultural and Democracy: The Human Development Sequence* (2005).

1

Citizens, Democracy, and Markets

Russell J. Dalton and Doh Chull Shin

Democracy and the market economy are two sides of a coin, or two wheels of a cart. Every nation that has embraced both democracy and a market economy has been successful

—*Kim Dae Jung*
(Inaugural address, 1998)

Two historic processes are transforming East Asia. The first process, and the better known, is the region's economic development. Today, East Asia represents one of the most dynamic parts of the global economy. As the world's fastest growing region, it is rapidly closing the economic gap between itself and the Western advanced industrial societies. In the past two decades, the region has experienced an average annual GDP growth rate of nearly 8 percent. As recently as 1970, some of the now affluent East Asian nations had income levels comparable to many poor African nations. Today, citizens in some East Asian nations are as much as four times wealthier than they were just a single generation ago. East Asia, including Japan, currently accounts for more than 20 percent of the world economy and 24 percent of world trade (World Bank 2002). In terms of both the magnitude and speed of change, no other region of the world has recently experienced economic transformation to a greater extent than East Asia.

Japan and the four East Asian tigers—South Korea, Taiwan, Hong Kong, and Singapore—are known as 'miracle economies' because their accomplishments are unparalleled in the history of economic development. They have registered large, sustained economic growth rates over decades, while keeping relatively low levels of inequality in wealth and income distribution. Following the policies of export-growth and state guidance of industrialization that Japan initiated in the early 1960s, three other countries in the region—Indonesia, Malaysia, and Thailand—have achieved rapid and sustainable economic growth. However, these examples of economic development were often based on incestuously close relationships between corporations and the government—sometimes called 'crony capitalism' or directed capitalism—that stopped short of free and open market competition.

In 1997, the worst financial crisis since World War II hit East Asia. The crisis ended the decades of rapid economic expansion and shattered the ideological foundation of crony capitalism (Dore 1998). Consequently, many Asian governments have sought to transform this system of directed or crony capitalism into market capitalism by restructuring financial institutions and corporate governance, privatizing public industries, deregulating private industries, and liberalizing international trade (Weiss 1999; Stigliz and Yusuf 2001). In Indonesia, Malaysia, South Korea, and Thailand, the costs of restructuring banks and other financial institutions alone range from 16 to 50 percent of their GDPs. Thus, the marketization process has followed an uneven course in Asia.

Communist China and Vietnam also have moved toward market capitalism in recent years with a 'socialist market economy' formula. Both countries, for example, are ending the practices of central planning of the economy. These two nations abandoned the collective farming system and granted individual households long-term use rights over land and the freedom to cultivate it as they wished. They also liberalized prices, foreign exchange, and external trade and investment. In the case of China, private enterprises currently produce 75 percent of its GNP. Most notably, the National People's Congress amended its Constitution in March 2004 to formally adopt the capitalist principle of private property: 'Private property obtained legally is inviolable'. At a slower pace, economic policy reforms are restructuring the Vietnamese economic system.

In overall terms, the economic transformation of East Asia has been nothing short of miraculous. Living conditions in many nations are now several times better than a generation ago. From Shanghai to Seoul, people today enjoy a lifestyle and life chances that are far removed from those of their grandparents. There are high-literacy rates in most nations of the region, increased access to information, and a globalized economy is increasing exposure to international norms. These economic changes are the most visible signs of a general process of social modernization in the region.

The second process of transformation has evolved slowly, and is perhaps less recognized outside of the region: Asia's participation in the third wave of democratization. The democratization wave began in 1986 when the 'people power' revolution swept the Marcos regime from power in the Philippines, recreating a democracy system of government. Taiwan and South Korea experienced historic transitions in the following year, with the introduction of free, competitive elections that began a relatively steady process of democratization. Mongolia made a rapid transition from Soviet vassal state to a democracy in the early 1990s. Military rule in Thailand ended in 1992 with a return to a civilian controlled government, and eventually the institution of free elections. In 1998, anti-government demonstrations brought an end to the 32-year rule of Suharto, charting Indonesia on a new democratic course that culminated in the 2004 presidential elections.

This democratization wave in East Asia means that more than 400 million people now live in new democratic political systems. These developments have significantly changed the political map of East Asia. In 1975, the Freedom House rated only one nation of the thirteen nations in East Asia as a free electoral democracy (this was Japan); by 2005, democracies exist in almost half of the nations in the region.[1] This trend has produced a dramatic change in the political rights and life chances of the people in many East Asian nations, but it is an incomplete process, since half the nations in the region remain non-democratic, or only partly free.

Some scholars argue that social modernization is increasing the potential for further democratization in East Asia (Neher and Marlay 1995; Diamond 2003; cf. Bueno de Mesquita and Downs 2005). Indeed, the modernization literature has long argued that economic development encourages democratic development (see the discussion in Chapter 2). Increased living standards, a more complex economy, increased literacy, and integration into the global system should eventually promote democratization in East Asia if the modernization thesis is correct. Thus, the potential for further democratic development exists. Bruce Gilley (2003), for instance, is provocatively asking how democratization will occur in China, and where it will lead. Imagine how the world could be transformed if China became democratic (also see Tang 2005).

However, other analysts maintain that national traditions and political culture may lead to different developmental courses. Prominent government leaders in East Asia directly challenge the applicability of liberal democratic politics to the region. Confucianism and 'Asia values' are regularly offered as a reason for the region's stunted democratic development (Lee 1994; Emmerson 1995; and see extensive discussion in Chapter 5). The adherence to traditional authority structures, the paternalistic norms, and rejection of individualism have sometimes been cited as factors retarding the development of democracy. Lee Kuan Yew's and Mahathir Mohamad's polemic statements on these points were widely cited in the popular and elite press, but more nuanced versions of this same logic have been offered by leading academic scholars of the region (Pye 1985, 1999; Scalapino 1989; Huntington 1996; Zakaria 2003; Chua 2003).

The evolution of political and economic reforms in East Asia will most immediately depend on the actions of political elites and other major political actors in these nations. At the same time, political culture theory maintains that longer-term development should be linked to popular orientations toward the political and economic systems (Almond and Verba 1963; Pye 1965; Inglehart 1997). Previous research has stressed the role of political culture in the development of democracy in Japan, South Korea and Taiwan (Richardson 1978; Xu 1999; Shin 1999). Culture can have an influential role in shaping future political and economic development in the region.

Thus, this book examines whether the values and orientations of East Asian publics are congruent with the development of democratic institutions and market economies in these societies. Although survey research on political culture is rapidly developing, the current body of evidence on East Asian political culture is incomplete and often limited to single nation studies. In addition, the questions of cultural congruence are central to understanding current conditions and future prospects for the region—and provide a critical case for testing congruence theory.

Until now, the nature of citizen values in East Asia has been debated by elites—with little systematic, representative cross-national evidence to substantiate claims on either side. The research evidence was often indirect, coming from observation of social norms, or nonrepresentative measurements of opinions. Scientific research on public opinion has typically been limited to nations that had consolidated their democratic development. Without broader evidence on the attitudes of people in the region, contending descriptions of political and economic values are inevitable.

Our project gives voice to the citizens of East Asia and adds this evidence on public opinion to the debate on the region's development. We draw upon a new set of coordinated national opinion surveys conducted as part of the World Values Survey (WVS) project (Inglehart et al. 2004). The WVS examines public opinion across a wide range of East Asian nations, and compares the Asian findings to the established Western democracies of the Pacific Rim. Most of the contributors to this volume are principal investigators who collected the WVS data, or who participate in the WVS network of scholars.

We have two broad research goals. First, much of the modernization literature treats political culture as an integral part of this process. East Asia is an important test case for this theory. To what extent has the past socioeconomic development of the region transformed citizen attitudes and values, or have historical and cultural traditions produced different developmental paths in these nations? Our project describes the level of support for democracy and markets across East Asia using representative national public opinion surveys. Although there is some empirical public opinion research in single nations, cross-national comparisons can improve our understanding of national patterns by placing each nation in a comparative perspective. Thus, our findings should illuminate the match of public values with political and economic systems in the region.

Second, the significance of opinions is partially dependent on the forces that are shaping them. Much of this volume is devoted to analyzing the sources of support for democracy and/or markets, especially the modernization processes that may be reshaping cultural traditions over time. Again, the WVS is an exceptionally rich resource for these analyses, because of the cross-national and cross-temporal breadth of the surveys, and the rich collection of questions asked in these surveys.

THE FRAMEWORK OF CONGRUENCE THEORY

One of the most powerful social science concepts to emerge in political behavior research—and one central to the study of citizen attitudes and behavior—is the concept of political culture. Tocqueville, for instance, wrote that democracy should develop as a habit of the heart reflecting basic values and patterns of social relations: 'The manners of the people may be considered as one of the great general causes to which the maintenance of a democratic republic in the United States is attributable' (Tocqueville 1945: 299). Almond and Verba's seminal study (1963), *The Civic Culture*, contended that the institutions and patterns of action in a political system are closely linked to the political culture of the nation. They described set of political values—tolerance, participatory norms, and political trust—that supported a democratic political process. Culturalist studies have been especially important in the early study of democratization, as analysts tried to identify the cultural requisites of democracy (Almond and Verba 1963, 1980; Eckstein 1966; Pye and Verba 1965). A similar argument could be made for the development of a modern, capitalist market (Inkeles and Smith 1974; Inglehart and Baker 2000).

Embedded in political culture research are several concepts that we draw upon in our project. Most basic is the concept of *congruence*. The political culture literature argues that stable political systems tend to have cultures and institutions that are congruent with one another. For instance, authoritarian states often depend on a deferential public that accepts the power of the state (or lacks the political skills and resources to challenge the state). The archetypical authoritarian example is Germany in the early twentieth century, where an undemocratic and intolerant public undermined the democratic Weimar Republic and eventually supported the consolidation of the Third Reich. Thus, the challenge for post-World War II Germany—and other non-democratic states—is to develop a political culture congruent with a democratic political order.

Even before the Third Wave democratic transitions, political culture studies were demonstrating the general principle of congruence. Drawing on the 1981 WVS, Inglehart demonstrated the congruence between broad political attitudes and democratic stability for twenty-two nations (Inglehart 1990, Chapter 1).[2] Putnam's research (1993) on regional governments in Italy provided even more impressive testimony in support of cultural theory. Putnam used an imaginative array of government performance measures to show that the cultural traditions of a region—roughly contrasting the cooperative political style of the North to the more hierarchic tradition of the South—were a potent predictor of democratic performance. Even more telling, Putnam showed that cultural factors were more influential than economic conditions in explaining democratic performance, and cultural factors reflected historical patterns of civic association. The Afrobarometer found a strong correspondence between public support for democracy and the extent of democracy across twelve African nations (Bratton, Mattes, and Gyimah-Boadi 2004).

Four aspects of congruence theory are relevant to the topics of this volume, and run through the analyses of various chapters. Briefly we can outline each as a framework for the analyses that follow.

The Congruence of Social and Political Values

A first aspect of congruence theory focuses on the sources of political values. The political culture literature views political values as derived from the broader pattern of authority relations in a society. Eckstein (1966, 1998), for example, argued that authority relations in the family, schools, social associations, and the workplace create norms that are then carried over to the world of politics. This is a major theme in the political culture literature. Almond and Verba (1963) saw the pattern of authority relations in the family and the schools as sources of the political culture. In the German case in particular, analysts argued that the authoritarian and patriarchal German family disposed the German public to accept these same patterns in the behavior of the Kaiser (Dahrendorf 1967). The literature also claimed that a democratic political culture is based on a highly developed associational life in society, the hallmark of what is now generally called 'civil society'. This stress on social associations spans the literature from Tocqueville's description of American democracy in the 1800s to the democratic transitions of Eastern Europe in the 1990s (Rueschemeyer Rueschemeyer, and Wittrock 1998; Howard 2003).

The congruence between social and political relations in East Asia is a central theoretical and political question of our project. Just as the German father was presumably the model for accepting the Kaiser, the hierarchic paternalistic traditions of many Asian families may lead to acceptance of autocratic political leaders. Lucian Pye, for example, summarized this view: 'Throughout the Confucian cultural area of Asia, the family was considered the proper model of government. Relations between ruler and subject were seen as analogous to those between parent and child' (1985: 61; also Pye 1999). Similarly, Lee Kuan Yew of Singapore and Mahathir Mohamad of Malaysia argued that Western liberal democratic was incompatible with Asian values and undersirable for the region (Emmerson 1985). More nuanced versions of this same logic have been offered by leading academic scholars of the region (Scalapino 1989; Huntington 1996; Zakaria 2003). In addition, it is claimed that the limited development of autonomous civil society groups in East Asia, even in democratic regimes, limits the social learning of democratic norms and civic virtues.

This argument about traditional, hierarchic pattern of authority relations in Asia has been challenged on two grounds. First, Friedman (1994*a*), Sen (1999), and others, stress the cultural diversity of East Asia, and the ability of democratic norms to take root in many different types of cultural traditions. In addition, other social values identified with Confucian traditions, such as norms of cooperation and collective interests, may provide a social basis for developing democratic political norms (also Fukuyama 1995).

Second, the social modernization literature suggests that the tremendous economic advances in many East Asian nations over the past generation should have changed public values. Increasing living standards provide new resources to become socially and politically active. An increasingly complex economic system creates new skills and a sense of personal efficacy among the public. And in a world of growing international trade and global interaction, modernization also increases exposure to liberal political norms, where closed states may have limited this exposure in the past (Sandholtz and Gray and 2003). In short, as social modernization transforms social relations and living conditions in East Asian societies, this should produce changes in political norms as well.

Scott Flanagan and Aie-rie Lee (2000, 2003), for example, demonstrated that social modernization variables are strongly related to support for more libertarian (less authoritarian) values in Japan and Korea (also see Nathan 2004; Shin 1999). One sees similar examples of changing family and work relations as a by-product of social modernization in China, Vietnam and other Asian societies. Others claim a substantial growth in civil society groups in East Asia, which are theorized to produce the social wellspring of democratic values (Alagappa 2004). In other words, the tremendous social change that many East Asian nations have experienced over the past generation may have altered the social relations that created 'Asian values'.

Thus, the first application of congruence theory examines whether social authority relations derived from family life and social relations in East Asia are congruent with democratic political norms in East Asia. This considers whether social relations fit the model of Confucian traditionalism as presented in the prior literature, and whether modernization processes are transforming social relations, and thus political norms.

The Congruence of Social and Market Values

A second aspect of congruence theory focuses on the social base of economic attitudes, paralleling our discussion of the social base of democratic values.

While Confucian traditions are often cited as an impediment to democratization, these same values are seen as conducive to economic growth (MacFaquhar 1980; Tai 1989; Levy Jr. 1992). Feelings of group solidarity and collective interest are a positive feature in developing economies. These norms are linked to the development of corporatist market systems in the Asian Tigers, and an economic model that stimulated growth. In short, while Confucian norms are supposedly incongruent with democratic values, they are seen as congruent with the economic development growth of the region.

If this economic congruence existed, the restructuring of many East Asian economic systems after the 1997 currency crisis may have altered this relationship. A corporatist economic system and protectionist economic policies are eroding in the face of a global economic system. Reforms in Korea, Japan, Singapore and other nations also asked economic interests and the public to accept greater competition, tolerate greater economic risk, and take greater individual responsibility in a new market system. At the same time, the Chinese and Vietnamese experienced an even more fundamental transition from a command economy toward a more competitive market system. Orientations toward such economic principles and values should broadly affect the development of the economic system (Harrison 1992; Brook and Long 1997; Inglehart and Baker 2000).

Thus, a second aspect of congruence theory is whether social modernization is creating economic values among East Asian publics that are more consistent with the closed economic systems and crony capitalism of the past, or the trends toward open, capitalist, market systems.

The Congruence of Political and Economic Values

A long theoretical and empirical debate exists about the relationship between political and economic values (and political development and economic development). Many scholars subscribe to the classic Seymour Martin Lipset (1959*a*) thesis that economic development and the concomitant processes of social modernization create the conditions in which democracy might develop (e.g. Vanhanen 1997; Przeworski et al. 2000). And some analysts suggest that the movement toward democracy is a course toward the rule of law and individual rights that underlie economic growth (Diamond 2003). That is, democratization is a source of economic growth and not just a consequence. The quote from former South Korean President Kim Dae Jung at the beginning of this chapter reflects the common belief that democratization and marketization are inherently linked, even if the direction of the causal relationship cannot be disentangled.

The possible separation between democratization and marketization is central to the literature on East Asia, and this dichotomy is a recurring theme in social science more broadly (Lindblom 1977, 1988).[3] For instance,

Singapore has followed a course of rapid development of a market economy and involvement in the global economic system, while consciously restraining democratization. China and Vietnam are the other prominent examples of where the state attempts to delink economic and political processes. In addition, the examples of crony capitalism in East Asia sometimes occur in nations with a consolidated democratic system.

Because of our interest in public values, this raises the more fundamental question of whether support for democracy and support for a capitalist market economy are congruent values. For instance, Sen (1999) argues that both value systems are built upon the premise of individual freedom and the rule of law, and thus they are reinforcing value systems. In the real world, a liberalized economy facilitates new and innovative activities among the masses, while democracy restrains extravagant and illegal activities among elites. Democracy and a market economy thus work as 'the twin pillars on which lasting development can thrive' (Bhagwati 2002). Bhalla (1997) provides cross-national evidence that neither democracy nor free markets alone produces significant development; such development is likely to occur only when they work together as complementary forces.

Consequently, our third element of congruence examines the relationship between public support for democracy and the values underlying a market economy. Are the individuals who accept the democratic principle also those who endorse the development of competitive market economies in East Asia—or do publics see a tension between these systems as some scholars maintain? In the postcommunist world of Eastern Europe, democratic and capitalist attitudes are moderately interrelated, and the causal flow seems to run more strongly from democratic attitudes to free market preferences than the reverse (Duch 1995; Gibson 1996*a*). In Africa, however, both attitude sets remain largely unrelated, although almost all sympathizers of free markets are firmly committed to democracy (Bratton, Mattes, and Giamah-Boadi 2004, Chapter 14). To date, the nature of relationship between democratic and capitalist attitudes seems to vary a great deal from one region to another. There is little evidence confirming the Washington Consensus about the complementarity of democratic and market reforms.

The Congruence Between Citizen Values and Institutional Structures

Ultimately, the congruence between the citizen values and institutional structures provides the rationale for political culture theory. If democracy is to endure, then it should be based on a political culture of democratic values; an effective market economy also presumes that citizens share the values embedded in this economic system. However, there is an asymmetry in the relationship between culture and regimes; authoritarian states can endure through coercion, since the regime does not rest on popular legitimacy

(Bueno de Mesquita and Downs 2005). For regimes that require popular legitimacy, however, congruence is more important: a democracy without democrats is unlikely to endure, and an open capitalist market system without popular support will be more difficult to sustain.

While we recognize the centrality of this aspect of congruence theory, the congruence between citizen values and institutions is a relationship that functions in a long-term perspective. In the midst of dynamic political changes in East Asia, the fit between mass values and institutional forms will be necessarily imperfect when examined at any single point in time. For instance, Indonesia has made dramatic democratization progress since 1998, moving several scale points on the Freedom House statistics (see Chapter 4). In the short term in such a transition, the culture may either lag or lead institutional change at various points. However, congruence theory suggests that if Indonesian democracy (or other new democracies in East Asia) is to endure, it will require that the public and the political elites broadly support the norms of the new democratic regime. In other words, Indonesians may have turned away from the authoritarian regime of Suharto, which stimulated the initial pressures for political reform in 1998, but then as democratic institutional reform has quickly changed the political regime, the current challenge may be for citizen values to internalize these new norms (Asia Foundation 2003). Similarly, based on the findings from our project, it appears that the Vietnamese and Chinese publics are relatively supportive of democratic norms and processes, more so than allowed by their current political systems. Thus, there is a potential for further democratization in these nations, but the current elites and political structures restrict these developments in order to retain power. Further social change in Vietnam and China should increase the popular pressure for eventual democratic reform—as congruence theory suggests.

In summary, cultural theory emphasizes broad processes of social change, rather than the immediate actions of political elites and regimes. In the long run, congruence theory should shape political outcomes and the stability of regimes. Otherwise, the institutions or culture will eventually shift to produce congruence. Thus, defining the social and political cultures of East Asia with this first wave of empirical survey data will help chart the prospects for Asia's future development.

DESCRIBING DEMOCRACY AND MARKETS

Democratization and marketization have transformed the world in the last half of the twentieth century. Where once democracy seemed like a small island in a sea of authoritarian states, with an uncertain future, it now is proclaimed as the inevitable endpoint of human political evolution (Fukuyama 1992). Similarly, the challenges to market-based economies, from both the left and the right, were a central theme in mid-twentieth century and globally during the Cold War competition. Now, the spread of a global economic system based on capitalist, laissez faire market economics and enforced by the WTO and the IMF seems destined to continue.

As an initial description of institutional conditions for the nations in this project, Figure 1.1 plots each nation on political and economic freedom in 2000 (approximately the time of our surveys), including the nations of East Asia, even if they are not part of the WVS. Democratic development is represented by the Freedom House index of political freedoms and civil liberties along the horizontal axis, which uses a Western, liberal definition of democracy (Freedom House 2002). Economic freedom on the vertical dimension is measured by the Heritage Foundation (2001), which measures the extent of property rights and other market principles. The four Western democracies of the Pacific Rim in our study—Australia, Canada, New Zealand, and the USA—all receive high scores on both dimensions, locating them at the upper right quadrant of the figure. As the long-term established democracy and market economy in East Asia, Japan also falls into the upper portion of this quadrant.

The course of economic and political change in East Asia, however, has not always followed global trends, with democratization and marketization tracking a single trajectory. For a substantial period, the tigers of East Asia

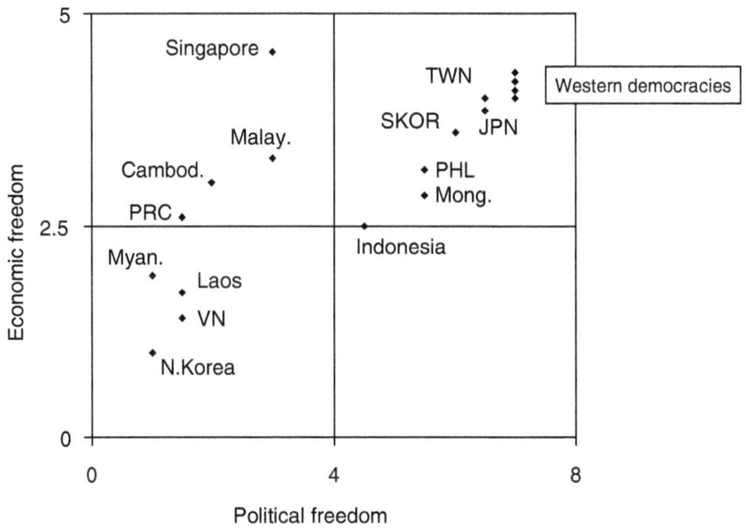

FIGURE 1.1. Pacific Rim nations on political and economic freedoms

Sources: 2000 data on political freedom from Freedom House and 2000 data on economic freedom from the Heritage Foundation. Political freedom is scored (1) low to (7) high; economic freedom is scored (1) low to (5) high.

pursued a course of economic modernization—while consciously resisting concomitant political reforms. Singapore is the most notable example, following a model in which economic development occurs relatively independently of political modernization. Deng Xiao Ping's China is another oft-cited example of this pattern. This pattern carries over at least partially to the present. Singapore is still notable for its high score on economic freedoms and development of a market economy, but its relatively lower score on the democracy dimension. Malaysia also fits this pattern and lies in the upper left quadrant of the figure; it is the other nation most clearly espousing an alternative model of development.

The People's Republic of China has consciously attempted to disassociate economic and political trends. China is now located above the scale midpoint on economic rights, in part because of the reforms required to become a WTO member. Yet, the regime simultaneously limits political modernization. There has been progress in some areas, such as local village elections, but there is continuing resistance to further democratization, and even some examples of regression over the past decade. Thus, China falls just into the upper left quadrant, similar to the position of Cambodia.

For a substantial time, political reform in Taiwan and South Korea also lagged behind the economic development of these two nations. However, rapid democratic progress since the mid-1980s has moved both nations ahead in terms of political rights and social liberties. Figure 1.1 thus plots nations as scoring relatively high on both dimensions; these two nations fall in the upper right quadrant slightly below Japan.

Another possible pattern is for a nation to advance in political democratization, in which economic freedoms and development of a market economy lag behind. In 2000, the Philippines, Indonesia, and Mongolia scored above the democratization midpoint; at the same time, their economic freedom scores were lower than the established democracies. These three nations are not in the bottom right quadrant, but they are close.

Several nations receive low ratings on both scales and thus fall into the lower left quadrant of the figure. The absolute lowest scores on economic and political freedoms occur in North Korea, which is located at the bottom left corner of the figure. Vietnam has made sustained efforts toward economic reform since the mid-1980s (*doi moi*), but these economic reforms are kept separate from reforms of the political system (Turley and Selden 1992). In overall terms, Vietnam receives low scores on both dimensions, as do Laos and Myanmar. Southeast Asia thus represents the least developed area on both dimensions.

This pattern also has historical parallels. Zimmerman (2002) describes this pattern as consistent with Leninism in the Soviet context, with strong commitments to state authority in both the domains. Indeed, it is a model widely seen in less developed nations, and sometimes advocated as a course of government-directed development (e.g. Huntington and Nelson 1976).

In overall terms, there is a clear relationship between both dimensions as the Kim Dae Jung reference at the start of the chapter implies, but the relationship is far from perfect. This figure also suggests that there is not a single pattern to the East Asian experience. Moreover, the congruence between these institutional forms is also uncertain. The Indonesian experience since 1998 is a graphic example of the potential for political development despite prior authoritarian rule and claims of the cultural limits to democratization.

While such institutional evidence is generally available, there is unfortunately little empirical evidence on how closely public orientations toward democracy and markets match these institutional arrangements across the region, as well as the causal processes that generate these opinions. Without this evidence, it is difficult to estimate the congruence of political culture with political processes in the region, or prospects for change in the future. This project addresses this void.

THE WORLD VALUES SURVEY

In order to study public attitudes in across a set of Pacific Rim nations, this book primarily relies on a new wave of surveys from the WVS project. The WVS is a unique resource in the social sciences. The first wave of the project was a coordinated survey of twenty-one nations conducted in the early 1980s by the European Values Survey group (Inglehart 1990). The second wave in the early 1990s expanded to forty-two nations, including many of the post-communist states in Eastern Europe (Inglehart 1997). The Third Wave in the mid-1990s included fifty-four nations, and expanded the data collection to several nations in the developing world. The fourth wave of the WVS includes representative national surveys examining the basic values and beliefs of publics in more than 65 societies, on all 6 inhabited continents, containing almost 80 percent of the world's population.

An international network of social scientists carries out this project, coordinated by an international directorate.[4] The international board develops the questions to include in the survey, and these are translated into the national language by each research institute. Most surveys are funded from national sources, and conducted by leading survey research firms. The data are then assembled in a single dataset, and made available to the international research community.

An exceptional feature of the 1999–2002 WVS is the range of new nations included in the survey, and in combination with the prior 1995–8 wave, the project now includes representative national surveys in eight East Asian nations: China, Japan, Indonesia, the Philippines, Singapore, South Korea, Taiwan, and Vietnam. Supplemental data are also available from Hong

TABLE 1.1. *World Value Surveys in the Pacific Rim*

	Wave III		Wave IV	
Nation	Date	Sample size	Date	Sample size
East Asia				
China	1995	1,000	2000	1,000
Hong Kong	—	—	2005	1,252
Indonesia	—	—	2002	1,004
Japan	1995	1,054	2000	1,362
Philippines	1996	1,200	2001	1,200
Singapore	—	—	2002	1,512
South Korea	1996	1,249	2002	1,200
Taiwan	1995	1,452	—	—
Vietnam	—	—	2001	1,000
Western democracies				
Australia	1995	2,048	—	—
Canada	—	—	2000	1,931
New Zealand	1998	1,201	—	—
USA	1995	1,542	2000	1,200

Kong.[5] This is one of the largest and most diverse sets of East Asian nations that has ever been surveyed on political and social values. In addition, researchers conducted the same survey in Australia, Canada, New Zealand, and the USA, which provides reference points to compare the opinions of East Asians to Western democratic publics. Table 1.1 lists the nations included in our core analyses, the dates of fieldwork, and the sample size for each survey. Additional information on survey sampling, research teams, timeframe, and other facts is presented in the appendix of this book.

Previous academic and political debates about the political culture of East Asian nations have explained the past development patterns of the region, and projected the potential for change in the future. The one missing element, however, has been to consult the citizens themselves. The WVS enables us to describe and explain how citizens in the region think about democracy and economic markets, and the values underlying their opinions.

POLITICAL CULTURE, POLITICS, AND MARKETS

This book analyzes public attitudes toward democracy and markets in four sections. The first section examines global processes of modernization and value change, and places the nations of our study into the global context. In Chapter 2, Christian Welzel and Ronald Inglehart present a model of human development as a general framework for understanding value change and the modernization process. Pooling all the nations from the WVS, they argue that the development of self-actualizing values is an essential element in modernization that is strongly linked to the expansion of democracy. Tan Ern Sen and Zhengzu Wang then examine the development of self-actualizing values more explicitly in the East Asian nations in our project. They ask whether this general model of value change equally applies to the nation of the region.

The second section examines support for democracy among the citizens in the Pacific Rim nations. In Chapter 4, Russell Dalton and Doh Chull Shin describe public orientations toward democracy across the nations of our project. They focus on public support for broad democratic principles and what they call 'democratic aspirations'. They also examine how the social influences of modernization, such as education and income levels, are related to democratic values. Their findings challenge the common claim about the lack of support for democracy in East Asia, and thus are more sanguine about the prospects for further democratization.

Research on East Asia has debated the impact of Confucian cultural traditions on support for democracy in the region. Chapter 5 by Dalton and Nhu-Ngoc Thuy Ong examines the attitudes toward social authority relations, and the impact of these attitudes on support for democracy. This is the most direct empirical test of the Asian values thesis, which heretofore has been debated by elites without evidence of what citizens actually believe. The next chapter examines the development of a civil society within the nations of East Asia, and the benefits of social activity in stimulating social trust, political engagement and democratic values. Wang, Dalton, and Shin analyze the juxtaposition of citizen evaluations of the current government with citizen support for a democratic regime. Their findings highlight the general separation between these two orientations in democratic nations, but a distinctly different process in the Asian non-democracies.

The third section of our research probes into citizen orientations toward capitalist markets. Shin and Dalton assess the broad cultural foundations of a capitalist market system in public values and orientations in East Asia. Chung-Si Ahn and Jiho Jang then use data from the Asian Values Survey to examine public support for market reforms in nine East Asian nations. They also examine the interrelationship between market orientations and attitudes toward globalization. In Chapter 10, Ken'ichi Ikeda and Tetsuro Kobayashi consider how attitudes toward risk avoidance vary across the region, and how these orientations may influence economic orientations and support for capitalist market values. Finally, Vietnam represents a special case of a nation currently experiencing the transition from a command economy to a market economy. Pham Minh Hac and Pham Thanh Nghi probe into Vietnamese orientations toward market reform, and the social distribution of these opinions within the Vietnamese public.

The fourth section of our study considers the intersection of democracy and markets in the belief systems of East Asian publics. Shin and Dalton study the relationship between these two dimensions across the Pacific Rim nations in the WVS. The conclusion discusses the implications of our findings for the future political and economic development of the region.

CONCLUSION

Our study adds to two distinct strands of the research literature that converge in East Asia. First, the third wave of democratization has altered the political map of East Asia, although this transformation remains incomplete. Often the explanation for the lack of democratic development focuses on the political culture of the region, claiming that social development or cultural norms were not conducive to democratization. Our findings will challenge this argument of cultural determinism. The contributors to this volume, and the findings of the WVS, speak to the diversity of citizen values across the nations of East Asia. This is not a single, distinct cultural zone when it comes to the democratic and market orientations examined in this book. Moreover, the lack of a distinct East–West gap in values is a theme that is repeated across chapters. Many of the values of democracy and citizen empowerment we examine appear to be 'human values', rather than Asian or Western values.

Thus, rather than a congruence of culture and political institutions, East Asia apparently represents a region where this broad systemic congruence is lacking. This suggests that the lack of democratic development in the region may lie primarily in elite power structures, the inability of challenging elites and social groups to erode entrenched autocratic structures, and the resistance to change at the top. Indonesia illustrates this pattern, making dramatic gains in democratic institutional development following the regime change in 1998. Democratic development in Indonesia is still uncertain and evolving, but institutional change apparently lagged behind the popular support for political change until the regime actually changed. Most Indonesians today favor a democratic regime, and their understanding of democracy has quickly grown as they have experienced a new democratic order (Asia Foundation 2003). Just as institutional change in Eastern Europe in the 1990s, or Spain and Portugal in the 1970s, moved forward the democratization process and built upon social change that was already affecting the citizens of these nations, the same potential is growing in East Asia.

Similarly, there is broad support for the principles and values of a market economy in the region. Indeed, much reform still remains to be done before open markets, property rights, and free and fair trade are established throughout East Asia. However, our findings suggest that the popular acceptance of market competition and belief in the benefits of this system are widespread in East Asia. Again, cultural values do not appear to be the major impediment to further progress.

Finally, this volume gives voice to the citizens of East Asia in a manner that goes beyond past research. This project represents the first major empirical study of public opinion on political issues that compares East Asia to established Western democracies. Moreover, the survey gives voice to publics in several nations where their own government is unwilling to recognize the right of free expression. It is empowering to the public to speak for themselves, instead of only through others. A decade ago, the project presented here would have been impossible—or not even imaginable. We therefore hope this volume stimulates the development of systematic empirical research that can address some of the other important questions of Asian politics and develop a truly comparative study of citizen politics in East Asia.[6] Empirical survey research opens a door to a better understanding of the values, beliefs, and behaviors of the citizens of East Asia.

ENDNOTES

1 We define East Asia as: Cambodia, China, Indonesia, Japan, North Korea, South Korea, Malaysia, Mongolia, Myanmar (Burma), Singapore, Taiwan, Thailand, and Vietnam.

2 This research has renewed the debate on whether the correlation between culture and democratic institutions is a causal relationship. See the exchange between Inglehart (1990, 1997) and Muller and Seligson (1994).

3 We would like to thank William Zimmerman and his study of public opinion in Russia for bringing this theoretical framework to our attention (Zimmerman 2002, Chapter 2).

4 Ronald Inglehart is the coordinator of the WVS, and an international executive committee oversees the project. We want to acknowledge the Institute for Future Studies in Sweden for support of several surveys in East Asia, and the Center for the Study of Democracy, UC Irvine, for support of the Vietnamese project. More information on the project is available at the website: http://www.worldvaluessurvey.org The data from the surveys are available from the Inter-university Consortium for Political and Social Research at the University of Michigan, and in Inglehart et al. (2004).

5 The 2005 'Hong Kong Creativity Index' survey was commissioned and funded by the Government of the Hong Kong Special Administrative Region, and was directed by Ng Chun Hung and Tsang Gar Yin. We received these data after the book manuscript was essentially complete, so these findings are included in the basic tables in Chapter 4, but not in the other substantive analyses of this volume.

6 A list of survey research sources on East Asia is available at: http://www.democ.uci.edu/resources/asia.php. This website lists sources for the WVS, Asia Barometer, East Asia Barometer, and other national and cross-national surveys covering East Asian nations. Many of these data-sets are available for free download.

Part I

Social Modernization and Value Change

2

The Human Development Model of Democracy: East Asia in Perspective

Christian Welzel and Ronald Inglehart

This chapter describes theory and evidence of a model that considers the emergence, existence, and flourishing of democracies as the institutional reflection of a broader process of human development. At various points, we highlight the applicability of this model to societies in East Asia.

Amartya Sen (1999) introduced the term human development. Its basic idea—the enhancement of human agency—was revised by Welzel (2002) in an attempt to give it a more explicit focus on human values and democracy. Welzel, Inglehart, and Klingemann (2003) followed this approach, and it was developed more extensively by Inglehart and Welzel (2005). This chapter summarizes the human development approach.

Our concept of human development integrates economic, cultural, and institutional changes into one theme: the strengthening of human agency (which is human development), or its weakening (which is human regression). Analogously to psychology where human development means the maturation of a person's ability to set his own preferences and actualize himself (Chirkov et al. 2003), the human development of whole societies means progress toward conditions that enable, stimulate, and entitle people to shape their lives based on their self-chosen preferences. Thus, the human development of entire societies is equivalent to the empowerment of their people in featuring freedom of choice.

From the viewpoint of self-determination theory (Deci and Ryan 2000; Ryan and Deci 2000), a development that features freedom of choice and empowers people deserves the attribute human because the potential to make autonomous choices, to follow intrinsic motivations, and to express and determine oneself is the most distinctive property of the human species. People's potential to self-actualization constitutes the human potential inherent in any society. Societies do not differ in this human potential. They differ in the social conditions that enable, stimulate, and entitle people to develop and actualize their human potential. The concept of human development intends to measure exactly these differences in the human condition. It assumes constancy in the human potential and variation in the social conditions that allow it to develop.

A cultural relativist might object that human development equals people empowerment, arguing that the focus on freedom of choice is alien to non-Western cultures. Indeed, many of the chapters in this book directly examine prior theorizing on the distinctiveness of Asian values (see Dalton and Ong, Chapter 5; Shin and Dalton, Chapter 8). But this claim would be like denying that the potential to reason, judge, and choose is part of human nature—which we think is undeniable. This position also contradicts empirical insights of cross-cultural psychology, which provide massive evidence that people whose activities are driven by intrinsic motivations (which means they act according to self-chosen preferences), increase feelings of fulfillment, subjective well-being, and general life satisfaction. 'Autonomy', 'agency', and 'self-actualization' are universal psychological needs that diminish life satisfaction when unsatisfied (Ryan and Deci 2001). Even people in 'collectivist' cultures systematically report lower levels of life satisfaction when they feel they have little choice in determining how their life turns out.

Much of what defines culture is its tendency to breed conformist values that constrain people's striving for autonomy, agency, and choice. Cultures are most 'successful' in this respect under pressing existential conditions. Existential pressures make people more prepared to prioritize group discipline and authority over individual autonomy and choice. It is therefore no coincidence that emancipative values that emphasize human self-expression tend to prevail in more affluent societies (Welzel, Inglehart, and Klingemann 2003; Inglehart and Welzel 2005).

Evidence from the WVS illustrates this point, showing that the individual-level linkage between life satisfaction and people's perception of choice is present throughout all cultural zones.[1] Figure 2.1 presents the correlation between these two survey questions across seventy-four nations in nine distinct cultural regions—there are consistently positive correlations. There is nothing uniquely Western in the fact that more freedom of choice tends to create higher levels of subjective well-being.

We think it is perfectly in line with human nature to center the definition of human development on 'people' empowerment, where people empowerment means diminishing constraints on people's potential to determine and actualize themselves, giving them a choice in making decisions affecting their lives. People empowerment makes people themselves the agents in shaping their lives.

People empowerment is a matter of the social conditions in which people live. These conditions are relevant in three aspects: economic, cultural, and institutional (see Table 2.1). Accordingly, people empowerment involves at

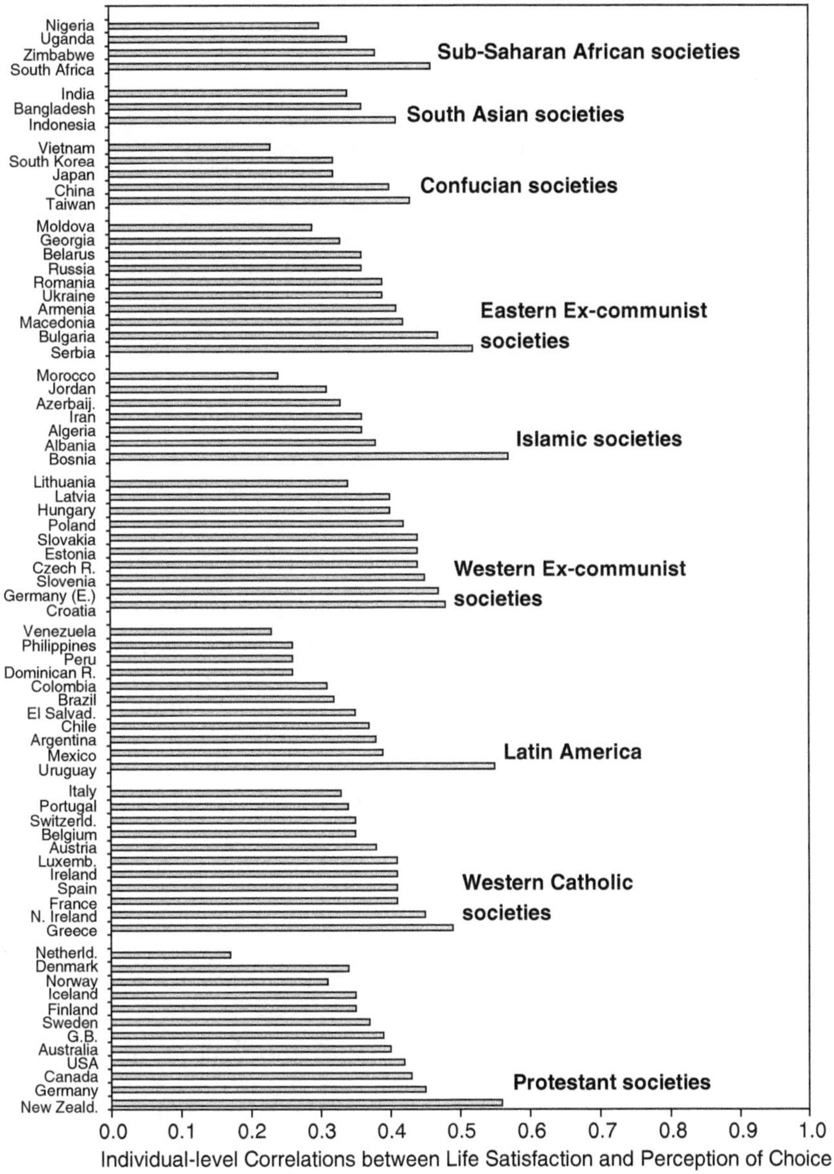

FIGURE 2.1. Life satisfaction and the perception of choice and autonomy
Source: Inglehart and Welzel (2005: 140).

TABLE 2.1. *The human development of societies*

Human development ...	SOCIOECONOMIC Dimension	CULTURAL Dimension	INSTITUTIONAL Dimension
... takes place when:	growing **Individual Resources** extend people's action repertory	rising **Emancipative Values** strengthen people's valuation of freedom	increasingly **Effective Liberties** widen people's enforcable rights
... determines:	the extent **able** to pursue	to which **willing** self-chosen	people are **allowed** priorities
... enlarges people's:	**Capabilities** of	**Aspirations** for	**Entitlements** to
	AGENCY		
... means in short:	**People Empowerment** (diminishing constraints on intrinsic human choice)		

Source: Adapted from Welzel (2002: 46).

least three things. First, people must be *enabled* to make their own choices. This is a matter of the socioeconomic conditions, which do or do not give people the means needed for human agency. Second, people must feel *encouraged* to make their own choices. This is a matter of cultural conditions, which do or do not support the values stimulating people to human agency. Third, people must be *allowed* to make their own choices. This is a matter of the institutional conditions, which do or do not give people the rights that entitle them to human agency. Thus, people empowerment operates on the level of people's capabilities, motivations, and entitlements to set their own goals in life and pursue self-chosen priorities.

EMPOWERMENT THROUGH CAPABILITIES: THE ROLE OF INDIVIDUAL RESOURCES

People's capabilities to pursue self-chosen activities depend fundamentally on available resources that people can access and use upon their choices. These resources include economic means, cognitive skills, and social connections. Each of these types of resources increases people's action repertory in manifold ways. The expanded repertory includes collective actions, too, which is noteworthy, as collective actions are a decisive factor in holding decision-makers responsible to what people want out of life.

Modernization is linked with an increase in economic, intellectual, and social resources. Through economic development, it increases and diversifies people's supply of goods and services and raises their financial incomes, making them capable to invest the time, money, and equipment needed for many activities, both individual and collective ones. Economic resources make people means-wise more capable.

Furthermore, modernization is linked with rising levels of education, more easily available information, and a mobilization of human intellect by expanding knowledge-intensive activities. All this increases people's cognitive skills, making them intellectually more capable to invent and undertake human activities.

Finally, modernization interweaves societies with an ever more complex web of human interactions, offering people a greater choice of possible connections to other people. The individualization trend linked with this development does not erode people's social connectivity. Individualization simply makes people freer to connect and disconnect as they choose. This might make social ties weaker, but it also makes them more 'bridging' (Granovetter 1973). Individualization empowers people socially, making them relation-wise more capable to initiate and join activities with others. In sum, modernization increases and diversifies people's resources, skills, and connections, making them more capable to follow their own preferences and pursue self-chosen activities.

EMPOWERMENT THROUGH MOTIVATIONS: THE ROLE OF EMANCIPATIVE VALUES

People empowerment has a psychological dimension as well. To become a widespread practice in social life, human agency needs not only people who are able to pursue self-chosen activities, but also people who are willing to do so. This is a matter of motivations, which are most powerful if they are intrinsic, and based on internalized values. However, people rarely internalize values through a conscious process of rational choice. Value orientations are, for the most part, acquired through the subconscious mechanisms of socialization. Socialization allows cultures to reproduce themselves, passing on their value system from one generation to the next. Thus, given value systems can and do discourage people to strive for self-actualization, despite the fact that this striving is innate to human nature.

Conformist values, which place collective discipline over individual autonomy, strongly discourage any activity that would set an individual too much apart from its related group. By contrast, emancipative values that emphasize human self-expression strongly encourage people to pursue self-chosen activities, even if this diminishes group conformity. Actually, group conformity is not seen as a value in itself when emancipative orientations arise. Quite the contrary; the opposite of group conformity—human diversity—becomes increasingly seen as a value that enriches social experience. Again, these insights are well anchored in cross-cultural psychology, which has long emphasized the difference between collectivist and individualist cultures

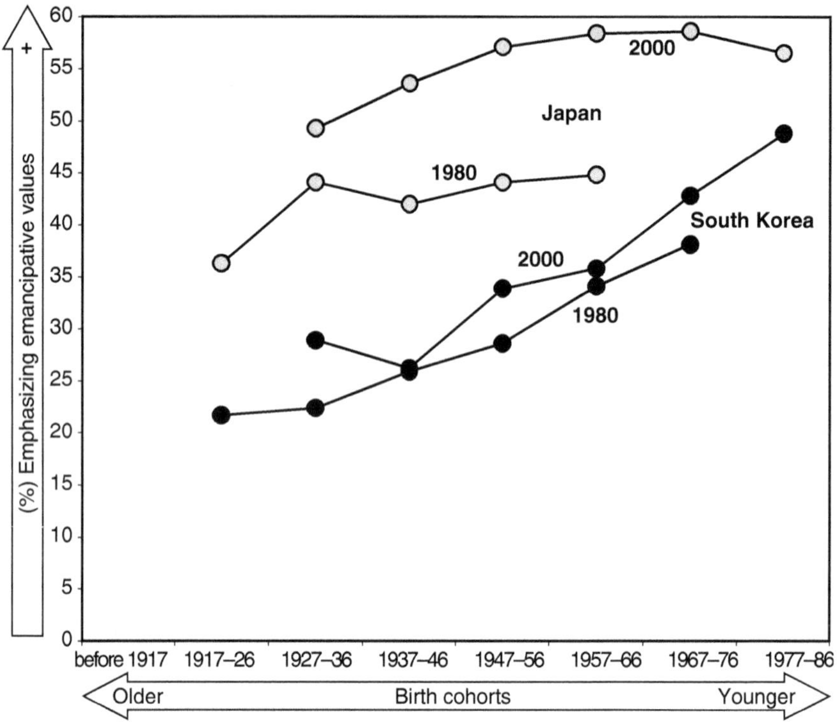

FIGURE 2.2. Generational value differences in Japan and South Korea
Source: World Values Surveys I and IV.

(Triandis 1995; Markus, Kitayama, and Heiman 1996; Hofstede 2001; Schwartz 2003; also see chapter by Ikeda and Kobayashi in this volume).

We prefer the term emancipative to individualist because individualist is too easily confused with egocentrism. In fact, emancipative values mean an appreciation of human autonomy in general, including *other* people's autonomy, leading to greater tolerance of human diversity. Emancipative values include a humanistic emphasis on human freedom in general, rather than an egocentric emphasis on one's own freedom only. Also, emancipative values are not anticollective in the sense that they withhold people from initiating and joining collective actions. On the contrary, emancipative values actually encourage people to initiate and join various new types of collective activities, especially elite-challenging actions that keep power holders responsive to the public (Welzel, Inglehart, and Deutsch 2006).

However, emancipative values are not a constant cultural trait of societies. Instead, societies move towards more emancipative values when existential

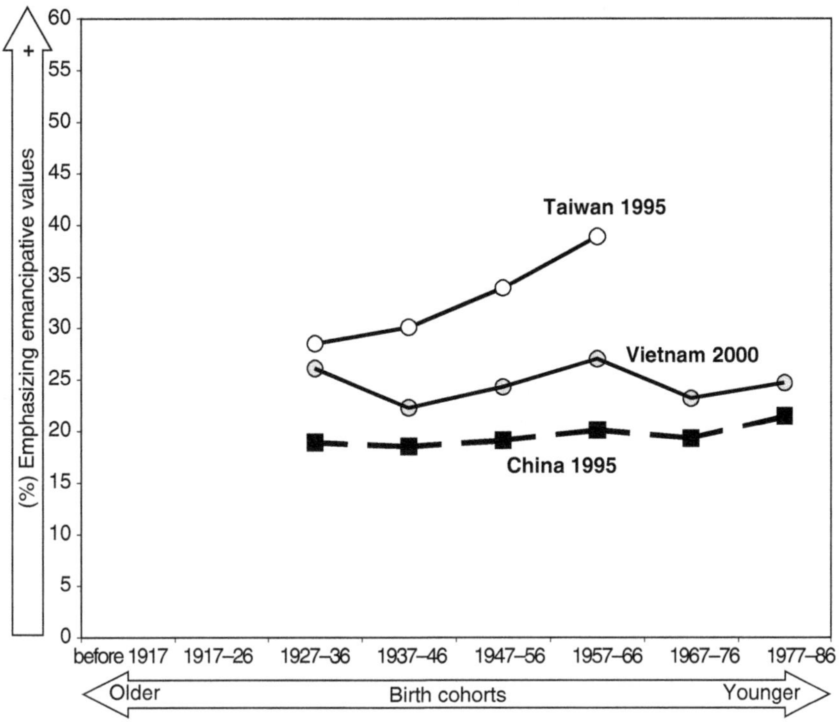

FIGURE 2.3. Generational value differences in China, Taiwan, and Vietnam
Source: World Values Surveys III and IV.

conditions become more permissive, giving the human striving for self-actualization more room. This happens even in societies in which conformist values have a long tradition. For example, German mass culture was traditionally seen as authoritarian and conformity oriented—a fact that in times of existential pressure, such as the Hyperinflation and the Great Depression, made it relatively easy for demagogues to foment xenophobia and feelings of existential threats, helping the Nazis to seize power. Only after a prolonged Economic Miracle in the 1950s and 1960s, did conformist values give way to a generational shift to emancipative values.

Today we observe a similar generational shift to emancipative values in all affluent postindustrial societies, including Confucian societies such as Japan and South Korea. From the WVS, we constructed an index of emancipative values. This index is based on questions tapping civil and political freedom, political expression, valuing human diversity, social trust, and life satisfaction.[2] Figure 2.2 plots the distribution of these emancipative values for

Japanese and Korean generations, across the first WVS in 1981 and the most recent survey in 1999–2001. There is a clear gradient toward emancipative values from older to younger generations in both nations. In addition, there is a shift toward emancipative values across generations between the two time points. This value change reflects receding existential constraints on human autonomy and choice.

Emancipative values do not reflect the universal force of globalization as the generational shift does not occur everywhere, but only where existential pressures on human autonomy recede. As Figure 2.3 illustrates, we do not yet observe pronounced generational differences in emancipative values in China and Vietnam, where the conditions facilitating these values are still underdeveloped. However, such differences do exist in Taiwan, which has undergone a developmental process similar to Korea. Thus, Confucian culture does not make societies immune against the emancipative effects of fundamental socioeconomic transformations.

Rising emancipative values are the major cultural force in the process of human development, motivating people to set their own priorities, define their preferred way of life, pursue self-chosen activities, and join forces with others who do the same. Emerging emancipative values transform modernization into a process of human development, giving rise to increasingly people-centered cultures.

EMPOWERMENT THROUGH ENTITLEMENTS: THE ROLE OF EFFECTIVE LIBERTIES

Human empowerment not only requires people to be capable and willing to pursue self-chosen preferences, but people must also be *allowed* to do so. This is a matter of rights, which entitle people to pursue their own choices. In complex modern societies, freedom of choice has both a defensive and an offensive aspect. The defensive aspect (negative freedom) shields an individual from interventions into its private decision-making freedom in such areas as the choice of occupation, residence, partner, religious beliefs, sources of information, or sexual orientation. This defensive aspect of freedom is protected by specifically *civil* rights. However, civil rights do not suffice to provide freedom of choice in societies, in which major aspects of people's daily lives are subject to political regulations. Hence, entitling people to influence the things that affect them also requires *political* rights. Political rights, including the right to associate with others, initiate and join public actions, sue officials, access administrative information, and vote in elections and referenda, provide offensive freedom (positive freedom). This type of freedom does not shield people from the state; it offers them opportunities to influence and direct its activities (Rose 1995).

Besides the legal specification of formal rights, both civil and political, there must also be the rule of law in order to make formal rights effective (Finer 1999; Rose 2001). Formal rights alone do not guarantee people any real freedom if power holders are not committed to the rule of law. Only the rule of law ensures that civil and political liberties are set into effect. Hence, our concern is with *effective* liberties, not formal ones. As these civil and political liberties define liberal democracy, effective liberties are equivalent to 'effective democracy'. Effective civil and political liberties operate on the level of entitlements, empowering people legally to pursue self-chosen activities. From this perspective, democracy is the institutional setting most suited to the human potential for choice and agency.

Empirical Linkages

Conceptually, individual resources, emancipative values, and effective liberties belong together, as each of these components makes a distinctive contribution to a common underlying theme: human empowerment. These three components are not only logically linked; empirically, too, these components are closely tied to each other. In fact, individual resources, emancipative values, and effective liberties converge in a robust and coherent dimension, which a factor analysis clearly demonstrates. Across a global sample of 74 nations, for which measures of all three variables are available, there is a 92-percent overlapping variance between national levels of individual resources, emancipative values, and effective liberties, with each of the three components showing a 0.96 loading on their common underlying factor: human development.

How do the linkages between the three components of human development operate? We argue that emancipative values gain momentum in societies to the extent to which existential constraints on human choice recede, which happens when growing individual resources make people materially, cognitively, and socially more capable to pursue self-chosen activities. Increasing capabilities of action nurture a basic sense of human agency. This leads people to question unlimited authority and makes them receptive to the idea of civil and political liberties, acting for the rights that effectively guarantee these liberties.

Evidence in History

This pattern of human development is evident throughout history. Whenever civil and political rights became effective, this happened for one particular reason: people who developed a basic sense of agency because they disposed of fundamental resources were inspired by an emancipative ethos leading them to articulate the demand for individual rights. For reasons of contrast, consider the history of preindustrial societies. This history is full of hunger revolts in which exploited peasants spontaneously rebelled against pressing hardship. In none of these revolts, however, did people have a program to implement rights that empower the people. The entire idea of individual rights, be it property rights or voting rights, was alien to an exploited peasant population in despotic agrarian empires from Eastern Europe to China. Instead, the idea of civil and political rights was born in free farmer societies in ancient Athens and the Roman Republic; it had been reinvented by free farmer societies and merchant republics in late medieval Europe, most notably in Northern Italy, the Lowlands, Switzerland, Iceland, England, and Scandinavia; and it had been expanded to establish early limited forms of democracy in the era of preindustrial capitalism through the liberal revolutions in Western Europe and Northern America, enacting principles such as 'no taxation without representation' (Finer 1999; McNeill 1990).

However, the liberal revolutions established only limited versions of democracy, none of which qualifies as a democracy under today's standards. The entitlement to civil and political liberties was far from being fully inclusive. But the first and foremost step was made with the very definition of these liberties, committing governments for the first time since classical Athens to the well-being of the people, even if the people were not yet defined comprehensively. It is significant that the implementation of effective liberties, however limited, has been pioneered by capitalist freeholder societies whose members experienced a significant degree of existential autonomy. This nurtures a basic sense of human agency—making people more critical toward authority and more receptive to the idea of civil and political rights—the very heart of democracy (or at least liberal democracy).

More recently, societies were likelier to democratize during the Third Wave when more abundant individual resources gave rise to emancipative values among the new middle classes whose members filled the ranks of civil and political rights movements, especially in middle-high income countries, such as the Philippines and South Korea (Huntington 1991; Diamond 1993). Alternatively, members of the middle classes entered state parties, such as the PRI in Mexico or the Kuomintang in Taiwan, liberalizing the system from within. In East European communist societies, the equivalent of the new middle classes have been the professionals who became an increasingly significant group in the economically more advanced part of the former communist bloc, including Hungary, Poland, Czechoslovakia, the GDR, and the Baltic states (Konrad and Szelenyi 1991; Joppke 1994). These professionals, too, entered state parties, such as the Communist party in Hungary, and liberalized the system from within; or, they established nascent civil rights movements, which launched massive democratization campaigns—once the Brezhnev Doctrine was abandoned.

The logic remains the same: Groups of people who gain a sense of human agency because they dispose of fundamental resources are more capable and motivated than others to launch liberation movements that engage for greater and more effective civil and political liberties. Once these groups become large enough, their demands become increasingly difficult to ignore.

Existential Experiences

Formal versions of liberal democracy can be imposed on any society by external powers or can be adopted by enlightened elites, even if the masses suffer from deficient individual resources and show little sense for emancipative values. Though it is not very likely that liberal democracy will be established under these circumstances, in some exceptional cases, it nevertheless happened, for instance, in postcolonial India and postwar Germany. But whether civil and political liberties become effective, enabling and stimulating people to *actually* practice these liberties, depends on resources and values, as Inglehart and Welzel (2005, Chapter 8) have shown.

Horrified by World War II, and with American and British support, the postwar West German elite adopted a democratic constitution—irrespective of the fact that the suffering German population was still characterized by an authoritarian culture that placed little emphasis on emancipative values. At the start there was little intrinsic support for democracy; the system was accepted merely because there was no alternative. At its start at least, West Germany was a democracy with few convinced democrats among the broader public (Almond and Verba 1963). Only after the Economic Miracle made people accustomed to more permissive existential conditions did an emphasis on emancipative values arise. These values stimulated the younger generation to use their formal liberties in more autonomous and self-assertive ways, both sexually and politically. This cultural shift became obvious by the protest movements of the late 1960s (Inglehart 1977; Conradt 1980; Dalton 1988). It was not the democratic institutions as such that led to a prodemocratic culture; it was a generational value change toward more emancipative orientations driven by vastly improved economic conditions. By contrast, emancipative values did not have a chance to emerge under such miserable conditions as the Hyperinflation and the Great Depression in Weimar Germany.

Both the evidence of historical cases as well as contemporary statistical evidence suggest that abundant individual resources bring more permissive existential conditions, giving rise to emancipative values that emphasize human agency and choice. This in turn tends to mobilize social pressures to establish and strengthen effective liberties, that is, liberal democracy.

Pressures to Democratize

If growing individual resources make people more capable and rising emancipative values make them more willing to enjoy effective liberties, it becomes increasingly likely that these people initiate and join social movements that demand greater and more effective liberties. In a democracy, this will result in social pressures to widen already existing liberties or extend their applicability. In an authoritarian system, such liberation movements challenge the whole political regime itself because the enactment of civil and political liberties puts an end to authoritarian rule. This makes liberation movements a risky adventure. Authoritarian elites may decide at any point to terminate such a movement by force, as it happened in 1989 in China.

But suppression is not an unlimited option. Quite the contrary. Confronted with a public whose members are capable and motivated to initiate and join widespread mass actions, the coercive option is likely to fail. Democracy movements can only be suppressed by military means if they are concentrated on a few places and limited to isolated groups of the population. Such was the case when members of the thin student population initiated prodemocracy demonstrations on Tiananmen Square in Summer 1989. However, when mass demonstrations spread all over the country involving virtually all groups of the population, as it was the case in the GDR, Czechoslovakia, and the Baltic States, military suppression becomes almost impossible. This was also the case with the people power movements that swept Marcos from power in the Philippines and ushered in democracy to Indonesia in 1998. This is not to say that coercive regimes cannot survive when they have lost support by the population. The sad truth is that they can—but only as long as the population does not dispose of the resources and does not emphasize the values that enable and stimulate it to launch a mass liberation movement. Once, however, individual resources become abundant and emancipative values emerge, no coercive regime can survive for long time (except if it has support from an external power). This has been the experience across the globe, and we believe the same principles apply to the nations of East Asia.

Experiencing Autonomy

Economic development helps give rise to emancipative values because it provides a basic sense of human agency. This is so because economic development increases individually accessible resources, including material means, cognitive skills, and social contacts. As these resources grow, they widen people's action repertory, nurturing a sense of agency. Sometimes, however, economic development can be suspiciously one-sided, as is the case in oil-exporting countries, which are exceedingly wealthy, but otherwise very traditional.

Oil-exporting economies produce high levels of material wealth without nurturing the basic sense of agency that gives rise to emancipative values. This is an important illustration of the fact that sheer material wealth alone does little to provide a sense of human agency, unless it is accompanied by high levels of education (which make people intellectually more capable) and high levels of social complexity (which connect people in more diverse ways, making them socially more capable). The activities needed to sustain a rent-seeking economy require little intellectual skills and little flexibility in people's social connectivity. A rent-seeking economy can become rich while continuing to keep people on a low level of skills and continuing to lock them in closely knit social groups. This highlights that the nature of a society's prevailing economic activities plays a decisive role in determining whether higher cognitive skills and more diverse social connections are favored. Only in combination with these factors does economic development nurture a basic sense of human agency.

If subsistence activities require individual creativity and initiative, they nurture a sense of individual competence, mastery, and agency. If they involve rather standardized routine work, they undermine this sense of agency. Thus, Nolan and Lenski (1999) provide evidence that people in hunter–gatherer societies had more individualistic values than people who grew up in the 'labor-repressive regimes' of agrarian empires. On our scale of emancipative values, hunter–gatherer societies would probably score higher than agrarian empires. Not coincidentally, hunter–gatherer societies have been relatively democratic, whereas the hallmark of agrarian empires was despotism (Ember, Ember, and Russett 1997).

By contrast, whenever civil and political liberties have been institutionalized in preindustrial times, it was in free farmer societies or free merchant republics, in which private property on land and free access to markets gave people some degree of existential autonomy, even if they have not been affluent. These societies have not been rich by today's standards; nevertheless, it was in exactly these societies that the philosophies of Humanism and Enlightenment established an emancipative ethos. Not coincidentally, free farmer and merchant societies in Western Europe and Northern America are the cradle of modern liberal democracy. The meritocratic middle classes in these societies have been the strongest proponents of the civil and political liberties that define democracy.

Industrialization did not strengthen this emancipative ethos. And the working class was not the most powerful social force in pushing for democracy, contrary to what Rueschemeyer, Stephens, and Stephens (1992) suggest. The working class demanded a welfare state and universal suffrage but often enough at the expense of civil and political liberties. Quite frequently, the working class helped to vote fascist, communist, and populist parties into office. Once in power, these parties restricted civil and political liberties or nullified them altogether. In any case, the working class did not place special emphasis on individual civil and political liberties, in line with what Lipset (1959*b*) once described as 'working class authoritarianism'. Thus, the rise and expansion of the working class did not bring or strengthen emancipative values.

The daily work performed by the blue-collar worker of the industrial age was standardized manual routines, nothing that nurtures human creativity and independent thinking. The Fordist organization of economic and social life in industrial societies with their gigantic factories, huge bureaucracies, uniform social classes, and prefixed role models has been rigidly standardized. People hardly experienced themselves as autonomous individuals in this standardized world. Even though the mechanical worldview of the industrial world gave rise to secular–rational values, it did not support emancipative values to the same extent. Uncoupled with emancipative values, the secular–rational worldview was perfectly compatible with communist, fascist, and other forms of totalitarian ideologies. True, industrialization brought universal suffrage and mass involvement into politics, but this happened as often in fascist, communist, or other forms of authoritarianism as it happened in democratic forms.

The postindustrial age brings another turn, as the rise of knowledge-intensive economies changes the nature of economic activities. Tasks in knowledge-intensive professions become more cognition-based and involve more intellectual creativity, which offers a wider scope for individual judgment and thinking. The change in the nature of economic activities goes along with more flexible ways in which the whole society is organized, destandardizing social classes, social roles, career patterns, and life courses—a trend that is usually referred to as individualization (Beck 2002). Individualization does not mean the destruction or reduction of people's connectivity, but rather more individual freedom to connect and disconnect as they choose, making social networks more diverse, flexible, and modular. This individualization trend nourishes a sense of autonomy/agency and an emancipative ethos that brings social pressures for a further differentiation and specification of civil and political rights and equal opportunities, including consumer rights, women's rights, children's rights, the rights of gays and lesbians, freedom of information rights, as well as increasing pressures on elites to govern transparent, accountable, and responsive.

This framework is especially relevant to East Asia. The past generation has seen a tremendous economic boom—most prominently in the Asian Tigers, but more recently there have been dramatic economic gains in China, Vietnam, and other nations. Moreover, literacy rates in Asia are often substantially higher than economic levels would suggest. Vietnam, for instance, is one of the poorer nations of East Asia, but has a 94 percent literacy level. And increasing Asian economies are being linked to the global economic regime, which should increase exposure to the emancipative norms of other nations. Thus, we expect East Asian nations will experience these same trends toward emancipative values and human development.

Clustering in Cultural Zones

Regardless of the reasons that cause individual resources, emancipative values, and effective liberties to correspond to each other, these three

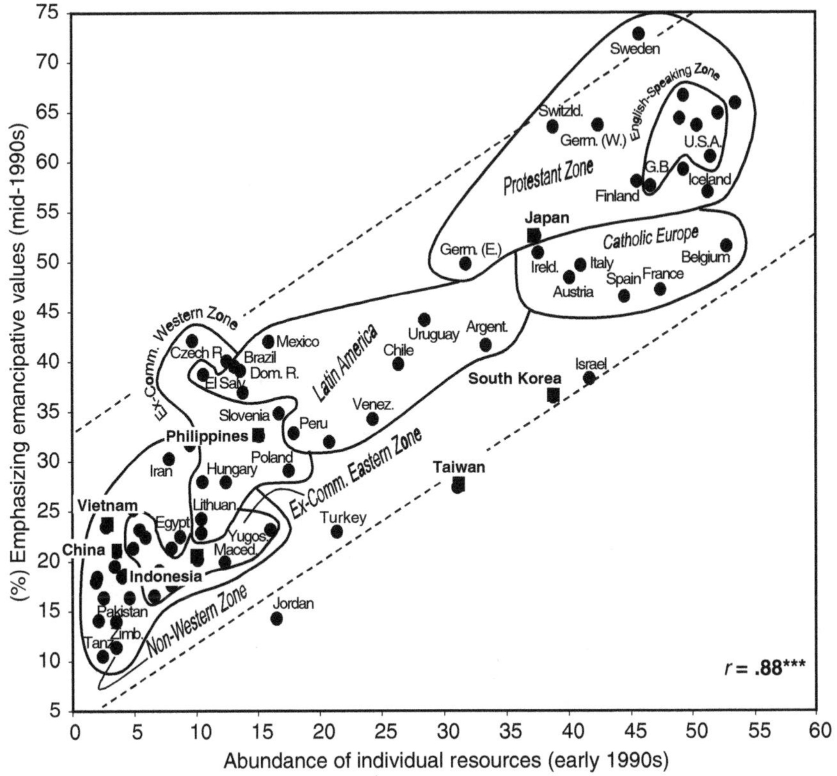

FIGURE 2.4. Individual resources and emancipative values

Source: Horizontal axis combines measures of the spread of material and intellectual resources and the complexity of people's social connectivity, using Vanhanen's 'index of power resources' (1997). Vertical axis summarizes measures of people's esteem of freedom and political expression as well as tolerance, trust, and satisfaction, using the *latest* available survey of WVS II–IV (average measure in 1996).

components are indeed closely linked. Figure 2.4 displays the relationship between the level of individual resources in a nation and emancipative values as measured by the WVS.[3] Knowing how widespread individual resources are in a society, we can explain 79 percent of the cross-national variance in emancipative values.

One of this book's themes is to explain the potential for democratization across East Asia. We believe that the human development approach provides a framework for assessing the important cultural values underlying democracy. For example, Figure 2.5 displays the global relationship between emancipative values in the early 1990s and a measure of the scope of effective civil and political liberties,[4] that is, the degree to which civil and political liberties are (*a*) formally codified and (*b*) respected by power-holders in

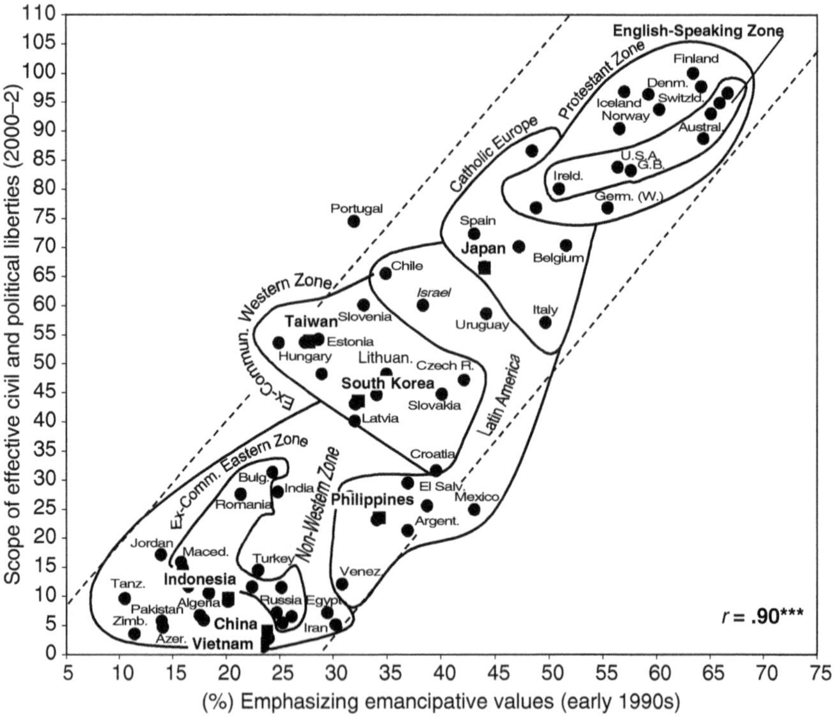

FIGURE 2.5. Emancipative values and effective liberties

Source: Horizontal axis summarizes measures of people's esteem of freedom and political expression as well as tolerance, trust, and satisfaction, using the *earliest* available survey of WVS II–IV (average measure in 1992). Vertical axis is a measure of the scope of civil and political rights in 2000–2 (using scores from Freedom House) weighed by the respect of the rule of law by elites in 2000–2 using the World Bank's control of corruption scores.

practice (also see Inglehart and Welzel 2005, Chapter 8). We see the scope of effective civil and political liberties as the very essence of effective democracy (or effective liberal democracy to be more precise) so that we use these terms synonymous in this and subsequent sections. In any case, knowing how widespread *emancipative values* are in a population, we can explain 80 percent of the cross-national variation in *effective democracy (or scope of effective civil and political liberties)*.

A country can score low in effective democracy for any of two reasons: either civil and political liberties are not even formally codified; or, they are codified but are not respected by power-holders. However, a country can only score high in effective democracy because both of two conditions are fulfilled: a country must have a full range of civil and political liberties, *and* power-holders respect these liberties. These conditions exist only where widespread emancipative values also exist.

It is noteworthy how coherently most nations cluster into cultural zones over the three aspects of human development in Figures 2.4 and 2.5. Most of the differences between this world's cultural zones are corresponding differences in three major aspects of the human condition: resources, values, and rights. There are, however, three exceptions. First, Arab countries, Sub-Saharan African countries, South Asian countries, and the Orthodox and Islamic countries of the former communist bloc are almost undistinguishable in all three aspects of human development. Hence, they are summarized under the heading 'Non-Western Cultural Zones'. This set of nations does not deviate from the general model, but represents a consistent combination of low individual resources, low emancipative values, and low effective democracy. Second, countries in the Latin American zone show a considerably wider differentiation in human development than most other cultural zones. But again, these nations conform to the general patterns of the human development model—individual resources increase, so do emancipative values and effective democracy. Third, the societies of East Asia clearly show the widest spread of all cultural zones, ranging from still very low human development in China and Vietnam to high levels in South Korea and Japan—placing Eastern societies into various cultural zones. Yet what is most noteworthy from the framework of this volume is the general conformance of East Asian nations to the global model of human development. East Asian nations are not generally lower in emancipative values than their level of individual resources suggests, as the Asian values and Confucian culture literature would argue (see review in chapter by Dalton and Ong). Moreover, Figure 2.5 indicates that as emancipative values develop in East Asian societies, this follows the general relationships with effective democracy as well.

Effect Thresholds

The linkages between societal levels of individual resources and emancipative values, and between emancipative values and effective democracy, are systematic and linear. Yet even strongly linear relationships such as these are not perfect. Nations are not positioned on a straight line. Rather, they are scattered along distinct but relatively broad corridors (i.e. confidence intervals), as depicted by the left and right dotted boundaries in Figures 2.4 and 2.5.

These corridors reflect thresholds in the effects of resources on values and of values on democracy, implying that each one-unit increase in resources is directly reflected in a corresponding increase in emancipative values, and not each one-unit increase in values is reflected in a corresponding increase in democracy. The size of the increase in individual resources that is needed to make corresponding increases in emancipative values very likely (say to 95 percent likely), and the size of the increase in emancipative values required to make corresponding increases in effective democracy very likely, is relatively large. It reflects the increase in *X* needed to make corresponding increases in *Y* very likely, which we call the 'effect threshold' of *X* on *Y*. Its size is depicted by the horizontal widths of the corridors demarcated by the dotted lines in Figures 2.4 and 2.5. Since relationships in the social and political world are never strictly deterministic, the existence of effect thresholds is what we usually expect.

Consider now Figure 2.4. If one moves from a point at the left boundary to the right, that is, along increasing resources, it is not very likely that the next society you encounter scores higher in emancipative values than the previous one, unless your move exceeds a horizontal distance as large as the resource-gap between Vietnam and Taiwan. In other words, there is a significant range of individual resources within which emancipative values vary arbitrarily. The same applies to Figure 2.5. As one moves from weaker to stronger emancipative values, starting at any point of the left boundary of the corridor, effective liberties vary arbitrarily unless one's movement on the horizontal axis exceeds a range as large as the value-gap between Taiwan and Italy.

These distances indicate the size of the threshold in the effect of resources on values and of values on liberties. These effect thresholds are constant because the corridors have parallel boundaries. You have to move the same distance in *X* from any point of the left boundary to make an increase in *Y* very likely.

The thresholds are rather large—so large indeed that the effects become fully apparent only when taking the entire global variation into account. Vice versa, most cultural zones are internally so coherent that the variation among their nations hardly overcomes the threshold of the effects of resources on values and of values on liberties.

Thus, restricting one's view to the limited variation within cultural zones would lead one to mistakenly conclude that there is no systematic relationship between individual resources, emancipative values, and effective liberties. Because only sizable increases in individual resources give rise to emancipative values, and because only sizeable increases in emancipative values bring more effective liberties, variation within coherent cultural zones is too small to adequately represent these linkages. Only East Asian societies are diverse enough as a cultural region to fully represent the covariance between resources, values, and liberties, with Vietnam and Japan ranging at opposite ends in each of these three components of human development. And as Wang and Tan show in more detail in the next chapter, there is a clear relationship between these variables among the nations of East Asia.

AGGREGATION AS ERROR REDUCTION

The linkages between resources, values, and liberties—which constitute human development—are strikingly evident. But these are societal-level linkages on a global scale. Thus, one should not be surprised if these relations are not represented to the same extent at the individual level *within* national samples. For example, the societal-level relation between individual resources and emancipative values points to a highly significant 0.89 correlation, whereas the equivalent individual-level relation is highly significant and positive as well, but reaches only a magnitude of 0.22 pooled across samples.[5]

The fact that the same two variables correlate more strongly when averaged to aggregate units, such as nations, than they correlate at the individual level, is well known. This pattern reflects two things: (*a*) the existence of measurement error in individual-level survey data and (*b*) the fact that these idiosyncratic individual variations are to a large extent random. As has been shown repeatedly, individuals in mass surveys give erratic answers (Converse 1970; Page and Shapiro 1992). In correlation calculus, this naturally increases the error term diminishing the correlation coefficient.[6]

Fortunately, many of the errors in mass surveys are random, so that downward and upward deviations from a given sample mean cancel each other out, leaving the mean values of given variables unaffected. In other words, aggregated variables are relatively robust. Thus, averaging data to aggregate units is nothing suspicious, but rather an efficient means to eliminate random measurement error. Logically, the same two variables correlate much stronger when the error term is diminished, which is exactly what happens when aggregating variables.

Gravity Effects

The difference between aggregate and individual correlations also points to another regularity. Sampling units, such as nations, are contexts of common socialization based on common education systems, common media, and common legal frameworks. For this reason, nations have gravity effects on their constituents: in given variables, constituents tend to cluster around their nation's central tendency. Logically, the within-sample relation between any such centered variables is the smaller (*a*) the more they are centered and (*b*) the larger the threshold in their relation is. Assume, for example, the following: (*i*) the effect of financial income on emancipative values has a large threshold such that only increases in thousands of dollars bring corresponding increases in people's emancipative values; (*ii*) most individuals cluster so closely around the mean income of their sample that most of the within-sample variation is in hundreds of dollars; (*iii*) mean national incomes vary largely such that the between-sample variation occurs in thousands of dollars.

Under these conditions, the relation between income and emancipative values will be weak or even absent at the individual level *within* samples, but will become apparent as soon as *between*-national variation is taken into account. This is logical when national units center the distribution of variables whose relation has thresholds—which is usually the case.

The same phenomenon characterizes the relation between the variables that constitute the syndrome of emancipative values. This syndrome is composed of five component values. The figures in brackets below show loadings on the common factor in order of (*a*) within-sample loadings, (*b*) pooled individual-level loadings, and (*c*) aggregate-level loadings:[7]

- a valuation of civil and political freedom reflected in liberty aspirations (0.54, 0.67, 0.87);
- a valuation of political expression reflected in participation in petitions (0.45, 0.65, 0.84);
- a valuation of human diversity reflected in an acceptance of homosexuality (0.47, 0.68, 0.78);
- a valuation of the life one lives reflected in general life satisfaction (0.13, 0.42, 0.82);
- a valuation of people in general reflected in interpersonal trust (0.34, 0.39, 0.61).

The magnitude of these factor loadings shows that the syndrome of emancipative values is most coherent at the level of aggregate nation-level measurements; that it is second most coherent at the pooled individual level; and that it is least coherent at the individual level within samples. For the reasons outlined above, this is perfectly logical when given variables show (*a*) sample-centered distributions and (*b*) sizeable thresholds in their relation.

The overlapping variance that ties the five components of emancipative values together only occurs over *large* variations in its components. Because of the gravity effects of nations, variations of this size do hardly occur within national samples. They only occur between samples from around the world. Still, even pooled individual-level data contain much random measurement error, which is canceled by aggregation. Hence, the components' coherence becomes most obvious at the aggregate level. The fact that the coherence of emancipative values is not as evident at the individual level within samples does not invalidate the presence of this syndrome at the societal level. It simply shows that within-sample variations are usually too small to adequately represent covariations that only occur on a large scale.

These insights have fundamental implications for area experts, including experts of Asian societies. For one will not find a coherent syndrome of emancipative values within Asian samples. To conclude from this that Asian people are genuinely different, however, would be entirely misleading. It simply demonstrates that regularities that appear between samples on a global scale are not fully visible within samples. This is as true for Asian samples as for any other sample. The incoherence of the emancipative values syndrome within samples is a general regularity, not an Asian specialty.

INTRINSIC AND INSTRUMENTAL SUPPORT FOR DEMOCRACY

The societal-level relation between emancipative values and effective democracy does not have an individual-level equivalent. Democracy is a system property that does not exist at the individual level. However, one might suppose that the effect of emancipative values on effective democracy because these values produce mass support for liberal democracy. For instance, Figure 2.5 showed a clear congruence between emancipative values and effective democracy. Thus, we might also assume that questions that explicitly measure support for democracy would have an even more direct effect on systemic democracy. Surprisingly as it may seem, this is *not* the case.

When we calculate the percentage of people in a country who express strong *overt support for democracy*,[8] this variable explains only 32 percent of the variation in effective democracy over 74 nations in the WVS. By contrast, the national levels of emancipative values explain 80 percent of the variation in effective democracy, *even though none of the components of these values refers explicitly to democracy*. Adding explicit support of democracy to emancipative values as an explanatory factor increases the explained variance by only 5 percent, and explicit democratic support is much weaker and less significant than the effect of emancipative values.[9] Hence, the effect of emancipative values on effective democracy does not operate by producing more people who express overt support of democracy; its impact is direct in creating a climate for democratic politics.

This is all the more noteworthy as we use an elaborated indicator of support for democracy that balances people's support of democracy against their support of authoritarian alternatives to democracy, such as military rule. Accordingly, the support for democracy measure is not inflated by people who react favorably on the term democracy without rejecting other political systems (also see discussion in Chapter 4 in this volume). This finding directs attention to the relationship between emancipative values and support for democracy. Should not these two variables be strongly related because democracy is the natural system preferred by people who emphasize human emancipation?

Indeed, there is a positive relationship between emancipative values and support for democracy. At the aggregate level, a society's mean emphasis on emancipative values correlates at 0.53 with percentages expressing strong overt support for democracy ($N = 71$). At the individual level, people's emphasis on emancipative values correlates with their support for democracy at 0.26 in the pooled global dataset (0.33 in a pooled Japanese, South Korean, and Taiwanese sample). These correlations are highly significant and point into the expected direction. But they are weaker as one might suspect. Why is this the case?

As Inglehart and Welzel (2005: 265–70) demonstrate, the relation between emancipative values and support for democracy exists at the societal level, because societies having relatively large numbers of people who emphasize emancipative values (i.e. above 45 percent) always produce a majority of people who overtly support democracy. Thus, relatively widespread emancipative values are a sufficient condition to produce majorities of overt democrats. What weakens the relation, however, is that the reverse does not hold true. Among societies with low proportions of people emphasizing emancipative values, the proportion of overt supporters of democracy is not necessarily low. Among societies with low levels of emancipative values, one can find a wide range in overt supporters of democracy from a low of almost 0 percent in Vietnam to a high of roughly 80 percent in Bangladesh.[10] Hence, emancipative values are a sufficient, but not necessary, condition to produce majorities of overt supporters of democracy.

Why this is so becomes obvious when one examines the attitudinal predictors of support for democracy at the individual level. Emancipative values are a significant individual-level predictor of overt support for democracy because emancipative people have an intrinsic tendency to endorse the civil and political liberties that define democracy. People who support democracy on the basis of emancipative values support it because of its inherent qualities, not as a means to other ends. This is what we call 'intrinsic' support. But many people with weakly emancipative orientations also support democracy—for other reasons. This is obvious from the fact that what people believe about the performance of democracies, namely how good they think democracies are at maintaining order and managing a prospering economy, is an even better predictor of support of democracy than emancipative values. This sort of support is detached from an intrinsic valuation of democracy's inherent qualities. It derives from performance expectations. Thus, democracy is valued as a means to other ends, not an end in itself. This is what we call 'instrumental' support.

The distinction between intrinsic and instrumental support is crucial and helps explain why emancipative values are a much more powerful predictor of systemic democracy than overt support for democracy. Even the most sophisticated measures of overt support for democracy are highly inflated by instrumental support motives. Only to a lesser extent do they measure intrinsic support for democracy. This makes it necessary to split the overt supporters of democracy into intrinsic supporters (who place relatively strong emphasis on emancipative values) and instrumental supporters (who place relatively little emphasis on emancipative values).

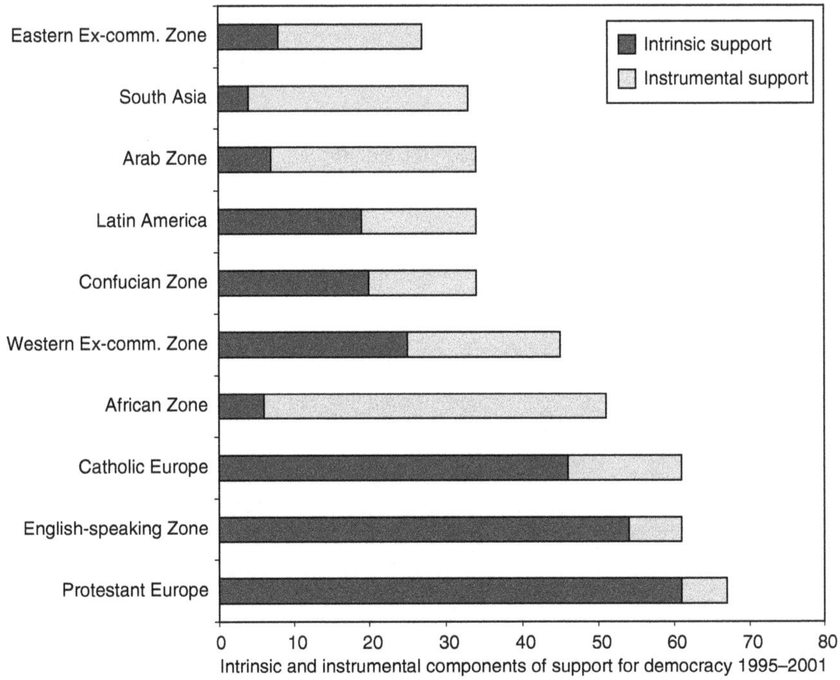

FIGURE 2.6. Partitioning support for democracy into its instrumental and intrinsic components

Source: WVS III and IV.

Figure 2.6 partitions overt democratic support into these two components: intrinsic support and instrumental support. This distinction is based on dividing strong overt supporters of democracy into those placing relatively strong emphasis on emancipative values (intrinsic supporters) and those placing relatively little emphasis on emancipative values (instrumental supporters).[11] This distinction yields highly interesting results. First of all, strong overt support of democracy does not differentiate the world very much any more. It has spread around the globe, showing high levels even in Sub-Saharan Africa. But intrinsic support continues to differentiate the world. It has not diffused into all corners of the planet. And most relevant to the analyses in this volume, overt support for democracy in the Confucian

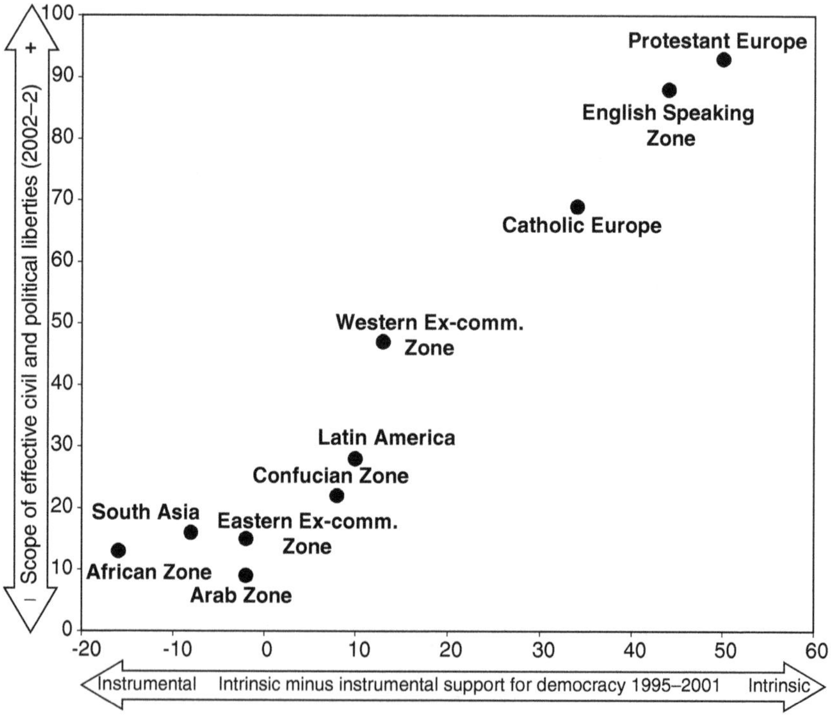

FIGURE 2.7. Effective democracy and intrinsic vs. instrumental support for democracy

Source: Horizontal axis is a percentage difference index calculated by subtracting national proportions of instrumental supporters of democracy from intrinsic supporters (data from earliest available survey from WVS III and IV) Vertical axis is a measure of the scope of civil and political rights in 2000–2 (using scores from Freedom House) weighed by the respect of the rule of law by elites in 2000–2 using the World Bank's control of corruption scores.

nations of East Asia is estimated to be an almost even mix of intrinsic and instrumental motivations.

To extend this logic one step further, Figure 2.7 shows how the *composition* of support of democracy across cultural regions, not its overall level, is related to the level of effective democracy. The extent to which intrinsic supporters exceed instrumental supporters places a cultural zone higher in the level of effective democracy (it should be noted that the national publics of the same cultural zones are very homogenous with regard to the intrinsic versus instrumental composition in support of democracy). In other words, intrinsic criteria constitute only a part of overt support for democracy. But this part is of major importance for a country's effective level of democracy, much more than support for democracy in general. These findings confirm the emphasis that human development theory places on the theme of emancipation. Support for democracy is relevant to real democracy only insofar as it is tied to emancipative values. Democracy is essentially an emancipative achievement, which makes it a central aspect of human development. Available evidence suggests that Far Eastern societies are no exception from this fundamental insight.

CONCLUSION

This chapter has described a model of human development that argues for a general process of human change. Table 2.2 provides a summary of the argument, breaking it down into a number of sequences to be followed by reading the table from top to bottom. The top half summarizes the mechanisms through which socioeconomic development helps give rise to emancipative values, namely by diminishing constraints on human autonomy through an increase of three major types of resources: economic, cognitive, and social. The lower half summarizes the mechanisms through which emancipative values help provide democratic progress. As emancipative values can emerge in both democratic and nondemocratic systems, there are two pathways through which these values affect democracy. If they emerge in a nondemocracy, the conditions of mobilizing a democracy movement improve. Also, the probability that parts of the younger elite cohorts will be affected by such value changes increases, making it more likely that a camp of liberal reformers will split off. All this increases the likelihood of adopting democracy where it is not yet in place. On the other hand, democratic institutions can have been in place for quite some time, such that emancipative values become more pronounced in an already democratic setting. In this case, these values fuel various social movement activities, many of which have in common that they struggle for equal opportunities for underprivileged groups, such as women, gays and lesbians, handicapped people, children, and the like. These movements are proponents of many of

TABLE 2.2. *The human development process*

SOCIOECONOMIC DEVELOPMENT

⇓ ⇓ ⇓

Economic growth and the welfare state increase people's *economic* resources, making them materially more autonomous	Rising levels of education, expanding mass communication, and increasingly knowledge-intensive work widen people's *cognitive* resources, making them intellectually more autonomous	Growing social complexity and diversification broaden people's *social* resources, making them relation-wise more autonomous

⇓ ⇓ ⇓

Diminishing constraints on autonomous choice nurture a basic *sense of human agency*, making people more receptive to the idea of individual freedom and self-expression

⇓

RISING EMANCIPATIVE VALUES

in nondemocracies			in democracies		
⇓	⇓	⇓	⇓	⇓	⇓
growing number of civil and political rights activists	growing mass support for civil and political rights movements	growing number of liberal reformers among elites	growing number of equal opportunity activists	growing mass support for equal opportunity movements	increasingly mass-responsive elites
⇓	⇓	⇓	⇓	⇓	⇓
Formal adoption of liberal democracy			Increasing effectiveness of liberal democracy		
⇓			⇓		

DEMOCRATIC PROGRESS

Source: Adapted from Inglehart and Welzel (2005).

the transformations that Cain, Dalton, and Scarrow (2004) portray as a third transformation of democracy, making existing democracies more people centered. Together, the adoption of democracy where it did not yet exist and the strengthening of democracy where it already does exist constitute democratic progress.

We have not found any evidence that Asian societies are distinct from these general regularities, which we think depict a universal pattern of human development that applies to Asia as to any other culture composed of human beings. In its essence democracy is the political order designed to maximize human choice. Quite naturally, this order tends to take root as people become more capable and willing to make their own choices. Asian people do not seem to differ in this regard.

These insights allow for some speculations. First of all, should economic growth continue as dynamically as it did recently in China and Vietnam, we expect these societies to show rising generational differences in emancipative values, with a younger generation of highly educated people in the booming urban middle classes showing growing emphasis on emancipative values. To be sure, we know that cultural traditions can have a retarding effect on the impact of socioeconomic development on emancipative values. The fact that the Taiwanese and South Korean publics show less emphasis on emancipative values than their level of individual resources suggests points in this direction. Perhaps socioeconomic development impacts on emancipative values with a less steep gradient in Confucian societies. But this does not mean that the fundamental relation between socioeconomic development and emancipative values is altogether invalid in Asian societies. Countries like Japan and China are located on our maps of human development exactly where one would predict them to be using the two relations we have elaborated on.

Based on these relations, we predict that if China and Vietnam continue to show the current rate of socioeconomic development (which they seem likely to do), emancipative values will become more prominent in these societies. As this happens, prospects for pressures to democratize from within these societies will rise. In highly developed societies, such as Japan and South Korea, emancipative values already have a prominent place. Given the generational differences in these values, it is plausible to predict a further increase in years to follow. According to the logic of our model, this implies that Japan and South Korea should experience many of the developments that Cain, Dalton, and Scarrow (2004) describe as the third transformation of democracy, which is a transformation that makes democracies more people centered.

Overall, we see the prospects for democracy in Asia in a rather positive light. Some caution is appropriate, however, as the logic of our human development model also functions in the reverse direction. Existential threats deriving from sudden economic shocks or terrorism can seriously weaken the emphasis on emancipative values, making the ground for authoritarian regimes more fertile again.

ENDNOTES

1 Like others in this volume, our analyses are based on data from the WVS. Appendix A describes the details of the surveys in East Asia. Additional information on the full set of nations in the WVS is available from the project website: www.worldvaluessurvey.org or from Inglehart et al. (2004).

2 Emancipative values summarize five aggregate component values in a factor-weighed combination, including: (*a*) a valuation of civil and political freedom (reflected in liberty aspir-

ations), (*b*) a valuation of political expression (reflected in participating in petitions), (*c*) a valuation of human diversity (reflected in an acceptance of homosexuality), (*d*) a valuation of fellow people (reflected in interpersonal trust), and (*e*) a valuation of one's life (reflected in life satisfaction). The index is created in such a way that it can be interpreted as the percentage of people emphasizing emancipative values. Also see the discussion below on pp. 40. For additional information on measurement and scaling details, see the Internet appendix to Inglehart and Welzel (2005) at: http://www.worldvaluessurvey.org/publications/humandevelopment.html, under 'Variables' (#49).

3 Individual resources are a composite measure taken from Vanhanen (1997), combining the level and distribution of material resources, intellectual resources, and a measure of social complexity that is supposed to indicate diversity in people's social connectivity. The index yields values of maximum 100. For more details see the Internet appendix to Inglehart and Welzel (2005) at: http://www.worldvaluessurvey.org/publications/humandevelopment.html under 'Variables' (#08).

4 Our measure of effective democracy combines the formal presence of civil and political rights and the elites' respect of rule of law ('elite integrity') in such a way that high scores in elite integrity cannot do more than simply reproduce a given level of civil and political rights (measured in percentiles of the possible maximum), whereas low scores in elite integrity can seriously downgrade a given level of civil and political rights. For measurement details, see the Internet appendix to Inglehart and Welzel (2005) at: http://www.worldvaluessurvey.org/publications/humandevelopment.html under 'Variables' (#21).

5 To calculate this correlation, a variable combining an individual's level of formal education (measured on a nine-point ordinal scale from no education to university-level education) and income level (measured in national currency deciles of available household income) has been constructed. For the magnitude of the correlation, it does not matter if one uses an additive or multiplicative combination of education and income.

6 This is a fundamental issue in comparative politics, dealing with the problem of using aggregated individual-level data as collective attributes of entire populations (see Seligson 2002; Inglehart and Welzel 2003).

7 That is, the first coefficient is based on analyses of the individual level data separately for each nation, and then averaged. The second coefficient is from a single analysis of the individuals in the pooled cross-national file, where individuals are still the units of analysis. The third coefficient is based on an analysis of national mean scores where nations are the units of analysis. For additional information on the measurement of these components, see the Internet appendix to Inglehart and Welzel (2005) at: http://www.worldvaluessurvey.org/publications/humandevelopment.html under 'Variables' (#43–49).

8 Following Klingemann (1999), we created an 'autocracy–democracy preference' index as follows: we first summed up the extent to which a respondent endorses the statements 'Having a democratic political system' (V166 in WVS III-IV) and 'Democracy may have problems but it's better than any other form of government' (V172). Approval of these statements can be expressed in four categories: 'very good' (recoded 3), 'fairly good' (recoded 2), 'fairly bad' (coded 1), and 'very bad' (coded 0) with the former and 'agree strongly' (coded 3), 'agree' (coded 2), 'disagree' (coded 1), and 'disagree strongly' (coded 0) with the latter. Thus, support for these statements adds up to produce a scale from 0 to 6, with 6 representing the highest support for democracy. In the second step, we summed up people's agreement that 'Having a strong leader who does not have to bother with parliament and elections' (V164) and 'Having the army rule' (V165) would be a good way to run this country. This also creates a 0–6 scale, measuring support for authoritarian forms of government. We then subtracted support for authoritarian rule from support for democracy, yielding an index from −6 (maximum support for autocracy) to +6 (maximum support for democracy). Finally, we calculated for each sample the percentage scoring at least +4 on this −6 to +6 index, classifying those respondents as 'strong' overt supporters of democracy.

9 To be more precise, regression results are as follows:

Predictors	Dependent variable: Scope of effective civil and political liberties 2000–2		
% Strong overt supporters of democracy[a]	0.55*** (5.61)	—	0.17** (2.96)
% Emphasizing emancipative values[b]	—	0.89*** (16.89)	0.82*** (14.63)
Adjusted R^2	0.29	0.80	0.83
N	74	74	71

Entries are standardized beta-coefficients with T-ratios in parentheses.
[a] Average measure is in 1998 (earliest available survey from WVS III-IV).
[b] Average measure is in 1992 (earliest available survey from WVS II-III).
Note: *** Significant at .01 level. ** Significant at 0.05 level.

See also Inglehart and Welzel (2005: 255).

10 This is not because the Vietnamese do not say favorable things about democracy. Quite the contrary. A relatively large proportion indicates that having a democratic system is a good idea. However, we have calculated support for democracy such that support for authoritarian alternatives is subtracted. Since a large number of the Vietnamese also says that having the army rule is a good idea, almost no respondent achieved a score of at least +4 on the −6 to +6 autocracy–democracy preference scale. Very few people in the Vietnamese sample could be classified as strong supporters of democracy.

11 Respondents scoring high in support for democracy (4 or higher in the autocracy–democracy preference index described in fn. 8) have been divided into (*a*) those having above-average emancipative values (i.e. scoring above the overall mean in individual-level emancipative values) and (*b*) those having below-average emancipative values. Group (*a*) has been classified as intrinsic supporters of democracy and group (*b*) as instrumental supporters. For each sample, the percentage of both groups has been calculated. Finally, a percentage difference index has been created by subtracting instrumental from intrinsic supporters. For further details on instrumental and intrinsic support of democracy, see the Internet appendix to Inglehart and Welzel (2005) at: http://www.worldvaluessurvey.org/publications/humandevelopment.html, under 'Variables' (#58–60). Note that for East Asian societies, this index could only be created for Japan, Taiwan, and South Korea.

3

Self-Expression, 'Asian Values', and Democracy: East Asia in Global Perspective

Zhengxu Wang and Ern-Ser Tan

The emergence of a socially and politically active public has been a major factor contributing to democratization across the globe. In various societies, we are observing a public increasingly more oriented toward secular–rational and self-expression values. This process of value change is itself an outcome of modernization, a process set in motion by economic growth, urbanization, and development in information technology and mass communications. Modernization scholars, such as Inglehart and Welzel (see Chapter 2), argue that the rapid economic gains experienced by the past generations globally have predictable consequences for political modernization and democratization across a broad range of countries, including those in East Asia.

At the same time, however, proponents of the Asian values position have questioned the applicability of the general 'modernization–democratization' model to the East Asian region. Essentially, the Asian values argument maintains that the culture of East Asian societies has somehow rendered their citizens more tolerant—even supportive—of strong government, and, correspondingly, we are unlikely to witness the expansion of civil society groups that are characteristic of democratizing nations (Alagappa, 2004; also see Chapter by Dalton and Ong).[1]

A third aspect of this debate suggests that, although traditionally Asian societies have developed a system of belief and culture different from that of the West, such a system does not prevent the emergence of modern (hence, prodemocratic) values. Better still, in the age of global exchanges and integration, the traditional values of Asian societies may themselves be transformed and, in turn, contribute to the development of global culture, including democratic values (Chan 1998; Tu 2000*a*, 2000*b*). Many of the chapters of this volume do, in fact, document the democratic aspirations among East Asian publics.

This chapter examines the relationship between modernization, value change, and democracy in East Asia. It begins by asking whether the phenomenal economic growth in the region is producing value changes supportive of democracy. More specifically, it seeks to determine the extent to which self-expression values are prevalent amongst the publics in East Asia. The answers to these questions first entails developing a measure of self-expression values appropriate for the East Asian context, and then using it to examine value change across East Asian societies. Following that, we examine the theme of Asian values, if these values are prevalent in the region, and have modified the relationship between modernization and democracy. In other words, we ask whether traditional Asian culture can change the character and trajectory of democratization. Our analysis resonates with those of Inglehart and Welzel (Chapter 2) in seeing human development as a universal process. Although cultural traditions and regional particularities may result in different patterns in human development, we believe there is an overall tendency of a society advancing toward democratic attitudes and democratic government on top of economic development.

MEASURING SELF-EXPRESSION VALUES

Scholars have argued that self-expression values are part of a core value dimension in the modernization process (Inglehart 1997; Inglehart and Welzel 2005). Self-expression is a cluster of values that has several elements: social tolerance, life satisfaction, public expression, and liberty aspiration.[2] This five-item measure of self-expression is a critical intervening variable connecting socioeconomic development and democratization. Correspondingly, self-expression values is a key component in a theory of democratization understood as a process of human development (see Chapter 2). Other studies of modernization and value change discuss many of these same concepts as important aspects of the modernization process (Inkeles and Smith 1974; Flanagan and Lee 2000, 2003).

Thus far, however, most of the key studies on self-expression values have utilized global or cross-country comparisons in which the units of analysis are nations. This chapter focuses on one region—specifically, the six Confucian societies in East Asia. We analyze value changes across subsocietal levels, such as generational cohorts in these societies. Such an analysis entails our developing a new measurement for self-expression values derived from data based on the region. We have three main reasons for undertaking this task.

First, the structure of belief systems may differ across regions because of historical and cultural traditions. Analyses aiming at building a single global dimension are not sensitive to such variations. Analyses conducted within cultural zones may generate results that differ from those at the global level.

Certain value items may show strong correlations at the regional level, but not at the global level, and vice versa. More precisely, the factors emerging from the two levels of analysis may not be similar. In addition, culturally more homogenous regions may produce value patterns that are more clearly identifiable at the regional level, than at the global level.

Second, the self-expression factor in the existing literature was created as part of an effort to represent cultural changes in two dimensions: the survival/self-expression dimension and the traditional/secular–rational dimension. Inglehart and Baker (2000) use ten variables to capture value changes on these two dimensions. A factor analysis of these ten variables directly results in two factor scores, one representing the self-expression values dimension and the other the traditional–rational dimension. We ask whether adding other theoretically relevant variables to the analysis results in different factor patterns. In our case, we include such variables as attitude toward gender equality, and views on authority at the workplace or within the family.[3]

Third, the self-expression factor in current scholarship includes 'public expression' as one of the five elements. The public's willingness to express their views through actions, such as petition or demonstration is, undoubtedly, an important element of the self-expression concept. Methodologically, however, a minor problem exists. The relevant WVS question was designed to measure protest *behavior:* it asks respondents whether they have signed a petition. Although protest behaviors probably reflect some underlying democratic values, we decided to use attitudinal measures that possess greater cross-cultural validity than behavioral measures. For instance, Dalton and van Sickle (2005) argue that protest is a consequence of democracy and democratic values, and therefore should be separated from values that predict democracy.

Thus, we first investigate whether there is a more reliable and inclusive measure of self-expression values for the nations of East Asia. At the same time, we are also conducting a theoretical examination of the meaning of self-expression values in the Asian context, especially across the wide range of national conditions that exist in the region

DEVELOPING A SELF-EXPRESSION FACTOR FOR EAST ASIA

We began with a factor analysis to define the self-expression value dimension among East Asian publics. We chose six societies to represent East Asia: Japan, South Korea, China, Taiwan, Vietnam, and Singapore. All of these societies may be described as possessing a significant Confucian heritage, but have had different developmental experiences in recent decades. Therefore, they allow us to examine the possible influence of a common tradition on societies that have followed different social, economic, and political trajectories.

Furthermore, such analyses allow us to test the validity of the Asian values argument. We selected the most recent wave of WVS for our analyses (see Appendix A for the time of survey and the sample size of each society).

To find the combination of variables representing self-expression values, we took an inductive approach. we included as many relevant variables as possible, and let the emerging patterns lead us to the best configuration of variables. We identified a pool of more than twenty variables from the WVS. The value concepts covered by these variables include the following items: liberty aspiration (e.g. whether political rights and freedom are more important than material interests), attitudes toward workplace authority (e.g. whether one should follow order unconditionally), attitudes toward family authority relationship (e.g. authority relationship between parents and children), attitudes toward gender equality, interpersonal trust, tolerance of outgroups; environmentalist beliefs (e.g. whether it is acceptable to sacrifice environment for economic development), attitudes toward religion (e.g. whether God is very important), attitudes toward one's personal life (e.g. whether friends are very important, leisure is very important), and political engagement (e.g. whether politics is very important).[4]

We conducted intensive analyses to find out which variables cluster together to form cohesive factors. We adopted several criteria when selecting the variables that potentially constitute our self-expression values factor. Most importantly, given that liberty aspiration (or postmaterialism) is the main component of self-expression orientation (Inglehart and Welzel 2005), we assign it the status of a core variable in the factor structure. If a variable has a high covariance with liberty aspiration, then it is likely to have a high loading when included in the factor analysis with liberty aspiration, which would increase its probability of becoming part of our self-expression values factor. Social tolerance is highly correlated with liberty aspirations; these two variables therefore became the core components of our self-expression values factor.[5]

In addition to liberty aspiration and tolerance, our measurement includes four themes that are not found in Inglehart's self-expression factor. These are rejection of patriarchy, rejection of paternalism, support for gender equality, and importance of leisure. Rejection of patriarchy is measured in terms of the extent of inclination toward equality in parent–child relationship. It is reflected in the responses to statements about whether children's respect for parents ought to be earned rather than expected, and whether parents should have their own lives to live, rather than living their lives entirely for their children (also see Chapter 5 in this volume). Rejection of hierarchic authority at the workplace is gauged by the question of whether one should question the logic and reasonableness of instructions before following them, or whether one should always follow instructions unconditionally. In short, these elements of self-expression values correspond to an emphasis on independence, autonomy, and rationality, as opposed to blind obedience and deference to authority.

Another dimension in our self-expression factor is gender equality, as measured by responses to statements such as whether 'men make better political leaders', 'a boy's education is more important than a girl's', as well as attitude toward women having a career, and women having the right to make their own marital, sexual, and maternal choices. A favorable attitude toward gender equality is part of the fundamental value change accompanying the modernization process, and that the move toward protection of women's rights is a good indicator of a shift towards a more prodemocratic worldview (Inglehart and Norris 2003). The last dimension in our analysis relates to the importance of leisure. This dimension measures the shift from an outlook focused on material security to one geared towards a postmaterialist concern such as quality of life (Inglehart 1990).

We combined these items into a factor analysis to identify if there is a common dimension of values (Table 3.1). Our final self-expression values measure includes attitudes toward liberty, participation, tolerance, gender equality, family, and workplace authority as all being significantly related to this underlying dimension. Within East Asian societies, there is significant coherence among these social values, although this may not always be

TABLE 3.1. *Factor structure of self-expression values in Confucian Asia*

	Factor loading
(1) Liberty aspiration (0–5)	0.524
Respondent gives more priority to liberty and freedom than material and physical security	
(2) Tolerance (standardized score)	0.666
Respondent feels that behaviors such as abortion and groups such as prostitutes are somewhat justified	
(3) Equal family relationship (standardized score)	0.658
Respondent thinks that parents should earn their respect by their behaviors, instead of requiring children to respect them unconditionally; and	
Respondent thinks parents have their own lives, instead of doing everything for the benefits of their children	
(4) Leisure is important (1–4)	0.464
Respondent feels leisure is an important part of one's life	
(5) Gender equality (1–4)	0.328
Respondent disagrees that men have more right to jobs than women	
(6) Reject workplace paternalism (1–3)	0.305
Respondent thinks that one should follow directions from one's supervisor only when one is convinced, instead of following directions unconditionally	

Source: Wave 4 (1999–2001) of WVS conducted in China, Japan, Korea, Singapore, Vietnam, and Wave 3 (1995) of WVS conducted in Taiwan. Extraction Method: Principal Component Analysis; One component extracted.

TABLE 3.2. *Correlation between self-expression values and component dimensions*

Variables	Correlation with self-expression values
Variables positively correlated with self-expression values factor	
1. Friends are important for my life	0.23
2. Independence is an important quality for children	0.12
3. Woman do not need to have children in order to feel fulfilled	0.14
4. Both husband and wife should contribute to household income	0.16
5. Men do not necessarily make better political leaders than women	0.22
6. A boy's education is no more important than a girl's	0.18
Variables negatively correlated with self-expression values factor	
7. One of my life goals is to make my parents proud	−0.15
8. Obedience is an important quality for children	−0.22
9. Hard work is an important quality for children	−0.24
10. Do not want to have heavy drinkers to be one's neighbor	−0.20
11. Good and evil are clearly cut	−0.15
12. Religion is very important	−0.12
13. God is very important	−0.14
14. Willing to fight in war for my country	−0.30
15. Proud of my nation	−0.25

*All correlations significant at $p = 0.001$.
Source: Wave 4 (1999–2001) of WVS conducted in China, Japan, Korea, Singapore, and Vietnam, and Wave 3 (1995) of WVS conducted in Taiwan, with a sample size of 1,500 for each country.

obvious at first glance. For instance, a person who considers freedom of speech to be more important than economic well-being will, among other things, also think that men and women should enjoy equal social opportunities; that disliked groups or behaviors should be tolerated; that the relation between parents and children should not be patriarchal; and that paternalism in the workplace should be replaced by persuasion, negotiation, and mutual respect.[6]

How then does our measurement of self-expression values differ from that of Inglehart and colleagues? Our measure has six value themes, while theirs has five (see Chapter 2, Footnote 2), albeit with different content. First, our measurement includes two value dimensions that Inglehart and his colleagues use: liberty aspiration (or postmaterialism) and social tolerance. This similarity indicates that self-expression is a worldview that stresses both liberty and tolerance—two dimensions that seem to constitute the core of these values. Liberty aspiration can be understood in terms of an individual's demand for two kinds of freedom: passive liberty, such as freedom of speech, and active liberty, such as participation in decision-making and politics. Tolerance is an inclusive attitude toward ethnic minorities and deviant groups. Although we excluded public expression, the liberty aspiration dimension does relate to attitudes pertaining to political participation. The last three dimensions included in our self-expression factor are rejection of paternalism, rejection of patriarchy, and support of gender equality.[7]

To better understand the concept of self-expression values, we will focus our attention on how it correlates with other value dimensions. In Table 3.2, the upper panel comprises those dimensions that are positively correlated with the self-expression factor, while the lower panel lists those dimensions that are negatively correlated with it.

This table shows that self-expression values are a syndrome of values that emphasize independence, creativity, liberty, and self-realization, while rejecting obedience, patriarchy, and paternalism (positive correlation with item 2 in the table; negative correlation with items 7 and 8). It also stresses tolerance (negative correlation with item 10), gender equality (positive with items 3, 4, 5, 6), and quality of life (positive with the first item, negative correlation with the ninth). Furthermore, self-expression values are supportive of secular rather than religious values (negative correlation with twelfth and thirteenth) (Inglehart and Norris 2004). Just as interesting is our finding that self-expression values run counter to strong nationalist sentiments (negative correlation with the last two items).[8]

IS THERE A CONFUCIAN ASIA?

Having derived a self-expression factor for East Asia, we next address the question of whether there is indeed a cultural region characterized by the prevalence of Asian values. In asking this question, our intention is not to revive the Asian values debate, nor are we suggesting that cultural specificities can be used to justify undemocratic governments. Rather, we are seeking to establish by empirical means whether there is a Confucian Asia distinct from South Asia and Central Asia, among other cultural zones such as Protestant Europe and Catholic Europe, on the "cultural map" advanced by earlier scholarships (Inglehart 2003; Inglehart and Baker 2000).

The six items in the self-expression factor shown in Table 3.1 form a coherent pattern among the publics of East Asian societies. Should these same variables form a similar pattern across different cultural zones, then there is probably no uniquely East Asian phenomenon as defined by self-expression values. If, however, the six value items produce a different value pattern for other societies, then we have some basis to argue that there are distinct cultural zones. We compare the factor loadings on the six value items for several East Asian countries that have a Confucian cultural heritage (China, Taiwan, Japan, Korea, Singapore, and Vietnam), with two countries in South Asia (India and Bangladesh), and two in Southeast Asia (Indonesia and the Philippines).

TABLE 3.3. *Factor analyses for Confucian and non-Confucian Asia*

	Confucian countries	Indonesia	Philippines	India	Bangladesh
Liberty aspiration (0–5) Respondent gives more priority to liberty and freedom than material and physical security	0.524	0.363	0.400	0.639	0.624
Tolerance (standardized score) Respondent feels that behaviors such as abortion and groups such as prostitutes and homosexuals are somewhat justified	0.666	n/a	n/a	n/a	0.624[a]
Equal relationship between parents and children (standardized score) Respondent thinks that parents should earn their respect by their behaviors, instead of requiring children to respect them unconditionally; and Respondent thinks parents have their own lives, instead of doing everything for the benefits of their children	0.658	n/a	−0.331	0.545	0.598
Leisure is important (1–4) Respondent feels leisure is an important part of one's life	0.464	−0.419	0.456	n/a	n/a
Gender equality (1–4) Respondent disagrees that men have more right to jobs than women	0.328	0.681	0.482	0.514	n/a
Against workplace paternalism (1–3) Respondent thinks that one should follow directions from one's supervisor only when one is convinced, instead of following directions unconditionally	0.305	0.590	0.656	0.547	n/a
Number of component extracted	1	3	3	2	2

Source: Wave 4 (1999–2001) of WVS conducted in China, Japan, Korea, Singapore, Vietnam, Indonesia, Philippines, India, and Bangladesh, and Wave 3 (1995) of WVS conducted in Taiwan.

Notes: An 'n/a' in the cell refers to this variable not loading with the Self-Expression Values factor for this country, but instead loads with another factor. As a result, its loading with the Self-Expression Values factor is very low and hence is not reported here.

[a]The factor of tolerance in Bangladesh has a structure which differs from that of the Confucian societies and India (see Inglehart and Norris 2003).

Table 3.3 shows the factor structures of the Confucian and non-Confucian countries in East and Southeast Asia. The same variables form *different* factors in these societies. For Confucian societies, these variables form a single factor, but for the non-Confucian societies, they form two or more factors. For the Confucian societies, the two highest loading value dimensions are social tolerance (tolerating outgroups and disliked behaviors) and rejection of patriarchal relations (support equal parent–child relationship), but this is not the case for the non-Confucian countries. Social tolerance does not have loading on the first dimension for Indonesia, the Philippines, and India, and rejection of patriarchy is not a loading variable for Indonesia. In other words, in these societies, people who value liberty and political rights may not at the same time support social tolerance or rejection of family patriarchy. In the case of Bangladesh, people who support liberty and political rights may not support leisure as an important part of human life, nor are they inclined toward gender equality.

From the above analysis, we may infer that the East Asian countries constitute a distinct cultural zone. Furthermore, given the historical and cultural connections between the East Asian countries, we may label this zone as Confucian Asia, as distinct from South Asia, Southeast Asia, Central Asia, or West Asia.

'ASIAN VALUES' AND DEMOCRACY: SINGAPORE AND ASIAN CULTURAL ZONES COMPARED

We next examine whether the publics of Confucian Asia are supportive of authoritarianism. As noted earlier, the proponents of Asian values have suggested, even asserted, that East Asians do not support Western liberal democracy. Given that Singapore is a major source and epitome of the Asian values argument, it makes sense to use Singapore as a critical case to investigate whether people in Confucian Asia are indeed less inclined toward prodemocratic values.

Our approach is to plot the positions of the East, Southeast, and South Asia countries included in the WVS on the two-dimensional space defined by Inglehart and colleagues (Inglehart and Baker 2000). In addition, for the Singapore case, we plotted not only its overall location, but also that of its main component ethnic categories: Chinese, Malays, and Indians. The resulting cultural map is shown in Figure 3.1.[9]

This cultural map displays several interesting features. Asia (excluding West Asia or parts of the Middle East) may empirically be grouped into three cultural zones: East Asia (China, Japan, South Korea, and Taiwan), South Asia (India, Pakistan, and Bangladesh), and Southeast Asia (Indonesia, the Philippines, and Vietnam).[10] In addition, perhaps not surprisingly, Singapore is located almost at the center of the cultural map.

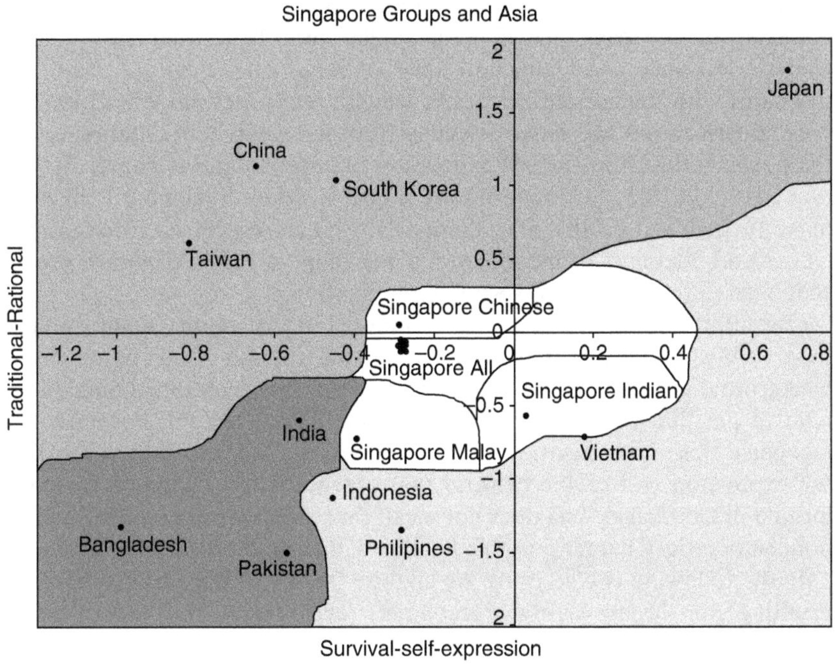

FIGURE 3.1. The map of Asian value space
Source: World Values Survey.

The more or less geometrically center position of Singapore may be attributed to two factors. First, Singapore is a culturally and ethnically heterogeneous society. Ethnically, its population comprises a Chinese majority (78 percent), Malay (14 percent), and Indian minorities (7 percent). Moreover, the population follows a mix of religious beliefs, primarily Buddhism, Taoism, Islam, Christianity, and Hinduism. This ethnic and cultural heterogeneity may account for Singapore's location on the cultural map relative to that of its geographical neighbors.

From Figure 3.1, one may infer that Singapore's position on the cultural map reflects some degree of cultural continuity between Singapore's ethnic groups and their related neighboring cultural zones. At least for the two major ethnic groups, Chinese and Malay, this is clearly the case: the Singapore Chinese are located close to China and the other northeast Asian societies, while their Malay counterparts are located close to Southeast Asia's Indonesia.

Second, Singapore's position on the cultural map can be explained by its relatively high degree of economic development and social modernization. If we agree that Singapore's extent of modernization is less than that of Japan, close to that of South Korea, and more advanced than Bangladesh and Pakistan, then it seems plausible for Singapore to be located 'east' of Bangladesh, Pakistan, and China and 'west' of Japan on the cultural map. This resonates with the current literature, which argues that modernization and postmodernization will move a society from the survival orientation end of the horizontal axis to the self-expression orientation end (Chapter 2). One may also infer that, with continuing modernization, Singapore is likely to move further east on this map. Similarly, we may expect countries such as China and Vietnam to move east on the map as they experience greater economic development and social modernization.

Overall, this analysis suggests two things. First, a country's cultural heritage visibly influences its trajectory of value changes. Singapore's ethnic background and cultural heritage have more or less determined Singapore's relative position on the cultural map. Second, one should, however, also recognize that modernization tends to produce a cultural shift toward the self-expression end of the cultural map. Hence, the fact that a society is located in Confucian Asia does not mean that its value structure will remain nondemocratic. Chapter 5 in this volume will expand on this theme.

In the following two sections, we analyze the rise of self-expression values resulting from the process of socioeconomic developments and modernization/postmodernization occurring in East Asia.

RISE OF SELF-EXPRESSION VALUES IN EAST ASIA: 1930s–1990s

We have shown that, while Confucian societies differ from South Asian and Southeast Asian societies, their publics are not necessarily more resistant to acquiring prodemocratic self-expression values. Indeed, if we look upon the self-expression values factor as a broad measurement of support for democracy, we would notice that most Confucian societies (Japan, South Korea, Vietnam, and Singapore) are more prodemocratic than some neighboring societies that possess democratic institutions (e.g. India and Bangladesh). As Inglehart and Welzel argue in Chapter 2, the existence of formal democratic institutions (such as elections) does not in itself guarantee quality democracy. Rather, the incidence of self-expression values may be a better indicator of the extent of a democratic political culture in a polity. To put it another way, democratic governance is sustained, if not brought about, by a public with well-developed self-expression values.

The development of such values is in turn a result of continued socioeconomic development and modernization and postmodernization. Given Confucian Asia's recent rapid socioeconomic development and modernization, we may hypothesize that there is a shift toward self-expression values within these societies. While time-series data covering several decades are not available, we can examine evidence of long-term value changes by comparing intergenerational changes in self-expression values. Differences between generations can reveal long-term trends of a given society, given that significant value shifts take place largely through generational replacements (Dalton 1977; Inglehart 1977; Jennings and Niemi 1981).[11]

Figure 3.2 plots the self-expression values scores of six age cohorts in several Confucian societies. The time periods marked on the X-axis are the years during which the respondents within each cohort were between 10 and 20 years of age, which are understood to be crucial years in the shaping of social values at the level of individuals (Mannheim 1952; Dalton 1977). For all six societies, there is a rising trend in self-expression values from the 1930s to the 1990s. The trend rises more sharply in Japan, Korea, and Taiwan, and less so in Singapore, China, and Vietnam.

Apart from this broad trend, several other findings are also significant. Five of these societies demonstrate the same level of self-expression values just prior to 1945, while Japan demonstrates higher level of self-expression values since the earliest generation for which we have data. This suggests that Confucian societies did share similar sociopolitical values before the

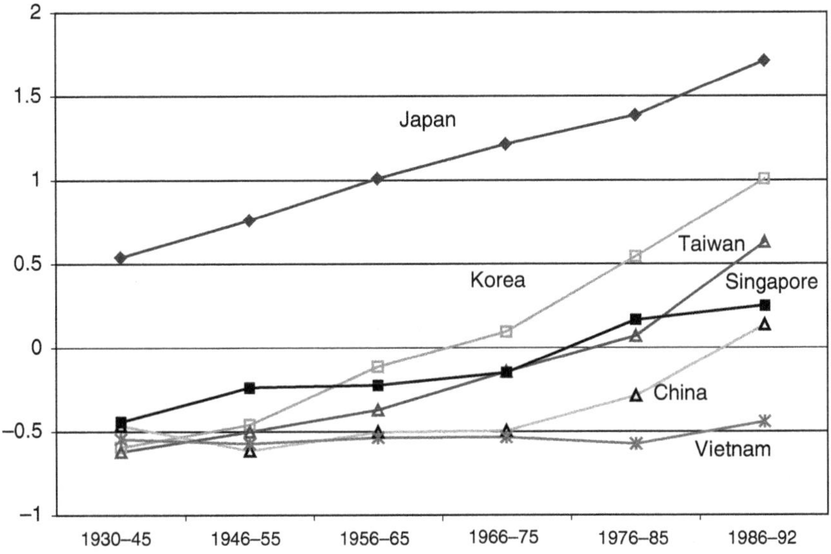

FIGURE 3.2. Intergenerational value shifts in six Confucian societies

Source: 1999–2001 (WVS) of Japan, Korea, Singapore, China, and Vietnam, 1995 WVS of Taiwan.

Note: The X-axis shows the time periods when each cohort was between 10 and 20 years old.

Self-Expression Values: A factor score of six variables: Liberty aspiration, tolerance, gender equality, attitude toward patriarchal family relationships, attitude toward paternalism at workplace, and importance of leisure.

commencement of industrialization, and that Japan was ahead of fellow Confucian societies in terms of self-expression values. We interpret Japan's relatively high level of self-expression values as corresponding to its having embarked on industrialization earlier. Indeed, by the 1930s, Japan was already a highly industrialized society. Thus, as early as the 1930s, the Japanese public was much more self-expression oriented compared to the publics of the other Asian societies, which were mostly agrarian.

In addition, once rapid industrialization and economic take-off are underway—and political institutions also begin to change—people's values shift dramatically toward greater emphasis on self-expression. Japan and the Asian newly industrializing economies (NIEs)—Korea, Taiwan, and Singapore—are prime examples.[12] Indeed, in all the three NIE societies, there is a clear leap from the 1946–55 cohort to the 1956–65 cohort. The 1960s was the period in which industrialization took off in these societies. As economic growth continued, so did the momentum of value shift beyond 1965. There is a high probability that the trajectory of value shifts in Korea and Taiwan will converge with that of Japan as they enter the postindustrial stage of economic development.

The relationship between economic development, modernization, and self-expression values applies even to socialist economies like China and Vietnam. Although self-expression factor scores in these two countries remains low and unchanging for several generations, once economic take-off begins, there is a corresponding shift in the social and political values of their publics. China's high economic growth began in the late 1970s and early 1980s. Since then, its economy has been growing at about 10 percent annually. In Vietnam's case, economic reforms were initiated during the mid- to late 1980s, which subsequently resulted in economic growth rates of between 7 and 10 percent. The figure shows that the shift toward self-expression values in these two societies also coincides with the timeline of economic take-off. In China, the value shift began with the 1980s cohort, while, in Vietnam, it was evident in the 1990s cohort.

EDUCATION AND SELF-EXPRESSION VALUES

Besides looking at generational differences, we also examine other dimensions of social change that may affect social values. We would argue that the extent of urbanization and mass information[13] as well as the proportion of people employed in the professions or the service or knowledge sector (finance, education, business) would encourage the growth of self-expressive values in a society (Inglehart 1990). More generally, a powerful element contributing to the rise of self-expression values is education. Educational attainment is probably the single most important variable that explains individual political attitudes (Jennings and Niemi 1974).

In Figure 3.3, we compare self-expression values of the six societies by education level.[14] The figure shows a clear picture that, in each society, higher level of education attainment translates into stronger self-expression values. Education seems to make the biggest impact in South Korea, as evident in the 'slope' of its data line. In contrast, the Vietnam case exemplifies a weaker impact of education on self-expression orientation, with the exception of college education (also see Chapter 4). The data line of Singapore in Figure 3.3 is above all other societies, other than Japan. This indicates that education in Singapore has a relatively stronger effect on self-expression orientation than in other societies. To put it another way, although the overall strength of self-expression values in Singapore is equal to or weaker than that of South Korea and Taiwan, it can be observed that at each level of education, a Singaporean is likely to be more self-expression oriented than his or her counterparts *with the same level of education* in South Korea or Taiwan.

These analyses suggest that increasing public access to education, especially higher education, can contribute directly to the rise of self-expression values of a society. We therefore have good reasons to be optimistic about the future, given the sustained expansion of education—even mass higher education—among the East Asian societies. In the case of China, the gross higher education rate (percentage of age cohort receiving college education) has increased from close to 4 percent in the early 1980s to 15 percent in 2001, and will likely to hit close to 30 percent by 2020 (National Education

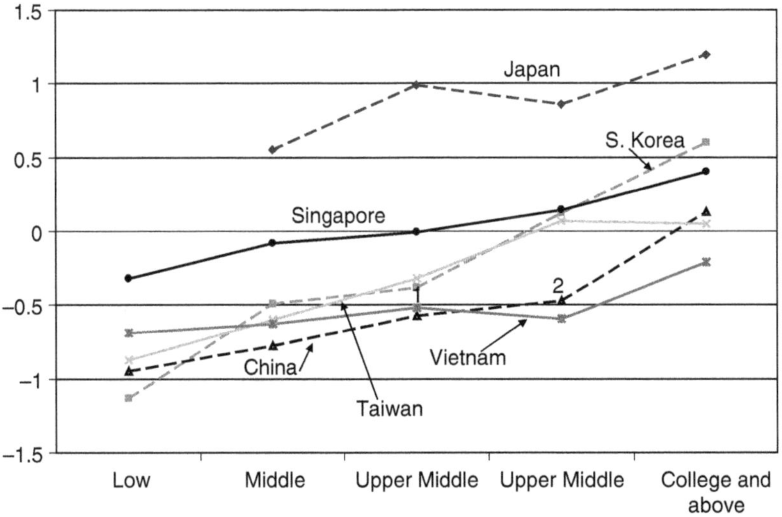

FIGURE 3.3. Education level and self-expression values in six Confucian societies
Source: China, Japan, South Korea, Vietnam, Singapore: WVS, 1999–2002; Taiwan: WVS, 1995.

Development Center 2003). Such advancements in mass access to education bode well for the strengthening of self-expression values in these societies.

BENIGN AUTHORITARIANISM?

Self-expression values are growing among East Asian societies, but a major controversy regarding the relationship between value and democratic institutions is still unresolved. The cosmopolitan or liberalist point of view presented in Chapter 2 sees the rise of self-expression values as a global certainty. Inglehart and Welzel argue that this universal process of human development will result in conditions favorable to the rise and effective functioning of democratic governance. In contrast, the culture-specific argument, including the more radical Asian values claim, maintains that Western democracy does not fit the sociocultural realities of Asia. It argues that Asian publics prefer a communal society of order and harmony, in which the society is a big family and the state is the paternalist father who takes care of his dependents. In contrast, this perspective argues that Western democracy is conducive to extreme individualism, competition and conflicts, and violations of social and communal norms (Zakaria 1994). Such a view (the Asian values view) of good society and good government can be termed as 'benign authoritarianism'. A moderate or centrist view sees the East Asian heritage as a valuable contribution to human understanding of good society and good government, rather than one that hinders the possibility of democratic governance (Chan 1998; Tu 2000*b*; O'Dwyer 2003).

We found some evidence supporting the argument that Asian publics may have a different view of what is a good society. The WVS asked respondents about the kind of society they prefer. One option is 'a society that assures safety and stability through appropriate regulations', and another is 'a deregulated society where people are responsible for their own actions'. The first option offers a vision close to benign authoritarianism: a state with power, but that uses power for supposedly 'good' purposes. The second option, in contrast, is close to a liberalist or even a libertarian vision of state–society relationship. The respondent is asked to choose from a 1–5 scale, where '1' is for the first option and '5' for the second option.

We would expect the publics in Western societies, including the USA, Canada, New Zealand, and Australia to be inclined toward the centrist or even liberalist position. This hypothesis, unfortunately, cannot be tested due to lack of data.[15] Of all the Pacific Rim countries, Mexico is the only non-Asian society that asked this question. The Mexican public in fact manifests a centrist stance: the mean score of this question in Mexico is 2.95.

In contrast, for all the Asian countries for which we have data on this question, only Japan's population has a mean score of close to '3'—the mean is 2.93 in Japan. Other Asian publics generally prefer a society with more regulation to ensure individual safety and stability. Of these countries, China (mean = 1.29) and Singapore (1.67) are closest to the benign authoritarianism position; Vietnam scores 2.40 and the Philippines 2.22.[16]

Another angle to investigate the benign authoritarianism preference is to examine the East Asian publics' orientation toward having a 'strong leader'. In Confucian traditions, the ideal state is one personalized in a sage-king (*ren jun* or *min jun*). A sage-king is viewed as a strong leader that takes care of his subjects as a responsible father would his family.[17] Such a sage-king is at the same time granted by the people the mandate and power necessary to protect the people. Hence, supporting a strong leader, insofar as the leader is believed to be trustworthy and capable—possessing legitimacy—is a major component of Confucian political culture. In contrast, a preference for a strong leader, however benign, is considered antidemocratic in the liberalist tradition.

The WVS provides a good opportunity to solve this puzzle. One question asks respondents whether they think having a strong leader is very good, good, bad, or very bad. At a somewhat superficial level, it could be hypothesized that if the Confucianist notion of sage-king is still strong, then the willingness to support a strong leader among Asian countries should correspondingly be high. Conversely, if self-expression values are an indication of prodemocratic mentality, then as the strength of self-expression values increases, the willingness to support strong leaders should *decrease*. Which of these scenarios fits the East Asian case?

A methodological note is, however, in order. The survey question does not refer to 'strong leaders' in general, but to a certain kind of strong leaders, one that 'does not have to bother with parliament and elections'. With this qualifier, the question conveys a negative image of strong leaders, while excluding such possible positive characteristics as efficiency, long-term vision, and consistency. Consequently, we would expect the magnitude of positive support for strong leaders, in the context of our data-set, to be somewhat smaller than it would have been with a more balanced qualifier.

Be that as it may, we are interested in the relationship between self-expression values and support for strong leaders.[18] We would expect the correlation to be negative (and significant)—negative correlation simply means that if someone is prodemocratic, he or she is also against having a strong leader. Our analysis here covers all the Pacific Rim countries, including some in Latin America, as well as the Non-Confucian countries in Asia.[19] The resulting twenty correlations are shown in Table 3.4.

As expected, for all the North American and Oceanic countries, and Mexico and Argentina in South America, the correlation between self-expression values and support for a strong leader is negative and significant.

TABLE 3.4. *Democratic aspiration and supporting strong leader*

Country	Using Confucian Asia self-expression values factor	Using Inglehart's global self-expression values factor
China	−0.01	−0.02
Singapore	0.00	0.06(**)
Taiwan	−0.17(**)	−0.04
South Korea	−0.22(**)	−0.18(**)
Japan	−0.11(**)	−0.02
Philippines		0.01
Indonesia		−0.05
United States		−0.16(**)
Canada		−0.17(**)
Australia		−0.17(**)
Argentina		−0.20(**)
Chile		0.03
Mexico		−0.12(**)

Source: WVS, Fourth Wave or the Last Available Wave.

Note: Table entries are the correlation between self-expression values and support for strong leader;the significant negative correlations are noted by (**).

This confirms that democratically oriented people are more likely to reject a government with a strong, authoritarian leader who is not checked by parliament and held accountable by elections.

The picture is, however, not as clear-cut in the case of the Asian countries. For the three Confucian democracies—South Korea, Taiwan, and Japan—the correlation between support for strong leader and one measurement (our measurement) of self-expression values is negative and significant. For the other Asian societies included in the analysis, there is either no significant relationship, or, in the case of Singapore, using Inglehart's factor, there is even a positive relationship.[20]

This finding suggests a more complex relationship between democratic orientation and institutional choice in East Asia. While it is logical from a Western liberalist point of view that a democrat would reject the government of a strong leader, in East Asia this linkage seems to be weak. It appears that democratically oriented people can tolerate, if not support, a government with a strong leader. Although the evidence presented here is limited, we need to take this finding into serious consideration. Does it reflect a cultural lag, a vestige of the past? Are people inclined toward strong leaders who can get things done? Would institutional design need to strike a balance between decisiveness, accountability, and debate?

SELF-EXPRESSION VALUES AND DEMOCRACY IN EAST ASIA

The ultimate question for the study of political culture is the congruence between culture and political institutions (see Chapter 1 in this volume). Certainly, in the short term, the development of political systems might be primarily affected by the action of elites or the unique circumstances of historical events and personalities. Ultimately, however, the persistence of a political system hinges on public values and expectations about governance. The development of a prodemocratic public is essential for democracy in two ways. First, it provides the conditions for the establishment of democratic institutions—public pressure is a necessary condition which steers the elite toward making political changes. Second, once formal democratic institutions are in place, the consolidation and quality of democracy largely depends on citizens' democratic orientations and behaviors (Putnam, Leonardi, and Nanetti 1993; Shin 2003).

Our analysis shows that, in recent decades, East Asia has seen the rise of self-expression values and, in turn, the emergence of democratic institutions. To test this idea, we first calculated the self-expression values score for each of the East Asian countries. We then used the Freedom House scores of democratic governance for the period from 1990 to 1999 to calculate a total 'democracy score' for each country.[21]

Table 3.5 indicates that self-expression is, by and large, positively correlated with scores for the quality of democratic governance. For instance, Japan has the highest score on the self-expression dimension among the

TABLE 3.5. *Mean self-expression score and Freedom House Rating*

Country	Self-expression score (2000)	Freedom House democracy rating 1990–9 (reversed)
Japan	1.069	129
Korea	0.219	117
Taiwan	−0.176	102
Singapore	0.0111	66
China	−0.396	22
Vietnam	−0.533	20

Source: Self-expression score: Calculated by the author based on data from WVS 1999–2001 (except for Taiwan, which is 1995 data); Freedom House Rating: Freedom House Inc. (www.freedomhouse.org).
Self-Expression Score: National mean of a factor score from Table 3.1 analyses.
Freedom House Rating: Freedom House rates each country every year by a number ranging from 2 to 14. The higher the number, the less democratic the country is. We reverse each country's coding from 14–2 so the higher the score, the more democratic the country/society is. See footnote 6 for additional details.

East Asian countries, as well as the best democratic record over the decade. At the other end of the spectrum, Vietnam has the lowest score on self-expression values and the lowest score on the Freedom House measure. Although only six cases are dealt with in this analysis, and we are using the Freedom House rating as the only indicator of the degree of democratic governance, one could argue that this finding provides a good indication of cultural and institutional congruence.

The eventual congruence between the cultural and the institutional is a likely outcome, as Chapter 2 and the literature have attested. The explanation could suggest that economic growth brings material security, enabling people to shift their priority from survival and physical needs to social and psychological needs, and thereby the pursuit of a greater sense of belonging, empowerment, and self-realization. To put it another way, economic growth and industrialization produce a public that is liberty-oriented, outspoken, tolerant, and tends toward proequality, or, broadly speaking, more inclined toward self-expression values. The latter affect democratic politics in two ways. First, self-expression oriented people are more likely to engage in political activities, such as protests or demonstrations, which exert some pressure on their governments to be more accountable and responsive. They also tend to adopt a more critical stance toward government institutions (Wang 2005*a*). Second, self-expression oriented citizens are more active in social and civic organizations, thus generating more social capital, a collective asset that facilitates democratic participation, contributing to the functioning of democratic governance and institutions (Wang 2005*b*; also see Chapter 6 in this volume).

Nevertheless, the development of democracy in East Asia at present is a complicated picture. The most optimistic example can be found in the case of Japan, where democracy of decent quality has long been functioning. Down the ladder, we have Taiwan, South Korea, the Philippines, Thailand, Indonesia, Malaysia, and also Mongolia.[22] But while democratic institutions can be grafted from one context onto another, the challenges of consolidation in these new democracies in Asia testifies to the difficulty of building Western institutions on a different cultural soil.[23] The implication is that the success of democracy lies in the creative integration of traditional Asian values and Western liberalist ideas. One can cite Singapore as an example, however imperfect, of a society that has somehow managed to weave Confucian visions of a good society and good government with Western ideas of parliamentary democracy. It is possible to argue, therefore, that while the development of democracy may often encounter difficulties, there is no reason to feel despair that East Asia is resistant to democracy, nor to adhere to the Asian values position, even if culture-specific and traditional values may continue to shape the character of democracy in the region and the rest of Asia.

CONCLUSION

This chapter has attempted to answer the question of whether self-expression values are rising in East Asia, and how will such value changes affect the evolution of democratic political institutions in this region? The answer contributes toward the debate between a universalistic argument that modernization and human development will lead to liberal democracy around the globe, and a cultural relativist argument that political institutions developed out of Western societies cannot be transplanted onto Asian societies. Our approach is an empirically inductive one. We used survey data to measure the changes in social values among six Confucian societies. We then examined the linkage between social values and political institutions to determine how people's social values affect their perception of what a good government is or should be, and what kind of political institutions they are likely to support.

We constructed an index of self-expression values in the six Confucian societies. In East Asia, we found the rise of a set of coherently linked social values among their publics: proindividual liberty and freedom of expression, tolerance of differences and diversity, participation in decision-making, support of equal relationship between individuals, and emphasis on self-actualization. These values are interchangeably called liberalist values, emancipative values, or modern values by scholars of values changes, human development, and individual modernity. Regardless of differences in terminology, we find a rising trend in self-expression values in East Asia, which provides yet another empirical support for the linkage between socioeconomic modernization and the emergence of a prodemocratic, cosmopolitan culture.

At the same time, however, our findings suggest that Confucian societies in East Asia share some common values and beliefs. While not in agreement with the Asian values proponents, we would nonetheless argue that there is a Confucian East Asia which is distinguishable from that of its geographical neighbors in South Asia and Southeast Asia. In regard to choice of political institutions, East Asian publics have a vision of a good society and good government that differs somewhat from that of their non-Asian counterparts. Specificially, Asian populations appear more willing to tolerate a paternalist state that provides for and protects its citizens. There are also indications that East Asian publics are likely to be more tolerant, even supportive, of strong leaders who can deliver good government—a kind of benign authoritarianism, if we may—even as they become more inclined toward self-expression and democratic values.

Our earlier analysis presented a table showing the relationship between level of self-expression values and support for democracy, and suggested that rising self-expression values will, in the long run, contribute toward greater democratization of state and society even in the East Asian region. The actual evolution of democratic governance, however, may be more complicated than such a linear correlation would suggest. It may be argued that Japan, South Korea, and Taiwan exemplify the successful integration of Asian modernity with democracy. Nevertheless, it is also true that many of their citizens are showing dissatisfaction with the character and pace of democracy in these countries (Chu 2005). In some parts of Asia, procedural democracy has not delivered what it promised in the Philippines, Thailand, Indonesia, India, Bangladesh, Mongolia, and Afghanistan. In Central Asia, the transition to democracy has experienced regressions and encountered much difficulty. These developments may provide a pretext for the view that democracy does not fit Asian countries.[24]

Having debunked such an extreme position, we would argue that the difficult road traveled in building democracy according to Western designs testifies to our finding (and those of Chapter 2) that quality democracy needs a social base: a society with well-developed self-expression values. Many countries in Asia are now at the crossroads where they could work on developing a polity that is democratic, and a government that is strong and decisive, yet competent and accountable. Undoubtedly, the fact that many are moving 'eastward' along the self-expression dimension bodes well for the process of democratization—whatever forms it may take—in Asia.

ENDNOTES

1 For the Asian values argument, see Zakaria (1994) and Chapter 5 in this volume.

2 The definition of these value dimensions are discussed in Chapter 2. *Life Satisfaction* is a person's overall sense about life. *Social Tolerance* is a person's attitude toward socially disliked groups (Gibson 1992). Homosexual people, minorities, immigrants, people with generally unaccepted behaviors (prostitutes, drug users, and heavy drinkers, for instance), are good examples of disliked social groups. *Public Expression* is a person's willingness to express his or her (mostly political) views with public behaviors: petition, demonstration, boycott, sit-in, and so on. *Postmaterialism Liberty Aspiration* gives priority to liberty (freedom of speech, participation in local and national government) over material and physical security (economic status, national defense, fighting crime).

3 Indeed, scholars of value change around the world have pointed out various variables that can be used in such analyses (Flanagan and Lee 2000, 2003; Nevitte and Kanji 2003).

4 The selection of this big pool of variables is based on three lines of existing literature: the Asian values debate (Chan 1998; Tu 2000*a*; Song 2002), the modernization of human values and individual modernity literature (Inkeles 1966), and the literature of modernization, postmodernization, and democratic attitudes (Inglehart 1977, 1997; Gibbins 1989; Fukuyama 1995*a*; Gibson 1996*a*; Inglehart and Baker 2000). According to these literatures, all of the selected value dimensions are likely affected by modernization and reflect the degree democratic orientation of an individual or a public. A technical note: we only chose the variables that are available for every society included in this study.

5 Several other criteria guide our analyses. First, all other conditions being equal, more variance is preferable to less. Hence, if several variables are measuring the same concept, the one with a 10-point scale is preferable to one with fewer response categories. Second, consistency across countries and time is important. For example, if several variables have high covariance, but one of them in a certain country shows a distribution pattern that is

notably different from the others, then we might have a case of systematic error, which means that we should consider not using this variable. Third, repetition of variables should be avoided. That is, if two (or more) variables measure the same (or a similar) concept, as the question wording and distributions both show, it is preferable to select only one of them. If possible, these two (or more) variables should be combined into a new variable.

6 A methodological note: Table 3.1 presents the factor loadings of these variables when the data of all six societies are included. For each individual society, although the loadings may vary, the general pattern holds fairly well. That is, all these six variables can be made one factor in the analysis of each individual society.

7 Our factor includes overall life satisfaction. We use 'leisure is important' to measure overall life satisfaction. In Inglehart's research, he normally uses the subjective level of happiness (Inglehart and Baker 2000). In Chapter 2 by Inglehart and Welzel, this dimension is replaced by social trust.

8 While industrialization in Western Europe is also the process of rising nationalism (see, e.g. Hobsbawm 1962), the age of postindustrialization sees the rise of these so-called 'postmodern' values such as environmentalism, support of different lifestyles (e.g. gaymarriage), and cosmopolitanism. With this is a decrease in nationalist sentiment (see Inglehart 1997) among others.

9 For the construction of this figure, we use Inglehart's Survival/Self-Expression and Traditional/Rational values measurement (Inglehart and Welzel 2005). In the following sections we return to our measurement of self-expression values. We make this methodological diversion for two technical reasons. First, although we constructed a separate self-expression factor score for the six Confucian societies, we are comparing the positions of these six societies to the other societies. The measurement of self-expression values has to be consistent for the comparison to be meaningful. Hence, we use the global measurement of self-expression values by Inglehart (including all the 80+ societies covered by the WVS). Second, to construct this figure we include the Tradition/Rational value measurement, which is also borrowed from Inglehart.

10 Such groupings are arbitrary, however. For example, Vietnam can be grouped with the East Asia group, Japan can belong to a group of only itself, and India can be grouped with the East Asia or the Southeast Asia groups (as it is close to Indonesia). Nevertheless, without further evidences on the causes of the different locations of these societies' public attitudes on this value space, we accept the current grouping as reflecting the geographical and cultural/civilizational lines in this region.

11 We are, nonetheless, able to give a partial examination to the long-term trends in two of these societies. For Korea and Japan, we have WVS data at four time points between 1981 and 2000. A factor score based on three variables that are measured in all the four surveys shows an observable trend of rising self-expression values over time. This part of our analysis is not presented in this chapter but is available upon request.

12 An early study documents this shift of Japanese value orientation as economic growth took place during the 1950s and 1960s (Ike 1973).

13 This argument originates from the earliest modernization theorists, such as Deutsch (1961), Lipset (1960), Finkle and Gable (1971), and Weiner (1966).

14 We code education into five levels: (*a*) elementary school education or less, including illiterate population where applicable; (*b*) above elementary but not above junior middle school education; (*c*) finished junior middle school but not senior middle school; (*d*) completed senior middle school but did not enter college, including attendance at technical institutions after middle school; and (*e*) entered college, including those with graduate education.

15 For comparison purposes, we could use Western European countries to substitute North American and Oceanic countries, but data for Western European countries on this question are not available either.

16 Other surveys also have similar findings. For example, a 1993 survey of China found 65 percent of the respondents agreed that having too many political parties would bring chaos

(data from Tianjian Shi of Duke University). In East Asia Barometer surveys, people found that, after democratization in Taiwan and South Korea, some people were dissatisfied with how democracy has generated chaos and disorder, and hence express that 'sometimes authoritarian government may be more preferable than democracy' (Chu, Diamond, and Shin 2001).

17 See *Analects* or other classical Confucianism writings, such as *Mencuis*.

18 In fact, the answers to this question in East Asia is not drastically different from many other countries (see Chapter 4 in this volume). Support for strong leader as measured by this question is relatively low in all these countries. In China, more than 90 percent say that having a strong leader who does not need to bother with parliament and elections is bad or very bad. This limited support for strong leaders in East Asia may show the fear lingering from the past when strong leaders existed (such as Mao of China, Lee in South Korea, and Kiang in Taiwan), or simply because of wording the question.

19 Except for the six Confucian societies, for which we use our own self-expression values as well as Inglehart's factor, the other countries' self-expression scores were based entirely on Inglehart's.

20 A methodological side note: If supporting democracy must mean rejecting a strong leader, then Table 3.5 shows our factor of self-expression values is better for measuring democratic aspiration of East Asian population, as our measure correlates to rejecting of a strong leader in Japan, South Korea, and Taiwan, while Inglehart's factor does not in any of the Asian societies. Vietnam is not included in this analysis because this question is not consistently measured in the Vietnamese survey.

21 Freedom House rates each country every year by 1 to 7 on two dimensions: civil liberty and political rights. We recoded these scores so that 7 represented the highest score, that is, a free, democratic country. The table adds up the rating of each country yearly from 1990 to 1999 (the highest possible score is 140 and the lowest 20).

22 Mongolia is an anomaly. Its democracy was not founded upon sustained economic growth. Hence, it does not seem to qualify as an example of modernization preceding democracy. Nonetheless, liberalists would certainly like to cite it as an example of the likelihood of democratic triumph.

23 For the discussion of consolidating democracy in this region, see Chu, Diamond, and Shin 2001; Shin 2003; Chu 2005; Shin and Wells 2005.

24 This is indeed the original Asian values view, or, more generally, Orientalist point of view.

Part II

Orientations Toward Democracy

4

Democratic Aspirations and Social Modernization[1]

Russell J. Dalton and Doh Chull Shin

The people power movement that forced Ferdinand Marcos from power in 1986 was the beginning of the third wave of democratization in East Asia, which was quickly followed in 1987 by the end of military rule in South Korea and the lifting of martial law in Taiwan. Democratization then spread to several other East Asian nations (Mongolia, Thailand, and Indonesia). However, democratic progress in the rest of East Asia has been incomplete. China and Vietnam represent two of the handful of nations where the Communist party still controls the state. Singapore and Malaysia have had a mixed political record over the past decade, and the Freedom House rated both as only partly free in 2000. In 2000, the Freedom House rated 44 percent of the nations in East Asia as democracies, and 33 percent were authoritarian or totalitarian states. There are few areas in the world where the diversity of political regimes is as great—and the overall prospects for further democratization as uncertain—as in East Asia.

There are many potential explanations for the still-limited democratic development in East Asia. The low level of economic development and social modernization in several nations restricts their potential political development. Inglehart and Welzel's analyses in Chapter 2 suggest that the democratic development of East Asian nations generally fits their positions on the social modernization continuum. Other scholars (and political elites) have questioned whether Confucian traditions and the political culture are compatible with established Western forms of democracy—a theme explored later in this volume (see Chapter 5). Other analysts point to the path-dependent forces that have shaped the political history in the region. Indeed, many explanations for the political status quo abound.

Missing from this debate has been the voice of the people themselves. What do people in East Asia think about the democratic process and the alternative forms of government? This chapter focuses on the attitudes and aspirations toward democracy across the nations in our project. As a first step, we describe the democratic experience of these nations. Second, we use the WVS to map citizen orientations toward democracy. The foundation of a democratic system is a public commitment to democratic values and principles that are described in this chapter. Third, we test the social modernization hypothesis by examining the distribution of opinions across sociodemographic groups that are differentially linked to modernization processes.

THE EXTENT OF DEMOCRACY

How broadly has the third wave of democratization affected the nations of East Asia? A first step is to define what we mean by democracy. Indeed, one of the complications of the democratization literature is the disagreement on the definition and measurement of this concept. One approach focuses on elections as a linchpin of the democratic process (Vanhanen 1997; Przeworski et al. 2000). The holding of competitive, free, and fair elections is essential to the meaning of democracy. This includes acceptance of the rule of law, so there is legal administration of elections and procedures for resolving electoral disputes. Unless different political views can compete in the electoral arena, and the electoral outcomes structure government policy to a substantial degree, a political system cannot claim to be a democracy.

But electoral democracy is a minimal threshold for defining democracy. Most political theorists and practioners have a more expansive definition. For example, Dahl held that democracy required social structures beyond the functioning of the electoral process that enabled citizens to independently form their preferences, and to collectively express and mobilize these preferences (Dahl 1971, Chapter 1). Similarly, Huntington (1991: 174–92) discussed how viable opposition groups and independent social interests are important in assuring that governments will actually tolerate electoral opposition and run fair elections. Thus, freedom of expression, freedom of the press, and freedom of association are essential elements of electoral democracy. These rights are especially important for political minorities and other groups that are vulnerable to oppression by the state. In addition, although the term 'civil society' was not yet in common usage when Dahl was developing his theoretical framework, the principles of civil society were very much present in Dahl's writings. In fact, Dahl wrote that autonomous organizations were an essential part of the democratic process (Dahl 1982: 31–40).

Democracy thus requires a set of political conditions and civil liberties that extend beyond elections. These conditions are necessary to ensure the meaningfulness of elections, and that democracy includes more than just elections. If an election is free, but the society is not, then the election is unlikely to have informed voters who freely cast their preferences for future government policy.

There have been numerous attempts to measure democracy and track its development in broad cross-national terms.[2] Because it is the most widely used data source, and because it taps a range of civic and political rights, we use the Freedom House scales to describe national levels of democratic development. The Freedom House uses experts to score nations on two scales. The *political rights scale* measures the extent to which people can participate freely in the political process to choose policymakers who make government policy. This is largely equivalent to the electoral dimension of democracy. The *civil liberties scale* evaluates the freedoms to develop views, organizations, and personal autonomy apart from the state. This involves characteristics such as the right to organize and freedom of assembly, an independent judiciary and respect for the rule of law, personal autonomy (such as freedom of movement and freedom to travel), and economic rights. We combined both scales to create a 'democracy score' for each nation.[3]

Figure 4.1 displays the democracy score of each nation in our project for the 1985–2003 period that brackets the public opinion data collected by the WVS. The four Western democracies in our study consistently score at the

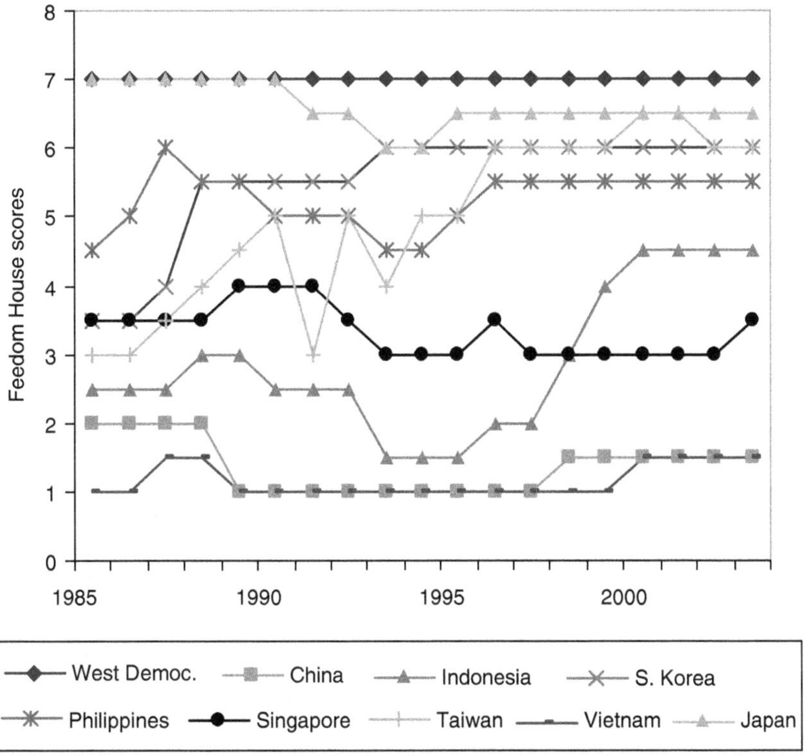

FIGURE 4.1. Freedom House summary scores, 1985–2003
Source: Freedom House; mean of political rights and civil liberties scales: (1) low and (7) high.

highest level on both scales across this entire decade. In fact, we include these nations in the project because they are reference points of established democracies to compare to the nations in East Asia.

The Asian nations display tremendous political variation. The most interesting cases are at the other end of the democracy scales: China and Vietnam. China was making progress on both dimensions during the 1980s, but then the Tiananmen protests in 1989 led the regime to reassert its control. Similarly, Vietnam began a process of economic liberalization (*doi moi*) in the mid-1980s. There have been small democratizing experiments in both nations during the 1990s (Thurston 1998; Shi 2000*b*), but both nations remain controlled by a dominant Communist party that prohibits true electoral democracy. According to Freedom House, both nations have made slight progress in providing civil liberties to their citizens, although this remains limited.

Singapore and Indonesia present more complex patterns. The dominance of the People's Action Party provides a vehicle for the party elites to control the Singapore government, and the government uses these powers to curb potential political opposition. Constraints on the press and other government actions limit the conditions necessary for elections to be meaningful. In addition, while social life enjoys relative freedom from state interference, there are significant constraints on free expression, assembly and other rights when they have a potential political content. Since the financial shock of 1997 and the subsequent recession in the Singapore economy, the government's use of its authority has strengthened. Thus, the Freedom House describes a general erosion of political rights and civil liberties over the decade of the 1990s.

Indonesia moved in the opposite direction. For most of the 1980s, Indonesia earned a 'partly free' rating from the Freedom House because of the Suharto regime's behavior. In the 1990s, pressures mounted against Suharto and his continued rule, and the government's response was to suppress its political opponents. Ethnic conflict in East Timor, Aceh and other regions put further strains on the government. Opposition protests mounted in the later half of the decade, partly in reaction to deteriorating economic conditions. Figure 4.1 thus displays a significant drop in the summary democracy score in the mid-1990s. In 1998, Suharto's regime was forced out of power. This ushered in a tumultuous period of reintroducing elections, a rapid turnover in the executive branch, and parliament asserting itself as a democratic body. By the end of the 1990s, Indonesia had made dramatic gains both in the extent of political rights and in the protection of civil liberties (an overall increase of 3.0 points between 1995 and 2001), although politics remains contentious.

Since the end of military rule in 1987, South Korea has made relatively steady progress in developing its democratic system and ensuring civil liberties. As a consequence of the financial crisis of 1997, power shifted to the political opposition—a key indicator in the development of democracy.

Democratic politics still remains contentious, however, as illustrated by the parliament's impeachment of President Roh Moo-hyun in early 2004. The end of martial law in 1987 began the democratization process in Taiwan, signaled by Lee Teng-hui's election as president, and then the victory by the opposition Chen Shui-bian in the 2000 presidential elections. Chen's close re-election in 2004 also demonstrates the contentious nature of democracy in Taiwan. South Korea and Taiwan have joined Japan as examples of consolidated democracies that ensure the basic political rights and civil liberties of their citizens.

Japan, of course, has the longest democratic history in the region, and this is reflected in its positive scores on the summary democracy scale over this period, with only a slight decline in the 1990s. The Philippines also has a generally positive record over this time span. The end of the Marcos regime in 1986 marked the Philippines' return to a democratic system. Much of the 1990s were a period of political tumult, first to recreate democracy and then the struggles of the Estrada impeachment. The Philippines enjoys a relatively high level of political rights and civil liberties, but this has been accompanied by contentious electoral politics.

In summary, the political context in our nations varies widely—representing as large a gap as is possible with the Freedom House measures. Over the past two decades there has been a general movement toward democracy among the East Asian nations in our project, but progress has been uneven, and Singapore experienced a significant regression according to Freedom House. Thus, the extent of democracy remains mixed across East Asia.

MEASURING ATTITUDES TOWARD DEMOCRACY

How do citizens across these nations view democracy? We expect that citizens in established democracies are strongly committed to democratic values and prefer democracy to other regime forms (Klingemann 1999; Dalton 2004). The prior literature is less clear, however, on what we might expect across the publics in East Asia.

Congruence theory predicts that orientations toward democracy will be generally consistent with the current regime form. This perspective suggests greater support for democracy in the more democratic nations of Japan, Korea, and Taiwan. Based on an earlier wave of the WVS, Klingemann described high levels of support for democracy in these three nations. Evidence from surveys in Korea and Taiwan reinforce this conclusion (Shin 1999, 2000*a*; Xu 1999).

We also expect that democratic orientations are less frequent—or at least less frequently expressed to strangers conducting a public opinion survey—in several East Asian nations. Indeed, the political culture literature has long stressed the lack of democratic norms among Asia publics (Pye 1985, 1999;

Scalapino 1989; and see Chapter 5 in this volume). Certainly one might question whether democratic values exist in China and Vietnam, where the regime is based on the dominant role of the communist party. The recent survey evidence of Chinese public opinion is mixed (Chen and Zhong 1998; Nathan and Shi 1993; Shi 2000*a*; Chu and Chang 2001; Chen 2004). Until the WVS, systematic national opinion data for Vietnam was nonexistent. Similarly, Singapore is widely cited as the archetypical case of where citizens accept a restriction of their political rights and liberties in exchange for the (past) economic progress of the regime. The commitment to democratic principles is equally uncertain in Indonesia; popular protests for democracy have been highly visible in the recent transition to democracy (Asia Foundation 2003), but the WVS was conducted when the democratic transition was just beginning.

The WVS provides an exceptional cross-national resource for studying how people view democracy (see Appendix A). In addition, we include recent data from the 2005 'Hong Kong Creativity Index' survey that replicated these democracy items from the WVS.[4] These cross-national comparisons should provide a context for better interpreting public sentiments in any single nation, as well a tool for investigating the interaction of political/economic structures with public opinion. Not all nations are included in both waves of the WVS, and the appendix to this book provides information on each survey. Equally important, the WVS includes several different measures of public orientations toward democracy, which we describe and analyze in this section.

Democracy Versus Other Regime Forms

Public support for democracy is a complicated attitude to measure. As we have noted, the concept of democracy is itself complex. If political theorists continue to differ on what democracy means, then equal diversity might exist in the minds of people who are asked to evaluate democracy or democratic potential in their nation. Understanding the meaning of democracy is especially uncertain in those nations where experience with democratic politics is limited or nonexistent. This is a serious concern that we discuss as the analyses proceed. In addition, opinions toward democracy might be conditioned by the nature of the current political regime. It may be as unlikely for an Australian to express their dissatisfaction with the principles of democracy as it is for a Vietnamese (or an Hungarian before 1989) to express opposition to their current government. Conversely, with the global spread of democracy, governments of all types claim to be democratic, and thus, ritual support for democracy may be seen as the social acceptable response to a public opinion interview. Democracy can be an elastic term, used by leaders in Washington and Beijing (see Chapter 1). The solution to these potential problems is to proceed cautiously, and with multiple items to tap different aspects of democratic sentiment.

The WVS included a battery that assessed orientations toward different regime types, presenting democracy as one of four options. Respondents were asked if they agreed or disagreed with a set of four statements:

I'm going to describe various types of political systems and ask what you think about each as a way of governing this country. For each one, would you say it is a very good, fairly good, fairly bad, or very bad way of governing this country?

- Having a strong leader who does not have to bother with parliament and elections
- Having experts, not government, make decisions according to what they think is best for the country
- Having the army rule
- Having a democratic political system

Separating these different regime principles attempts to lessen a purely rhetorical endorsement for democracy. Respondents can express support for nondemocratic alternatives in the first three items before the democratic alternative is presented. In addition, the response set normally encourages individuals to agree with questions, which facilitates potential nondemocratic responses on the first three items. In other words, we measure support for democracy primarily by assessing disapproval of autocratic regime forms.

Figure 4.2 presents the percent of the public in each nation giving the prodemocratic responses to each of the four items. The prodemocratic responses are to *disagree* with the first three items, and *agree* with the fourth.[5] The first clear pattern is the breadth of prodemocratic (or antiautocratic) sentiment across this diverse set of nations. A majority in each nation is positive toward democracy, even in the nations that Freedom House would rank as only partly free or not free (this battery was not asked in a comparable way in Vietnam). Indeed, the similarity in support for democracy (and rejection of autocratic regimes) between the established Western democracies and East Asian nations is especially striking.

Support for a democratic regime may arise from the positive aura attached to the term that results from the democratization wave of the past decade, and the rhetorical endorsement of 'democracy' from very different regimes. For instance, even North Korea's official title is the 'Democratic Republic of North Korea'. Thus, it is equally important to observe that people also express disapproval of nondemocratic regime forms. Large majorities in most nations disapprove of government by a strong leader who exercises power without democratic controls.[6] One might rightly ask whether Chinese peasants understand the term democracy, but they certainly understand

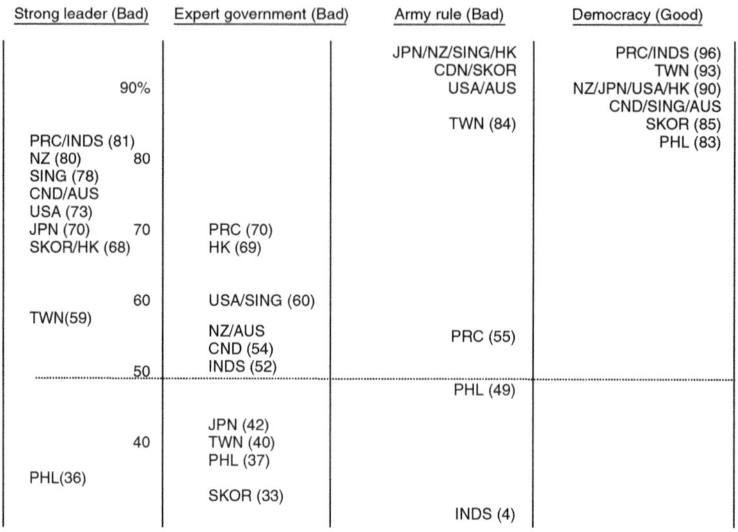

FIGURE 4.2. Orientations toward political regimes by nation

Source: 1995–8, 2000–01 WVS; 2005 Hong Kong Survey. Figure entries are per cent giving prodemocratic responses on each item (V164 to V167).

government by oligarchic leaders. It is especially striking to see broad disapproval of such a governing system in nations such as China and Singapore, where the autocratic experience still exists. Citizens in Hong Kong are also broadly critical of government managed by experts or by oligarchic leaders, and are very positive toward a democratic regime; this can be seen in the continuing tensions between Hong Kong residents and the regime in Beijing.

The majority of citizens in most East Asian nations also reject other non-democratic regime forms: military or expert rule. The most notable exception is also illustrative. In 2001, only 4 percent of Indonesians said that army rule is bad—far lower than in any other nation. This presumably reflects the military's positive role in easing Suharto from office in 1998 and the *dwi-fungsi* tradition in Indonesian politics (Sundhaussen 1988). Until the 2004 election, the democratically elected parliament reserved seats for the military and police. The military also plays an active role in Indonesian politics, and terrorist concerns have reinforced this involvement. In the other nations of East Asia, however, the public generally disapproves of military rule.[7] Opinions on the role of experts are more varied (and more ambiguous in terms of democratic theory), but there is only modest support for this alternative.[8]

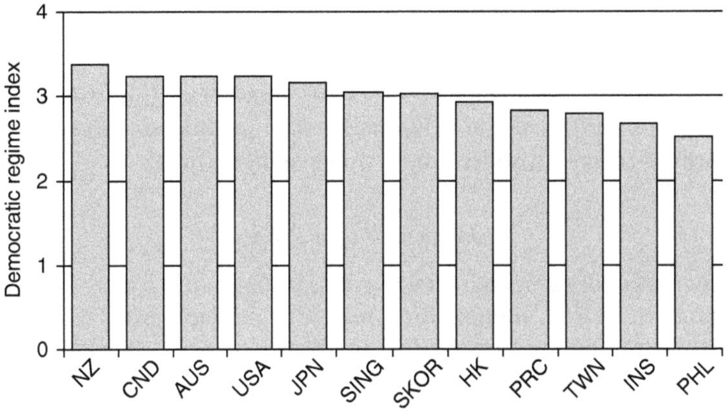

FIGURE 4.3. Democratic regime index by nation
Source: 1995–8 and 1999–2002 WVS 2005 Hong Kong Survey.
Note: Figure entries are the mean scores on the four political regime items of Figure 4.2. The coding of the democratic regime index is: 1) support nondemocratic regime and 4) support democratic regime.

The general support for a democratic regime (or opposition to autocratic regimes) is seen by combining these four items to create a democratic regime index.[9] Figure 4.3 presents the national mean scores on this index.[10] A score of 4.0 on this scale is the highest level of prodemocratic sentiment, and a score of 1.0 is autocratic or nondemocratic. In all eleven nations, the mean score tends toward the democratic end of the scale. As we would expect, citizens in the four Western democracies clearly favor a democratic structure over nondemocratic regimes (the four-nation average is 3.27). Prodemocratic sentiments are slightly less common in the nations of East Asia (2.87)—although the size of the East–West gap is quite modest. Citizens in both Hong Kong and the PRC score above the midpoint on this scale.[11] Taiwan scores lower than one might expect, given its recent democratic record, and there are two factors to consider. First, this is the only nation where the data are only from the 1995 time point. Second, the democracy items were only asked of rural respondents in Taiwan, which should depress support for democracy.[12] Finally, the lowest support for democracy occurs in the Philippines, which has struggled with its democratic development since Marcos was overthrown. This suggests that poor democratic performance may erode democratic aspirations.

Certainly we should question whether people in all of these nations fully understand the democratic process when they answer these questions.[13] Aspirations for democracy—and negativity toward autocratic regimes—are common among East Asian publics. This does not mean that people are equally pleased with the policies of the current government or the behavior of the current incumbents of power. As Wang and his colleagues show (see Chapter 7), support for a democratic regime often co-occurs with criticism of the government in democratic systems. However, the viability of democracy is based more on these regime orientations than evaluations of incumbent governments, and citizens in these Pacific Rim nations see democracy as the best form of regime to address their policy preferences.

Democracy as a Process

Another aspect of democracy involves the performance traits of democratic governments. Indeed, support for a regime in principle is far different from evaluations of how that regime will perform in practice. This is a common criticism of democracy, communism and other regime forms.[14] Thus, people might express support for democracy in the abstract, but then worry about how the process actually functions. These concerns are compounded because much of criticism of democracy by autocratic East Asia politicians focused on the supposed performance weaknesses of democracies, such as their inability to maintain order or direct economic development.

To tap such sentiments, the WVS asked respondents about various traits that might be attributed to a democratic system:

> I'm going to read of some things that people sometimes say about a democratic political system. Could you please tell me if you agree strongly, agree, disagree, or disagree strongly, after I read each one of them?
>
> - In a democracy, the economic system runs badly
> - Democracies are indecisive and have too much quibbling
> - Democracies aren't good at maintaining order
> - Democracy may have problems but it's better than any other form of government

These items allow respondents to express doubts about democracy, without directly rejecting democratic principles. Moreover, the focus is on broad features of democratic governance, and not short-term judgments about a specific government. The first three items are also phrased so that criticism of democracy is easy to express as approval of the statement. The disadvantage is that by explicitly asking about democracy, these questions might tap affective support for the democratic ideal. We should also point out that the fourth item testing the Churchillian principle that 'democracy may have problems but it's better than any other form of government' has been widely asked in other surveys (Rose, Haerpfer, and Mishler 1998).

Figure 4.4 presents the percentage who give prodemocratic responses to each of the four items (disagree with the first three items and agree with the fourth). The fourth item asks whether democracy is the best form of government; it shows that support for democracy is remarkably widespread even in

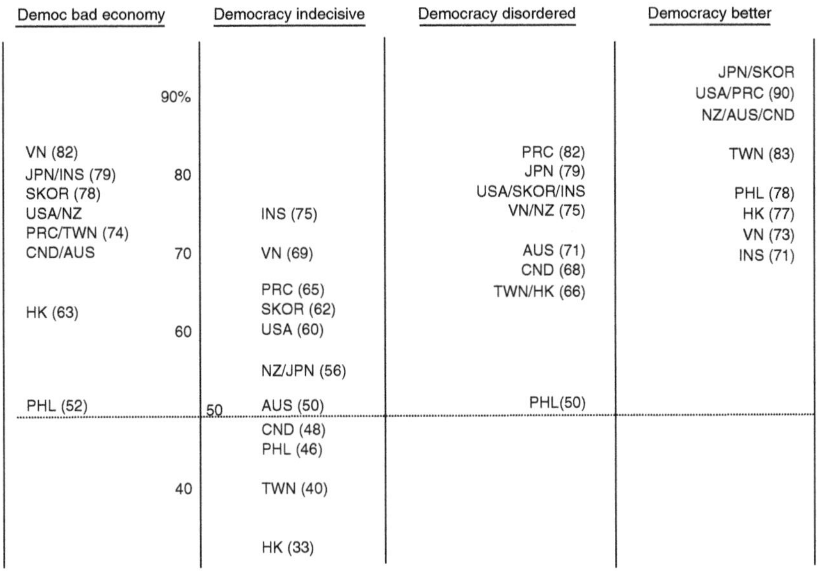

FIGURE 4.4. Attitudes toward democratic process by nation
Source: 1995–8, 2000–1 WVS; 2005 Hong Kong Survey. Figure entries are percent giving prodemocratic responses on each item (v167 to V172).

nations that lack a democratic government, such as in China (95 percent), Hong Kong (73 percent), and Vietnam (73 percent). When most people in these nations say that democracy is better than other forms of government, this suggests that democracy is now seen as a basic human value. Indeed, surveys from Eastern Europe in the early 1990s detected similarly positive sentiments toward democracy virtually as the Berlin Wall was being breached (Dalton 1994; Rose, Haerpfer, and Mishler 1998; Rohrschneider 1999).

The other items in Figure 4.4 tap potential criticisms of the democratic process: it weakens the economy, is indecisive, and does a poor job in maintaining order. Given the presumed emphasis on agreement and aversion to conflict in Asian societies, it is striking that large majorities reject the view that democracy is not good at maintaining order. Similarly, most people reject the view that the economic system runs badly in a democracy. This is in stark contrast to the claims running from Lee Kuan Yew to Samuel Huntington that one must chose between economic development and democratic development—most people in East Asia reject this claim.[15] Opinions are more divided on whether democracies are indecisive and have too much quibbling, and these concerns are also common in the Western democracies. The greatest doubt about the indecisiveness of democracy is in Hong Kong, and this may reflect a realistic appraisal of how democracies have responded to Hong Kong's political position.

The overall cross-national pattern is seen in Figure 4.5, which presents national means scores on the four-item scale.[16] The striking pattern is the limited evidence of an East–West divide.[17] Citizens in the established democracies are generally positive about these features of the democratic process. The exceptional case is again the Philippines, where the public scores at the mid-point of the scale. However, people in less-democratic nations are generally not significantly more skeptical about democracy than the Western publics. Moreover, because these process questions tap some of the themes about democracy's supposed limitations from the perspective of an Asian values critique, it is significant that most people in East Asia do not agree with these criticisms.

Moreover, the cross-national findings of the WVS are now being confirmed by other East Asian opinion surveys. For instance, the 2002 Pew Global Attitudes Survey assessed public opinion in a smaller set of Asian and Western democracies. One item asked about support for 'democracy as it exists in the United States'. One might question this choice of wording, but the reference to the USA ensures that respondents are not confusing the term with democratic socialism or other claims to democracy practiced in non-democratic states. A citizen of Hanoi, for instance, does not think of the CPV's version of democracy in answering this question. Table 4.1 shows that majorities of the public in Vietnam (62 percent), Japan (62 percent), South

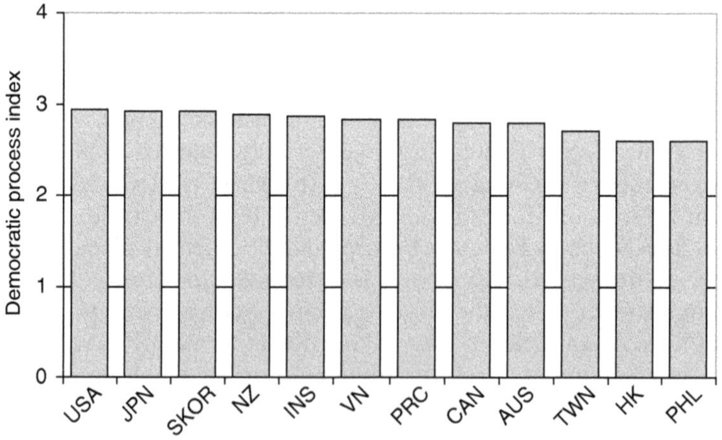

FIGURE 4.5. Democratic process index by nation
Source: 1995–8 and 1999–2002 WVS; 2005 Hong Kong Survey.

Note: Figure entries are the mean scores on the four democratic process items of Figure 4.4. The coding of the democratic process index is: 1) critical of the democratic process 4) supportive of democratic process.

TABLE 4.1. Support for democracy

	Favor US-style democracy (%)	Democracy over strong leader (%)	Good democracy more important than strong economy (%)
Western Nation			
United States	—	63	61
Asian Nations			
Indonesia	52	65	30
Japan	62	—	—
Philippines	69	41	55
South Korea	58	61	47
Vietnam	68	—	66

Source: Pew Global Attitudes Survey, 2002. Table entries are the percentage agreeing with each statement.

Korea (58 percent), and Indonesia (52 percent) were favorable toward democracy, even using this wording. Another question compared whether the nation should rely on a democratic government or a strong leader. Indonesians and South Koreans broadly preferred a democratic government at levels comparable to Americans (the Philippine public is relatively low). Finally, when asked whether good democracy or a strong economy is more important—even though we consider this a false choice—only in Indonesia does a majority prefer a strong economy. Perhaps most striking is the breadth of support for democracy in Vietnam in the Pew Global Survey, even when it includes a reference to US democracy barely a quarter century after the American–Vietnamese War.

In addition, initial results from the East Asia Barometer find majorities in support of democratic principles for most of the nations they surveyed (Chu 2003; Shin and Wells 2005). The Gallup Voice of the People Survey (2005) also finds broad support for democracy in Asia, registering higher than in Latin America or Eastern Europe. Similarly, other research on Chinese public opinion uncovers surprising support for democratic principles (Yougnian 1994; Nathan and Shi 1993; Shi 2000*a*; Chu and Chang 2001). Chen and Zhong (1998) found nearly universal support for multiparty elections, minority rights, and a free press in a survey of Beijing, and Zweig's (2002) surveys in poor rural Chinese villages similarly found that support for democratic principles was widespread. In short, most of the publics we surveyed agree with the Churchillian premise that democracy may be the worst form of government—except for all the other forms.

In summary, our findings describe political cultures of East Asia that are radically different from traditional descriptions of the region. Instead of the hesitancy (or outright opposition) to liberal democracy that some previous scholarship had suggested, contemporary public opinion surveys are finding a breadth of support for democracy as a regime and the working of the democratic process across most nations in East Asia. In fact, the difference between Asian and Western publics in these attitudes is suprisingly small. This reaffirms an emerging finding from the WVS that democratic aspirations are widely distributed across the globe (Inglehart and Welzel 2005).

SOCIAL MODERNIZATION AND DEMOCRACY

Current public support for democracy in most East Asian nations undoubtedly arises from several sources. One of the most basic explanations, however, links these opinions to the process of social modernization. With increasing educational levels, rising living standards, technological advancement, and economic globalization, much of the world has been changing rapidly in the last several decades. As a society modernizes, citizen values should be affected, as Inglehart and Welzel argue in Chapter 2. This is true in both the developed and the developing worlds. In developing nations, however, these forces of social modernization are often seen as prerequisites for citizen support of the democratic process and 'modern' attitudes (Lerner 1958; Inkeles and Smith 1974; Pye 1997). With modernization and rising socioeconomic standards presumably comes a broadening of world views, a tolerance for diversity, and a more sophisticated understanding of politics and society. Larry Diamond's discussion of the potential impact of modernization on China illustrates the logic of this argument:

> As it gathers more momentum and begins to generate a more urban, educated, wired and middle-class society over the next two decades, economic development is going to generate enormous pressures for political change in China. People are going to want more say over their own affairs. They are going to expect less hierarchical control from the state and ruling party, and more accountability of political leaders to the citizenry. There will be decidedly less tolerance for corruption and abuse of power, and more readiness and ability to organize in protest of it. There will be significantly greater aspirations for personal and political freedom, and for greater pluralism in sources of information and choices of leaders. (Cited in Gilley 2003: 65)

Thus, from Martin Lipset's early study of *Political Man* (1960) to Inglehart and Welzel's analyses of human value change (Chapter 2; and 2005), researchers posit a strong relationship between socioeconomic conditions and orientations toward democracy.

Recent research in democratized nations seems to validate this proposition. Political values typically differ between socioeconomic groups, or between traditional and modern sectors or society (such as rural–urban differences). In the newly democratized states of Eastern Europe, support for democracy correlates positively with education, socioeconomic status, and city size (Dalton 1994; Rohrschneider 1999; Rose, Haerpfer, and Mishler

1998; Zimmerman 2002). Education also predicts support for democracy in Korea, Taiwan, Hong Kong, and China (Shin 1999; Chu and Chang 2001).

Economic modernization thus suggests that higher status individuals—measured by education and income—will be more supportive of democracy. This reflects both their personal conditions of life and an increased exposure to norms that might encourage democratic values.

Table 4.2 presents the correlations between social status measures and the democratic regime index.[18] Consistent with modernization theory, education and income are positively related to prodemocracy attitudes in all four Western democracies, often with strong effects. The average education correlation, for instance, is approximately 0.20. Income effects are weaker, although they also run in the expected direction.

The picture in East Asia is more complex. Social status is significantly related to support for democracy in the three consolidated democracies in the region. However, the average education correlation is noticeably weaker than for the Western democracies. These patterns are weaker still in the nondemocratic nations in the region. For instance, the average education correlation in China and Vietnam is barely positive. These same cross-national patterns are repeated for income.

One can better visualize these patterns in Figure 4.6, which presents the educational differences in support for a democratic regime across three groups of nations. The solid line in the figure represents the level of support for a democratic regime by education averaged across the four Western democracies. Support for a democratic regime steadily increases with educational level—even though all these respondents function within a democratic political system. The line for the consolidated democracies in East Asia (Japan, South Korea, and Taiwan) displays a more modest education gradient, though still significant. Among the remaining nations, however, there is essentially no difference in support for a democratic regime across education groups.

This educational relationship is an intriguing finding. In addition to the self-expressive effects of education that Inglehart and Welzel describe (Chapter 2), education also socializes individuals into the norms of the regime. Thus, higher education may inculcate greater support for democracy to the extent to which the national political system is itself democratic. This leads to greater support for democracy when students are socialized in democratic regimes. But this effect is substantially attenuated when the regime is socializing nondemocratic values. Indeed, one might presume that the political content of education in Beijing University is much different than in the Australian National University, and the content of education influences the process of value formation. But as democratization occurs—as in the consolidated Asian democracies—these two effects of education become reinforcing, leading to a stronger commitment to education among the better educated.

Table 4.2. The correlates of support for democratic regime

	USA	CND	AUS	NZ	Avg.	JPN	SKOR	TWN	Avg.	SING	PHL	INS	PRC	VN	Avg.
Education (highest level)	0.30	0.21	0.27	0.12	0.23	0.14	0.10	0.19	0.14	0.05	0.09	0.02	0.08	0.03	0.05
Education (age finished)	0.20	0.19	0.15	—	0.18	0.11	—	0.17	0.14	−0.06	0.14	0.00	0.05	0.02	0.03
Income	0.15	0.21	0.13	0.05	0.14	0.08	0.07	0.11	0.09	0.06	−0.02	0.04	−0.02	0.06	0.03
Urbanization	−0.03	0.02	0.06	0.03	0.02	−0.05	—	0.10	0.03	−0.07	0.11	0.08	—	−0.20	−0.02
Political interest	0.22	0.27	0.35	0.16	0.24	0.15	0.01	0.12	0.09	0.10	−0.05	0.08	0.11	0.12	0.07

Source: 1999–2002 WVS. The table presents the Pearson *r* correlation between each variable and the support for democratic regime index (Figure 4.3). For Vietnam, we use the alternative index of democratic values (Figure 4.5).

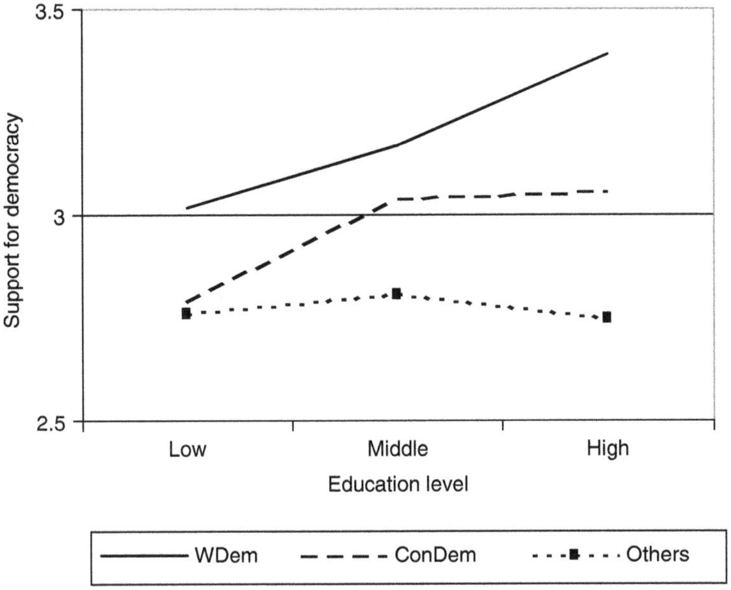

FIGURE 4.6. Education and support for a democratic regime
Source: 1999–2002 WVS.
Note: Figure entries are the mean on the four political regime items of Figure 4.3 by educational level. The results are presented separately for Western democracies, the Asian consolidated democracies, and the other nations in East Asia.

Another potential modernization variable is urbanization. The movement from peasant life to the more cosmopolitan conditions of the city have been widely posited as encouraging modern values and support for political development. Urban life typically exposes the individual to a broader world view, a more diverse environment, and the orientations and skills that encourage participatory demands. For example, the 'border effects' hypothesis suggests that citizens in Shanghai, Ho Chi Minh City and similar locales are exposed to the influences of globalization and this broadens their life experiences and world view, promoting more cosmopolitan values.

Empirically, however, rural and urban residents display only weak differences in democratic attitudes. The strongest relationship is in Vietnam, and indicates that democratic support is lower in urban areas.

A final, albeit indirect, test of the modernization thesis examines whether political engagement is related to support for democracy. Certainly in a democratic nation we expect the most politically interested would also more strongly espouse democratic orientations, and this presumption is embedded in the political culture and development literature. As individuals become more cosmpolitan, are exposed to the media, and become participants rather than subjects, this should generally encourage democratic values. The question is whether this applies even in nondemocratic regimes.

The last row in Table 4.2 demonstrates that political interest is strongly related to support for a democratic regime in the Western democracies. This relationship is modestly positive in the consolidated Asian democracies, and weaker still in the less-developed nations of East Asia. The pattern underscores the conclusion from the social status relationships. Modernization can encourage the development of democratic values, but these influences interact with the nature of the political regime. In democracies, these effects are strengthened, but in nondemocratic states, the contradictory norms of the regime attenuate these effects.

POLITICAL CULTURE AND DEMOCRACY

Scholars have engaged in a long debate on the political culture of Asian societies. One side of this debate suggested that Confucian traditions and political history had produced a political culture potentially incongruent with a democratic political system. The lack of democracy in most of East Asia was cited as evidence supporting this position, and even those nations that had made the democratic transition functioned under the spectre of this cultural stereotype. On the other side, experts suggested that cultural traditions were open to multiple meanings and applications, and that democracy was not a regionally distinct phenomenon that could only prosper in Western Europe. Bruce Gilley (2003), for example, has recently argued that the potential for democratization even in the People's Republic of China has been underestimated.

Noticeably absent from this debate, however, has been the voice of the people in East Asia—what they actually think about democratic principles and the democratic process. The WVS describes citizen orientations toward democracy in the nations of the Pacific Rim. Although caution is warranted, since democracy is a complex concept, the WVS describes broad support for democracy as a regime form, and rejection of the nondemocratic alternatives of oligarchy and military rule. Similarly, most people are positive about the democratic process, rejecting the common claims of democracy's critics that it weakens the economy and leads to disorder. Indeed, when large majorities in China and Vietnam endorse the view that democracy may have its problems, but it is better than other forms of government, it is an indicator of how widespread democratic aspirations have become. Moreover, broad support for a democratic regime and the democratic process that transcends the East–West divide.

Certainly, one must be cautious in interpreting these findings. In several of these nations, the average citizen is unlikely to understand the full benefits and limitations of a democratic system.[19] It is not realistic to think that when the Vietnamese express support for democracy, it carries the same meaning as when citizens are surveyed in established, advanced industrial democracies. A similar problem existed in the first public opinion surveys in Eastern Europe after the fall of Communism. But we also find that citizens in nations with oligarchic leadership are willing to criticize this system of government, as well as military rule—they know how these systems work, and can meaningfully reject them. Thus, democratic aspirations seem to be a common element of the human condition in the nations of the Pacific Rim, whether West or East.

Perhaps the strongest caveat comes from the survey findings in the Philippines. Despite the democratic progress since Marcos's overthrow in 1987, the Philippine public displays only modest support for a democratic regime and support for the democratic process. This may be an enduring trait of the Philippine political culture, but this also may reflect the public's disenchantment with the uneven political record of democracy in their nation. Corazon Aquino struggled to govern after replacing Marcos, while also facing repeated coup attempts. After the relatively stable interlude of the Ramos administration, the government of Joseph Estrada was dogged by corruption charges, impeachment, and then a divisive power struggle until he was forced to resign in 2001. Evidence from Latin America and Eastern Europe suggests that a very poorly performing democratic system can erode support for democratic principles and aspirations (Rose, Haerpfer, and Mishler 1998).

A potential empirical challenge to our conclusions comes from some of the contributors to the East Asia Barometer. Chu, Chang, and Hu (2003) present data on support for democracy and authoritarian regime for eight East Asian nations. They conclude that support for democracy is 'surprisingly low', and they speculate about the persisting appeal of authoritarian regimes in the region. We question their conclusions on two fronts. First, survey questions must be interpreted in terms of a reference point, since response distributions are partly a function of question wording. The East Asia Barometer does not have comparable survey evidence from stable Western democracies, in which some citizens are also critical of the political system (Dalton 2004). Second, when they do compare the responses from Eastern Asia to those of East Europe in the mid-1990s, there is virtually no difference between these two regions. This evidence is cited to discount the extent of democratic norms in East Asia. Alternatively, it is a positive sign if East Asian nations generally match the democratic values in postcommunist Eastern Europe as many of these nations join NATO and the EU.

The experience in Eastern Europe is also illuminating because it suggests that democratic aspirations are the beginning of a process of building a democratic political culture that accepts the frustrations and conflicts that come with the democratization (Rohrschneider 1999). People seek freedom and rights, but it is more difficult to openly extend these rights to one's opponents. Elections and a fair judiciary are positive values until one's party loses an election or an electoral appeal. We have less evidence on whether the citizens in the nondemocratic states of East Asia understand and accept these democratic principles as an extension of their democratic aspirations. In fact, these norms might only be internalized by actually working within a democratic process. For example, Taiwanese surveys find a broad shift toward democratic values of freedom and pluralism that follows the nation's democratization process (Xu 1999), and increased understanding of democracy came with Indonesia's transition in 1998 (Asia Foundation 2003).

Our analyses of the social correlates of support for democracy also provide some insights into the process of cultural change in East Asia. Economic and social modernization undoubtedly contributes to support for democracy in the region. For instance, the better-educated in Vietnam and China have a broader world view, more access to information, and more self-expressive values. This leads to greater support for democracy as well—but the direct impact of education is quite modest. Social status and other modernization variables apparently interact with regime norms, so that as democratization occurs, the modernizing impact of social status apparently strengthens. Thus, educational differences are greater in the consolidated democracies of East Asia, and greater still in the Western democracies.

Public attitudes are of course only one part of the democratization process. The course of democratization, at least over the short term, is more likely to depend on the strategic decisions of national elites than on the responses of citizens to a public opinion survey. In the long run, however, a democratic system requires a democratic public to survive and function. Especially when placed in the larger context of the global findings from the WVS (Inglehart and Welzel 2005), it appears that democratic aspirations are a common belief—more common than previously recognized.

ENDNOTES

1 Our thanks to Ronald Inglehart, Hans-Dieter Klingemann, Nhu-Ngoc Ong, Dorothy Solinger, and William Zimmerman for their advice on this chapter.

2 Vanhanen (1990: 11–26) reviews the previous empirical studies that have scored nations in terms of their democratic development.

3 Similarly, the Polity project gives Australia, Canada, New Zealand, and the United States perfect democracy scores of 10 in 1999 (http://weber.ucsd.edu/~kgledits/Polity.html). The Polity data also describe the same general cross-national patterns as the Freedom House measures. The scores on the 0–10 scale in 1999 were: China 0, Vietnam 0, Singapore 2, Indonesia 8 (although it was scored 0 in 1998 before the regime change), South Korea 8, Taiwan 9, and Japan 10.

4 The 2005 'Hong Kong Creativity Index' survey was commissioned and funded by the Government of the Hong Kong Special Administrative Region. We want to thank Ng Chun Hung for providing us with access to these data. We received these data after the book manuscript was essentially complete, so these findings are included in the overall cross-national marginals, but not in the other substantive analyses of this chapter.

5 We do not distinguish between the two waves of the WVS and simply combined the available data for each nation across the 1995–8 and 1999–2002 waves. Missing data were excluded from the calculation of percentages.

6 A partial time comparison is available for Korea. In 1972–3 Chong Lim Kim and Young Whan Kihl did a national opinion survey; they asked if 'elite rule is desirable' and 65 percent agreed (cited in Kim 1978: 71–2). In the 2001 WVS, only 28 percent were favorable to government by a strong leader without democratic controls.

7 The next most positive rating for the military comes in the Philippines. This may reflect the role the military played in restraining the Estrada administration and finally prompting his resignation in 2001.

8 Even in Western democracies, a reformist element in public administration has called for a greater role of experts within the policy process. For instance, Alan Blinder (1997) wrote about removing politics from American policymaking while he was at the Federal Reserve. He suggested extending the model of independent Central Banks (such as the Federal Reserve) to other key policy areas, so that decisions would be taken out of the hands of elected politicians and come under the control of nonpartisan experts. See discussion of this general theme in Mair (2005).

9 We conducted a factor analysis of these four items to verify they form a common dimension. One factor emerged from these analyses (Eigenvalues = 1.73, 42 percent of the total variance), with all four items loading on this first dimension: strong leaders (0.792), experts (0.577), army rule (0.740), and support for democracy (−0.475). In separate analyses, the factor structure is stronger in the advanced industrial nations (USA, Canada, Japan, Australia, and New Zealand) than in the remaining nations, but the same pattern applies. Then, we simply summed together responses to the four items (reversing the polarity of the democracy item) and divided the total by four. The resulting scale runs from 1) prefer nondemocratic regimes and disapprove of democracy to 4) prefer a democratic regime and disapprove of nondemocratic regimes.

10 We have two time points for three nations, and the overall democratic regime scale is relatively stable over these two waves:

	Japan	S. Korea	USA
1995–8	3.16	3.03	3.33
1999–2003	3.18	3.01	3.18

11 There is a tendency for respondents in both nations to take modest positions on the agree/disagree scale. Although large majorities express prodemocratic responses in Figure 4.3, for example, few select the 'strong' response category. Thus, the mean scores on the overall index are more moderate than the agree/disagree percentages would imply.

12 The Taiwanese survey did not ask this question in the urban half of the sample (in towns greater than 10,000 population). Since urbanization is related to support for democracy (see Table 4.2), this likely depresses the overall support for democracy registered in Taiwan. This rural sampling also applies to the democratic process variable described below.

13 Evidence from the Thailand survey in the East Asian Barometer project is very illuminating. Albritton and Bureekul (2003) asked an open-ended question about what the respondents meant by the term democracy. Nearly half the respondents replied with examples that fit traditional notions of liberal democracy, and an additional third mentioned personal freedoms or civil liberties that are very consistent with Freedom House definitions of civil liberties. Also significant was what was not mentioned: 'Most surprising was the low response rate in terms of traditional 'Asian values' as commonly understood—good governance, social equality, or duties to society. Only one respondent mentioned 'openness or

government transparency', and no one mentioned 'solving employment', 'providing social welfare', or 'finding someone a job'.

In contrast, the survey in China found that 42 percent did not give a definition of democracy, a much higher level of non-response than in Taiwan or Thailand (Shi 2003).

14 For example, a standard question in postcommunist nations asks whether individuals think socialism was a bad idea, or a good idea badly carried out (Rohrschneider 1999).

15 These data also illustrate the value of the cross-national research approach. Shin (1999:31) noted that during the 1990s, Koreans still appeared to question whether prior authoritarian governments were more effective than democracy in dealing with the nation's problems. But when placed in cross-national context, Korean support for the democratic process is relatively high compared to the Western democracies and other East Asian nations.

16 The four items were added together to produce an additive scale, and then divided by four. The resulting scale is scored: 1) critical of the democratic process 4) supportive of democratic process.

	Japan	S. Korea	USA
1995–8	2.91	2.92	2.94
1999–2003	2.93	2.92	2.92

17 We have two time points for three nations, and the overall democratic process scale is relatively stable over these two waves:

18 Because this scale was not available in Vietnam, we use the democratic process index in this one case.

19 For instance, Shin, Park, and Jang (2005) express doubts about the democratic values of Koreans, but many of these same caveats exist in the literature on advanced industrial democracies. Without comparable cross-national measures, it is difficult to assess whether the citizens of East Asia differ from those of established Western democracies.

5

Authority Orientations and Democratic Attitudes: A Test of the 'Asian Values' Hypothesis[1]

Russell J. Dalton and Nhu-Ngoc T. Ong

Among the many explanations for the course of political and economic development in East Asia, the theme of Asian values has played an especially prominent role. The Singaporean patriarch Lee Kuan Yew popularized the claim that the authority orientations particular to Confucian culture explained the unique pattern of political development in East Asia (Lee 1994; Emmerson 1995). The Confucian tradition of respect for authority and family and the emphasis on community over individual rights are presented as antithetical to Western images of liberal democracy. In less polemic terms, this same principle is prominent in scholarly research on East Asian political culture (Pye 1985; Lau and Kuan 1988; Scalapino 1989).

As we discuss below, this proposition has generated considerable scholarly attention. Researchers ask whether such cultural traditions still exist, and whether they are inconsistent with democratic development. And as shown in Chapter 4, the WVS and other new East Asian public opinion surveys suggest a breadth of support for democracy that was unexpected, given previous scholarship.

Although the theme of Asian values is widely debated, cross-national empirical research on what citizens in East Asia actually believe is largely lacking from this discussion. This chapter examines some of its underlying assumptions of the Asian values thesis and tests these ideas drawing on the WVS. We first describe orientations toward authority in various social settings. Then we consider whether these orientations significantly affect support for democracy among East Asians, with comparisons to the West. The findings give voice to the publics of East Asia in this debate on the content and consequences of Asian values, and provide evidence on the cultural conditions relevant to democratization in East Asia.

THE ASIAN VALUES DEBATE

Since the collapse of the Soviet bloc, democracy is the dominant ideological option (Fukuyama 1992). However, several Asian leaders have articulated an alternative model—often to justify the continuation of their autocratic rule. Asian cultural identities are offered as an alternative to universal concepts such as 'democracy' and 'human rights' that are presented as products of the liberal West. Former Singaporean Prime Minister Lee Kuan Yew cited Confucian cultural traditions as a justification for a special Asian course:

> The expansion of the right of the individual to behave or misbehave as he pleases has come at the expense of orderly society. In the East the main object is to have a well-ordered society so that everybody can have maximum enjoyment of his freedoms. This freedom can only exist in an ordered state and not in a natural state of contention and anarchy. (1994; also see Emmerson 1995)

Mahathir Mohamad of Malaysia and other prominent East Asian leaders have expressed similar views.

According to Asian values proponents, because of Confucian traditions, East Asian societies are paternalistic, duty-based, and community-oriented—characteristics that promote harmony and consensus. In contrast, Western societies are rights-based and individualistic, which is congruent with the competitive elements of a democratic system (see Wang and Tan Chapter 3; Lau and Kuan 1988; Rozman 1991). Moreover, similar descriptions of the Confucian cultural heritage are a well-established theme in the political culture literature on East Asia. Lucian Pye (1985) argued that these social values produce an allegiance to authority that appears inconsistent with democratic norms. Robert Scalapino (1989) similarly stressed the limited potential for democratic development in East Asia because of cultural traditions that emphasized communalism with limited toleration for opposition groups. Francis Fukuyama (1998) summarized the Asian values position in the following terms:

> It describes an ethical world in which people are born not with rights but with a duties to a series of hierarchically arranged authorities, beginning with the family and extending all the way up to the state and emperor. In this world, there is no concept of the individual and individual rights; duties are not derived from rights as they are in Western liberal thought. While there is a concept of reciprocal obligation between ruler and ruled, there is no absolute grounding of government responsibility in either the popular will or in the need to respect and protect an individual's sphere of autonomy.

Perhaps the strongest statement comes from Yung-Myung Kim (1997: 1125) who states, 'Confucian ideas are antithetical to Anglo-American democracy'.[2]

In contrast, other scholars question the premises underlying the Asian values hypothesis. For instance, Friedman (1994*a*) and Sen (1999) stress the cultural diversity of East Asia, and the ability of democratic norms to take root in many different types of cultural traditions. Fukuyama (1995) sees the democratic potential of Confucianism to counterbalance some of the negative tendencies of an individualistic, atomized society as exists in some liberal democracies. Theodore de Bary (1998) similarly argues that elements of Confucianism can provide a basis for democratic governance. Another viewpoint holds that Confucian orientations of community may help an individual expand social networks and accumulate social capital, which are normally seen as beneficial to democracy. Indeed, Confucius's actual writings in the *Analects* are so large and diverse, that many elements stress values that are conducive to democratic development (Ames 1999). The issue is not Confucianism—but how it is interpreted in relationship to current political matters.

Social modernization in East Asia, moreover, may transform social and political norms. With modernization comes urbanization, the breaking up of traditional social networks, and the spreading of a competitive mentality, some of the factors contributing to the growth of individualism in Asia. Flanagan and Lee (2000), for example, demonstrate that social modernization variables are strongly related to support for more libertarian (less authoritarian) values in Japan and Korea. Thus, modernization may erode the very values and lifestyles that create the norms encapsulated in Asian values. The chapter by Welzel and Inglehart (in this volume) went one step further, arguing for a broad model of human development where cultural traditions such as Confucianism plays a minor role. Furthermore, rather than the persistence of traditional authority relations, recent descriptions of Japan, Korea, and other East Asian nations often stress the lack of traditional authority relations (Shin 1999; Nathan 2004).

National conditions and histories also vary widely across East Asia, which raises the question of whether there is a single East Asian culture. Although most of the region is linked to Confucian cultural traditions, this is certainly not universal. Indonesians are overwhelmingly Islamic, and Filipinos are disproportionately Catholic. The Communists in China and Vietnam shun Confucianism. Furthermore, for centuries, other philosophies such as Taoism and Buddhism are interwoven into fabric of East Asian life and traditions. Even Pye (1985) acknowledged that adherence to Confucianism varies greatly across the nations linked to this tradition. Thus, it is problematic to talk of a single East Asian political culture or philosophy that reaches from Japan to Singapore.

The dialectic between the East and the West is voluminous, and we have only sketched the outlines of this discussion. However, this debate does not offer a social scientific model for theorizing and testing these contrasting positions. To develop this theoretical framework, we re-cast this debate in the framework of Harry Eckstein's *congruence theory* (see Chapter 1). In essence, congruence theory holds that political systems tend to be based on authority patterns that are congruent with the authority patterns of other units of society (Eckstein 1998). For instance, the hierarchic and paternalistic authority structures of the German family and social life in Weimar and the Wilhelmine Empire were more congruent with the political norms of the Kaiserreich than democracy under the Weimar Republic. More generally, *The Civic Culture* treated family and school authority relations as structuring the political culture (Almond and Verba 1963). Putnam's analysis of political development in Italy (1993) is a reflection of congruence theory: political structures reflect the norms of social relations in the society that they govern. Inglehart's research linking (1997, 2000) self-actualizing values and democratic development is another example. Many of these same arguments are made for the impact of cultural traditions in East Asia; Confucian traditions are seen as more congruent with authoritarian political structures.

This framework leads to a two-step research plan. First, we use the WVS to assess the support for hierarchical, authority relations in family and other social relations. Elite debates about the political culture in Asia have been strikingly lacking in such empirical evidence on how the citizens actually describe their orientations toward authority. Then, we consider whether these orientations are linked to the public's support for democracy. These analyses thus address both sides of the Asian values debate, and provide broader evidence on congruence theory as applied to the East Asian experience.

ORIENTATIONS TOWARD AUTHORITY

This research is based on seven East Asian nations and four Western democratic countries that participated in either the 1995–8 or 2000–2 waves of the WVS. We examine all the surveys from East Asia, identifying China, Indonesia, Japan, the Philippines, Singapore, South Korea, Taiwan, and Vietnam as the East Asian set. Pye (1985) classified most of these countries as having significant Confucian influences (although Filipinos are predominately Catholics and Indonesians Muslims); thus, we expect evidence of strong attachment to the concept of Asian values in most of these nations. Australia, Canada, New Zealand, and the USA are established Western democracies that provide a benchmark for comparing political culture in East Asia to the West. Most of the analyses that follow combined the samples from the third and fourth wave of the WVS in order to increase the number of nations and the empirical base of the analyses.

There is a long tradition of empirical research on attitudes toward authority within Western societies that often begins with questions about the compatibility of these orientations and democratic commitments (e.g. Adorno et al. 1950; Milgram 1974). One goal of the WVS was to tap such orientations (e.g. Nevitte 1996), so we are fortunate that a variety of different questions ask about authority in various life domains.

One set of questions focuses on family relations and orientations toward one's parents. Numerous authors have claimed that familism is one of the foundations of Asian cultural traditions (Pye 1985; Lau and Kuan 1988; Yang 1988). The survey asked respondents whether one should always love and respect one's parents regardless of their faults, whether it is the parents' duty to do what is best for their children, and whether one of the main goals in life is to make one's parents proud.[3] Table 5.1 presents the responses to these questions. If one treats the Western democracies as a control group, then respect for parents and allegiance toward one's parents are surprisingly strong among Western publics. For instance, 78 percent of Americans and 79 percent of Canadians say that one's parents should be respected regardless of their faults. Japanese sentiments are actually less deferential to parents than the Western average (73 percent). Respect for parents is somewhat stronger in other East Asian nations: 91 pecent in Taiwan, 94 percent in Singapore and South Korea, and 99 percent in Vietnam. Parental respect is also relatively high in the two East Asian nations without a Confucian heritage: 95 percent in the Philippines and 90 percent in Indonesia.

The item on parental duty shows some cross-national variation, but virtually no systematic difference between East Asia and the Western nations. The other item asks whether one's main life goals are to make your parents proud; positive responses average only slightly higher among the East Asian publics. On the whole, one would conclude that respect for parental authority is important in both cultural regions. The difference between the two regions averaged across these three parental questions is about a 6 percent gap.

Other questions examined orientations toward authority outside of the parental relationship: belief that child rearing should emphasize obedience,

TABLE 5.1. *Support for authority by nation*

	Western democracies				East Asian nations							
Question	Aust.	Can	NZ	USA	JPN	SK	TWN	PHL	INDS	Sing	PRC	VN
Family relations												
Respect parents	74	79	64	78	73	94	91	95	90	94	85	99
Parents duty	79	82	71	85	46	50	79	90	82	83	64	87
Make parents proud	69	82	58	79	56	60	64	93	91	94	69	97
Other social domains												
Teach obedience	28	35	—	31	5	14	33	44	53	47	35	56
Work instructions	49	58	35	66	29	16	17	42	25	26	24	46
Respect authority	73	69	53	74	5	16	46	72	37	53	49	80
High on index	57	66	—	71	7	16	36	83	61	69	35	86

Source: 1995–8, 2000–2 WVS. Table entries are the percentage giving a response supportive of authority on each item; high scores on the authority relations index represent selecting four or more authority items on the six questions.

one should follow instructions of superiors at work even if one disagrees, and a desire for greater respect for authority in the society. The bottom panel of Table 5.1 shows that when one moves outside of the family, the overlap in sentiments across the East–West divide is even more apparent. For instance, 35 percent of Americans and 31 percent of Canadians mention obedience as a value that parents should instill in their children—and the average across the 8 East Asian nations is 36 percent. There is more variation in these opinions among East Asian nations rather than between East and West.

The other authority items also do not follow a clear East–West division. Agreement that one should follow a superior's instructions at work even if one disagrees is slightly higher among the established Western democracies. None of the East Asian publics is more likely than Americans to say that one should follow instructions at work. In addition, beliefs that society should give greater respect to authority are generally much higher among the established Western democracies than in the East Asian nations. Taken alone, one might think that the low percentages calling for more respect for authority in Japan (5 percent), South Korea (16 percent), and Taiwan (46 percent) may occur because people believe that the authority already garners too much respect in these nations—except that the other questions in the table fail to demonstrate strong orientations toward authority in these three nations. In other words, these three nations display modest support for authority, and believe that respect for authority is still too high.

Beyond the individual questions, these separate items tap a common dimension of respect for authority.[4] Thus, we created an additive index measuring support for authority with the six questions included in Table 5.1.[5] The three Western democracies with full data have more than half the public with high scores on this index (i.e. agreeing with four or more authority items out of six): United States, 71 percent, Canada 66 percent, and Australia 57 percent. In comparison, Indonesia (61 percent), Singapore (69 percent), and Vietnam (86 percent) have a majority with high scores, and only minorities hold these views in Japan (7 percent), South Korea (16 percent), the PRC (35 percent), and Taiwan (36 percent).

Thus, this initial empirical evidence already yields one striking finding: acceptance of authority is not sharply different between these East Asian nations and a set of established Western democracies around the Pacific Rim.[6] This finding runs counter to most of the past qualitative research, which claims that respect for authority is greater in these East Asian societies. Using the cross-national breadth of the WVS, we demonstrate that the level of authority relations in East Asian nations is not substantially different from authority orientations found in Western democracies.[7]

It is possible that the wording of the survey questions created these patterns as a methodological artifact—but we discount this explanation. The new wave of public opinion surveys in East Asia is generally finding similar patterns. For example, Ahn and Kang (2003) include three items on individualist versus collective orientations in their survey of Korean public opinion. They conclude, 'South Koreans are evenly divided between individualism and collective orientations' (2003). Flanagan and Lee (2000) previously described authority relations in Japan and Korea using data from earlier waves of the WVS. They found these two publics were nearly evenly divided in terms of their libertarian versus authoritarian orientations. Preliminary analyses of family authority questions from the East Asian Barometer find that the model of family hierarchy and family loyalty 'are rejected by over three-fifths of the respondents in the average Asian country' (Chu 2003; Nathan 2003*a*: 9).

There are several possible explanations for our findings and the contrast to earlier cultural studies of East Asia. Most of these East Asian nations have experienced a considerable process of social modernization during the later twentieth century, in which many of these traditional cultural traditions may have attenuated with increasing social and geographic mobility, and the move from rural to urban lifestyles (Flanagan and Lee 2000). This might apply especially to the non-family aspects of authority orientations, where opinions overlap the most between East and West.

Partial evidence backing for this modernization hypothesis comes by comparing generational differences within each nation (also see chapters by Welzel and Inglehart, and Wang and Tan in this volume). In the four Western democracies, support for authority is only slightly higher among older generations ($r = 0.06$). In contrast, the age gradient is much steeper in East Asia, especially in the three Asian democracies that have experienced economic and political modernization during the late twentieth century (Japan $r = 0.24$, South Korea $r = 0.27$, and Taiwan $r = 0.19$). In fact, the relationship in all East Asian nations is stronger than the average for the four Western democracies.[8] Thus, authority orientations are more strongly felt among older Asian generations, and these sentiments are distinctly weaker among the young.

Another explanation is that previous descriptive studies of East Asian political culture overstated an Asian stereotype, or focused on socially observed behavior rather than personal attitudes that are internal to the individual. Admittedly, the social traditions in many East Asian nations still place a priority on hierarchy and deference to elders that seems exceptionally strong by Western standards (as noted in our literature review). But social customs are not the same as individual beliefs. Rituals of ancestor devotion can be as ceremonial as a Western Christian who goes to church each Sunday, even while doubting core teachings of the church. Indeed, Eckstein (1988: 797) described a pattern of ritual conformity as 'compliance without commitment' to prevailing social rules as one typical response when governing authority is not congruent with popular values. Moreover, excessive ritual may cause counterreactions, as might be apparent in the Japanese rejection of the need for greater respect for authority.

In summary, recent empirical evidence—our findings and those of other recent surveys—suggests that past descriptive characterizations of the pattern of authority relations held by people in East Asia are not reflected in current public opinion. While a nation's historical traditions may shape orientations toward authority, there is not a sharp East–West clash of values in this domain.

TESTING CONGRUENCE THEORY

Our analysis next examines the link between social authority orientations and support for a democratic regime. If authority relations in the family, workplace, and social life are a basis of political orientations, as congruence theory implies, then the acceptance of hierarchic authority patterns would not be a fertile basis for democratic values.

To test this hypothesis, we use the 'Democratic Regime Index' presented in Chapter 4.[9] The index is based on a battery of items that measures support for nondemocratic regimes and then democracy. The question asked for agreement or disagreement with the following items:

(1) Having a strong leader who does not have to bother with parliament and elections;
(2) Having experts, not government, make decisions according to what they think is best for the country;
(3) Having the army rule; and
(4) Having a democratic political system.

Prodemocratic responses are defined as disagreeing with the first three autocratic items and *agreeing* with the fourth (see Appendix B for index construction).

Chapter 4 demonstrated that support for democracy (and opposition to autocratic regimes) is remarkably widespread across East Asia—including the nondemocracies of the region. This alone argues that Confucian historical traditions are not directly translated into political values, even though norms of family and work relations do not display hierarchic authority orientations. However, we can test the congruence thesis more directly by linking social authority orientations to support for democracy.

We begin by correlating the six measures of authority relations and the democratic regime index (Table 5.2). In the advanced industrial democracies, there is normally a modest, albeit statistically significant, relationship between authority patterns and democratic values. For instance, Americans who say that parents should always be respected are somewhat less likely to endorse democracy over authoritarian political regimes ($r = -0.10$). The

Table 5.2. *Correlations between authority orientations and support for democratic regime*

	CAN	USA	NZ	Aus	*West avg.*	JPN	SK	TW	PHL	INS	Sing	PRC	VN	*East Avg.*
Parental respect	−0.15*	−0.10*	−0.13*	−0.14*	*−0.13*	−0.03	−0.00	−0.09*	0.07*	−0.01	0.02	−0.07	−0.04	*−0.02*
Parental duty	−0.05	0.01	−0.01	−0.03	*−0.02*	0.05	−0.08*	−0.06	0.03	−0.03	0.00	−0.02	0.10*	*−0.01*
Make parents proud	−0.18*	−0.08*	−0.15*	−0.12*	*−0.14*	−0.03	0.02	−0.10*	−0.14*	0.04	−0.02	−0.02	0.01	*−0.03*
Teach child obedience	−0.09*	−0.09*	—	−0.13*	*−0.10*	−0.02	−0.06	−0.06	−0.02	0.01	0.02	—	−0.03	*−0.03*
Follow work instructions	−0.04	0.01	−0.02	−0.06	*−0.04*	−0.01	−0.05	0.01	0.00	−0.09*	−0.10*	−0.03	0.04	*−0.03*
General respect for authority	−0.05	−0.02	−0.09*	−0.12*	*−0.07*	−0.19*	−0.14*	−0.11*	−0.03	−0.05	−0.14*	−0.08*	0.23*	*−0.06*
Authority index and democratic regime	−0.15*	−0.09*	−0.14*	−0.18*	*−0.14*	−0.04	−0.10*	−0.17*	−0.04	−0.08*	−0.09	−0.05	—	*−0.08*
Authority index and democratic process	−0.20*	−0.07*	−0.17*	−0.19*	*−0.16*	−0.09*	−0.02	−0.10*	0.03	−0.01	—	−0.06	0.12*	−0.01

Source: Combined surveys from the 1995–8 and 1999–2002 WVS; * means the Pearson's r is significant at 0.05 level.

same pattern appears for the 'make parents proud' item for the Western democracies.

This pattern does not carry over to East Asia, however. Some nations display a positive relationship and some a negative relationship, and the overall average is close to a null relationship. A notable anomaly is Vietnam, where respect for authority often is positively related to support for democracy. Even though we use a different democracy index in Vietnam, we do not believe this explains the anomaly, since the two indices are positively correlated in the other nations where both were asked.

The same general pattern applies for the three other authority questions in the lower half of the table. Those who mentioned obedience as a trait to socialize are significantly less likely to endorse democratic values among the Western democracies. Among the nations of East Asia—including Japan—this relationship is essentially nonexistent. The only item that shows a pattern of strong congruence in East Asia is the question on greater respect for authority—though we noted earlier that few respondents in the nations where this relationship is strongest actually subscribe to these beliefs (see Table 5.1).

The final evidence comes from the overall authority scale in the last rows of the table. The relationship between authority orientations and the democratic regime index is generally stronger in Western democracies (average $r = -0.14$)—consistent with congruence theory (although these relationships are not large). The average correlation is only -0.08 across East Asian nations.

Some might suggest that democracy has become such a dominant political model that Asian publics see little alternative except to support a democratic regime. If this were the case, then it would be a striking findings by itself. But to probe these sentiments more deeply, we also examined attitudes toward the democratic process (see Chapter 4). Indeed, much of the criticism by Lee Kuan Yew and others focused on the supposed economic and political inefficiencies of democracy, which is captured by the process index. The last row of the table shows that the relationships between authority orientations and the democratic process index are significantly greater in the Western democracies than in East Asia.

It is important to note that there is supporting evidence from the East Asia Barometer surveys. Albritton and Bureekul (2004) analyzed the relationship between authority measures and democracy scales in Thailand. They also find only a weak, nonsignificant relationship between familial values and support for democracy. In fact, the direction of the relationship in Thailand is reversed to that predicted by theory. Thus, the findings presented here are also apparent in other empirical studies of public opinion.

These weak relationships are significant because they contradict the widely claimed—but seldom tested—thesis that Confucian traditions and resulting authority orientations in East Asia will undermine the development of democratic values. It is true that deference toward authority has a negative impact within the Western democracies, which is one reason this thesis developed in the political culture literature. But the same pattern is not apparent in East Asia. This is not because variance is restricted on either the dependent or the independent variables, since similar distributions exist in West and East. The absence of a systematic relationship in the East Asian nations suggests that other elements of Asian culture may have counterbalancing effects such as the emphasis on community and collective values (e.g. Fukuyama 1995*b*; de Bary 1998). Furthermore, the high levels of support for democracy across East Asia provide additional evidence that Confucian traditions are not directly translated into political norms.

Multivariate Analyses

Before concluding that authority orientations are without strong effects, we want to consider whether these relationships are affected by other factors that influence democratic values. For instance, the dramatic social modernization in East Asia may be shifting opinions, and this may appear in age or social status differences that are related to authority orientations. Alternatively, other established predictors of support for democracy, such as social trust, might have confounding influences on these relationships. Across such a wide range of regimes, the role of financial or policy satisfaction also might affect these relationships.

To test for such effects, we include the index of authority relations with a set of other variables in a multivariate model predicting support for a democratic regime (Table 5.3).[10] Education and political discussions are included to see if sophisticated and involved citizens were more supportive of democracy. A measure of financial satisfaction taps whether immediate economic performance is related to support for a democratic regime. Social trust is based on Putnam's (1993) analyses of support for democracy in the West. We also add age to see if there are generational patterns in these attitudes.

In most Asian nations, the impact of authority orientations is quite modest, far short of the cultural determinism that is implied by the Asian values thesis. The other predictors do not attenuate this relationship because they are only weakly related to support for democracy. Among the Western nations, the impact of authority relations weakens slightly in the multivariate model, and is now outweighed by other predictors such as education, age, or political engagement. Moreover, the Vietnam survey shows the same pattern as the bivariate relationship, with authority patterns positively related to support for a democratic regime (see Table 5.1).[11]

The Confucian constellation of China, Japan, Korea, Singapore, Taiwan, and Vietnam thus do not speak in unison about the relationship, if any, between social authority orientations and democratic values. The weak

TABLE 5.3. *Multivariate analyses of support for democratic regime*

	CAN	USA	NZ	AUS	JPN	SK	TW	PHL	INS	Sing	PRC	VN
Authority Index	−0.10*	−0.08*	−0.13*	−0.12*	−0.08*	−0.10*	−0.14*	−0.04	−0.07*	−0.08*	−0.04	0.11*
Education	0.14*	0.09*	0.08*	0.12*	0.12*	0.09*	0.07	0.09*	−0.03	0.06	0.05	0.01
Age	0.17*	0.18*	0.09*	0.12*	0.16*	0.06	0.05	0.03	0.01	0.15*	−0.01	−0.03
Financial satisfaction	−0.01	0.00	0.11*	0.01	−0.04	0.04	−0.05	0.01	−0.02	−0.02	−0.03	0.12*
Social trust	0.13*	0.08*	0.07*	0.14*	0.07*	0.01	0.04	0.06	0.06	0.02	—	−0.02
Discuss politics	0.16*	0.15*	0.17*	0.18*	0.06	0.07*	0.20*	0.00	0.06	0.11*	0.08*	0.03
Multiple *R*	0.30	0.30	0.29	0.36	0.21	0.16	0.28	0.12	0.11	0.19	0.12	0.18

Source: Combined surveys from the 1995–8 and 1999–2002 WVS.

Note: Table entries are standardized regression coefficients; pairwise deletion of missing data was used in these models.

* Coefficients significant at 0.05 level

relationships between authority patterns in the Asian family and support for democracy contradict the view that democracy will have difficulty taking root in Asia, particularly within countries strong in Confucian traditions. The democratic potential of these nations should be judged by factors other than the social relationship between parents and their children.

CONFUCIAN TRADITIONS AND CONGRUENCE THEORY

Our research should, at the least, contribute empirical evidence to other criticisms of the Asian values thesis, which claims that Confucian-based authority relations are a significant impediment to democratization in East Asia. Multiple opinion items point to a pattern of social authority norms in East Asia that is not dramatically different from the established Western democracies of the Pacific Rim (or Europe). Moreover, other recent opinion surveys in East Asia are providing evidence in support of the findings presented here. Thus, the cultural explanation for the place of Asia and, more specifically, countries with a Confucian tradition, in current history seems to be much weaker when viewed in terms of this evidence from public opinion surveys. National levels of authority orientations within East Asia are not strongly linked to Confucian heritage (comparing the Catholic Philippines and Islamic Indonesia to the Confucian nations in our survey), and not markedly different from the Western democracies of the Pacific Rim.

We think there are several reasons why our empirical findings conflict with previous qualitative and descriptive studies of East Asian political culture. For countries with a history of political authoritarianism, a habit of thinking that the culture impeded democratization was probably built into scholars' perception of East Asia. This deterministic mode of thinking might have arisen from generalizing from the observable actions of authoritarian elites and social traditions, to presuming that these patterns represented the values of the citizenry. People in authoritarian countries, however, do not necessarily hold beliefs consistent with what their leaders value. In fact, individual citizens of such countries may not conform to what their rulers say they should. Amartya Sen (1999: 248) reached a similar conclusion: 'to see Asian history in terms of a narrow category of authoritarian values does little justice to the rich varieties of thought in Asian intellectual traditions. Dubious history does nothing to vindicate dubious politics'.

In addition, generalizations about the undemocratic political culture of East Asia may have been true in the past, but the social modernization in the region during the late twentieth century has changed public opinion. The generational shift away from authority orientations is much greater in East Asia than in Western democracies although in both regions, elders decry the declining respect for authority in their respective societies (also see chapters by Welzel and Inglehart, and Wang and Tan, in this volume; Flanagan and Lee 2000, 2003).

In summary, the evidence presented here and in other recent public opinion surveys suggest that Confucian cultural traditions—to the extent that they do exist in contemporary East Asia—are not an impediment for the formation of democratic norms among contemporary publics in the region. This does not mean that democratization will immediately follow, but it does imply that mass political culture is not the impediment to democratization as some analysts and political leaders have claimed.

Our results also raise questions about treating all of East Asia as adhering to a single model of Asian values. The nations of the region differ widely in their economic condition and their political histories. East Asia spans the range from Vietnam to Japan, from South Korea to Indonesia and the Philippines—these are very different nations, with different social, religious, and political traditions. The citizens also differ significantly in their orientations toward family and authority relations. At least in terms of the authority orientations examined in this chapter, there is not a single, unified East Asian political culture.

Diverse values exist among the citizens in East Asia. This observation may be one of the most optimistic and liberating views for democratic prospects in the region. Our initial findings provide some evidence toward the possibility of democratization without having to change the cultural traditions of the region. The speed of democratization will inevitably be faster than the slower pace of change in social relations or cultural traditions, but as long as no incongruence is perceived, and the political is kept separate from the nonpolitical spheres of values, then experiencing democratic development may not require a cultural shift.

ENDNOTES

1 The first author would like to thank the POSCO Fellowship program at the East–West Center in Hawaii for their support of this project, especially Dr Choong Nam Kim.

2 One could also note, however, that the other aspects of Confucian traditions appear more compatible with democracy. The emphasis on harmony and the responsibility of leadership, for instance, are consistent with classic democratic theory. Similarly, the value of the community also may be beneficial in developing a democratic culture. Thus, Fukuyama (1995*b*: 8) also notes that 'there are fewer points of incompatibility between Confucianism and democracy than many people in Asia and the West believe'.

3 See Appendix B for more information on these six items. The questionnaire with the specific wording of items is available at: www.worldvaluessurvey.org

4 We entered the six items into a principal components analysis, and the following table presents the first unrotated dimension in each nation. The 'teach obedience' question was not asked in New Zealand. Like Flanagan and Lee (2000), the results suggest a single dimension underlies these items, although in some instances the limited variance on items restricted the correlations; this is most clearly apparent in the Vietnamese results.

	CAN	USA	Aust	NZ	JPN	SK	TW	PHL	INS	Sing	PRC	VN
Respect parents	0.63	0.63	0.67	0.69	0.50	0.35	0.56	0.76	0.33	0.46	0.57	−0.14
Parent duty	0.31	0.36	0.34	0.53	0.46	0.67	0.61	0.77	0.62	0.64	0.63	0.40
Parents proud	0.59	0.49	0.59	0.65	0.62	0.12	0.47	0.12	0.35	0.56	0.14	0.60
Teach obedience	0.44	0.43	0.45	—	0.32	0.47	0.46	−0.03	0.52	0.38	0.58	−0.22
Follow instructions	0.57	0.38	0.35	0.30	0.42	0.16	0.35	−0.14	0.49	0.25	0.36	0.56
Respect authority	0.54	0.59	0.61	0.44	0.48	0.63	0.23	0.00	0.35	0.45	0.45	0.60
Eigenvalue	1.65	1.45	1.61	1.47	1.35	1.24	1.31	1.21	1.26	1.35	1.41	1.26
Percent variance	27.6	24.2	26.8	29.4	22.5	20.6	21.7	20.2	20.9	22.4	23.4	20.9

5 The scale was computed as the simple sum of the approval of authority option on each of the six items. The scale thus runs from 0 to 6 in each nation, except in New Zealand, where one item was not available. See Appendix B.

6 In a presentation of these data, a discussant claimed the questions were insufficient to tap attitudes toward authority in East Asia since they were derived from a survey first conducted in Europe. We disagree because we see these questions as broadly applicable across diverse national contexts, as was the intent of the WVS. In addition, previous published studies of East Asia have interpreted these data as valid (e.g. Flanagan and Lee 1991, 2000); and other studies have compared East Asia to the West using some of these WVS items (Flanagan 1982; Inglehart 1997; Flanagan and Lee 2003; Welzel, Inglehart, and Klingemann 2003).

7 The four Western democracies examined here are not markedly different from the findings in Europe from the 1999 European Values Survey that included these same questions (Halman 2002).

8 Generational comparisons potentially reflect the impact of five or six decades of history, and long-term time series dating back to the 1950s or 1960s might display such trends. However, these trends are not apparent for the shorter time span of the WVS. Three items were included with comparable wording over the four waves of the WVS in Japan and Korea: respect parents, teach obedience, and respect for authority. The average giving the authority response across these three items had not changed significantly over this two decade time span:

	1981	1990	1995	2000
Japan	28	32	29	27
Korea	38	42	41	41

9 The democratic regime index is not available for Vietnam, so the Vietnamese analyses are based on the democratic process index that is also described in Chapter 4.

10 The regression models in Table 5.3 are not strictly identical across all ten nations. In about half the nations, we used the 'age left school' variable as a measure of education; in the other half, we used a country-specific ranking of educational levels. The authority relations index lacked one item in New Zealand, the social trust variable was not included in the Chinese

survey, and an alternative democracy scale was used in Vietnam as noted in footnote 9. For these reasons, we present standardized regression coefficients in the table. Comparing results where possible with the unstandardized coefficients yielded essentially similar results.

11 Perhaps the meaning of democracy for the Vietnamese is different than other East Asian countries. Like China, Vietnam has been experimenting with grassroots democracy, where the people contribute to policymaking at the local level. In these exercises, however, Vietnamese authorities always emphasize the importance of democratic practice within boundaries, meaning that the people should be aware of actors who try to 'take advantage' of democracy and promote ideas harmful to societal structure and harmony. Hence, the value patterns shown in the analysis may indeed reflect governmental constraints.

6

Civil Society, Social Capital, and Democracy[1]

Russell J. Dalton

Many researchers hold that a vibrant civil society is integral for the democratic development of a nation (Diamond 1994; Linz and Stepan 1996; Inkeles 2000; Edwards, Foley, and Diani 2001). Participation in autonomous social groups supposedly produces the interpersonal skills and resources that benefit democratic participation, encourage tolerance and trust in others, broaden world perspectives, and provide practice in deliberation and decision-making. These citizen-building benefits seemingly create the 'social capital' that supports democratic politics. Thus, the democratic transition literature on Eastern Europe maintains that civil society is a stimulus for regime change and a foundation for consolidating democracy in post-communist nations (Rueschemeyer, Rueschemeyer, and Wittrock 1998; Howard 2003).

At the same time, there are frequent questions of whether Western liberal ideals of group participation and civil society apply to East Asia (Brook and Frolic 1997; Alagappa 2004). Although public protests are a prominent part of many democratic transitions in East Asia—and visible examples of periodic opposition to authoritarian regimes—the depth of such social activism is uncertain. The Asian values debate discussed in Chapter 5 also suggests that the pluralism and autonomy that are hallmarks of a vibrant civil society may be lacking in some Asian nations. In other East Asian nations, the government intentionally limits the formation of social groups and their public activities, so an autonomous civil society barely exists. Thus, social group activity may not be widely practiced in Asian societies, and this may impede the democratization of the region.

This chapter examines the theme of civil society across our set of Pacific Rim nations. East Asian nations display striking variation in their political conditions. Civil society actions were especially visible in the democratic transitions in South Korea and Taiwan. Similarly, the Philippines is well-known for the public protests that overthrew the Marcos regime and led to the resignation of Joseph Estrada in 2001. The type of autonomous civil society discussed in democratic theory should be lacking in China and Vietnam because of the still-dominant role of the communist party. Even in these nations, however, participation in social groups may be extensive; and even in a communist state, social group activity may have some of the consequences suggested by the civil society literature.

Much of prior research on civil society groups in East Asia focuses on the number of groups existing in a nation, but our research examines individual participation in civil society groups. The new wave of the WVS measures membership and participation in social groups. We compare the level of civil society activity in East Asia to the Western democracies of the Pacific Rim. In addition, we consider whether civil society activity encourages the development of democratic norms and behaviors as the theory would suggest.

GROUP MEMBERSHIPS AND CIVIL SOCIETY

In the past decade, theorists and political practitioners have stressed the importance of civil society in the process of political development. Perhaps the most visible work is by Robert Putnam (1993, 2000) who maintains that the social capital formed by participation in associations develops a nation politically, as well as improving the political norms and skills of its citizens. Such a model has a long theoretical tradition within Western political culture, most notably described in De Tocqueville's *Democracy in America*.

Even in associations as diverse as environmental groups, labor unions, or rabbit-breeding clubs, social group activity can produce organizational skills that carry over to the political world. Interacting with other members creates social skills that are transportable to politics. Several studies show a strong relationship between group activity and political participation across a wide range of nations (Verba, Nie, and Kim 1978; Booth and Richard 1996; McDonough, Shin, and Moisés 1998). Given the activities of government in contemporary societies, these groups provide a forum for discussing how politics affects the group and the interests of its members. Even in nations where democracy is uncertain, participation in civil society—generally interpreted as voluntary participation in social groups that are autonomous of the state—is often seen as a step toward developing a democratic political culture. For instance, Booth and Richard (1996) demonstrated that group activity is related to greater support for democracy across a set of Latin American nations. This is why social groups are described as a potential training ground for democracy.

The civil society literature also stresses the role of social groups in the political process. An extensive civil society sector provides a buffer between citizens and the state, protecting individuals from the potential intrusions of state power. These groups can create a sphere for political discourse and debate separate from state actors. Civil society groups also serve as agents to articulate public interests and press governments to act on public policy matters. Pippa Norris (2002, Chapter 8), for instance, found that aggregate levels of social group activity in a nation are strongly related to levels of social tolerance, political engagement, democratic development, and good governance (also see Inglehart and Welzel 2005). Howard (2003: 43) summarizes this position by stating: 'civil society can and indeed *must* develop in order to establish a more deeply rooted, legitimate, and effective democracy' (also see Diamond 1994; Rueschemeyer, Rueschemeyer, and Wittrock 1998).

From the outset, however, some analysts have questioned whether this civil society model applies to East Asia, especially those nations linked to Confucian traditions. While some scholars see the collectivist aspects of Confucianism as supporting group action, others stress the deference to authority embedded in these same traditions (Chan 1996; Steinberg 1997; Schwartz 2003). Civil society groups should embody pluralism and autonomy, and the skeptics maintain that these orientations are lacking in Asian cultural traditions. Others claim that the social networks based on family or local community in many Asian nations inhibit the type of broader collective networks that are essential to a vibrant civil society (Fukuyama 1995*a*: 83–96). Moreover, while autonomous social groups are accepted or encouraged in the democratic nations of East Asia, they are limited in other nations. China and Singapore have restrictive registration regulations and monitoring activities that limit and control social groups. Thus, social groups in several East Asian nations are not independent of the state and do not exist in an autonomous civic space; rather, they function primarily as corporatist agents linked to government agencies (e.g. White, Howell, and Shang 1996; Brook and Frolic 1997).

Still, the broad processes of social modernization we have discussed in this volume may have encouraged a more active civil society sector across East Asia. The recent volume by Alagappa (2004) describes a flowering of civil society groups across Asia, and claims that skepticism of the civil society potential of the region is overdrawn. Even in China, social modernization—the marketization of the economy, increasing affluence, expanding international interaction, and a more complex society structure—have stimulated a growth of government sanctioned and informal social groups (White, Howell, and Shang 1996; Saich 2000). One government account claims that these groups are spreading like wildfire across the Chinese landscape.

Prior research thus provides a varied picture, although it is primarily based on evidence from individual nations. For instance, even in Japan, with its extensive postwar democratic history, nonprofit organizations were discouraged by tax laws and government regulations until fairly recently. While neighborhood associations flourished, membership in autonomous civil society groups was limited until the past decade (Takao 2001; Inogouchi

2002; Schwartz 2003). Thus, cross-national studies typically describe low levels of social group membership in Japan (Howard 2003: 79).

South Korea apparently has a more active civil society. University students and labor activists played a prominent role in the antigovernment demonstrations that stimulated the nation's democratic transition in 1987–8 (Kim 2000). Even though political protest decreased after the transition, the number of groups proliferated and Koreans remained active in these groups.[2] Shin (1999, Chapter 4) describes a relatively high level of civic engagement in associations in the mid-1990s, which was roughly comparable to levels found in other established and consolidating democracies (McDonough, Shin, and Moisés 1998; Shin 1999: 131).

The Philippines is typically cited as a case where an active civil society directly contributed to the democratization process. Various social groups and interests united in the antigovernment activities that led to Ferdinand Marcos' ousting in 1986 and Estrada's resignation in 2001. These are widely cited as examples of Philippine 'people power' (Franco 2004). Yet beyond these periodic dramatic outbursts of antigovernment protests, it is unclear how engaged the average Filipino is in civil society activity. Thus, although the Philippines has a democratic system and embraces the imagery of an active citizenry, the breadth of civil society activity is uncertain.

In the nondemocratic nations of Asia, the context and content of group membership is fundamentally different. Participation in social groups may not generate the type of participatory experiences that might occur in democratic nations. Chinese scholars, for instance, sharply disagree on the relevance of the civil society concept to China, and the extent of meaningful social group activity (White, Howell, and Shang 1996; Brook and Frolic 1997; Saich 2000).[3] The type of state-led social groups typically found in China and Vietnam is not what is meant by civil society activity. Indeed, there are clear distinctions in China between official organizations (*guanban*) and popular or informal organizations (*minban*); the latter are restricted, leaving limited space for truly autonomous social groups (*zizhihui*). Similarly, the internal workings of social groups in such a setting may—or may not—generate the types of organizational skills and social norms that are the essence of the civil society thesis. Research is divided on the extent of civil society activity in Vietnam (Sidel 1995; Thayer 1995; Lockhart 1997; Kerkvliet 2001).

The Singapore government also actively restricts autonomous civic engagement (Koh and Ling 2000, 2004; Kadir 2004). Autonomous, challenging groups are not tolerated by the state—which is exactly the type of group that epitomizes civil society. The government also restricts freedom of association and only permits registered political associations to engage in organized political activities. Even if some autonomous groups do exist (Kadir 2004), their membership and public involvement are limited, and they exist in a restrictive political environment. Thus, the potential for political discussion and the development of social capital is sharply circumscribed.

In summary, the context for civil society activity in East Asia is tremendously varied. The experiences of the public are likely equally varied, both in the extent of social group activity and in the norms or skills learned from this activity. Our study is in the unique position to compare these activity levels and effects systematically across a large set of East Asian nations.

CIVIL SOCIETY ENGAGEMENT

Civil society is a term with many meanings. Typically, the term refers to civic groups and social organizations, ranging from sports clubs to fraternal organizations, women's groups, and economic associations such as labor unions and professional associations (Linz and Stepan 1996).

Much of the past research on civil society in East Asia focuses on the organizations themselves, counting the number of groups and describing their activities. This is an important element of civil society. However, civil society can be a hollow term if these organizations do not have significant memberships and engage citizens in their activities. For instance, the number of organized social groups has dramatically increased in Japan, China, and other Asian nations (White, Howell, and Shang 1996; Pharr 2000; Schwartz 2003).[4] However, it is unclear whether these new groups mobilize a significantly larger share of the public.

We assess the actual degree of individual participation across nations. Since we are interested in citizen attitudes and behavior, these should be shaped by individuals' participation in civil society groups. The WVS asked two questions of respondents that were designed to measure social group involvement (see Appendix A for information on these surveys). The first question asked if respondents were members of a social group in fourteen different areas and an additional 'other' category:[5]

Please look carefully at the following list of voluntary organizations and activities and say which, if any, do you belong to:

- Social welfare services for elderly, handicapped, or deprived people,
- Religious organizations,
- Education, arts, music, or cultural activities,
- Labor unions,
- Political groups and organizations,
- Local community action on issues like poverty, employment, housing, racial equality,
- Third world development or human rights,
- Conservation, environment, animal rights groups,

- Professional associations,
- Youth work (e.g. scouts, guides, youth clubs, and so on),
- Sports or recreation,
- Women's groups,
- Peace movement,
- Voluntary organizations concerned with health,
- Other organizations.

This question format typically is used in studies of social group membership and it assesses the range of major social groups to which individuals belong. Some of these groups may be more relevant than others in producing politically relevant skills and norms—and below we make such distinctions. As an initial step, this battery provides a broad assessment of the degree of social engagement in each nation.[6]

Table 6.1 describes the percentage of the public in each nation that belong to a group in each of the fourteen sectors. The table displays wide cross-national variation in social group activity. The USA has a high level of group membership, consistent with previous findings (Norris 2002, Chapter 8; Putnam 2002). On average, an American belongs to 3.26 social groups. At the other end of the range is China, where the average person is a member of only 0.39 groups.[7] In addition, membership levels in Asia reflect the traditions and organizational context of the nation rather than economic or political development. For instance, membership levels are low in Japan (0.84) despite the nation's affluent and democratic history.[8] Membership levels in Korea and the Philippines are near those of Canada. As we expected, participation in social groups is limited in Singapore. Wang and Tan (in this volume) discuss the relatively high levels of self-expressive values among the Singapore public, so we attribute these low levels not to the lack of potential interest by the public, but rather to government restrictions and discouragement of such activity.

Vietnam is another distinctive case. The Vietnamese population is engaged in an active social life that rivals the level of group membership in the USA. At least in part, the level of group membership reflects the Vietnamese government's efforts to engage the public in social groups that are initiated and directed by the government. The Vietnamese Women's Association, the Ho Chi Minh Youth Union, the Vietnam Farmers Association, the Vietnamese Confederation of Labor and other groups have historically served as avenues for the government to communicate with key social sectors in Vietnam, and often these groups claim large national memberships (Porter 1993, Chapter 3). This produces a high degree of social group membership among the Vietnamese public, although one might question whether such mobilized membership has the consequences envisioned by civil society theory.

Equally important as the total level of group activity is the type of groups to which people belong, and this is equally varied. Membership in political

Table 6.1. *Membership in various social groups*

Group	USA	Canada	Japan	S. Korea	Philippines	Singapore	China	Vietnam
Social welfare services	16.8	13.2	9.4	9.4	8.0	7.1	2.9	26.1
Religious organizations	57.1	29.5	10.6	42.1	30.8	19.8	3.6	10.5
Education or culture	37.3	21.4	11.0	19.1	5.4	14.0	2.2	17.4
Labor union	13.6	14.4	6.5	5.6	4.0	4.3	6.9	11.4
Political group	19.2	6.3	3.5	2.7	4.1	0.4	8.3	28.6
Local community action	12.9	8.0	1.2	6.9	6.7	2.4	1.5	26.3
Third World/Human rights	5.5	5.1	1.7	2.3	4.8	0.5	0.4	1.5
Conservation and environment	15.6	9.1	3.2	6.2	8.0	1.0	1.2	7.6
Professional association	28.0	17.9	4.8	8.8	4.0	4.4	1.2	13.4
Youth work	26.3	11.2	2.1	4.3	7.5	8.3	1.1	15.5
Sports or recreation	36.0	27.5	14.1	24.7	12.3	15.1	3.2	18.8
Women's group	14.3	8.1	3.8	3.7	10.3	1.2	3.3	28.5
Peace movement	4.5	2.1	2.0	1.8	11.3	0.9	0.9	9.2
Health organization	16.7	11.1	3.1	9.8	9.3	3.6	2.7	14.9
Other group	21.8	11.2	6.9	4.3	1.6	3.6	—	3.7
Mean number of memberships	3.26	1.96	0.84	1.43	1.31	0.86	0.39	2.33

Source: WVS, 1999–2002.

groups—parties and political organizations—can, if voluntary, have great potential to socialize politically relevant skills and norms (Warren 2000). However, the skills and norms within these groups may vary dramatically depending on the political system. For instance, political activity is high in the USA and Vietnam; certainly it is an understatement to say that the content of political learning should differ in these examples. Economic associations are another common civil society activity in Western democracies; roughly a third of Americans and Canadians report membership in a labor union or professional association. Engagement in such economic groups is distinctly lower across East Asia. Membership in environmental groups, human rights groups, and, perhaps, community associations, may be closer to the classic image of civil society groups. Such activity tends to be higher in democratic nations that encourage these activities—the USA, Canada, Korea, and the Philippines—but the Vietnamese also report high membership levels in these groups. Membership in religious groups is especially high in the USA, Korea, the Philippines, and Canada; but state policies limit religious engagements in China and Vietnam.

For four nations—Japan, South Korea, Canada, and the USA—we have comparable longitudinal data to track group membership over time (the 1981, 1990, and 1999 WVS). Civil society activity has grown significantly in all four nations over this time span (Figure 6.1). For instance, before the democratic transition in 1981, group membership levels in South Korea were quite low (mean = 0.51), comparable to the levels in China today. With the democratic transition, there was a blooming of civil society activity and

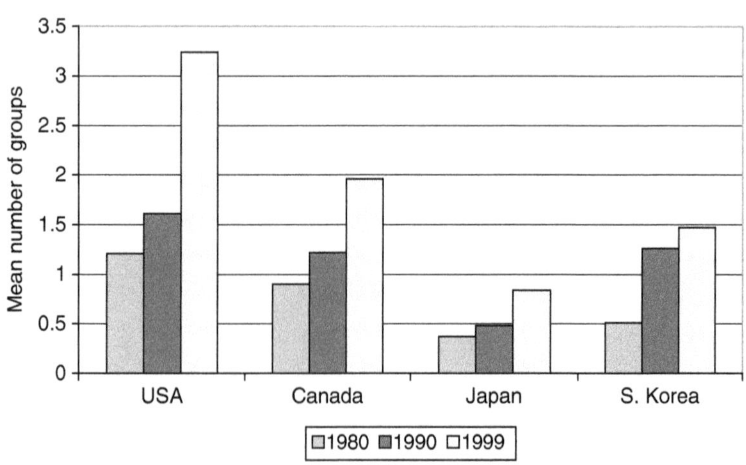

FIGURE 6.1. The trend in group membership over time
Source: 1981, 1990, and 1999–2002 WVS.

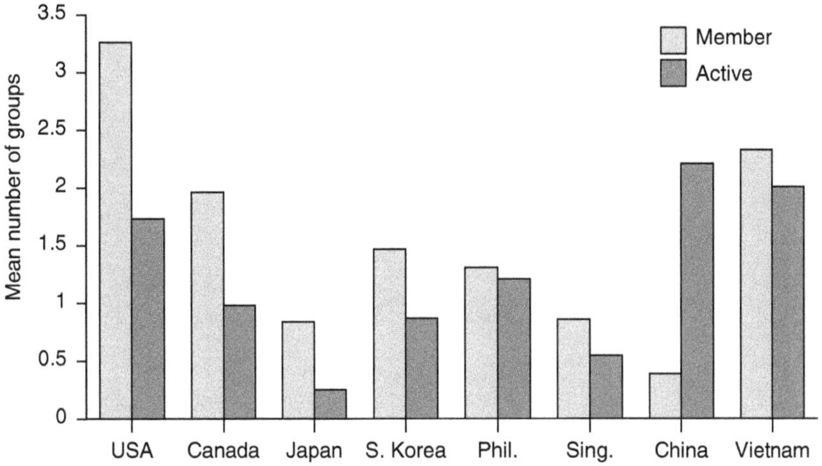

FIGURE 6.2. Membership and activity in various social groups
Source: 1999–2002 WVS.

membership more than doubled by 1990, and then increased again by 1999. The robustness of Korean civil society also shows in comparison to Japan; at each time point, Korean membership levels exceed those in Japan, even before Korea's democratic transition. Moreover, the level of group membership in Korea in 2002 is comparable to the USA or Canada in the first two waves of the WVS. In short, these time comparisons reaffirm the point that civil society groups strengthen democracy, and democracy strengthens civil society.

Membership in an organization may be a passive activity, but the civil society theory presumes that individuals are actively engaged. Therefore, the WVS asked a second question about voluntary activity for these same groups.[9] For instance, many people participate in voluntary activities—helping the elderly, working on environmental projects, volunteering in sports activities, or participating in community events—without being a formal member of a social group. Such activity may be even more powerful a source of social capital than formal group membership.

Table 6.2 describes the percentage of the public in each nation that had done unpaid voluntary work in each of the fourteen sectors. Typically, active engagement is lower than the reported membership in social groups. For instance, Americans report they are members of 3.26 social groups on average, but they are doing voluntary work for only 1.73 groups on average. This is still high in comparative terms, since other nations display this same drop-off. China is an exception because the Chinese survey asked about *willingness to work* for group, rather than actual activity.[10] Group membership in social

TABLE 6.2. *Voluntary activity for various social groups*

Group	USA	Canada	Japan	S. Korea	Philippines	Singapore	China	Vietnam
Social welfare services	14.0	9.5	5.4	9.1	10.1	7.1	56.0	28.7
Religious organizations	38.0	18.4	3.2	26.9	29.7	19.8	4.3	9.6
Education or culture	19.8	11.2	3.9	19.1	4.0	14.0	16.4	15.8
Labor union	3.2	3.4	0.6	8.5	3.3	4.3	7.2	9.8
Political group	7.0	2.7	1.2	2.2	4.0	0.4	9.9	23.8
Local community action	7.2	5.1	0.4	6.9	6.5	2.4	14.1	25.8
Third World/Human rights	2.9	2.5	0.3	2.3	5.3	0.5	4.6	1.3
Conservation and environment	8.5	4.5	1.2	6.2	8.8	1.0	27.7	7.9
Professional association	10.8	6.1	1.3	8.8	2.4	4.4	3.6	13.3
Youth work	21.8	8.1	1.0	4.3	6.4	8.3	9.8	10.4
Sports or recreation	18.8	12.8	3.3	24.7	12.2	15.1	17.7	13.9
Women's group	8.3	4.6	1.2	3.7	9.0	1.2	15.0	18.1
Peace movement	2.0	1.0	0.7	1.8	10.5	0.9	16.0	26.9
Health organization	11.1	8.4	1.5	9.8	9.3	3.6	24.0	6.8
Mean active groups	1.73	0.98	0.25	0.87	1.21	0.55	2.21	2.01

Source: WVS, 1999–2002.

Note: The WVS asked about voluntary activity in the past year, except for the Chinese survey, which asked about the willingness to do voluntary work.

groups is quite low in China (0.39 groups), but the willingness to work with groups is exceptionally high (2.21)—reflecting the different survey question and perhaps past patterns of collective action under the communist regime.

The highest level of voluntary activity is in Vietnam (Dalton and Ong 2005). Remarkably high percentages of Vietnamese say they volunteer in social welfare organizations, peace organizations, local community groups, and political activities.[11] This is evidence of state-mobilized activity; the government uses social groups as transmission belts to the public and encourages local cooperatives to organize efforts to address community issues.

A contrasting pattern is found in Japan and Singapore. Few Japanese belong to a social group (mean = 0.84) and activity is markedly low (0.25). On average, Singaporean respondents report a mean level of activity in only 0.55 groups. In neither of these two nations, therefore, is there widespread civil society activity that might be the training ground for democratic skills and values.

In summary, social group membership and activity vary substantially across the nations of the Pacific Rim, and the cross-national pattern seems to cut across a democratic/nondemocratic divide. Participation in social groups is low in both Japan and Singapore, despite their very different political regimes and acceptance of democratic participation. Participation is high in both Korea and Vietnam, again despite quite varied political contexts. At least at the cross-national level, there is an apparent independence between national levels of self-expressive values as discussed in previous chapters (Inglehart and Welzel; Wang and Tan) and participation in social groups. We also expect that the content of experience within social groups is equally varied across nations, and this ultimately is the most important factor in shaping the consequences of civil society activity, or in even deciding whether group activity fits the usual definition of civil society.

THE CONSEQUENCES OF GROUP MEMBERSHIP

Does group membership produce the type of positive benefits identified by the civil society literature, even when participation occurs outside of a democratic regime? Or, does mobilized membership in nondemocratic nations represent an example of the 'dark side' of social capital, where groups socialize members into a set of values supportive of the dominant regime, regardless of its form?

Social Trust

One of the theorized consequences of social participation is the social norms that result from these activities (Putnam 1993, 2000; Warren 2000). Extensive social group participation may weaken traditional ascriptive patterns of authority, as individuals work with others to address common interests. In addition, expanding social networks may break down parochial attitudes and lead to more cosmopolitan views of the world. This supposedly fosters cooperative orientations and acceptance of others that facilitate a modern political and economic system. In short, the experiences of working with others in a social group create 'social capital'.

Thus, research frequently focuses on social trust as an indicator of the content of social relations in a nation. Social group activity was a prime source of social trust in Putnam's analyses (1993, 2000) of social capital (also Inglehart 1997). The literature on civil society and political development repeats this theme (Rueschemeyer, Rueschemeyer, and Wittrock 1998; Inkeles 2000; Norris 2002).

Of course, such effects depend on the nature and content of the interactions that occur within groups, some of which may reinforce (or diminish) such patterns. For instance, Aspinall's discussion (2004) of social groups in Indonesia repeatedly stresses that *civil relations* within groups and between groups are necessary to generate a *civil society*. Thus, when groups were highly conflictual in Indonesia, participation in these groups was unlikely to generate social trust. The same point is made about the dark side of social engagement in Western democracies, ranging from the polarized environment of the Weimar republic to the impact or reactionary social groups (Putnam 2000: Chapter 22; Bermeo 2003). Moreover, Lucian Pye and others maintained that the traditional agrarian and Confucian traditions in some parts of East Asia limit trust to a relatively narrow circle of family and close friends (Fukuyama 1995*a*; Pye 1999). The cultural impact of communism is also unclear, since prior research demonstrates that levels of social trust vary widely across Eastern European nations in the 1990s (Newton 1999). If participation in social groups systematically increases trust in others, as the theory suggests, then examining this question across East Asia provides a robust test of civil society and social capital theories.

The WVS contains a standard survey question tapping trust in others.[12] There is considerable cross-national variation in the level of social trust. Only a minority of Americans (35 percent) and Canadians (39 percent) believe others can be trusted, which is roughly comparable to other surveys for these two nations (Newton 1999). Social trust is higher in several East Asian nations: China (55 percent), Japan (43 percent), and Vietnam (41 percent). Conversely, there are low levels of social trust in South Korea (27 percent), Singapore (17 percent), and the Philippines (8 percent). If one simply extrapolated from these levels of social trust, it would appear that national levels of social trust and social group engagement are essentially unrelated.

We are interested in whether social group activity is correlated with a more trusting view of others. The top two rows in Table 6.3 present the correlations between group membership (and activity) and social trust. There

TABLE 6.3. *The correlates of social group activity*

Correlates	USA	Canada	Japan	S. Korea	Philippines	Singapore	China	Vietnam
Social trust								
Number of group memberships	0.10	0.14	0.06	0.08	0.08	0.16	0.05	−0.10
Number of groups active	0.07	0.10	−0.01	0.03	0.07	0.08	0.09	−0.12
Discuss politics								
Number of group memberships	0.23	0.20	0.27	0.08	0.12	0.16	0.19	0.22
Number of groups active	0.16	0.14	0.21	0.06	0.11	0.11	0.17	0.21
Political interest								
Number of group memberships	0.20	0.20	0.24	0.07	0.15	0.14	0.10	0.27
Number of groups active	0.12	0.15	0.18	0.06	0.14	0.11	0.17	0.25
Protest activity								
Number of group memberships	0.20	0.26	0.19	0.12	0.20	0.07	—	0.08
Number of groups active	0.13	0.22	0.13	0.04	0.16	0.04	—	0.06
Self-expressive values								
Number of group memberships	0.12	0.15	0.14	0.18	0.04	0.23	—	0.04
Number of groups active	0.08	0.15	0.06	0.07	0.05	0.17	—	0.04
Democratic regime index								
Number of group memberships	0.12	0.11	0.00	−0.01	−0.07	−0.10	−0.04	0.00
Number of groups active	0.08	0.12	0.02	−0.04	−0.05	−0.08	−0.01	0.04
Social trust	0.14	0.18	0.08	0.03	−0.10	0.02	−0.01	−0.03

Source: WVS, 1999–2002; the democratic process index was used for Vietnam because the regime index was not included in the survey. Table entries are Pearson correlation coefficients.

is a positive, albeit modest, correlation in the USA and Canada of the sort that provided the initial basis for the social capital argument. More directly relevant to our interests, the same generally positive relationship applies across most of East Asia. For instance, even mobilized group action in China has approximately the same positive impact on social trust (0.09) as in the USA (0.07) or Canada (0.10). The only clear deviation from this pattern is Vietnam, where the mobilized and corporatist aspects of group activity stimulate less trust in others.[13]

Political Engagement

A second potential effect is political engagement. Participation in autonomous social groups is supposedly a training ground that provides the social skills and resources that facilitate political involvement (Diamond 1994; Rueschemeyer, Rueschemeyer and Wittrock 1998; Warren 2000). Group participation presumably nurtures a feeling of efficacy that may carry over to political engagement. At an even more basic level, group members may have access to additional information about political and social events, and this may stimulate an interest in politics. For all these reasons, social group activity is typically a strong predictor of political participation in established democracies (Verba, Nie, and Kim 1978).

The question, of course, is whether these same patterns appear across the nations of East Asia, where regime norms differ in their tolerance of citizen action. Especially in nondemocratic states, participation in mobilized social groups may not encourage further political involvement, while those in more autonomous groups may be hesitant to become involved because of their differences with the regime. Our data can answer these questions.

The next set of rows in Table 6.3 tests the political engagement thesis. Two questions ask whether the respondent regularly discusses politics or is interested in politics. There are strong positive relationships in the USA and Canada as prior research indicates. Even more important, this same pattern carries over to the democracies in East Asia—Japan, Korea, and the Philippines—and the three nondemocracies of China, Singapore, and Vietnam. To give some interpretation to these correlations, among the Chinese, only 21 percent of those who do not belong to a social group discuss politics frequently, whereas this rises to 43 percent among those who belong to two or more groups. Thus, the politicizing impact of social group activity apparently transcends regime form.

An even more rigorous measure of politicization is participation in protest activities. Taking part in such behavior requires greater initiative to become active. In addition, protest is typically a contentious activity, and represents the autonomy of civil society groups to challenge the government—although in nondemocratic systems, protests are also mobilized or facilitated by the state.

Table 6.3 displays the correlation between social group involvement and protest activity.[14] Social group activity is most strongly linked to protest in the two Western democracies, where both correlations are quite strong (USA = 0.20 and Canada = 0.26), implying that protest has become a clear extension of civil society activity. The relationships are nearly as strong for the three consolidated democracies in East Asia, suggesting a similar mobilizing effect in these nations. However, the relationships are markedly weaker in the two nondemocratic nations (the protest battery was not asked in China). Singapore and Vietnam represent contrasting practices of discouraging social group activity in the former case and encouraging state-led activity in the latter case, but they both share a political context where citizens cannot challenge the regime. Thus, in both cases the mobilizing potential of social group action appears attenuated by the norms of the regime.

Democratic Values

The third potential impact of social capital is as a source of democratic norms. Beginning with Tocqueville, social scientists have maintained that civil society activity teaches individuals the norms of participation, self-expression, and ultimately democratic choice. If a Vietnamese community association can plan a Tet festival, for example, the next step is to ask why citizens are not also involved in making political decisions affecting the community. Thus, a variety of studies link the extent of group activity to the learning of democratic norms (Putnam 1993; Booth and Richard 1996) and the development of democratic institutions (Diamond 1994; Inkeles 2000; Norris 2002).

However, these relationships may not consistently hold across East Asia. In nations where democracy is the dominant political paradigm, social capital should strengthen support for democratic norms and procedures. It is less predictable that social group engagement will generate the same democratic norms in a nondemocratic setting. Participation in a social group in nondemocratic states may produce political skills and interest, but it also may convey and reinforce the values of hierarchy and authoritarian decision-making that underlie an autocratic regime. At the least, a nondemocratic state may discourage the open expression of democratic preferences. Since our survey taps affective orientations toward the theme of democracy—rather than detailed knowledge or acceptance of the principles of democracy—it is unclear how social capital might affect these orientations.

We began by correlating social group membership to the survival/self-expressive values that Inglehart and Welzel (in this volume; 2005) have described as a cultural basis of democracy. Table 6.3 displays a significant relationship between social group activity and self-expressive values. In part, this might be expected because self-expressive values include measures of political engagement, but the index also includes indicators of tolerance, life satisfaction, and social norms.[15] It is especially noteworthy that group participation is closely linked to self-expressive values in Singapore. This suggests that participatory socialization can occur even in environments where the regime does not encourage these norms; this effect is what leads autocratic leaders to restrict such activity.

The last rows in Table 6.3 examine the relationship between social capital—group activity and social trust—and support for democracy, as measured by the Democratic Regime Index.[16] There is a modest positive relationship between these variables in the USA and Canada, demonstrating the Tocquevillian effect of social capital. For instance, Americans who belong to three or more social groups are 14 percent more likely to score high on the Democratic Regime Index compared to those who belong to no groups ($r = 0.12$), and those who trust others are 17 percent more likely to score high on the index ($r = 0.14$). However, in most Asian nations the relationship is negligible, and in the less democratic nations there are weak effects in the opposite direction.[17] That is, in the least democratic nations of East Asia, there is a slight tendency for our measures of social capital to reduce support for a democratic regime. In these nations, this might reflect the socialization of group activity to prevailing regime norms—consistent with the Tocquevillian logic, but under a regime with nondemocratic norms.

Differentiating Group Influences

We have focused on overall group membership and activity, but the research literature also highlights the differential impact of various types of social groups (Stolle and Rochon 1998; Stolle 2003). Groups that are more proximate to politics—such as political groups and public interest associations—are more likely to inculcate politically relevant norms and develop politically relevant skills. Economic associations—labor unions and professional associations—may play a somewhat more modest socializing role, since their economic concerns bring them into contact with the political domain, but secondary to the associations' prime economic mission. Self-help and identity groups may have an even more restricted political impact. And at the boundaries of political relevance may be groups like sports clubs and other leisure activities; individuals can learn politically relevant skills and values from these associations, but to a significantly lesser extent than in more explicitly political organizations. We compare these broad categories of groups, realizing that there is further variation even within each broad category.

Distinguishing between distinct associational sectors may also tap the different relationship between social groups and the state across nations. For instance, the nature of party and political groups obviously varies between the democratic and authoritarian nations of the region; while these groups may socialize democratic norms in democratic regimes, they may promote the values of the state in authoritarian regimes. Thus, a member of the American AFL-CIO presumably has different socializing experiences than a member of the Chinese ACFTU, and the relationship between the union and the state is dramatically different. Similarly, social groups that are mobilized by authoritarian governments—such as women's groups and youth groups—may be explicit transmission belts for the values of the regime, while such groups may have less political relevance in Western democracies. Much of the theoretical discussion and empirical analysis of differential group effects has been done in democratic nations; the potential systemic variation is far greater among the nations of East Asia.

Table 6.4 presents the relationship between membership in different types of social groups and two value dimensions: self-expressive values and the democratic regime index.[18] Because we are now dealing with small numbers of members in individual groups, we combine nations to examine three different regime forms: Western democracies of the USA and Canada; the Asian democracies of Japan, South Korea, and the Philippines; and China and Singapore as nondemocracies.

The complex interaction between social group membership and regime form appears throughout Table 6.4, especially in support for a democratic regime. Membership in a political group or a union/professional association is positively related to support for democracy in the USA and Canada as the Tocquevillian logic would suggest. However, this effect is essentially nonexistent when the three East Asian democracies are combined—and there is a weak negative relationship in the two nondemocracies. Even though these correlation coefficients are small, the differential impact of these relationships can be considerable. In percentage terms, in Western democracies support for a democratic regime is 17 points greater among members of political groups when compared to nonmembers, but in the Asian nondemocracies, it is 14 points lower among members of political groups when compared to nonmembers. This 31-points swing in opinions is a substantial difference across regime forms. Economic associations (unions and business associations) and civic associations show similar patterns, although with weaker differences, since these groups are not as explicitly political in their focus. These regime effects are further attenuated among social associations (women and youth) and health/welfare groups. Interestingly, only members of religious organizations are more likely to express support for democracy in the non-Asian democracies, which we suspect is because autonomous religious activism is not encouraged by the state in

TABLE 6.4 *Membership in different social groups and value orientations*

Group membership	Self-expressive values			Democratic regime index		
	Western democracies	Asian democracies	Asian non-democ	Western democracies	Asian democracies	Asian non-democ
Political group or party	0.09	0.06	0.05	0.12	0.00	−0.05
Union/professional	0.13	0.07	0.08	0.14	0.03	−0.01
Civic association	0.06	0.01	0.00	0.05	−0.12	−0.04
Woman/youth group	0.02	0.01	0.13	−0.01	−0.11	−0.06
Health/welfare group	0.05	0.02	0.03	0.02	−0.06	−0.06
Religious organization	−0.02	−0.01	0.14	0.03	−0.05	0.04
Sports club	0.08	0.04	0.19	−0.05	0.00	0.01
Total group memberships	0.12	0.06	0.23	0.08	−0.07	−0.06

Source: WVS, 1999–2002. The Western democracies are the USA and Canada; the Asian democracies are Japan, Korea, and the Philippines; the Asian nondemocracies are China and Singapore. Because the democratic regime index was not available for Vietnam, it was not included in these analyses. Table entries are Pearson correlation coefficients.

either China or Singapore, so members of religious organizations may see democracy as a way to gain greater religious freedom.

While regime effects in support for democracy are distinct, the impact of social group activity on self-expressive values is less conditioned by regime form. Most groups stimulate self-expressive values in the Western democracies, although the effects are somewhat stronger for political groups and labor/business membership. Effects are weaker in the Asian democracies, but follow the same pattern. Perhaps the most notable pattern is the stronger impact of group membership in the nondemocracies of East Asia. Moreover, the positive effects are again greatest among groups that are least likely to be politicized and controlled by the state: sports clubs and religious organizations. These groups may provide the social niches where citizens are able to organize and make decisions with fewer restrictions by the state.

CONCLUSION

It has become a common mantra in the development literature to see civil society and social capital described as a prime source of economic and political modernization, and a cure for whatever ails society. This chapter used new empirical evidence from the WVS to examine the social engagement of East Asian publics, and the impact of engagement on political orientations.

The vitality of civil society activity in East Asia is widely debated. Claims that new social groups are spreading like wildfire compete with claims that Confucian traditions and state actions make the concept irrelevant to Asia. The WVS is the first survey to describe systematically the levels of social group membership across a large set of East Asian nations. We find considerable variation in national levels of group membership and activity. State policies clearly discourage social group membership in China and Singapore; even formal members of labor unions do not think of themselves as members of this social grouping. This presumably robs these nations of the benefits of a vibrant civil society, or in these cases, limits popular demands, as the state prefers.

At the other extreme, there are high levels of group membership in Vietnam and Korea, despite the widely different political context of these two nations. Perhaps as a reflection of the mobilization efforts of the regime, Vietnamese membership in social groups is higher than in most other East Asian nations. This involves state-mobilized groups, such as unions, youth groups, or women's groups. In addition, we find relatively high levels of membership in nonstate groups, such as cultural associations or sports groups. Group membership in Korea has also grown substantially with democratization, and now most Koreans are socially well-connected.

The cross-national data suggest that group activity does not follow a single pattern across East Asia—just as it does not follow a single pattern across

Western Europe, or advanced industrial democracies in general. State policies can accentuate or restrict the development of civil society and the content and nature of group activity. National cultures also play a role, as seen as the low levels of activity in Japan relative to Korea. In addition, aggregate levels of group membership and activity are not clearly linked to the level of democratic development of nations within this set of nations. The effects of civil society participation may function within nations, but the simple level of membership does not appear to be strongly linked to democratic development across this set of East Asian nations.

A primary rationale for studying civil society is the list of social and political benefits that group engagement and social capital presumably produces (Putnam 2000, 2002; Edwards, Foley, and Diani 2001). The civil society literature presumes that the correlations between group activity and various attitudes and behaviors reflect causal relationships, although the evidence suggests that causal flow does run in both directions. For instance, membership and participation in group activity broadly encourages political interest and political discussion, even in nondemocratic states where autonomous civil society is discouraged. Social group membership even encourages protest activity, which is significant because protest is not encouraged by nondemocratic governments. But democratization also creates space for civil society to expand—as seen in the third wave democracies examples.

We also find that, with the single exception of Vietnam, group activity apparently encourages social trust, a critical component of social capital. Social trust is often described as providing the cooperative orientation that is essential to democracy (Putnam 1993, 2000), and thus it is noteworthy that several Asian nations display levels of trust above those found in the USA and Canada. Overall, the breadth of the effects of group membership on participation and trust across democracies and nondemocracies, and across affluent and poor nations, signals the impact of group activity more convincingly than past research, which has typically focused on advanced industrial democracies or the new democracies of Eastern Europe.

Ultimately, participation in civil society activities should facilitate democratic development. We saw evidence of this effect in the strong relationship between group activity and self-expressive values. Participation in a social group apparently increases feelings of efficacy, trust, and self-actualization that provide a cultural base for democracy (Inglehart and Welzel in this volume; 2005). Again, the striking finding was the presence of these effects even in a society such as Singapore, where the state discourages autonomous action, but when group activity occurs, it appears to generate the social capital that facilitates self-expressive values among the participants.

While the participatory effects of social group engagement apply across nations, the impact of group activity on political values varies with regime form. Engagement in the civil society found in Western democracies does encourage the development of democratic values among the active citizenry. However, in the nondemocratic states of East Asia, involved citizens are less supportive of a democratic regime. This may be a case where explicit regime norms are embedded in the content of group action, and in nondemocratic states, this erodes the democratizing aspect of group activity. We would need additional research on the content of group activity to answer this causal question definitively. At several points, however, our findings reinforce the point that *civil society groups* must exist in a *civil society* (rather than an authoritarian society), in order for democratic values to be reinforced.

In summary, our findings speak to the development of group activity—and presumably a meaningful civil society sector—across several East Asian nations, and the positive impact of group activity in shaping citizen values and behaviors. When combined with evidence that social modernization is increasing the development of an independent civil society in Asia, this should contribute to the democratization of the region. The more people who join organizations that have some degrees of independence from the state, the more conducive the political climate is to forming a civil society, and the more a civil society supports democratic development.

ENDNOTES

1 Our thanks to Nhu-Ngoc Ong who coauthored a paper on social capital in Vietnam that explored many of these same topics (Dalton and Ong 2005), and Dorothy Solinger, Yang Su, and Zhengxu Wang for their comments on these analyses.

2 Kim (2000, Chapter 6) shows that after the democratic transition there was a dramatic growth in citizen movement organizations (*Simin undong tanch'e*), such as environmental groups, consumer organization, religious groups, and people's movement groups (*Minjung undong tanch'e*), such as young groups and other social groups. This suggests that the potential for civil society existed before the transition, and the creation of this civil space independent of the state was quickly filled by new organizations. See Figure 6.1 for additional time series data from the WVS.

3 The uncertainty in the literature is illustrated by Frolic's description of civil society (1997) in China. He begins his essay with the sentence: 'If the prospects for China's immediate democratization are uncertain, the vision of the emergence of a Chinese civil society, a sphere of activity marked by a growing degree of autonomy from state power, is more promising.' Frolic then concludes his essay with the following sentence: 'For the present, however, expectations of the imminent emergence of a Chinese civil society in the Western sense are premature if not misleading.'

4 For instance, Yutaka (2003) presents comparative data on the number of registered NGOs in Japan, Korea, and the USA. Based on these data he argues that civil society activity is several times higher in Japan than Korea, which is contrary to the evidence of the actual number of citizens who are members or participants in these groups.

5 We do not present data for Taiwan because it was not surveyed in the 1999–2002 WVS, and the prior WVS wave had a different question on group membership and lacked the democratic values indices that are analyzed below. Indonesia did not include the group membership question in the 1999–2002 wave.

6 There are also potential choices in how to translate group descriptions or references that might affect the level of membership for specific categories. Thus, one might be cautious about

comparing the precise level of membership in any group across nations. To minimize these measurement problems, most of our analyses will focus on total group membership with the hope that such wording differences will balance out across a large number of groups.

7 There is an interesting contrast between self-reported membership in labor unions and official union membership statistics. The following table displays the percentage of the total employed labor force that were reported as labor union members from 1999 union statistics (from national statistics as reported by the ILO Bureau of Statistics).
A portion of the difference with the survey statistics in Table 6.1 is due to comparing the total public to those in the employed labor force. However, the large discrepancy for China is also found in other public opinion surveys. This suggests that Chinese workers who are

	USA	Can	Japan	Korea	Phil.	Sing	China
ILO statistics	13.9	30.6	22.2	11.9	27.4	18.0	89.7
WVS	13.6	14.4	6.5	5.6	4.0	4.3	6.9

mandated to be members of a union do not view this as a voluntary activity.

8 Similarly, the 1998 International Social Survey Program asked about voluntary activity in four types of organizations (political, charitable, religious, and other). Japan scored below the midpoint of the two dozen nations in the study, with levels of voluntary activity comparable to many East European nations (Bulgaria, Poland, and Russia). Also see (Howard 2003: 79). Together, these data portray an image of a relatively isolationist Japanese public.

9 The question wording is: 'And for which, if any, are you currently doing unpaid voluntary work?'

10 The Chinese survey asked: 'Which of the following organizations are you *willing* to do volunteering work for?' (italics added).

11 The very high level of peace activity may occur because the survey took place in October 2001, and like most other nations, Vietnam was responding to the September 11 terrorist attacks in the USA and subsequent events.

12 The question wording is as follows: 'Generally speaking, would you say that most people can be trusted or that you need to be very careful in dealing with people?'

13 Dalton and Ong (2005) found a nonlinear relationship between the total number of group memberships and social trust in Vietnam. Social trust is low among those who do not belong to any social group (40 percent trustful), and increases with membership in one (49 percent) or two groups (48 percent). But among the hyperactive—those who belong to five or more groups—social trust dips to its lowest level (27 percent trustful). We suspect this reflects the impact of those allegiant to the regime who are active in the largest number of social groups.

14 The protest index is a simple count of participation in four activities: a lawful demonstration, an illegal strike, a boycott, or occupation of a building. The scale ran from 0 protest acts to all 4 acts.

15 The self-expressive values index includes: liberty aspirations, tolerance of homosexuality, trust in other people, protest activity, and life satisfaction. For additional information, see Inglehart and Welzel (in this volume).

16 The index is described in Appendix B. The Vietnamese survey did not include this battery, so we used the Democratic Process Index for Tables 3 and 4.

17 Preliminary analyses of the East Asian barometers (Chu, Hu, and Chang 2004) also find a weak relationship between total group memberships and democratic/authoritarian regime attitudes across their set of nations. However, the strongest impact was in Korea and Taiwan, two of the consolidated democracies in their set of nations.

18 Economic groups include both labor unions and professional business associations; civic groups are local community groups, environmental groups, human rights groups, or peace groups; women and youth groups were combined as social groupings; health and social welfare groups were also combined.

7

Political Trust, Political Performance, and Support for Democracy

Zhengxu Wang, Russell, J. Dalton, and Doh Chull Shin

While most of our analyses reported in this volume focus on broad value orientations related to democratization and marketization in East Asia, the sentiments are also linked to citizen orientations toward the current political regime and its performance. Political culture theory argues that a regime's perceived legitimacy is a key factor in promoting political stability, and presumably adherence to the norms of the regime (Almond and Verba 1963; Diamond 1999; Gilley 2006). In new democracies, a high level of political trust facilitates the consolidation process, while a lack of trust may contribute to political instability or a return to authoritarianism. In an authoritarian regime, an accurate measurement of the public's trust in government provides an indication of how strongly the regime is holding its grip among the public.

This chapter examines the relationship between orientations toward contemporary governments and support for democracy across the nations of the Pacific Rim. We begin with mixed expectations about the level of political trust in the three Western democracies in our study. The traditional description of a democratic political culture argued that a supportive, allegiant public was a key element in sustaining a democracy (Almond and Verba 1963; Eckstein 1966). In virtually all economically advanced democracies, however, declining public trust in government institutions and in politicians has become manifest in recent decades (Norris 1999*a*; Pharr and Putnam, 2000; Dalton 2004). Researchers attribute the declining public support for government institutions in advanced industrial democracies to citizens' changing expectations of government, leading to the development of 'critical citizens' or 'dissatisfied democrats' (Norris 1999*a*; Klingemann 1999). These scholars argue that long-term economic and political development since the 1950s have produced a public that is less deferential to authority and increasingly ready to challenge government through various protest actions (Norris 2002). Furthermore, recent longitudinal studies in Japan and Korea note a similar decline of political trust over the past two decades (Tanaka 2001; Shin 2001).

One might also expect to find low levels of political trust in repressive authoritarian societies. Indeed, such dissatisfaction is typically seen as generating pressure for political reform in cases such as the Philippines, Indonesia, and the earlier democratic transitions in South Korea and Taiwan. Moreover, since we have found broad support for democratic values across East Asia, this suggests that support for authoritarian governments would be limited among their populations. However, recent survey data often contradicts this expectation—indicating that the level of political trust is actually high in several nondemocratic nations (Ahn and Kang 2002; Inglehart and Welzel 2005; Tang 2005; Wang 2005*a*).

This raises serious intellectual and practical questions. What is the meaning of political trust in nondemocratic nations—is it a sign of political support or the hesitancy to express opposition to an autocratic state? More fundamentally, what is the relationship between support for the government and support for democratic norms? Are these distinct political values, or are they interconnected? Furthermore, the findings for several East Asian nations are in striking contrast to the widely observed phenomenon of low, and declining, levels of political trust in the advanced industrial societies. For example, the Chinese public expresses higher levels of confidence in government than citizens in most advanced industrial societies, although rich democracies provide both a higher standard of living and more personal freedom than is available to the average Chinese citizen. In theoretical terms, is this pattern a challenge to traditional notions of what constitutes a democratic political culture?

THE ELEMENTS OF POLITICAL SUPPORT

The concept of political support is complex. Political trust or political support can be analyzed on several levels. Before we begin, therefore, some theoretical clarification is needed. Discussions of popular orientations toward politics often intermix different aspects of citizen evaluations, such as feelings of political alienation, cynicism, or distrust. Sometimes the evidence of public discontent is no more than dissatisfaction with the current government, even though this might be considered a normal and healthy aspect of the democratic process. The theoretical distinctions between different levels of support and different objects of political support are often blurred (or ignored) in the debate over public trust and confidence in democracy. In other instances, the theoretical significance of public opinion findings is uncertain because the wording of the survey questions is ambiguous. Thus, a simple but necessary starting point is to explicate a conceptual framework for studying political support.

We begin with David Easton's description (1965, 1975) of the various elements of political support as a framework for our research.[1] Easton distinguished between support for three levels of political objects: *the political community*, the *regime*, and *political authorities.*

This chapter focuses on the elements of regime support and support for political authorities. Regime support refers to public attitudes toward the constitutional order of a nation. Easton (1965, Chapter 12) distinguished between different elements of the regime. Regime principles define the broad parameters within which the political system should function—such as the democratic (autocratic) regime index analyzed in previous chapters. At the broadest level, this involves choices about whether political relationships should be organized as a democratic, authoritarian, or other political form. A shared consensus on such values would seem to be a prerequisite for a stable political order, and history has sadly shown what can occur when the democratic consensus fails. A second major component of the regime consists of the norms of behavior, which Easton called the operating rules or the rules of the game. These involve the specific rules or norms governing political action. For instance, democracy can take multiple forms that involve different assumptions about the role of the citizen, the political rights of individuals, the acceptance of dissent and political conflict, and other features of the political process. This conception comes closest to what we have labeled the democratic process index. In addition, it involves orientations toward principles such as majority rule, minority rights, free expression, and other aspects of the democratic process. Finally, regime support also can include orientations toward political institutions, such as evaluations of parliament, political parties, the courts, and other institutional actors.[2] The public must accept the institutions of governance as legitimate, and accept the decisions made by those who control these institutions.

We distinguish between these different aspects of regime support for several reasons, both theoretical and empirical. Theoretically, 'regime support' is a broad term that includes different elements. For instance, there are important distinctions between support for the norms of a regime and support for the specific institutions of a regime. Indeed, one can observe how public demands for institutional changes, such as the recent electoral reforms in Japan, and New Zealand, represent the public's desire to better realize the norms of the democratic system by changing the political institutions. Acceptance of democracy as a principle is more central to defining the political community, while acceptance of the specific institutions of democracy are more instrumental judgments.

Easton defined the political authorities as those individuals who currently hold positions of political authority, such as prime ministers or legislators, or in a broader sense, the pool of political elites from which government leaders are drawn. For instance, how do citizens evaluate the present incumbents of office rather than the office itself? Evaluation of political authorities is an important element of the political process. Images of political elites and the current government are essential elements in the legitimacy of a political system. In short, in a well-functioning political system the citizens support the incumbents of government who make authoritative political decisions, as well as endorsing the general principles of the political system.

It is often difficult to draw such fine theoretical distinction in public opinion surveys. Empirical research finds that support for the political authorities frequently carries over to support for political institutions and the political system (Muller and Jukam 1977; Canache, Mondak, and Seligson 2001). Public opinion survey questions measuring political support frequently overlap between levels. Does a general 'trust in government' question, for example, measure support for the incumbents or for the regime? Despite these empirical problems, it is important to begin with this theoretical distinction.

This framework is also important because public orientations toward different objects of support carry different political implications. For instance, discontent with political authorities in a democracy normally has limited systemic implications. Citizens often become dissatisfied with political officeholders and act on these feelings to select new leaders at the next election. Dissatisfaction with authorities, within a democratic system, is not usually a signal for basic political change. Negative attitudes toward political officials can exist with little loss in support for the office itself or the institutional structure encompassing this office. As the object of dissatisfaction is generalized to the regime, the political implications broaden. A decline in support for the political process might provoke a basic challenge to constitutional structures or calls for reform of the procedures of government. For a nondemocracy, it may signal the public's willingness to seek a more fundamental change in the regime form.

Measuring the Dimensions of Political Support

Our first empirical step, therefore, is to determine whether the theoretical distinctions between different levels of political support are empirically observable in public opinion among the nations in this project. The WVS provides a valuable resource to address this question. Because of the project's interest in comparing system orientations across a wide diversity of nations, the survey included many questions that were intended to tap different levels of political support. Klingemann (1999) showed that separate dimensions of support emerge for the combined results of the more than forty nations in the 1995–8 wave of the WVS. We want to examine the structure of opinion for the set of East Asian and Western democracies we are studying.

To determine whether citizens distinguish between different objects of support, we factor-analyzed a large set of questions that appear to tap support for political authorities, political institutions, and democratic/autocratic regime norms.[3] We also included three measures of personal satisfaction—life satisfaction, satisfaction with one's financial situation, and feelings of happiness. These are not measures of political support, but they have have been linked to a civic culture, and we will include these variables in the analyses below (Inglehart 1997, ch. 6). Our analyses divide the Pacific Rim nations into three groups: Western democracies (the USA, Canada, Australia, and New Zealand), Asian democracies (Japan, South Korea, Taiwan, Indonesia, and the Philippines), and Asian nondemocracies (China, Vietnam, and Singapore). We grouped nations together to focus on broad differences in regime form; in addition, not all questions were asked in each nation, which would have severely restricted individual nation-by-nation analyses.[4]

The support measures tend to be positively interrelated on a first unrotated dimension that captures what is common across all the items, indicating that positive images of politics tend to be generalized across levels. However, when we rotate the factor analyses, we find three distinct dimensions of political attitudes (Table 7.1). The first dimension reflects support for political institutions—the government, parliament, political parties, civil service, and the army—and trust in government and satisfaction with national politicians.[5] (In other analyses for the Western democracies that included more items on political incumbents, trust in government and trust in institutions load on different dimensions, see Dalton (2004, Chapter 3)).

The second dimension taps support for democratic norms, including items from the democratic regime index and the democratic process index. The question, 'democracy may have problems, but it is better than other forms of government', is the one item that is not strongly related to this dimension in either Asian subset, which suggests it may evoke different meanings among the Asian respondents. However, the other seven items in the democratic regime and democratic process indices form a common dimension. Western and Asian publics do distinguish between their images of government (and the present institutions of government) and their attitudes toward democracy.

The third dimension groups the personal satisfaction items, which are only weakly related to either the democratic norms dimension or the support for government dimension. In part, this is a statistical artifact of the methodology of rotated factor analyses, but this also suggests that personal evaluations are somewhat distinct from political evaluations for these survey respondents. Previewing the analyses presented below, one can also note that the democratic attitude items in the nondemocracies also weakly load on this satisfaction dimension.

These results are similar to previous findings from earlier waves of the WVS (Klingemann 1999; Dalton 2004), except that there is a clearer distinction between support for politicians/government and confidence in political institutions in advanced industrial democracies. Still, the similar results reinforce

TABLE 7.1. *Dimensions of political support*

	Western democracies			Asian democracies			Asian nondemocracies		
Questions	Govt.	Democracy	Satisfaction	Govt.	Democracy	Satisfaction	Govt.	Democracy	Satisfaction
Confidence government	0.84	−0.05	−0.01	0.79	−0.07	−0.05	0.83	−0.05	−0.01
Confidence parliament	0.82	−0.11	−0.01	0.83	0.07	−0.05	0.83	−0.07	−0.06
Confidence in parties	0.77	−0.03	−0.02	0.78	0.02	−0.04	0.79	−0.04	−0.01
Confidence in civil service	0.64	0.06	−0.02	0.66	0.00	−0.02	0.66	0.02	−0.12
Confidence army	0.38	0.14	−0.08	0.52	0.03	−0.01	0.67	−0.05	0.01
Satisfied with politicians	0.63	−0.07	−0.06	0.51	0.09	−0.10	0.51	−0.07	−0.27
Government for big interests	−0.52	0.13	0.06	−0.46	0.01	−0.00	−0.22	0.18	0.05
A strong leader	0.14	0.59	0.01	0.23	0.51	−0.03	0.00	0.40	0.07
Expert decisions	0.06	0.46	0.03	0.02	0.38	−0.07	−0.02	0.24	0.10
Army rule	0.23	0.54	0.03	0.42	0.25	−0.07	0.26	0.40	0.23
Democratic system	0.10	−0.63	0.00	0.11	−0.26	−0.11	0.27	−0.24	0.22
Democracy: Economy	−0.16	0.70	0.00	0.07	0.78	−0.00	−0.16	0.67	0.07
Democracy: Indecisive	−0.18	0.65	−0.01	−0.01	0.76	−0.02	−0.15	0.74	−0.01
Democracy: Order	−0.13	0.69	−0.00	0.08	0.77	−0.04	0.01	0.76	−0.10
Democracy: Best	0.04	−0.53	−0.02	0.00	0.05	−0.10	0.03	−0.12	0.07
Life satisfaction	−0.05	0.05	0.87	−0.06	0.04	0.86	−0.07	0.10	0.81
Financial satisfaction	−0.11	0.07	0.73	−0.04	0.10	0.83	−0.04	0.10	0.80
Happy with life	−0.05	−0.03	0.75	−0.08	−0.03	0.59	−0.31	0.00	0.58
Eigenvalues	3.43	3.03	1.88	3.40	2.38	1.87	3.54	2.12	1.91
Variance explained (%)	19.1	16.9	10.4	18.9	13.2	10.4	19.7	11.8	10.6

Source: WVS (most recent wave for each nation).

Note: Varimax rotation with pairwise deletion of missing data.

the view that these are separate dimensions of opinion among Asian publics.[6] For instance, some people are relatively supportive of democracy, while remaining skeptical about political institutions. Thus, these publics do differentiate between levels of political support—these are not simply interchangeable formulations of a general feeling of political satisfaction or malaise.

CONFIDENCE IN GOVERNMENT

The differentiation of political orientations is important, both normatively and analytically. Normatively, it is important, for example, that we distinguish trust in institutions versus support for democracy as a principle. If one is interested in regime change, for example, prevailing levels of satisfaction with the incumbent politicians is less important than trust in institutions. Trust in institutions may indicate the level of popular support for the present regime, and thus the legitimacy of the overall system. Demands for political reform are likely to grow when the key institutions command low levels of confidence.

In the rest of this chapter, unless noted otherwise, 'political trust' refers to citizens' attitudes toward government institutions: the national government, the parliament, political parties, and the army. Support for democracy refers to the democratic regime index (see Chapter 4), although the results for the democratic process index are quite similar.

If Almond and Verba were correct that the democratic civic culture is supportive and allegiant, then the world has turned upside down. Table 7.2 shows that confidence in the institutions of democratic government—the government, parliament, and political parties—is very low in the four Western

TABLE 7.2. *Confidence in government institutions*

Nation	National government	Parliament	Political parties	Civil service	Army	Average
United States	38	38	23	55	82	47
Canada	42	40	23	52	67	45
Australia	26	31	16	38	68	36
New Zealand	16	15	6	29	63	26
Japan	27	22	18	32	67	33
South Korea	30	11	11	67	64	37
Taiwan	70	46	36	60	76	58
Philippines	53	61	46	71	74	61
Indonesia	52	43	33	59	74	52
China	97	95	93	66	97	90
Vietnam	98	97	92	79	97	93
Average	50	45	36	55	75	

Source: WVS (these questions were not asked in Singapore).

Note: Table entries are the percentage expressing "a great deal" or "quite a lot" of confidence in each institution.

democracies. Barely a quarter of these four publics express confidence in these institutions. It is striking that confidence in the civil service and the army—two nonrepresentative institutions—exceeds confidence in political institutions in all nations in our study. Although we do not stress any specific differences in political support across these Western democracies, these responses reaffirm earlier findings on the limited support for government in Western democracies today (Norris 1999*a*; Pharr and Putnam 2000; Dalton 2004).

Confidence in democratic institutions is somewhat higher in the democracies of East Asia. Even here, however, the citizens of the three consolidated Asian democracies—Japan, Korea, and Taiwan—express less confidence than the citizens in the Philippines and Indonesia.

The most striking finding is the extremely high level of expressed confidence in political institutions in China and Vietnam. In China in 2001, for instance, 97 percent of the respondents say they have 'a great deal of confidence' or 'quite a lot of confidence' in the national government, 95 percent are confident in the parliament (National People's Congress), and 92 percent confident in the political parties (basically the Communist Party).

The WVS asked another question about satisfaction with national politicians (Figure 7.1).[7] Again, there is a striking support for government in the three least democratic nations in our study. The established Western democracies fare better in these comparisons, falling near the midpoint of this scale. In addition, the oldest consolidated democracy in East Asia, Japan, has only 8 percent of the public who are satisfied with the national politicians.

These results are not unique to the WVS. Ahn and Kang (2002) compared public images in eight East Asian nations across a variety of dimensions. Their typical finding was that levels of democratic development were negatively correlated with positive images of the political system. For instance, the highest levels of perceived responsiveness of government were in Malaysia, and the lowest in Japan and South Korea. Malaysians and Singaporeans were most likely to describe their government as just and respectful of human rights; Japanese and Koreans were least positive about their nation in these same terms. Discussing the broader international findings from the Gallup Millennium Survey, Inoguchi says (2000: 4–5):

> It is those quasi-democratic and semi-authoritarian countries that are accorded highest scores for subjective democratic governance along with such seemingly highly democratic countries as Switzerland, Netherlands, Denmark, Sweden and UK. It is those highly democratic countries such as Japan and South Korea that are given low scores of democratic governance along with Cameroon and Colombia. . . . Those quasi-democratic and semi-authoritarian countries are given bonuses to their democratic scores despite some illiberal practices.

Similarly, the East Asia Barometer found that support for government institutions was lower in Japan, South Korea, and Taiwan than in the

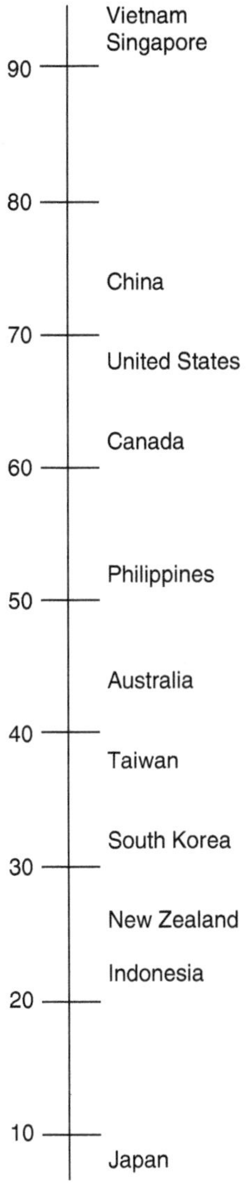

FIGURE 7.1. Satisfaction with national politicians
Source: 1999–2002 WVS.
Note: Figure displays the percentage who are "very" or "fairly" satisfied.

People's Republic of China (Albritton, Bureekul, and Guo 2005). Tang (2005: Chapter 3) also showed that popular support for China's one-party structure was relatively high in 1999, even while many of the same Chinese expressed support for democratic reforms. In a more recent survey, conducted in rural China between 1999–2001, 81 percent of the respondents expressed 'relatively high' or 'very high' levels of trust in the central government, while those expressing 'relatively low' or 'very low' account for less than 4 percent (Li 2004).

If one characterizes this situation in the Western democracies as *Wan Ma Qi Yin*, 10,000 horses all silent, should we take the situation in China (and Vietnam) as *Yi Zhi Du Xiu*, 1 single flower blossoming?

POTENTIAL EXPLANATIONS FOR POLITICAL SUPPORT IN NONDEMOCRACIES

As students of democracy, should we be pessimistic because the one-party regimes in East Asia enjoy high level of political support? Admittedly, it is disconcerting that objective measures of democratic development, press freedom, and corruption seem negatively related with public confidence and satisfaction with government. As comparativists we should sort out the problem of causality. Why is there high level of public trust in government in China, Vietnam, and Singapore? Typically, survey research is not done in authoritarian states, and the WVS has first opened this door. Now we have to attempt to disentangle the meaning of these patterns.

There are several possible explanations for these cross-national patterns (Gilley 2006). One possibility is that citizens under an authoritarian regime are threatened so they cannot express their real opinions. Or phrased more benignly, these regimes may successfully propagandize their citizens, so they are persuaded that the government is an excellent one. Alternatively, is there something intrinsically good about the political reality in these nations that they are able to secure genuine public support? For instance, while the economies of Asia's democracies have struggled over the past decade, the growth rates in China and Vietnam have been exceptional. Thus, citizens may be responding to their dramatically improving living standards, while citizens in Japan, Korea and other nations struggle with economic decline. Or, have citizens in established democracies simply learned to be critical citizens so that willingness to express dissatisfaction has become an indictor of democratization? In this section, we consider several rival hypotheses, and then in the following section, we examine the correlates of government support.

Fear and Indoctrination

One explanation for the high level of public support for government in China, Vietnam, and Singapore is that, in an authoritarian country, citizens are intimidated by the state. As a result, they cannot express their genuine attitudes toward the government. We can call this the 'fear' hypothesis. If people are intimidated by the state so that they will not openly voice their distrust, then one should find a strong positive correlation between the level of citizens' political fear and their expressed trust in government. However, other studies suggest that this is *not* the case. For instance, Chen and Shi (2001) found the correlation between political fear and trust in government among Chinese respondents was very weak, ranging from 0.04 to 0.14. Similarly, in presenting other survey evidence on trust in government among the Chinese public, Wenfang Tang (2005) discounts fear as a primary explanation for government support. Given the general trend of decreasing state penetration and increasing societal autonomy in China in the recent decade (Goldman and MacFarquhar 1999), political fear presumably plays a diminishing role in the expressed level of political trust at the time of the WVS in 2001–2.

Another potential explanation can be called indoctrination theory. Such an explanation sees the citizens as immersed in the information generated, managed, and distributed by the state. Researchers find that media does play a role in shaping citizen's attitudes, including trust in government (Miller, Goldenberg, and Erbring 1979; Robinson 1976). These studies of Western democracies find that exposure to media content critical to the government lowers trust in government. Thus, contemporary political leaders from Putin to Berlusconi attempt to control the media as an agent of the state. Can we expect that citizens in China show high trust in government because they only receive positive content regarding to the government? Without question, a propaganda state still exists, although a weakened one (Lynch 1999). Again, research raises doubts about this explanation. Chen and Shi (2001) found that, around 1993, exposure to media in China actually has a *negative* effect on citizens' trust in government. They thus conclude the propaganda state is failing its task of generating public support by its control of information. Since then, the state monopoly of media, or at least the monopoly of media content, has generally decreased. The media in China and Vietnam now have less state intervention (Zha 1995). Under such circumstances, it probably will be even harder to find the direct effect of indoctrination through citizens' consumption of political news.[8]

Economic Performance?

Another explanation is that citizens are satisfied with the performance of the government. This is plausible because China, Vietnam, and Singapore have sustained a remarkably high rate of economic growth for more than two decades, and the large majority of the populace has benefited from this. Even with the financial crisis of 1997, Singapore remains an affluent nation. In contrast, Korea and Japan have suffered from markedly slower economic progress over the decade preceding this survey, and some researchers have linked this to decreasing faith in government (Pharr 2000; Ahn and Kang 2002). Moreover, previous political culture studies in Germany and Japan argued that economic growth was a key element in developing a democratic political culture in these nations following World War II (e.g. Baker, Dalton, and Hildebrandt 1981; Richardson 1978).

To test the performance thesis, we should measure performance as *perceived by* the citizens. That is, we should measure individual's *satisfaction* with life conditions that might be attributable to government performance. Below we will use two questions to tap life conditions: satisfaction with one's life and satisfaction with one's financial conditions. If rising living standards are driving support for government in China, Vietnam, and Singapore, this should be apparent in a strong relationship between life conditions and political support.[9] Thus, increased individual well-being may lead to higher satisfaction of the incumbent government and positive assessment of government institutions.

Before Critical Citizens?

As mentioned earlier, the 'critical citizens' theory suggests that trust in government is decreasing in advanced industrial societies because citizens are learning to be more critical of government and less deferential to political elites. Inglehart (1990, 1997; Inglehart and Welzel 2005) has argued that social and economic modernization gives rise to a new political culture that is conducive to the rise of critical citizens and contentious citizen politics. Postmaterial or self-expressive values tend to correlate with decreased confidence in public institutions (Inglehart 1997), and people with these values tend to reject authority. This reduces support for the military, government, and other hierarchical institutions (Inglehart 1999; Dalton 2004, Chapter 5).

Although this seems inconsistent with political culture models of democratic development, there may be some consistency. For instance, Almond and Verba (1963) contrasted the civic culture of a democracy with the subject culture of nondemocratic systems. A subject culture would emphasize allegiance and unquestioning support for the state. As citizens develop more participatory roles, they also may develop the autonomy to question the actions of government.

Moreover, the democratic process may itself encourage dissatisfaction. Democracy is generally an adversarial process among contending political elites. Elections are civics lessons for the citizenry and provide a means of popular control of government, but they also provide a venue for half the nation's political elites (the opposition) to criticize the government and its past actions. In addition, once the election is over, the new opposition continues to criticize. Thus, one hears government leaders in many developing nations dismiss competitive democratic elections as too contentious and polarizing for their nation, favoring one-party elections in their place. While such claims often are mere justification for autocratic rule, they may contain a grain of truth as well. Democracy may teach individuals to be critical citizens.

Across East Asia, recent economic development, industrialization, and postindustrialization are also leading to the rise of self-expressive values (Wang and Tan in this volume; Welzel and Inglehart in this volume). If so, why are we not observing a rise of critical citizenship in China, Vietnam, and Singapore? Our explanation is that, although there is a rise in self-expressive values, the extent of these values and their effect on political trust is still marginal. Declining trust in government in Western democracies did not become manifest until the 1970–80s, after several decades of rapid and very high levels of economic development. Moreover, the one-party states in Asia still lack the open competition of political ideas and opposition that come with democratization.

Thus, we would characterize the current situation in China, Vietnam, and Singapore as the era 'before critical citizens'. It is premature to expect a widespread rise of critical citizens, as the rapid rate of economic development is producing high levels of satisfaction among a still predominantly materialist public that has only recently emerged from subsistence-level poverty. For now, economic development may still serve to enhance public support for government in these Asian nations.

MODELING CONFIDENCE IN GOVERNMENT

To test these explanations of political support, we combined measures of economic performance, self-expressive values, and other potential predictors into a multivariate model. To measure political support, we use the average of three indicators: confidence in the national government, confidence in parliament, and confidence in parties. We refer to this indicator as 'trust in political institutions'; it serves to measure the regime's legitimacy among the public. In addition, we separately analyze satisfaction with national politicians (Figure 7.1) since this item has a clearer focus on the incumbents of government and is available for all the nations in this project.

Our predictors of political support are based on the hypotheses described below:

A: Performance hypothesis: Economic development results in citizens' high satisfaction with living conditions, which in turn leads to high trust in government. We test this hypothesis with an index combining life satisfaction and financial satisfaction.[10]

B: Critical citizen hypothesis: Citizens with stronger self-expressive values tend to distrust the government. This uses the self-expressive values scale described by Welzel and Inglehart in Chapter 2.[11]

C: Before critical citizens hypothesis: Personal satisfaction will have a stronger impact on political support in the nondemocratic nations of Asia, while self-expressive values will have a relatively stronger impact in Western democracies and the democracies in East Asia.

In addition, our analysis controls for age, gender, and educational background, variables that are thought to have an impact on political trust. We control for a citizen's psychological involvement with politics to see if engagement encourages/discourages political support, measured by the respondent's *interest in politics*. We also control for feelings of national pride, on the expectation that nationalism may provide a basis for government support, especially in nondemocratic regimes that build upon nationalist sentiments.

Table 7.3 presents two sets of regression analyses. Those in the top panel predict trust in political institutions (which excludes Singapore, since these questions were not asked). The second panel is a model that predicts satisfaction with the politicians in the national government, which was asked in all nations (see Figure 7.1). To focus on the pattern across regime types, we combine the nations into three groups: Western democracies, Asian democracies, and Asian nondemocracies, following the patterns in Table 7.2.

The models for both political support questions indicate that personal satisfaction is positively related to political support across all three regime forms, which partially substantiates the performance hypotheses. However, the regression coefficients for satisfaction are all quite modest, and there is not a large, systematic variation across regime forms. As we might expect, the effects of personal satisfaction are stronger for satisfaction with national politicians—a measure of specific support for incumbents—than for confidence in political institutions—which tends to be more diffuse support. Still, personal satisfaction is only modestly related to satisfaction with national politicians in Western democracies ($\beta = 0.127$), Asian democracies ($\beta = 0.107$), and Asian nondemocracies ($\beta = 0.134$). Thus, economic development does lead to positive evaluations of the government, but these effects appear muted.

The influence of self-expressive values is also modest. In Western and Asian democracies, self-expressive values decrease confidence in political institutions and satisfaction with the government, but the relations are very weak—in part because of the other variables being controlled in the model, which also overlap with these values. For the Asian nondemocracies, self-expressive values lead to ambiguous results across the two models, and the impact of values is not statistically significant for either measure of political trust.

What, then, generates support for government? One of the strongest predictors, and one that varies markedly by regime form, is national pride. People with higher levels of national pride are more likely to give positive evaluations of government performance; being allegiant to the government is linked to national identities. Moreover, these effects are much stronger among Asian nondemocracies. For instance, national pride has a modest impact on institutional trust in Western democracies ($\beta = 0.126$), a stronger influence in Asian democracies ($\beta = 0.291$), and even stronger effects in China and Vietnam ($\beta = 0.316$). These cross-regime patterns are even stronger for satisfaction with government.

TABLE 7.3. *Predicting political support*

	Western democracies		Asian democracies		Asian nondemocracies	
Confidence in political institutions	*b*	*β*	*b*	*β*	*b*	*β*
Personal satisfaction	0.035 (0.005)	0.099	0.036 (0.005)	0.111	0.014 (0.009)	0.054
Self-expressive values	−0.007 (0.012)	−0.009	−0.080 (0.013)	−0.096	0.033 (0.026)	0.048
National pride	0.142 (0.016)	0.126	0.241 (0.013)	0.291	0.244 (0.028)	0.316
Political interest	0.148 (0.010)	0.210	0.074 (0.012)	0.093	0.104 (0.020)	0.186
Age	−0.043 (0.012)	−0.050	−0.000 (0.014)	−0.000	0.044 (0.025)	0.061
Education	0.032 (0.016)	0.029	−0.104 (0.015)	−0.109	−0.032 (0.031)	−0.036
Gender	0.007 (0.018)	0.005	−0.047 (0.020)	−0.035	0.018 (0.036)	0.017
Constant	2.54 (0.074)		2.02 (0.078)		0.988 (0.134)	
R^2	0.278		0.359		0.425	
(Estimated *N*)	(6,042)		(5,083)		(1,834)	
Satisfaction with national politicians						
Personal Satisfaction	0.054 (0.006)	0.127	0.037 (0.005)	0.107	0.043 (0.006)	0.134
Self-expressive values	−0.002 (0.015)	−0.002	−0.074 (0.014)	−0.084	−0.035 (0.019)	−0.041
National pride	0.154 (0.020)	0.112	0.191 (0.014)	0.217	0.316 (0.020)	0.339
Political interest	0.010 (0.013)	0.011	0.034 (0.013)	0.040	0.040 (0.014)	0.060
Age	−0.121 (0.015)	−0.114	−0.049 (0.016)	−0.050	0.016 (0.018)	0.018
Education	0.038 (0.020)	0.029	−0.070 (0.017)	−0.069	−0.097 (0.022)	−0.090
Gender	0.014 (0.022)	0.009	0.009 (0.022)	0.006	−0.017 (0.026)	−0.013
Constant	2.57 (0.093)		2.37 (0.085)		1.472 (0.096)	
R^2	0.199		0.262		0.387	
(Estimated *N*)	(6,183)		(5,268)		(3,288)	

Source: WVS; the estimated *N* is the *N* for the dependent variable in each model.

Note: The table presents unstandardized and standardized regression coefficients from OLS regression analyses; the standard errors of the *b* are presented in parentheses.

Political engagement is also related to political support, and these effects tend to be stronger in Asian nondemocracies. This may be evidence of the mobilizing style of these nondemocracies. Most of the other demographic controls are only weakly related to political support. Perhaps the most interesting pattern occurs for age. In Western and Asian democracies, older citizens tend to be less supportive of government—a pattern consistent with earlier studies of political support in the West. However, in Asian nondemocracies, the old are more supportive of the government. This suggests that social modernization in these nations may be gradually changing the political orientations of younger generations.

A final noteworthy pattern in Table 7.3 is the pattern of explained variance across regime types. In both models, the lowest level of explained variance is in the Western democracies, which typically implies that orientations toward government diffuse feelings not strongly connected to personal well-being or an individual's ideology or political values. The models explain more variance in the Asian democracies, and even more in the Asian nondemocracies. For instance, the Multiple R square for government satisfaction varies from 0.199 in Western democracies, to 0.262 in Asian democracies, to 0.387 in Asian nondemocracies. This indicates that political support is more closely linked to satisfaction, values, and other political attitudes in the nondemocracies. Rather than diffuse support, images of government are more typically examples of specific support.

ORIENTATIONS TOWARD GOVERNMENT AND DEMOCRACY

The final step of our analyses links evaluations of government to public support for democracy. The logic of the political culture model is that sustained support for government (or dissatisfaction with government) eventually generalized into orientations toward the regime. As Arthur Miller (1974) argued in his initial description of Americans' decreasing trust in government, if sports fans grow tired of rooting for a habitually losing team, they eventually lose interest in the sport overall. Similarly, positive performance—by sports teams and by governments—may generate broader enthusiasm.

Thus, we repeated the model from the previous analysis to explain support for a democratic regime, the index analyzed in Chapter 4, and the items are part of the democratic values dimension in Table 7.1. In addition to the predictors used in the previous analyses, we added satisfaction with the politicians in the national government as an additional explanatory factor. This enables us to judge whether democratic norms are an extension of evaluations of the present government. If support for a democratic regime is deeply rooted in the political culture, the influence of the current government should be limited. But if this aspect of the political culture is still in the formative stage, then government performance may be a stronger influence on democratic values.

Table 7.4 presents a series of multiple regression analyses for Western democracies, Asian democracies, and Asian nondemocracies.[12] As we suspected, democratic values are essentially independent of satisfaction with government in both the Western democracies and Asians democracies. (The weak negative correlation is an indication of the dissatisfied democrat pattern; those dissatisfied with government performance tend to have stronger democratic values.) The weak relationship between these two attitudes is what should occur in a stable democratic political culture. One does not want evaluations of the Bush (or Koizumi) administration to shape public support for democracy as an ideal. At the same time, the relationship between support for the government and democracy is stronger in the Asian nondemocracies (as was seen in Table 7.1). In these nondemocratic settings, those who are most critical of government tend to be stronger advocates of a democratic regime ($\beta = -0.124$).

Other predictors point to the differential processes between democratic and nondemocratic nations. For instance, personal satisfaction has a weak positive relationship with democratic norms in democratic regimes; but in nondemocratic regimes, the most satisfied are *less likely* to support

TABLE 7.4. *Predicting support for a democratic regime*

	Western democracies		Asian democracies		Asian nondemocracies	
	b	*β*	*b*	*β*	*b*	*β*
Government satisfaction	−0.023	−0.033	−0.077	−0.108	−0.128	−0.124
	(0.010)		(0.011)		(0.022)	
Personal satisfaction	0.003	0.009	0.012	0.048	−0.050	−0.152
	(0.004)		(0.004)		(0.007)	
Self-expressive values	0.115	0.170	0.114	0.180	−0.103	−0.105
	(0.010)		(0.010)		(0.019)	
National pride	−0.028	−0.029	−0.142	−0.225	−0.131	−0.135
	(0.014)		(0.010)		(0.021)	
Political interest	0.104	0.172	0.038	0.062	0.195	−0.281
	(0.009)		(0.010)		(0.014)	
Age	0.115	0.154	0.089	0.129	−0.096	−0.105
	(0.011)		(0.011)		(0.019)	
Education	0.146	0.155	0.082	0.114	0.078	0.070
	(0.013)		(0.012)		(0.023)	
Gender	−0.075	−0.066	−0.021	−0.021	−0.086	−0.065
	(0.015)		(0.015)		(0.026)	
Constant	2.822		2.206		1.559	
	(0.068)		(0.066)		(0.134)	
R^2	0.378		0.364		0.4550	
(Estimated *N*)	(5,641)		(4,651)		(2,811)	

Source: WVS; the estimated *N* is the *N* for the dependent variable in each model.

Note: The table presents unstandardized and standardized regression coefficients from OLS regression analyses; the standard errors of the *b* are presented in parentheses.

democratic norms holding other factors constant. Those who are well off are often hesitant to embrace values that imply a disruption in the regime that produces their satisfaction. As Inglehart and Welzel have argued, self-expressive values increase support for democracy in Western and Asian democracies, but there is not a significant relationship in the Asian nondemocracies. Similarly, the politically interested are more supportive of democracy in the two groups of democratic nations, but the relationship is reversed in Asian nondemocracies. Chapter 4 also showed that education has a strong positive relationship with democratic norms in democratic regimes ($\beta = 0.155$ in Western democracies; $\beta = 0.114$ in Asian democracies), but this effect is attenuated in nondemocratic regimes ($\beta = 0.070$).

GOVERNMENT AND REGIME

Political cultures are multidimensional. They include images of the government, the norms and institutions of the political regime, the role of citizens within the political process, and the political community. This chapter focuses on two of these elements: attitudes toward government and support for a democratic regime across our set of Pacific Rim nations.

Perhaps the most striking finding is the high level of expressed support for government in many nations—especially the nondemocracies of East Asia. Large majorities state their confidence in government in China, Vietnam, and Singapore, even while simultaneously expressing confidence in the government, parliament, and the dominant political party. Moreover, trust in government is markedly lower in the democracies of East Asia and even in the established Western democracies of the Pacific Rim. Other recent studies of East Asian public opinion reveal a similar pattern (Ahn and Kang 2002; Albritton, Bureekul, and Guo 2005). This is a reverse of what the political culture literature typically argues as the pattern of congruence sustaining a democracy. Almond and Verba (1963), for instance, stressed that a supportive and allegiant public was a key element of a democratic political culture, and this refrain has been repeated in the political culture literature.

We suspect these findings partially reflect the expansion of survey research to nondemocracies, where the calculation of opinions follows a different process. Many different factors may be at work. In less democratic settings, some individuals may be unwilling to critcize the government because they fear negative repercussions. These effects are likely strongest for the survey questions we examined in this chapter: questions that ask about trust and confidence in the current government. However, other recent studies in China suggest that these effects are modest (Shi 2001: 405–7; Chen 2004: 35–6). Other effects are less direct. The limitations on the media in nondemocracies should limit the number of voices that are critical of the government and the spread of information about the failures of government.

In other words, many citizens may be honestly reflecting what they hear about government in the media—and what they hear is largely positive. In addition, democracy itself may breed 'critical citizens'. The adversarial nature of elections and democratic competition tends to highlight government-opposition divisions, stimulating dissatisfaction by supporters of the opposition. When an autocratic government claims to represent the nation, more people may feel included than when a democratic government claims to speak for a majority.[13] Finally, the critical citizens thesis argues that in the long run, high levels of economic development encourages value changes that decrease deference and respect for authority, which includes government as well as other hierarchical institutions.

The set of East Asian nations in our study reflect a unique mix of these factors because they span nearly the full range of democratic and economic development. But similar patterns appear in other cases where the WVS has included autocratic nations. The nine nations with the highest levels of expressed trust in the government included Vietnam, China, Azerbaijan, Bangladesh, Jordan, Tanzania, Uganda, Taiwan, and Iran (Inglehart et al. 2004, Table E079). The nine nations with the lowest trust are: South Korea, Bosnia, Japan, Australia, Argentina, Peru, New Zealand, the Dominican Republic, and Macedonia. When more Iranians express confidence in their government than the Swiss in theirs, one clearly senses that images of incumbent governments are not strongly related to the economic and political development of a nation—or are inversely related at the extremes.

While we believe that these systemic factors are important influences on expressions of trust in government across diverse political systems, our findings suggest that performance records also influence these opinions. The tremendous economic changes in East Asia have transformed the living conditions of most people in the span of a decade or two. The recent economic records of China and Vietnam are especially impressive. The high level of public support the Chinese and Vietnamese regimes currently enjoy partially derives from their economic performance. This is reminiscent of the way in which the economic miracles of postwar Europe and Japan helped consolidate public support for the governments of these countries.

Even more than government support, our research demonstrated that the democratic aspirations of citizens in the Asian nondemocracies are more strongly conditioned by satisfaction with one's personal situation and satisfaction with the government (Table 7.4). One may speculate that if economic performance deteriorates or, in the long run, a public emerges that takes prosperity for granted, then public support for the regime will decline (Huntington 1991). But such a performance-based model would also imply weakening support for democratic norms, or require that the social bases of democratic support in China, Vietnam, and other nondemocracies change. For the time being, it seems that as long as economic performance remains salient, and continues to be positive, public support for the state is likely to remain high. Thus, in the case of China, for example, the diagnosis that a crisis of governance is emerging (Pei 2002) seems unfounded—at least insofar as mass support is concerned. Nathan's assessment (2003*b*) that China's authoritarian regime has demonstrated resilience may be more accurate.

In the longer term, the democratization of the political culture may occur through different processes. We found that the social bases of democratic values differ markedly between the democratic and nondemocratic nations of East Asia. In democracies, education, political engagement, and self-expressive values all work to reinforce democratic norms. However, the contrasting norms of autocratic regimes attenuate or even reverse these effects. This interaction between regime form and the correlates of support suggests that democratization can develop its own process for deepening regime norms—once the democratic transition occurs and functions effectively. This has been the model in the consolidated democracies of East Asia. In addition, in consolidated democracies, performance criteria have much less impact on democratic norms, as these values become diffuse elements of the political culture. Thus, as modernization theorists have demonstrated (Welzel and Inglehart in this volume), public demands for more political rights and civil liberties may increase rapidly once socioeconomic development reaches high levels, and these changes in regime form can reinforce this democratization process.

ENDNOTES

1 Almond and Verba's distinction between different elements (1963) of a political culture is also useful, but because it does not distinguish between the relative importance of different elements, we have found Easton's framework more useful. Also see Dalton (2004, Chapters 1 and 3).

2 Easton tends to include institutional support within the categories of authorities. However, I reserve the category of authorities to represent distinct and individual actors to separate these evaluations from those generalized beyond a single candidate or government official.

3 We used a principal components analysis to extract factors and a varimax rotation of the factor structure. The Eigenvalues suggest four or five dimensions, but routinely the fourth and fifth dimensions reflected subsets of the first three dimensions. Therefore, we constrained the analyses to three dimensions. We used pairwise deletion of missing data, since some items were not asked in every nation.

4 For instance, as noted in Chapter 4, the democratic regime index was not asked in a comparable way in Vietnam, and the democratic process battery was not asked in Singapore. We also did not include other support questions that were missing in multiple nations.

5 Political parties are generally not considered government institutions in democratic systems. However, in the context of the Asian nondemocracies, where there is virtually only one party (the Communist Party or the PAP), and the party hierarchy dominates the state (thus the term party-state), *the* Party is indeed a key government institution. In empirical terms, however, the parties item loads strongly on the government dimension in both the Western democracies and the Asian nondemocracies.

6 We also conducted an oblique factor analysis (oblimin), allowing the dimensions to be intercorrelated. This analysis showed that support for the government and support for democracy are only weakly related for Western democracies (−0.03) and Asian democracies (0.07). However, these two dimensions are positively correlated for the Asian nondemocracies (0.16), which implies that evaluations of these governments and democratic norms are negatively interrelated!

7 The question asked: 'How satisfied are you with the way the people now in national office are handling the country's affairs? Would you say you are very satisfied, fairly satisfied, fairly dissatisfied, or very dissatisfied?'

8 Unfortunately, the WVS did not include a battery of media usage questions, so this hypothesis cannot be systematically tested with our current data.

9 We do not use questions asking explicitly about government performance because this seems to be a tautological relationship; people who are satisfied with government would respond positively to both questions. Government performance should influence support for the government, but it is difficult to assess causality with a single survey. Rather, we looked for measures of life conditions that were explicitly nonpolitical to minimize reciprocal causation.

10 We averaged the individual's overall financial satisfaction and overall life satisfaction, both of which were measured on a 1) dissatisfied to 10) satisfied scale. This averaging results in a variable that ranges from 1 to 10.

11 For the critical citizens theorists, besides value change, individual's educational and professional backgrounds and age are all important indicators of critical citizenship. That is, younger generations, those more educated, and people employed in the professional or knowledge sectors (lawyers, finance, entertainment, and information industries, etc) are more likely to be critical citizens. In this study, we include education as a control variable. The findings suggest that education level and self-expression values already include the large portion of the variation in professional background.

12 We use the satisfaction with politicians in the national government as a predictor because it was asked in all the nations, while confidence in political institutions was not asked in Singapore. However, in additional analyses, we found broadly similar results using the political institutions index. Vietnam is not included in these analyses because the democratic regime index was not asked.

13 This point is illustrated by the strong relationship between national pride and government support in the nondemocratic nations in East Asia, which is almost three times stronger than in the Western democracies (see Table 7.3).

Part III

Orientations Toward Markets

8

Exploring Weber's Theory of Capitalism in Confucian East Asia

Doh Chull Shin and Russell J. Dalton

> The concept spirit of capitalism is here used in this specific sense, it is the spirit of modern capitalism. ... Capitalism existed in China, India, Babylon, in the classic world, and in the Middle Ages. But in all these cases, as we shall see, this particular ethos was lacking.
>
> —Max Weber, 1904–5

Over the past several decades, many of the nations of East Asia have experienced a profound economic transformation. Income levels in East Asia were near those of Africa only a generation ago. As recently as 1975, GNP per capita in South Korea was roughly comparable to Zimbabwe and the Ivory Coast; Taiwan's income per capita was comparable to Algeria or Turkey; and even Singapore was similar to Gabon (Taylor and Jodice 1983). Then, an economic miracle transformed the region. The East Asian Tigers dramatically improved their economies and the living standards of their citizens. Even many of the less affluent nations in East Asia, such as China and Vietnam, have experienced profound economic growth over the past decade (also see Chapter 11 by Pham and Pham).

This economic transformation became the engine for socioeconomic modernization in the region, as well as potentially stimulating the democratization process. Educational levels increased, and literacy rates rose dramatically. East Asian economies not only grew in size, but also in complexity. Peasants moved to the cities, and manufacturing and trade became the driving forces for economic growth. Most of the nations of East Asia were increasingly tied to international trade and exposed to new norms of economic, social, and political life. Exposure to more information and more diverse sources of information occurred in nearly all nations, even those where the government tried to restrict these developments. In short, many of the forces of socioeconomic change emphasized in social modernization theory applied to East Asia over the past generation.

These experiences generated claims of a superior model of economic development in East Asia (Hofheinz and Calder 1982; Morishima 1982; Vogel 1991). Even when market economics was accepted, the state was seen as the guiding force for development. In Japan, MITI's involvement in economic investment and innovation became legendary. The Asian Tigers similarly followed a model of state-centered development and economic decision-making. The close relationship between business and government was seen as essential to the Asian model of economic development. And, of course, when China began to develop its economy and international trade opportunities, this was directed by the state. The result, it was argued, was a more efficient and effective economy.

This was supposedly another form of Asian values at work. It was widely argued that Confucian values provided an Asian model for economic development that contrasted with Weber's model of the Western economic growth. Instead of individual initiative and rational self-interest that Weber identified with capitalist development in the West, Asia development was apparently based on a collectivist approach (MacFaquhar 1980; Tai 1989; Levy Jr 1992). The developmental state paradigm emphasized the importance of governmental intervention to promote economic growth. The Asian model claimed that it was not individual effort, but the collective efforts managed by government, which generated growth.

The economic optimism of the East was punctured during the last decade, however. Japan has suffered a persisting recession of its economy beginning in the 1990s. The 1997–8 economic crisis abruptly turned East Asian economic powerhouses into international paupers. Moreover, this experience ushered in an era of reform for government-regulated economic systems in several nations. During the reformation, the model of a government-directed economy metamorphosed into market-oriented systems (Weiss 1999; Drysdale 2001; Stiglitz and Yusuf 2001; Whitehead 2002). Furthermore, the experience shattered the ideological foundation of East Asia's crony capitalism, which promoted incestuously close relationships between corporations and the government (Dore 1998).

The IMF and other international lending agencies directly or indirectly pushed many governments in East Asia to withdraw themselves from direct engagement in economic enterprises and to impose austerity and structural adjustment programs. The same agencies also prompted banks and other major corporate enterprises to undertake reforms to bring them into better agreement with the fundamental principles of market capitalism, particularly accountability, transparency, and rule by law (Beeson 2002). In the wake of the 1990s financial crisis, East Asia loosened itself from the hubris of its version of capitalism and embraced the principles and practices of market capitalism.

In postcrisis East Asia, the cacophony of claims about the superiority of Asian values and its models of economic development eventually has faded

(Dore 1998; Fukuyama 2003). Increasingly, the Anglo-American type of market capitalism emerged as the orthodox and superior doctrine for organizing economic life (Dean 1999; Weiss 1999; Woo-Cumings 2000; Lee 2002; Weber 2002). Despite the cultural and governmental diversity of East Asia, from communist China and Vietnam through authoritarian Malaysia and Singapore to democratic Japan, Korea, and the Philippines, the policy-makers in these countries are clearly enthralled by the virtues of market capitalism. What is less clear is whether their mass publics acknowledge and embrace those virtues as the basis of their economic system.

This chapter asks if there is a solid cultural foundation to anchor a transition to orthodox market capitalism in East Asia. Max Weber (1976) once observed that the lack of capitalist spirit among East Asians would prevent capitalism's development in the region. Before the 1997–8 crisis, other analysts argued that East Asia had found a new route to capitalist development. Once again, Weber's question is now ascendant. Our presupposition for this study is that economic system change, like political regime change, can succeed only when most ordinary citizens endorse its structural makeup and observe its behavioral norms.

Like others in this volume, we study citizen attitudes in the Asia-Pacific region with data from the WVS conducted during the 1999–2001 period.[1] We focus on six East Asian countries—China, Japan, the Philippines, South Korea, Singapore, and Vietnam. In addition, we include two North American countries on the Pacific Rim, Canada, and the USA, to compare how well rooted the structural and normative components of capitalism are in the publics of both regions.

This chapter has seven sections. In the first, we review previous research on economic liberalization and marketization. In the second, we explicate the notion of capitalism's principles of economic liberalism and individualism, and present the distribution of opinions across nations. The third section distinguishes attitudes toward four distinct types of capitalist economies. The fourth section introduces measures of citizen orientations toward capitalism as an economic system and a distinct mode of personal conduct. The next section describes the extent of Confucian values that are relevant to economic choice. The sixth section analyzes the relationships between these norms and market attitudes. The final section highlights key findings and discusses their theoretical and strategic implications.

PRIOR SURVEY RESEARCH

In the past decade, scholars have produced a spurt of studies about economic values and attitudes among the mass publics in countries making the transition to market capitalism. Since the end of communist rule more than a decade ago, all the countries in East and Central Europe have struggled to establish viable market economies to replace their bankrupt socialist systems. The New Europe Barometer and several other survey research programs have regularly monitored the dynamics and trajectories of popular reactions to the ongoing processes of privatization and marketization (Duch 1993; Evans and Whitefield 1995; Gibson 1996*b*; Rose 1998).

In Latin America, where neoliberal economic reforms have progressed during the past two decades, and in Southern Europe, where the current wave of global democratization began more than three decades ago, numerous cross-national and national public opinion surveys have examined the dynamics of public responses to the economic reforms (Stokes 1996, 2001; Maravall 1997; Weyland 1998). More recently, in Africa, the Afrobarometer program is monitoring public support for market reforms across countries in the region (Bratton, Mattes, and Gyimah-Boadi 2004).

Conceptually, these studies treated market capitalism primarily as a matter of economic freedom or liberalization. Substantively, these analyses have mostly compared the levels, sources, and distribution of attitudes toward capitalist markets across countries and within population subgroups. In terms of the levels, the mass publics of Africa, Eastern and Central Europe, and Latin America extend from weak to moderate support to economic liberalization, and their support remains relatively stable over a short period of time. Among the various segments of the mass citizenry, free-market reform appeals most strongly to the young and well educated, those who have the resources to benefit from such reform. In some countries, such as Russia, attitudes toward a market economy are moderately related to perceptions of the performance of the economy, indicating that support for liberal economic reform will grow when the economy changes for the better.

In East Asia, few survey-based studies have addressed the reactions of ordinary people to the surging forces of marketization and globalization, especially in the aftermath of the 1997 economic crisis.[2] The AsiaBarometer has begun to track consumption patterns of contemporary Asian publics (Inogouchi et al. 2005), and other international studies have examined Asian reactions to the process of economic globalization (chapter by Ahn and Jang; Pew 2003). Hefner (1998) provides some initial evidence of market cultures in China, Taiwan, and Southeast Asia. These studies show the rise of market capitalism in a variety of forms, and the expansion of mass participation in market activities.

Still, much of the debate on public economic attitudes in East Asia lacks firm empirical evidence. We have relatively little survey evidence about how Asian publics think about the basic values underlying a competitive, capitalist market system, and whether their opinions differ from the Weberian model posited for Western societies (like the Protestant traditions of the USA and Canada). Least known is how widely held Asian or Confucian traditions shape their orientations toward market capitalism, which presumably favor the traditional state-centered model of economic development.[3] Indeed, our research examines this ongoing debate about the congruence of Confucian values and support for market principle (*The Economist* 1998; Tu 1991).

This chapter, and the following chapter by Ahn and Jang, address these deficiencies in the existing literature by treating citizen orientations toward market capitalism as a multidimensional and multilevel phenomenon, identifying the distinct patterns of those orientations, and analyzing their linkage with the traditional cultural values of East Asia.

THE NOTION OF MARKET CAPITALISM

What constitutes market capitalism, now recognized as the world's dominant mode for organizing private and public economic activities? What organizational characteristics distinguish capitalism from alternatives such as socialism? What characteristics differentiate market capitalism from other types of capitalism? The answers to these questions uncover popular perspectives about the proper role for states and markets to play in managing economic life at the macro and microlevels.

According to neoclassical economic theory, it is the market, not the state, which should play the preeminent role in promoting national economic wealth and individual prosperity (Williamson 1993; Stiglitz 2002). The less the state intervenes in national and personal economies, the better those economies. This preference for markets over states follows the premise that incomplete information and political biases about economic affairs prevent states from accurately forecasting individual preferences, effectively translating preferences into collective policies, and efficiently converting those policies into economic goods and services.

In the neoclassic perspective, therefore, efficiency in goods and services depends on the freedom of individual citizens. They exercise this freedom as producers, traders, and consumers. They particularly need the freedom to buy and exchange properties, products, and services in an open market, competing against others for the maximization of their economic gains. In the real world, private property ownership and open market competition are interdependent, forming a symbiosis whose constituents reinforce each other. These two economic activities are fundamental to success in the sense that inhibiting them forecloses many other economic opportunities and possibilities. Therefore, private ownership of businesses and competition in an open market are regarded as the defining structural characteristics of capitalism (Stiglitz 1999).

Together, these two characteristics anchor the ideal of free economic life and represent the liberal principle of economic organization. The economies that rule out these two liberal organizational characteristics choose instead a foundation of authoritarianism, as practiced in various socialist and communist economic systems that employ state ownership and planning. To speak of economic reform for such authoritarian systems, therefore, means enlarging freedom on the part of private economic actors while reducing the state's regulation of their activities.

Another defining issue of economic organization concerns the relative importance that individual citizens and institutions should have in the marketplace. Should individual citizens or their governments assume the primary responsibility for their economic welfare? Is it individual striving or collective prosperity that should determine rewards for individual workers? The doctrine of laissez-faire capitalism says that the state should play a minimal role in the economy and espouses the principle that 'individuals bear sole responsibility for their own economic affairs' (McClosky and Zaller 1984: 145). By emphasizing personal merit and responsibility, this principle of economic individualism contrasts sharply with that of economic collectivism, which posits that government and external agencies should set collective goals and manage the welfare of individual citizens. To marketize an economic system, therefore, necessitates reducing the role of government and other agencies while expanding personal autonomy and responsibility.

As conceptualized, market capitalism is an economic system that incorporates both economic liberalism and individualism as its fundamental principles for organizing economic activities. Unlike the communist economic systems in Eastern and Central Europe, it allows individual citizens to become property owners and take part freely in other economic activities. Unlike social democratic systems in Scandinavia and Western Europe, it provides more incentives to be self-reliant and responsible for one's own successes or failures in managing economic affairs. To reform a government-directed system into a laissez-faire system is to promote personal freedoms and initiatives, and to reduce governmental intervention and obligations that inhibit market capitalism.

Structural reforms alone are insufficient to create an economic system of fully functioning market capitalism. Such an economic system requires individual citizens who can observe the norms of economic behavior that Max Weber characterized a hundred years ago as the spirit of capitalism. In *The Protestant Ethic and the Spirit of Capitalism*, Weber (1904–5) argued that the Protestant Reformation emphasized an individualistic, rational, cause-and-effect outlook.[4] Upon becoming pervasive, it promoted economic advancement in Great Britain and other regions of Europe by promoting the Commercial Revolution. He referred to industry and frugality as the most important elements of the individualistic and rational economic outlook.

More recently, many political economists have explained spectacular economic advances in East Asia over the past several decades as resulting from such strong achievement motives among its people (Berger 1988;

Hofstede and Bond 1988; Chan 1996; Davis 1998). However, this literature has also argued that Confucian traditions create a collective orientation that differs from the individualism that Weber stressed. Thus, instead of an individualist model of capitalism based on independent markets and individual initiative, the East Asian variant stressed state-centered development, collective action, and the moderation of individual action.

This literature raises basic questions related to the theme of cultural and institutional congruence that runs through our study. On the one hand, the past economic development of East Asia, especially among the Asian Tigers, was often attributed to a set of Confucian traditions and Asian values that supported economic development through a collective model. This was a pattern of apparent congruence between cultural traditions and economic systems. On the other hand, the recent movement toward capitalist market systems in many East Asian nations would presume a cultural base in the Weberian norms of individualism and competition that are apparently less common among Asian publics. Thus, the question of the congruence of these trends to capitalist markets and citizen values in East Asia parallels our analyses of congruence in the political domain.

Indeed, the potential clash of Western and Eastern economic norms is at the heart of the research in this chapter. At the macrolevel of economic structure, a market capitalism is an economic system that maximizes the role of markets and minimizes the role of states in managing the public and private economies. To sustain this system requires a set of social values congruent with this system. Our analyses ask if citizens in East Asia believe one pursues economic well-being through achievements of hard work, thrift, independence, and responsibility of the Weberian model, or through collective action, interdependence, and state action of the putative Asian model. This chapter examines which value syndrome exists among the publics of East Asia.

MEASUREMENT

Market capitalism as an economic system incorporates both liberalism and individualism, two different approaches to managing economic life. While emphasizing individual citizens' freedom to get ahead economically, individualism emphasizes their striving and responsibility as autonomous economic agents. Because freedom deals with the process of making economic decisions and responsibility deals with the consequences of those decisions, people may not consider these two basic principles of capitalism equally attractive. People in different economic situations who command differing resources may embrace none, only one, or both of the principles.

To tap citizen attitudes toward these two principles, the 1999–2001 WVS asked two pairs of questions.[5] The survey tapped the principle of *economic liberalism* by asking one question about the private ownership of businesses and industry and another question about competition in the marketplace. To measure the principle of *economic individualism*, the survey asked two separate questions on income differences as incentives for individual striving and the locus of primary responsibility for personal welfare (also see Chapter 9 by Ahn and Jang in this volume). As Appendix B shows, respondents could express their procapitalist or anticapitalist attitudes by choosing a number on a 10-point scale. For each question and each pair of questions, their responses were averaged for cross-national and cross-regional comparisons. Responses in the top half of the scale indicate procapitalist attitudes.

Citizens take guidance from specific norms that emphasize the rational pursuit of individual interests and economic prosperity, norms that Weber (1976, Chapter 5) called 'capitalist rules of action'. For the present analysis, we used a list of the ten norms probed in the 1999–2001 WVS.[6] The WVS asked respondents to choose five norms from this list that they would want their children to learn. In our study, we used only four of the ten norms: hard work, thrift, independence, and responsibility. Weber (1976, Chapters 2 and 5) described these four norms as typifying the spirit of capitalism or capitalist achievement motives. How many of these four norms WVS respondents selected as one of the five qualities children should be encouraged to learn at home constitutes our indicator of overall normative support for capitalism.

To determine whether adherence to Confucian values orient East Asians away from market capitalism, we selected a pair of items tapping orientations to authority and community (also see chapter by Dalton and Ong in this volume). These are key components of Confucianism that Weber argued would inhibit economic success in East Asia because they discourage competition and innovation.[7] Responses endorsing the virtues of obedience and unselfishness are indicators of attachment to the Confucian values of hierarchical collectivism.

LEVELS OF SUPPORT FOR MARKET CAPITALISM AS AN ECONOMIC SYSTEM

We begin our analyses by examining support for the economic values that presumably support a capitalist market economy. We ask if Asians support the principles of liberalism and individualism linked to a market system, and if they view these principles as favorably as their peers in North America do. To address these questions, we calculated mean scores on a 10-point scale, tapping orientations toward these principles and percentages expressing procapitalist orientations.[8]

Let us begin with the measures of economic liberalism on the left side of Table 8.1. Of the six Asian countries listed in the table, four scored above the midpoint on the 10-point scale rating the private ownership of businesses and

TABLE 8.1. *Economic orientations by nation*

	Liberalism			Individualism		
Regions	Private ownership	Competition	Mean	Merit pay	Self-reliance	Mean
Asia						
China	4.4	7.9	(6.2)	6.2	5.8	(6.0)
Japan	6.3	6.7	(6.5)	5.7	6.6	(6.2)
Korea	6.2	6.9	(6.5)	6.5	3.1	(4.8)
Philippines	4.6	6.9	(5.7)	6.6	5.6	(6.1)
Singapore	5.8	7.6	(6.7)	7.0	4.8	(5.9)
Vietnam	5.9	7.1	(6.4)	6.3	6.5	(6.4)
North America						
Canada	7.1	7.3	(7.2)	5.3	6.1	(5.7)
USA	7.5	7.6	(7.5)	5.7	6.7	(6.2)

Source: 1999–2001 WVS.

Note: Table entries are the mean scores on the individual questions and the two summary indices. All are measured on 10-point scale. For economic liberalism, 10 represents greater support for liberalism. For economic individualism, 10 represents greater support for individualism. Mean on 10-point scales.

two scored below it. China (4.4) and the Philippines (4.6) are the only two countries where less than two-fifths of the population favored the private ownership of business and industry. In the former, this presumably reflects the legacy of the communist system (although this is less apparent in Vietnam); the lack of support for private ownership in the Philippines might reflect popular opposition to the narrow elite class that dominates the Philippine economy. In Japan (6.3), Korea (6.2), Singapore (5.8), and Vietnam (5.9), majorities favor private ownership over a government-managed economy. Even in Korea, however, where the level of favorable views is highest, less than two-thirds support increased private ownership of businesses and industry. When all six Asian countries are considered together, they score 5.5 on the 10-point scale, the exact midpoint. Furthermore, all six East Asian countries score considerably lower than either of their two non-Asian peers, Canada (7.1) and the USA (7.5). These findings indicate clearly that East Asians as a whole are less supportive of privatization.

On attitudes toward competition, all six East Asian countries score well above the midpoint on the scale. This finding, together with what is presented in the next chapter by Ahn and Jang, indicates general support for competition among economic actors. Such support is highest in China (7.9), Singapore (7.6), and Vietnam (7.1) and lowest in Japan (6.7), Korea (6.9), and the Philippines (6.9). Considering all six countries together, their mean scores average 7.2 on the 10-point scale. Even in China and the

Philippines, where relatively small minorities prefer private ownership to governmental ownership of businesses, large majorities favor more competition. Surprisingly, little difference exists between the Asian and Western set of Pacific Rim countries. As a group, Asian countries stand at 7.2 on the 10-point scale, compared to 7.5 for the two Western countries.

To measure the overall level of support for the principle of economic liberalization, we averaged responses to these two questions (see Appendix B).[9] As Table 8.1 shows, all six Asian countries scored higher than the midpoint on the 10-point scale, indicating general favorability toward economic liberalism. Across regions, however, East Asian support (mean 6.3) lags behind support among North American publics (7.4).

In addition, the number of unqualified supporters for economic liberalism in East Asia varies a great deal from country to country. Supporters of both private ownership and competition range from lows of 26 percent in China and 32 percent in the Philippines, to highs of 51 percent in Singapore and 56 percent in Korea (see Table 8.2). Of the six countries in the region, only Korea and Singapore have majorities that endorse both characteristics of economic liberalism. In the rest, full economic liberalism receives minority support. Even in Japan, the region's most advanced capitalist nation, less than half the population fully supports economic liberalization. In all East Asian countries, however, those who fully support capitalism as an economic system outnumber those who do not support it at all. Even in the communist countries of China and Vietnam, supporters outnumber nonsupporters by a substantial margin, indicating popular favor for a capitalist, rather than a socialist, system. Among Asian nations, full supporters of capitalism account for a little over two-fifths (42 percent). For Canadians and Americans, full supporters account for more than two-thirds (69 percent) of the public.

An equally important dimension of economic values is *economic individualism*. When the WVS asked whether large income differences are needed as incentives for individual effort, Asian publics generally favored such differences. Endorsement of merit-based reward is the highest in Singapore (7.0) and the lowest in Japan (5.7). It is surprising that support for income inequality is also relatively common in China and Vietnam, where their communist heritages (and currently large income inequality) might have moderated such sentiments. Moreover, support for such a reward system appears to be greater in East Asia than in North America. The USA and Canada have a combined mean of 5.5, exactly the midpoint on the 10-point scale. This regional difference is our most surprising finding because of the higher support for inequality in East Asia, which also contrasts with the presumed cultural traditions of the region.

Another question from the WVS asked whether individual citizens or their governments should take greater responsibility in providing for their economic well-being. Responses among Asian publics are generally mixed.

TABLE 8.2. *Percentages expressing favorable orientations toward capitalism by nation*

Regions	Private property	Economic liberalism				Economic individualism				
		Competition	None	One	Both	Income difference	Own welfare	None	One	Both
Asia										
China	29.4%	78.5%	17.7%	56.7%	25.6%	56.3%	49.0%	28.1%	38.4%	33.4%
Japan	57.8	71.4	17.6	35.6	46.8	61.4	51.4	21.4	44.5	34.1
Korea	64.4	78.8	10.7	33.4	55.9	66.9	13.9	31.1	57.0	11.9
Philippines	39.4	73.5	18.7	49.8	31.6	64.0	48.8	22.9	41.3	35.8
Singapore	56.5	85.0	8.7	39.2	51.2	76.9	37.8	15.7	54.0	30.4
Vietnam	51.7	69.7	22.2	34.2	43.6	56.2	61.9	24.6	32.7	42.7
North America										
Canada	77.7	80.3	8.8	24.5	66.7	50.0	61.2	25.2	38.5	36.4
USA	81.8	80.2	9.2	19.5	71.3	55.6	69.3	18.2	38.8	43.1

Source: 1999–2001 WVS. Based on the four economic values presented in Table 8.1.

In Japan and Vietnam, much more than half the populations preferred self-reliance to governmental guarantee. In China and the Philippines, the populations were evenly divided between the two options. In Korea and Singapore, large majorities rejected the self-reliance option in favor of the governmental welfare option. In Canada and the USA, in contrast, more than three-fifths endorsed the same option. East Asians are generally less supportive of individual responsibility than their peers in North America.

Combining both questions into a scale of economic individualism, East Asians are not much behind North Americans in these values. In both regions, only minorities support this aspect of market capitalism fully. In Vietnam, there are as many full supporters as in the USA, and the Philippines have as many full supporters as Canada. Table 8.2 indicates that those who do not support economic individualism at all are less numerous in Japan (21%) and Singapore (16%) than in Canada (25%). On balance, East Asians and North Americans are about equally likely to embrace the principle of economic individualism.

In summary, East Asians tend to support the capitalist economic institutions of private ownership and competition, albeit less than among non-Asian capitalist countries on the Pacific Rim. Yet East Asians do generally support economic individualism, desiring individual citizens to steer their own economic destiny. Here, their support approximates that of Americans and Canadians.

THE MOST AND LEAST PREFERRED TYPES OF CAPITALIST ECONOMIC SYSTEMS

What sort of capitalism do East Asians prefer? We combined our two measures of economic values to define preferences for different institutional structures. Assuming that private ownership and open market competition are the defining characteristics of capitalism, we classified as capitalists only those who embraced both of these structural characteristics. We then differentiated capitalists into three subcategories according to attitudes toward the ideals of economic individualism. The capitalists who endorsed the ideals of rewarding individuals according to merits and for assuming the primary responsibility for their own personal welfare we called *market capitalists*. Those who rejected these two ideals in favor of reducing income differences and maintaining government social guarantees we called *state capitalists*. The capitalists who were favorably oriented to only one of these ideals of economic individualism we called *mixed capitalists*. Respondents who failed to embrace both private ownership and open market competition we called *non-capitalists*.

Table 8.3 presents the distribution of opinions across the nations in our study. Between the two polar capitalist choices, market capitalism receives more favor than state capitalism in East Asian countries. In four countries—China, Japan, Singapore, and Vietnam, market capitalism is more popular than state capitalism. In these countries less than one-tenth of their respective populations support state capitalism, and market capitalism is more popular than state capitalism. In Korea and the Philippines, on the other hand, state capitalism is more popular than market capitalism. In these two countries, more than one-tenth of their respective populations support state capitalism. Of all the six East Asian countries, Korea stands out as the country with the highest support for state capitalism and the lowest support for market capitalism. Only 4 percent of Koreans support market capitalism, while nearly five times as many (19 percent) support state capitalism. In this respect, Korea contrasts most strikingly with Japan, where 18 percent of the population supports market capitalism and only 3 percent state capitalism.

Perhaps because neither model is fully embraced by East Asian publics, we find that mixed capitalism is the most common choice in each nation. The support for a mixed capitalist model is highest in Korea (33 percent), Japan (29 percent), and Singapore (28 percent). It is lowest in the two communist countries of China (11 percent) and Vietnam (16 percent) and the Philippines (12 percent).

Similarly, in the USA and Canada, no single type of capitalism has the favor of a majority of the people. In Canada, mixed capitalism is preferred and state capitalism is the least popular, reflecting the same pattern found in most East Asian countries. In the USA, however, market capitalism is the most popular, and state capitalism is the least popular. There market capitalism is significantly less popular than mixed capitalism. In the USA,

TABLE 8.3. *Preferred types of capitalism*

Regions	Types of Capitalism				Total (%)
	Non capitalism	State capitalism	Mixed capitalism	Market capitalism	
Asia					
China	74.4%	5.4%	10.9%	9.3%	100
Japan	49.4	3.3	28.5	18.3	100
Korea	44.1	19.3	32.6	4.1	100
Philippines	68.4	11.1	12.3	8.2	100
Singapore	48.8	8.2	27.8	15.1	100
Vietnam	56.4	9.3	16.2	18.1	100
North America					
Canada	33.3	17.1	25.9	23.6	100
USA	28.7	13.2	28.4	29.3	100

Source: 1999–2001 WVS.

Note: See text for the construction of this typology.

supporters of market capitalism outnumber nonsupporters of capitalism. Such is not the case in any East Asian country. In both respects, popular support for capitalism in East Asia is qualitatively different from what is observed in the USA, where individualism and economic liberalism are strongly engrained in the political culture (Lipset 1990). Even in the USA, however, a large majority of the population avoids embracing market capitalism as the most preferred economic system.

COMMITMENT TO THE NORMS OF CAPITALIST CONDUCT

The norms of economic liberalism and economic individualism presumably are derived from broader social norms that exist within a society. Max Weber argued that the values of thrift, individual responsibly, and initiative provided the moral basis of capitalist thought, and that these values were to be found within the Western tradition. These themes have been hotly debated in the scholarly literature, with the implicit challenge that one does not have to be Protestant to have a capitalist ethic (Sen 2001). Indeed, many of the traditional values of Confucian culture seem strongly conducive to these same norms of economic development, and these norms are frequently cited as reasons for the economic advances of the five Tigers of East Asian development (Tu 1991; Jochim 1992; Gong and Jang 1998).

Fortunately, the WVS allows us to move beyond the economic values we have just presented to examine the commitment to Weberian social values between East Asians and North Americans. We looked at the four norms of hard work, thrift, independence, and responsibility, and counted how many of these norms respondents listed as important qualities that children should learn. Table 8.4 reports the percentages listing each of these norms. The number of these norms listed in each country is also reported in the right side of the table as a measure of overall achievement orientations.

The table shows interesting similarities and differences within and between the two groups of countries on the Pacific Rim. In all the countries in both groups, thrift is rated as the least important of the four capitalist norms considered in the present study. In most East Asian countries and both North American countries, this norm rates as an important norm in less than half the populations. Only in China (57 percent) and Korea (68 percent) did majorities rate it as important. These countries are the only two countries where each and every one of the four chosen norms gets majority support from the populations. Unlike thrift, hard work was viewed as an important norm by majorities in all Asian and non-Asian countries, with the exception of Japan (27 percent). In Canada and the USA, and in the three economically advanced East Asian countries of Japan, Korea, and Singapore, independence and responsibility are the two norms rated important by the largest majorities. In other Asian countries, on the other hand, hard work is more

TABLE 8.4. *Attachment to capitalist norms*

	Capitalist norms				Index scores					
Regions	Hard work	Thrift	Independence	Responsibility	0	1	2	3	4	$\bar{X}$
Asia										
China	85.8%	57.2%	74.1%	63.6%	5.5%	2.5%	19.0%	51.8%	21.2%	(2.8)
Japan	27.1	48.1	81.8	90.7	1.8	5.0	43.8	42.3	7.0	(2.5)
Korea	71.6	67.5	77.3	92.3	0.2	2.3	18.6	46.7	32.3	(3.1)
Philippines	72.8	45.2	68.8	66.5	0.4	9.4	38.8	39.9	11.5	(2.6)
Singapore	63.7	38.2	72.3	80.8	0.3	7.7	39.7	41.5	10.8	(2.6)
Vietnam	75.5	48.1	56.4	70.3	0.6	9.2	39.0	41.7	9.5	(2.5)
North America										
Canada	50.6	28.5	62.0	77.2	1.2	18.0	46.6	29.8	4.4	(2.2)
USA	59.6	22.8	62.0	72.6	1.5	18.8	45.8	29.8	4.2	(2.2)

Source: 1999–2001 WVS.

valued than either independence or responsibility. The higher the country's level of economic development, the less importance its people ascribe to hard work as a capitalist norm of conduct.

Comparing East Asians and North Americans reveals the surprising finding that East Asians are significantly more committed to the capitalist norms than their North American peers. On the 5-point index summing up responses affirming the four norms, all six East Asian countries scored significantly higher than either North American country. On average, persons in Canada and the USA endorse 2.2 of the four norms. In East Asian countries, the average ranges from 2.5 to 3.1. In North America, only one person in three (34 percent) endorsed three or all four norms. In Asia, the fully or mostly committed constitute three in five persons (59 percent). Undoubtedly, normative support for capitalism is stronger in East Asia where structural support for it is weaker. This finding disconfirms Weber's assertion (1951, Chapter 8) that Confucianism precludes economic actors in East Asia from embracing capitalist norms of conduct.

CONFUCIAN VALUES AND SUPPORT FOR CAPITALISM

What constitutes Confucian values? Have those values supported or deterred economic development in East Asia? Many in the scholarly community and policy circles have vigorously debated these questions for decades (see the chapter by Dalton and Ong; see also Bell 2000; Bell and Ham 2003; Huntington 1996; Koh 1995; Pye 1985). These debates identify respect for hierarchy and concern for collective well-being as two key distinguishing features of the Confucian culture. To determine whether East Asians still hold these two Confucian cultural values, we examined the proportions of WVS respondents who endorsed unconditional obedience to superiors and unselfish service to other people as the two important norms of public life. Table 8.5 presents the percentages embracing these two Confucian values among the publics of East Asia and North America.

In all six East Asian countries, as in Canada and the USA, majorities hold the value of collectivism emphasizing service to other people. In this respect, the two regions of the Pacific Rim are more similar to than different from each other. In endorsing hierarchical social life, however, they are markedly different from each other. In two North American countries, majorities prefer hierarchism to egalitarianism in organizing social life. In all the East Asian countries, however, minorities opt for the value of hierarchism. Contrary to what is known in the literature on Confucianism, hierarchs are less numerous in East Asia than in North America. Why do East Asians value hierarchical social life to a lesser extent than North Americans? Apparently, East Asians and North Americans both prefer an alternative to the particular type of social life in which they have been living.

TABLE 8.5. *Attachment to Confucian values*

Region/country	Confucian values		Index scores			
	Obedience	Service	0	1	2	(mean)
Asia						
China	16.0%	81.2%	15.4%	71.8%	12.7	(1.0)
Japan	28.0	60.1	29.1	53.7	17.2	(0.9)
Korea	49.3	64.7	14.8	56.4	28.8	(1.1)
Philippines	48.0	94.3	3.3	51.1	45.6	(1.4)
Singapore	25.9	78.7	16.5	62.5	21.0	(1.0)
Vietnam	42.2	71.0	18.2	50.4	31.4	(1.1)
North America						
Canada	57.4	91.2	3.6	44.2	52.2	(1.5)
USA	64.1	93.8	2.1	37.9	60.0	(1.6)

Source: 1999–2001 WVS.

When the two values of hierarchism and collectivism are considered, it becomes more evident that the two core values of Confucianism are less pervasive in East Asia than in North America. In Canada and the USA, hierarchical collectivists, that is, those who embrace the two values, constitute the majorities of their populations—52 percent of Canadians and 60 percent of Americans. In all six Asian countries, on the other hand, they constitute minorities ranging from 13 percent of the Chinese to 46 percent of Filipinos. In five of these countries, moreover, adherents of hierarchical collectivism constitute no more than one-third of their populations.

A more notable finding is that people in five of the six East Asian countries—China (16 percent), Japan (29 percent), Korea (15 percent), Singapore (17 percent), and Vietnam (18 percent)—are detached from the primacy of hierarchical collectivism to a greater extent than their peers in Canada (4 percent) and the USA (2 percent). Evidently, East Asians no longer remain strongly attached to the Confucian culture of hierarchical collectivism about which Weber was so critical. In fact, their detachment from the key perspectives of Confucianism exceeds North Americans', as was also demonstrated in the chapter by Dalton and Ong.

Table 8.6 examines the bivariate relationships between the index of Confucian values on the one hand, and structural support for capitalism (a combination of economic liberalism and economic individualism from Table 8.2) and normative support for capitalism (the index from Table 8.4) on the other. The Pearson correlation coefficients in the table reveal that the level of hierarchical collectivism is generally not related to structural support for capitalism. Only one of these relationships in the first column of the table is statistically significant, and the correlations also are negligible in magnitude. In virtually all nations, with the exception of Singapore, people separate their images of a desirable economic system from their personal social

TABLE 8.6. *Correlations between attachment to Confucian values and support for capitalism*

Region	Types of capitalist support	
	Structural support	Normative support
Asia		
China	−0.02	0.07*
Japan	0.03	0.05
Korea	−0.03	−0.06*
Philippines	0.00	−0.02
Singapore	−0.12*	−0.07*
Vietnam	−0.04	0.06*
North America		
Canada	−0.01	−0.03
USA	0.03	−0.02

Source: 1999–2001 WVS; table entries are Pearson correlation coefficients.
Note: * = Coefficients significant at 0.05 level

values—reminiscent of what Dalton and Ong (in this volume) found for attitudes toward a democratic political regime.

In striking contrast, however, the variable measuring the overall level of attachment to Confucian values is significantly related to normative support for capitalism in as many as four of the eight Pacific Rim countries surveyed. In two dragon states of these four, Korea and Singapore, the Confucian values are negatively related with such support. In two Communist countries, China and Vietnam, on the other hand, the same variables are positively related. This finding suggests that political as well as economic factors may shape the impact of Confucian norms on popular support for capitalism.

To determine the importance of Confucianism relative to other factors that might shape popular support for capitalism in East Asia, we conducted a multivariate analysis with four categories of variables derived from prior research on these attitudes: (*a*) demographics (gender and age), (*b*) human resources (education and income), (*c*) assessments of the personal economy, and (*d*) social capital (trust and civic engagements).[10] OLS regression is used to estimate the independent impact of each Confucian value variable while simultaneously controlling for the others in the model.

Comparisons of *betas* across rows in Table 8.7 reveal that both cultural variables have relatively little impact on support for the structural principles of a capitalist economic system. Neither cultural variable matters significantly in five countries—Japan, Korea, the Philippines, Canada, and the USA. Even in the other three Asian countries—China, Singapore, and Vietnam—where they do seem to matter significantly—the two variables

TABLE 8.7. *Predicting structural support for capitalism*

	China	Japan	Korea	Philippines	Singapore	Vietnam	Canada	USA
Demographics								
Gender	−0.08*	−0.03	−0.11*	−0.04	−0.06	−0.10	−0.05	−0.05
Age	−0.12*	−0.10*	0.02	−0.03	−0.05	−0.12*	0.07*	0.09*
Resources								
Education	0.03	0.07*	0.06	0.08*	0.03	0.00	0.05	0.00
Income	0.02	0.01	0.07*	0.01	0.13*	0.11*	0.07*	0.15*
Culture								
Obedience	−0.07*	0.05	−0.01	0.02	−0.09*	0.03	0.03	−0.03
Service	0.04	0.01	−0.02	−0.01	−0.05	−0.08*	0.03	0.00
Social capital								
Trust	0.00	0.05	−0.05	−0.01	0.02	0.07	0.03	−0.02
Associations	−0.05	−0.05	0.02	0.03	−0.02	0.02	−0.03	0.03
Economic								
Well-being	0.14*	0.09*	0.05	0.03	0.03	0.03	0.00	0.04
R^2	(0.05)	(0.04)	(0.03)	(0.02)	(0.05)	(0.05)	(0.03)	(0.02)

Source: 1999–2001 WVS.
Note: * = Coefficients significant at 0.05 level

together contribute less than 1 percent of the prediction of structural support for capitalism beyond the other variables in the model.[11] This finding suggests that, even when individuals do adhere to Confucian norms of hierarchical collectivism, this does not pose an obstacle to the support for a capitalist market system in East Asia.

Table 8.8 shows that the two Confucian cultural variables are more influential in shaping support for the behavioral norms of capitalism than its structural principles. In all Asian countries, with the exception of the Philippines, either cultural variable affects support for those norms significantly. Only in three of these five countries—Japan, Korea, and Singapore–they are negatively related. Even in these three countries, their net contribution to the prediction of normative support is much smaller than that of either demographic or socioeconomic variables. This finding confirms that Confucian values are quite limited in inhibiting Asians from embracing capitalism.

In both Asia and North America, as in other regions of the world, socioeconomic resources matter most significantly. As expected from modernization theory, people in both regions tend to be most supportive of capitalism when they command the highest levels of education and income. In terms of age, young people are not always most supportive of capitalism. In Asia, they are the most supportive of capitalist structural principles, while older people are the most supportive of its behavioral norms. In North

TABLE 8.8. *Predicting normative support for capitalism*

	China	Japan	Korea	Philippines	Singapore	Vietnam	Canada	USA
Demographics								
Gender	−0.02	0.04	0.00	−0.02	−0.01	−0.06	−0.03	−0.04
Age	0.00	0.13*	0.08*	0.03	0.08*	−0.14*	0.15*	0.04
Resources								
Education	0.16*	−0.01	0.01	0.03	0.08*	−0.06	−0.01	−0.05
Income	0.11*	0.01	−0.05	−0.02	−0.01	−0.08	0.08*	0.03
Culture								
Obedience	−0.04	−0.07*	−0.06*	−0.01	0.03	0.07*	−0.02	0.00
Service	0.13	0.00	−0.02	−0.04	−0.14*	−0.02	−0.02	0.04
Social capital								
Trust	−0.06	−0.01	−0.02	0.02	−0.01	−0.09	−0.05	−0.03
Associations	−0.07*	−0.07*	−0.14*	0.09*	−0.03	0.05	−0.02	−0.09*
Economic								
Well-being	0.03	−0.02	0.03	0.00	−0.04	−0.03	0.00	0.00
R^2	(0.07)	(0.02)	(0.03)	(0.02)	(0.04)	(0.05)	(0.02)	(0.02)

Source: 1999–2001 WVS.
Note: *=Coefficients significant at 0.05 level

America, however, older people tend to support its principles and norms more strongly than younger ones. Social capital, as measured by levels of interpersonal trust and associational membership, matters significantly in six of eight Pacific Rim counties. However, in four of these six countries—China, Japan, Korea, and the USA–it detracts from rather than contributes to popular support for capitalism, contrary to what the theory of civil society claims. Finally, the sense of economic well-being does not matter significantly in most of the countries. Only in China and Japan, satisfaction with one's own economic situation strengthens structural support for capitalism.[12]

SUMMARY AND CONCLUSIONS

Max Weber once observed that capitalism would not develop in East Asia because Confucian culture held in contempt the individualistic and rational outlook that promoted capitalism in Western and Northern Europe. The WVS findings presented above clearly reveal that the hierarchical and collectivistic values of Confucianism are no longer widely shared among the publics of East Asia, although when present, those values do inhibit the embrace of the achievement motivation that Weber characterized as the spirit of capitalism.

Most people in East Asia now hold egalitarian and individualistic values to the same extent as their peers in Canada and the USA. Many East Asians upholding such capitalist values have yet to fully embrace the organizational principles of economic liberalization and individualism. Consequently, market capitalism, which best fulfills these principles, is not the economic system most favored in the region. The latest WVS findings indicate that the people in all six East Asian countries prefer the economic system of mixed capitalism, which values both individual striving and communal prosperity. The preference for mixed capitalism exceeds favor for market capitalism, with its emphasis on individual merit over communal interest.

Our most important finding is that in all East Asian countries, large majorities support at least some liberalization of their current economic system. Large majorities also support some individualization of their current economic system. Nonetheless, only small minorities support economic liberalization to the fullest extent. In particular, smaller minorities support economic individualization to the fullest extent. On the basis of these findings, we can appreciate the progress in economic liberalization accomplished in East Asia, and conclude that its countries do possess the cultural foundation that, over the long haul, can and will facilitate a gradual and selective transformation of its crony capitalism into a full exercise of market capitalism.

This cultural foundation for market reform, however, does not appear to be as solid as the cultural foundation which the 1999–2001 WVS and the 2002–3 East Asia Barometer Surveys recently found to exist for democratic reform.[13] In every East Asian country, a large majority fully embraces democracy as the most preferred political system. Since many of these democrats have yet to become market capitalists, it is likely that in Confucian East Asia, the marketization of crony capitalism will proceed more slowly than the democratization of authoritarian politics in the political system.

ENDNOTES

1 More information on the surveys is presented in Appendix A of this book. More information on the project is available on the website: www.worldvaluessurvey.org

2 Public reactions to the Asian economic crisis are examined in Harris and Robb (1998), Kim and Shin (2004), and Robb (1998).

3 Market cultures in China, Taiwan, and Southeast Asia are examined in Hefner (1998).

4 Recent works on religion and economic development are reviewed in Ball (2001), Lee (2004), and Sen (2001).

5 The specific wording of the questions is presented in Appendix B of this volume. Both pairs of questions were combined into summary indices. A principle component analysis of the pooled eight-country data confirms that four items fell into two distinct dimensions, liberalism and individualism, as suggested by our notion of capitalism. Across the six East Asian countries, however, the two items in each pair were neither highly nor consistently correlated with each other. From this finding, it is evident that East Asians are far from being cognitively constrained or structured in thinking about market capitalism, which they have yet to experience fully.

6 These norms include independence, hard work, responsibility, imagination, tolerance, thrift, determination, religious faith, unselfishness, and obedience. From these ten norms, respondents were asked to choose as many as five that they personally consider important for child education.

7 For critical reviews of Weber's theory of capitalism, see Bellah (1968), Davis (1987), and Eisenstadt (1968).

8 See Appendix B of this book for the questions and index construction. The original responses to the items on private property and competition were rescaled so that a score of 1 means strong opposition to capitalism and a score of 10 means strong support for it.

9 This index was constructed by adding the scores on the two 10-point scales and then dividing the sums by two.

10 Civic engagements are measured in terms of the number of associations with which respondents are affiliated (see Chapter 7).

11 This percentage is estimated by the square part correlation coefficient, which measures the difference between the values of two coefficients of multiple determination.

12 Another set of OLS regression analyses was performed to determine whether attachment to capitalist norms contributes to support for a capitalist economic system independent of Confucian values and other control variables. The results of these analyses reveal that it has no significant impact on such support in seven of the eight countries considered here. Singapore is the only country where it shows a significant positive impact.

13 More information on the East Asia Barometer Surveys is available on the website: www.eastasiabarometer.org

9

Public Support for Market Reforms in Nine Asian Countries: Divergence of a Market-Based Economy

Chung-Si Ahn and Jiho Jang

A wave of market reform and globalization has swept across the world since the 1980s, and the nations of Asia have felt hits impact as greatly as countries in Latin America, Eastern Europe, and other parts of the world. For the past two decades, communist China and Vietnam have moved their state-directed economies toward an open economic system with private ownership. In November 2002, the 16th Congress of the Chinese Communist Party adopted an inclusive doctrine that allowed bourgeois capitalists to obtain party membership. In addition, a powerful wave of capitalist development had steadily transformed the economies of South Korea, Taiwan, and many other East Asian nations.[1] However, the region's 1997 economic crisis occasioned calls for the restructuring of the existing capitalist systems that had transformed countries, such as South Korea and Thailand, from economic paupers in the 1970s to powerhouses by the early 1990s.

For decades, crony capitalism (or the developmental state) allowed economic policy decisions based primarily on personal connections or political considerations instead of transparent competition (Bardhan 1997; Wei 1999; Kang 2002; Pagano 2002). Thus, the developmental model that brought about economic success for the past two decades was doomed to failure because of the 'rampant corruption', 'the prevalence of money politics', and 'systematic inflexibility' arising from a 'tradition-bound culture that resisted political modernization' (Lingle 1998: 284; Kang 2002, Chapter 1). For example, the Kim Young Sam government in Korea was, at first, reluctant, but eventually succumbed to the region's 1997 grave economic crisis and asked the IMF to bail out the Korean economy.

The IMF customarily attached conditions to loans in order to restrain its borrowers, and these conditions were a series of policy limitations and performance targets, in line with the 'Washington Consensus' which heralds the neoliberal market economic policies.[2] The IMF programs included fiscal and monetary austerity, financial market reorganization, corporate restructuring and improvement of corporate governance structure, liberalization of trade and capital markets, labor market flexibility, and enhancement of corporate transparency. In short, the program was to promote the marketization of the Korean and other East Asian economies.

The Korean government's effort to quickly resolve the crisis initially centered on overcoming the liquidity crisis, and then on market reforms, such as corporate restructuring and rapid opening of the domestic market.[3] Moreover, korea's experience of the crisis was felt to varying degrees in Taiwan and other East Asia economies. To restructure corporate governance, which was considered at the root of the financial crisis, Taiwan set up the Commission of Financial Supervision and Management, a Financial Restructuring Fund, and consolidated banks with large amounts of nonperforming loans (Chow 2002). Thailand and Malaysia also set up corporate debt-restructuring committees and relaxed the regulations preventing the foreign ownership of domestic companies. Likewise, other East Asian countries attempted to liberalize their economies by passing a variety of new laws and regulations.

Nonetheless, the evolution and success of market reforms are based not only on the actions of elites and powerful interest groups, but also on public support for the reforms. As others have argued in this volume, the further development of market capitalism in East Asia depends on the extent to which ordinary citizens embrace its principles and values.

Recent years have witnessed increasing challenges against liberal economic reforms in the region, especially from people who believe their livelihoods have been negatively affected by the new forms of global economic competition. For instance, thousands of antiglobalization protesters demonstrated at the EU–Asia summit in Seoul in 2000, Taiwanese farmers produced massive protests against opening agricultural markets to foreign competition, and even in China there are reports of mass protests by workers laid off by state enterprises. Some critics worry that Asian citizens may fall into a new form of dependency under the sway of international capital, and that the class structure may be stratified with the middle levels shrinking. Indeed, many people wonder whether neoliberal policy could produce such unfavorable consequences as rising unemployment, regressing income distribution and deep poverty, in addition to the macroeconomic consequences of low growth rates, unbalanced price structures, and financial instability. Thus, as Shin and Dalton also note in the Chapter 8, public reactions to the market reform are a force shaping the contours and dynamics of capitalist economic development in East Asia.

This chapter examines public attitudes toward market reform. While most chapters in this volume use the 1999–2002 WVS, we add another perspective on public opinion as measured by the eighteen-country 'Asia–Europe Survey'. Our analyses focus on the following research questions: To what extent do the mass publics of nine Asian countries support various kinds of market reform? Does their support for market reform tend to converge or diverge? Since market reforms in Asia have been mainly influenced by globalization forces, we include two other questions: Does support for globalization promote support for market reform? Which countries in the region are most and least supportive of these changes?

LITERATURE REVIEW

The changing condition of capitalism has been a major driving force of recent market reforms around the world. For example, Mittleman (2000) traces the origin of the present phase of market reform to the deep recession experienced by the Western countries in the 1970s. That recession produced new strategies for the restructuring of production from Fordist to post-Fordist strategies? that emphasizes more flexible, capital and technology-intensive operation. The intensification of these strategies in the West, facilitated by state policies and technological advances, resulted in the weakening of trade union power, the reduction in social expenditures, deregulation, privatization, and above all, an emphasis on enhancing competitiveness. Indeed, free-market competition was elevated to an ideology claiming that the market should be freed from political and social control.

Today, many governments and international organizations, including the IMF, the World Bank, and the WTO, accept various types of neoliberal ideology and implement policies of deregulation, privatization, and market liberalization. The aggressive neoliberal policy measures, together with great advancement of information technology and increasing specialization of the market, have bred winner-take-all markets, with a possible consequence of class conflict due to the widening gap between the small number of the rich and the large majority of the poor (Mittleman 2000: 17). Albrow (1996) also suggests that capitalism is a major factor in the opposition to the state control and of free flow of goods and services across borders and boundaries. Similarly, Guillen (2001: 236) notes that globalization is an ideology, often 'associated with neoliberalism and with technocratic solutions to economic development and reform'. In a nutshell, the logic of globalization is equated with neoliberal ideology and free-market capitalism.

Do globalization and its processes produce 'one world of global capitalism', embracing market capitalism? Do all countries and citizens favor the shift toward market capitalism, or do they diverge in their views of globalization and reforms for market capitalism? Convergence theorists argue that globalization and market reform push countries to converge on a universally superior pattern of organization and economic behaviors. According to these theorists, economic crises have promoted the shift toward free-market reforms in regions as diverse as Africa, Asia, the former Eastern bloc, and Latin America (Remmer 1991; Bermeo 1992; Widner 1994; Stallings 1995; Garron 1998; Haggard 2000). These theories also seem justified in postcrisis Asia, where economic crisis apparently resulted from the international market working against excessive government intervention, cronyism, corruption, and other forms of rent seeking (Kaminsky and Reinhart 1998; Krugman 1998). The conventional wisdom in the wake of the crisis is that Asian economies are vulnerable to a range of political constraints and economic imperatives that compel them to embrace the increasingly ubiquitous market-centered, neoliberal approaches.

Nonetheless, our research questions the thesis that national diversity has rapidly disappeared in East Asia. The existing literature on globalization and market reform does not adequately explain the divergent paths to market capitalism in East Asia. Theoretically, the convergence literature implicitly assumes that those elements can be detached from the societies and grafted as single components into quite different institutional configurations. Furthermore, existing studies routinely assume that economic policymaking settings are fairly institutionalized, national actors have discernable preferences and strategies, and social groups have reasonably stable coalitions among themselves (Widner 1994; Williamson 1994; Stallings 1995).

Conclusions based on these assumptions are likely to be invalid where institutions are fragile, actors' preferences and strategies are uncertain, and social coalitions are unstable—that is, where assumptions derived from an established market economy do not prevail. Furthermore, the existing research efforts rely solely on objective measures of the economy, ignoring its subjective assessments (see, e.g. Furman and Stiglitz 1998; Lim 1998; Laurence 1999; Woo, Sachs, and Schwab 2000). Examining the subjective public dimensions of market reform is crucial, because they ultimately determine the success or failure of reform policies.

To fill these gaps, our analysis emphasizes two areas absent in the existing literature. First, unlike the existing literature that looks only at the objective dimension, our framework explores the perceptual dimension of market reforms and globalization. Our research adds rich empirical evidence from survey analyses and enables us to test prior theories about public attitudes regarding market reform and globalization in East Asia. Second, we believe that one of the most valuable aspects of this study is its comparison of Asian countries. This comparative approach allows us to better interpret public sentiments in any single nation and provides a valuable research tool for investigating the interaction of economic structures with public sentiments. In other words, by comparing China, Japan, Korea, Taiwan, and five other nations in the region, one can better interpret the findings in each nation and better understand the different forces affecting them all.

MEASUREMENT

We examine citizen support for the values underlying market reforms by analyzing the eighteen-country Asia–Europe Survey that was collected in October–November, 2000 by Nippon Research Center in Japan under the auspices of Takashi Inoguchi.[4] Of the eighteen countries surveyed, we selected the nine East Asian countries for analysis: China, Indonesia, Japan, Malaysia, the Philippines, Singapore, South Korea, Taiwan, and Thailand.

In their daily lives, citizens are exposed to the various forms of market policies without being aware of any academic theory. The neoliberal argument has two closely interrelated components of market reform—one more 'economic' and the other more 'political' (Chang 1999). The economic component is the recommendation for a wholesale liberalization, that is, 'getting the prices right'. The right prices, to the liberals, are prices that will prevail in totally unregulated (domestic and international) markets. Internationally, this means the opening up of trade and following the comparative advantage dictated by the country's resource endowments. On the domestic side, 'getting the prices right' means the freeing of product and factor market constraints. The political component of the neoliberal reform is depoliticization of the economic policymaking and implementation process. According to neoliberals, any political determination of economic outcome essentially leads either to social waste or to the dominance of minority interest over the majority interest. They argue, therefore, that any pursuit of self-interest that is not disciplined by market forces will lead to socially harmful results, making it necessary to depoliticize the economy. In their view, depoliticization occurs through the contraction of the state through deregulation.

Thus, in this study, market policies as a comprehensive procedure incorporates three different principles: an open market, a free market, and government deregulation. As the chapter appendix shows, the survey asked three pairs of questions to tap public attitudes to each of these principles. First, an open market emphasizes transactions with the rest of the world, including trade in goods and services, movements of capital, transfers of information and technical knowledge, and migration of labor. To measure the principle of open markets, the survey asked two questions: one about the freedom to import foreign goods, and the other about the freedom of foreigners to buy domestic land.

Second, a free market is contrasted with a planned economy, where one party may be ordered to buy or the other to sell. In a free market, neither the quantities traded, nor the price at which trade takes place, is controlled by third parties. Indeed, a free market is based on individual economic actors' freedom to buy and sell voluntarily. Thus, to measure the principle of a free market, the survey asked two separate questions: one on competition in the marketplace, and the other on business actors' economic freedom, as an incentive for making much profit.

Third, governmental deregulation demands the removal or relaxation of the government's intervention in economic activities. It enables the government to lower the costs of social services or to reduce its responsibility for economic activity. To measure the principle of deregulation, the survey asked two more questions: one about government responsibility for ensuring job security or social welfare, and the other about government intervention in economic problems.

We measure support for market policies among the Asian countries in four steps. The first three steps assess each principle or dimension of market reform—open market, free market, and deregulation. The last step measures overall support for neoliberal market policies. At the first step of measuring support for market reforms, we calculated the percentage of each of five different responses to each question for the entire sample of the nine Asian countries to identify a pattern of orientations in Asia as a whole. Next, to examine national differences in the general level of citizen support, we rescaled responses into three broader categories—negative, neutral, and positive. Finally, to measure support for each market principle as a whole among Asian countries, we combined the two rescaled items into a three-point index by counting the numbers of items to which respondents expressed promarket attitudes.

The development of a market-based economy occurs in varying degrees across the region. Therefore, we cannot assume that inexorable convergence is taking place; we expect to find divergence among attitudes toward the market across nations. Throughout East Asia, the public attitudes toward market policies are expected to follow separate courses.

THREE DIMENSIONS OF MARKET REFORM

Open Market

To tap support for open markets, the survey asked whether foreign imports should be allowed and whether foreigners should be allowed to buy domestic land. We present the combined nine-nation pattern of responses in the left-hand panel of Table 9.1 (the questions are listed in the appendix to this chapter). Only 27 percent of Asian respondents endorse the free trading of foreign goods in an open market, and nearly half of them (49 percent) hold negative views to foreign imports. A small minority support the right of foreigners to buy domestic land; less than one-fifth of Asians surveyed (23 percent) agreed with the statement that foreigners should be allowed to do so, and one-half of them (50 percent) disagreed. The rest of them neither agree nor disagree with foreign direct investment in domestic land.

Table 9.1. *Public attitudes toward market reform in Asia*

	Open market		Free market		Deregulation	
	Foreign imports	Foreigners buy domestic land	Competition	Economic freedom	Government for social welfare	Government intervention
Strongly agree(%)	5.1	4.8	37.5	17.4	0.8	1.9
Agree	22.0	19.8	48.6	35.9	2.9	6.4
Neither agree nor disagree	22.9	23.6	10.3	26.4	10.3	20.5
Disagree	31.5	28.9	2.7	15.4	44.6	46.8
Strongly disagree	18.5	22.9	0.9	4.9	41.4	24.4
Total %	100.0	100.0	100.0	100.0	100.0	100.0
Total (*N*)	(8,813)	(8,646)	(8,891)	(8,594)	(8,996)	(8,659)

Source: Asia–Europe Survey; all nine Asian nations are combined in this table.

The statistics clearly indicate that many Asians do not favor an open market; they seem to approve of the government controlling an open market by not allowing imports or foreigners buying land. However, the statistics do not indicate that all Asians are against all aspects of open market. Instead, our findings suggest that we look to see how these countries vary in their attitudes toward open markets. Table 9.2 reports the percentages of favorable attitudes in each country and compares mean scores on a three-point scale from −1 (no support) to 1 (support).[5]

First, there are differences in support for an open market across the nine countries. For example, much more than half of the population in Singapore (64 percent) favors foreign imports. Surprisingly, the percentage of Asians reporting a favorable attitude toward foreign imports is higher in China (42 percent) than in any other Asian country except Singapore. Opinions toward foreign investment also vary widely, from 36 percent in Japan to 14 percent in Thailand. Support for foreign imports and land investments are especially low in Thailand, Malaysia, South Korea, the Philippines, and Indonesia. Interestingly, all five of these countries endured similar experiences during the economic crisis of 1997. Therefore, we might reasonably conclude that these publics are cautious of foreign economic activity in their domestic markets because of the past economic crisis. For them, an open market may appear to invite dangerous economic situations without warning.

Second, even within a country, support varies depending on the kind of open market described. In Singapore, 32 percent support foreign investment in land, which is only half the number who approve foreign imports. Similarly, Koreans' support for foreigners purchasing domestic land (21 percent) is almost twice as high as support for foreign imports (14 percent).

To measure the overall support for an open market, we counted how many questions respondents answered favorably and formed a three-point index ranging from 0 (none of two questions) to 2 (both of them). All nine Asian countries score below the midpoint of 1 on the three-point scale rating an open market. The mean score of China is the highest at 0.7. These low numbers indicate that, although support for an open market in the region varies significantly from country to country, a majority of Asian countries do not welcome an open market.

Free Market

One of the major goals of market reform is to bring about significant improvements in society's response to free market, characterized by Adam Smith's 'invisible hand'. The survey tapped public attitude towards two basic free market principles—competition and economic freedom. One question asked for agreement with the statement that competition is good because it stimulates people to develop new ideas. The next question asked whether

TABLE 9.2. Favorable attitudes toward market reform by nation

	Open market					Free market					Deregulation				
	Imports		Foreigners to buy land		Overall support	Competition		Economic freedom		Overall support	Government irresponsibility		Government non-intervention		Overall support
	Percent	Mean	Percent	Mean	Mean	Percent	Mean	Percent	Mean	Mean	Percent	Mean	Percent	Mean	Mean score
China	42.1	0.0	30.5	−0.2	0.7	92.1	0.8	55.8	0.2	1.5	4.1	−0.8	4.6	−0.8	0.1
Indonesia	16.0	−0.4	16.0	−0.4	0.2	86.6	0.8	62.1	0.0	1.1	1.2	−0.9	5.0	−0.7	0.0
Japan	28.2	0.0	35.7	0.2	0.6	60.6	0.5	49.3	0.3	1.0	1.8	−0.7	14.2	−0.2	0.1
Korea	13.9	−0.5	21.5	−0.3	0.0	87.1	0.8	76.7	0.7	1.5	2.4	−0.8	20.3	−0.3	0.2
Malaysia	15.4	−0.5	15.4	−0.5	0.4	93.1	0.9	37.8	0.4	1.5	3.0	−0.8	7.1	−0.7	0.1
Philippines	20.0	−0.4	25.9	−0.3	0.5	84.8	0.7	55.9	0.1	1.3	3.0	−0.8	7.1	−0.7	0.1
Singapore	64.4	0.4	31.6	0.0	0.5	91.7	0.8	68.1	0.5	1.6	4.2	−0.8	7.4	−0.6	0.1
Taiwan	39.6	0.0	24.0	−0.2	0.5	88.9	0.8	39.0	0.0	1.2	2.4	−0.8	3.7	−0.8	0.1
Thailand	15.0	−0.6	14.0	−0.6	0.3	91.7	0.8	48.7	0.3	1.5	2.6	−0.8	7.8	−0.7	0.1
Asia	26.1	−0.2	22.5	−0.2	0.6	83.6	0.8	52.5	0.3	1.4	2.8	−0.8	7.8	−0.6	0.1

Source: Asia–Europe survey.

Note: Mean scores on items are based on a three-point recoded scale. Mean score on overall support are average of number of items the respondent supported (0) none to (2) both.

respondents agree that society is better off when businesses are free to make as much profit as they can (see appendix to this chapter).

The center panel in Table 9.1 shows the combined distributions for all nine Asian nations. It is clear that East Asians tend to support free-market principles. A large majority (86 percent) agrees with the principle of competition. This is consistent with the findings from the WVS across East Asia (see Chapter 8). Furthermore, more than half of these publics (51 percent) endorses the economic freedom to purse profits; however, those who do not endorse this freedom cannot be ignored, because they constitute 20 percent of the entire population in these nations. Consequently, we cannot claim that the principle of a free market has become a deep-rooted value in East Asia as a whole.

Table 9.2 reveals the national divergence of free-market orientations. A vast majority of the public endorses competition in Malaysia (93 percent), China (92 percent), Singapore (91 percent), and Thailand (91 percent). Even in China, most people support competition! This overwhelming support indicates that many Chinese favor free-market values over a planned economic system, which should facilitate the marketization reforms in China. However, Table 9.2 reports that the lowest level of support (61 percent) for competition is reported in Japan, although Japan is the most advanced country in East Asia.

Compared with support for competition, Asians are significantly less supportive of economic freedom. A minority in Malaysia (37 percent), Taiwan (39 percent), Thailand (48 percent), and Japan (49 percent) agree with the statement that businesses should be free to make as much profit as they can. In contrast, in Korea, where citizens favor an open market to the least extent, favorable orientations toward economic freedom is as high as 77 percent. This shows that even within a county, the level of public support for market reform significantly varies according to the particular sort of market reform measures in question.

When favorable responses toward competition and economic freedom are jointly taken into account, clear distinctions appear among the nine nations. The means of all nine countries score at or above the midpoint on the three-point scale rating free market. Japan has the lowest mean rating (1.0), while Singapore (1.6) has the highest, closely followed by China (1.5) and South Korea (1.5). Thus, we can say that popular support for a free market in East Asia is generally solid.

Deregulation

To tap public attitudes toward market policies concerning governmental deregulation, the survey asked two questions to determine whether the national government should have a smaller role regulating economic activity. The first question dealt with the government's responsibility for ensuring that everyone either has a job, or is provided with adequate social welfare. The second question asked about government intervention to deal with today's economic problems.

The right-hand columns of Table 9.1 show strong support for governmental regulation in Asia. A large majority (86 percent) hold a positive view of government responsibility. Moreover, 41 percent of Asians 'strongly disagree' with the government taking no responsibility for job security or social welfare. Only a tiny minority (3 percent) reports that government should not take responsibility for providing job security and social welfare. This suggests that most Asians believe that government has to take at least some responsibility for these economic issues. Again, these patterns are broadly consistent with the findings from the WVS, which Shin and Dalton report in Chapter 8. Similarly, a substantial majority (70 percent) of those surveyed embraces government intervention in economic problems. Only a very small minority of less than 2 percent strongly agrees with the government's nonintervention in their economy.

The nine Asian countries are very much alike in their responses to the deregulation questions (Table 9.2)—a pattern they did not exhibit with respect to the two other pairs of items measuring market reform. On the scale tapping support for government nonresponsibility, there is very little difference across these nations; supporters account for less than 5 percent of their populations. This suggests very little or no enthusiasm for an economic system that limits government responsibility for economic welfare.

At the same time, most Asian countries are more supportive of reducing government intervention in the economy than government responsibility for economic welfare. For example, in Japan, the percentage favoring the former is 14 percent, favoring the latter compared to 1 percent. Korea also reports a similar pattern. The percentage of Koreans agreeing with the former is 20 percent, and the percentage favoring the latter is 2 percent. These statistics indicate that Asian publics consider the help they can receive from government in the areas of job security and/or social services as being more valuable than the help they can receive from government intervention in national economic problems.

Table 9.2 compares levels of overall support for deregulation within each nation. Similar to the other two pairs of market reform, we created a three category index of support for government intervention ranging from 0 (neither item) to 2 (both items). A great majority of respondents (above 90 percent) in every country except Japan and Korea fell into the lowest category, favoring neither deregulation item. In contrast, the percentage of respondents who favor both items is as little as 1 percent in China and the Philippines, and 0 percent in Indonesia. Overall, these findings clearly indicate that East Asians remain strongly supportive of governmental intervention in the market. A significant majority still remembers their governments providing social services and wants their governments free to intervene for the purpose of curing economic hardships.

Overall Support for Market Reform

To what extent do East Asians embrace all three dimensions of market reform we have examined? To address this question, we combined all three pairs of questions into a three-point index ranging from a score of 0 (low support) to a score of 2 (high support for market reform).[6] Table 9.3 shows percentages of these index scores in the nine East Asian countries, and their means on this index.

As expected, there is a great deal of cross-national variation in the overall level of support for market reform. In Japan, a large majority of nearly two-thirds (63 percent) do not support market reform leading to an open market, a free market, and deregulation. Among a small minority of supporters (37 percent), less than one-tenth (8 percent) is highly supportive. Such reticence may explain the difficulties the Koizumi government has faced in instituting economic reforms in Japan. In contrast, more than half the population in every other East Asian country supports market reform either somewhat or highly. Six countries—Korea, Thailand, Malaysia, the Philippines, Taiwan, and Singapore—register a mean level of support above the midpoint (1.0) of the three-point index. These figures indicate that East Asians, in general, tend to support market reform, which is consistent with the general reformist trend of governments in the region.

TABLE 9.3. *Level of overall support for market reform value*

	Score Points				
	0	1	2	Total	Mean Score
China	35.6%	39.3%	25.0%	99.9%	0.9
Indonesia	40.4	44.1	15.5	100.0	0.8
Japan	63.1	28.8	8.1	100.0	0.5
Korea	28.0	37.0	35.0	100.0	1.1
Malaysia	28.7	32.6	38.7	100.0	1.1
Philippines	26.1	33.7	40.2	100.0	1.1
Singapore	33.5	31.3	35.2	100.0	1.0
Taiwan	33.0	34.4	32.5	99.9	1.0
Thailand	21.4	42.0	36.6	100.0	1.2

Source: Asia–Europe survey; all nine Asian nations are combined in this table.

Note: Table combined the six separate questions on support for market reform. See endnote 6 for the construction of this index.

DOES GLOBALIZATION PROMOTE SUPPORT FOR MARKET REFORM?

Thus far, we compared levels of popular support for market reform across the nine countries of East Asia. As a final step in our analysis, we examined whether support for globalization promotes support of neoliberal market policies. Globalization has become a lightning rod in the intellectual debate on market reform. To its critics, globalization means the dependence of national economies on an international economic regime and the exploitation of individual nations, economies, and their peoples. To its supporters, globalization offers the promise of improving living standards and the diffusion of liberal social norms.

Globalization affects people's daily lives in one way or another, but how they perceive its impact varies depending on which particular domains of their lives globalization forces are perceived to affect. To measure attitudes toward globalization, the Asia–Europe survey asked a battery of questions on whether various aspects of globalization have good or bad effects. Table 9.4 displays the distribution of responses for all nine Asian samples combined. In aggregation, about one-third of the Asian people think globalization in each of these areas has a 'good effect' and about one-tenth a 'bad effect' (see chapter appendix for question wording). By a substantial margin of good effect over bad effect, East Asians are more likely to think that the domains of job security, living standards, and consumer choice benefit from globalization. There are also positive balances for access to news and entertainment. The

TABLE 9.4. *Percentages expressing effects of globalization on life in Asia*

Globalization effect	Good effect	Bad effect	Neither good nor bad	No effect	Do not know	Total
What you can buy in the shops	36.2	11.1	32.0	15.8	4.9	100.0
The kind of food available in restaurants	32.3	11.1	31.6	19.2	5.8	100.0
The kind of people who live in neighborhood	27.0	10.0	35.9	21.0	6.0	99.9
Job security	30.5	16.6	27.7	16.5	8.7	100.0
More use of English among people	45.3	9.2	25.0	13.8	6.7	100.0
Your standard of living	37.7	10.3	32.1	15.3	4.5	99.9
Films and entertainment programs on TV	33.6	14.7	34.1	13.3	4.4	100.1
The kind of things reported in the news on TV	44.6	9.9	30.1	11.2	4.3	100.1

Source: Asia–Europe survey.

Pew Global Values Survey similarly found broad support for globalization across East Asia.[7] Our analyses of the Asia–Europe Survey also find significant cross-national variation in these sentiments; Malaysians, Filipinos, and Thais see the greatest benefits, and the Japanese the fewest benefits.[8]

From this prevailing pattern in favor of globalization, we expected that general sentiments toward globalization would influence sentiments toward market policies. If people saw the benefits of globalization, they might be more willing to accept marketization. We first created an index of globalization support from the questions in Table 9.4.[9] Next, we examined the bivariate relationship between views of globalization and orientations toward market principles (Table 9.5). The Pearson correlation coefficients for all nine Asian countries demonstrate that favorable orientations toward globalization are significantly correlated with support for market reforms (see the last column of Table 9.5). The magnitude of this positive relationship is the smallest in China and the largest in Japan.

At the same time, the relationship between globalization and market reform varies with the particular kind of its dimensions. The relationship between globalization and a free market, for example, is similar to the pattern of significant and positive relationships found between globalization and overall support for market reform. In all East Asian countries, their relationships are positive in direction and statistically significant in magnitude. In most of these countries, however, the relationships between globalization and opening domestic markets to foreigners are highly mixed in both direction as well as magnitude. Only in four of the nine countries—Japan, Taiwan, Singapore, and Thailand—are the two variables significantly and positively related to each other. The rest of the countries have neither positive

TABLE 9.5. *Correlations between public orientations for globalization and support for market reform*

Globalization	Open market	Free market	Deregulation	Overall market reforms
China	0.01	0.12*	−0.06	0.06**
Indonesia	0.03	0.21*	0.10*	0.20*
Japan	0.25*	0.20*	0.09*	0.29*
Korea	0.06	0.12*	0.05	0.13*
Malaysia	0.03	0.07**	0.04	0.08*
Philippines	0.00	0.23*	−0.02	0.15*
Singapore	0.08*	0.22*	0.00	0.17*
Taiwan	0.07**	0.14*	0.05	0.16*
Thailand	0.11*	0.14*	−0.05	0.15*

Source: Asia–Europe survey.

Note: Table entries are Pearson correlation coefficients; * significant at the 0.01 level (2-tailed) and ** significant at the 0.05 level (2-tailed).

nor significant relationship between globalization and support for an open market. In the case of deregulation, globalization has neither a significant nor positive relationship in seven of the nine East Asian countries. Only in Japan and Indonesia, the two variables have a positive relationship of statistical significance. In conclusion, the impact of support for globalization on support for market reforms is usually positive, but varies considerably in magnitude according to the types of market reforms.

ASIAN PUBLICS AND MARKET REFORM

According to convergence theories, economies in East Asia are converging toward systems sharing the same characteristics of laissez-faire economies through globalization and various market reforms. Nevertheless, our study shows that, contrary to convergence theories, people across countries continue to exhibit fundamental differences in their public economic values in spite of increasing international interdependence. No matter how the arguments for convergence are fashioned to accommodate similarities in international pressures and policy responses, differences continue to exist, even among countries such as those in East Asia that have similar cultural and regional backgrounds. Because national governments maintain distinct domestic politics that are generated from the orientations of ordinary citizens, and because political outcomes demonstrate such great variance, convergence does not necessarily follow unidimensional trends.

Conceptually, this chapter examines multiple dimensions of market principles: support for an open market, a free market, and deregulation among nations. Instead of a single pattern of market opinions, the survey findings differentiate between public support for each principle. This facilitates a more meaningful understanding of acceptance of market principles.

Substantively, popular support for free-market reform in East Asia is more solid than support for the other two market values. The statistics clearly indicate that many people in East Asia strongly hold beliefs and values associated with free-market principles—such as competition and economic freedom—while they do not tend to favor opening the market to foreigners. East Asians tend to oppose an open market, especially when it is viewed as being harmful for their lives in a nation-bounded society. They approve of the way in which the national government controls undesirable effects of the open market. Moreover, East Asians as a whole do not support the deregulation of governmental intervention in the economy. A significant majority of East Asians still remembers the positive results of government intervention in the authoritarian past. They insist that their government should be responsible for social services and intervene to mitigate economic hardships.

However, we cannot assume that all East Asians are against all aspects of market reform. In different countries, there are very different public orientations. Furthermore, even within individual countries, the level of public support for market reform significantly varies according to the sort of market reform in question. For example, in Korea, where attitudes toward an open market are the least favorable, the percentage of citizens with a positive view of economic freedom is the highest.

This chapter especially indirectly shows the relationship between political culture and economic support. No matter what the political backgrounds and/or government systems, the more optimistic economic expectation of the public, the more support for economic reform. One of the most interesting cases is China, one of the two remaining communist nations in the region. In China, supporters for competition outnumber nonsupporters by a substantial margin. More Chinese are promarket reformists than East Asians in any other country. Many of these same patterns were described in Chapter 8, in which the Chinese scored relatively high on economic individualism. This positivity toward markets may be overstated, as individuals might have responded to the recent economic gains of marketization as they look back on the antiquated communist system of the past. Still, the relative openness of the Chinese public toward market values suggests that widespread hesitancy will not be an impediment to further market reforms. This is similar to the pattern that apparently exists in Vietnam as well (see Pham and Pham in this volume).

As an interesting contrast, the Japanese economy has suffered through a decade of recession as well as the financial shock of the late 1997, yet we found that the Japanese public is the least supportive of market reforms of any of the nine Asian nations we studied. This might be because the Japanese economy is already more modernized than other East Asian systems, and Chapter 8 demonstrated that support for the capitalist structural principles of private ownership and free competition is high in Japan. However, recent economic history suggests that the need for substantial economic reform in Japan does exist. Our findings suggest that public resistance may be one reason why Prime Minister Koizumi has been so ineffectual in actually implementing reforms.

Public opinion in Korea and Taiwan seems is to fall between these two polar examples. In both countries, as in Japan, support for free markets is widespread across their respective population (66 percent in Korea and 59 percent in Taiwan). In sharp contrast, however, support for open markets and governmental deregulation is confined to the very small segments of the populations (2% in both countries). This particular pattern of asymmetric reactions to market reform accords with the mixed type of capitalism identified in Chapter 9. Since active governmental involvement in the economy figures prominently in this type of capitalism, the Koreans and Taiwanese, like the Japanese, are likely to oppose the reforming of the public sector while supporting that of the private sector of their national economy.

The survey findings also display broad support for globalization across East Asian publics, focusing on improving living conditions and opportunities. People see globalization improving their life chances, rather than the dependency and exploitation that antiglobalization forces claim. East Again, this suggests that reforms to engage East Asian economies in the international economic regime will not generate widespread public opposition. In addition, we examined the relationship between attachment to globalization and support for market principles. In all nine East Asian countries, the overall impact of globalization on market principles is usually in a positive direction, yet it varies considerably in magnitude among the different types of market reforms. Given our findings, we conclude that the course of globalization and market reforms in East Asia does not move in a common unidimensional direction, and globalization and market reforms are not uniformly accepted among the public in this region. Also, even if globalization promotes support for market principles, its impact on the support varies considerably, depending on the type of reform.

Is different support of market principles within a country a result of individual social status or national culture? Is the variance of East Asian countries' support for different market reforms reflecting different domestic economic situations? Is the relationship between globalization and market principles in the East Asian survey findings unique only for the East Asian region? These answers lie in the next step of our study. Hence, the next critical research problems facing the study of East Asian support for market economy and globalization are both analyzing domestic social factors in terms of support for market principles, and comparing East Asian data with European data, especially focusing which Eastern European countries experienced drastic market reforms.

APPENDIX: SURVEY QUESTIONS

The following items were used to create the three market indices and the globalization index analyzed in this chapter.

A. *Public Orientations Toward Open Market*

Q 208: Now, I have some statements here that people make from time to time. You might agree or disagree with them. Please tell me how much you agree or disagree with the following statements. Do you strongly agree, agree, neither agree nor disagree, disagree, or strongly disagree:

(a) (Japan) should limit the import of foreign products.
(b) Foreigners should not be allowed to buy land in (Japan).

B. Public Orientations Toward Free Market

Q 306: Now, I have some statements here that people make from time to time. Please tell me how much you agree or disagree with the following statements. Do you strongly agree, agree, neither agree nor disagree, disagree, or strongly disagree:

(a) Competition is good because it stimulates people to develop new ideas.
(b) Society is better off when businesses are free to make as much profit as they can.

C. Public Orientations Toward Deregulation

Q 306: Now, I have some statements here that people make from time to time. Please tell me how much you agree or disagree with the following statements. Do you strongly agree, agree, neither agree nor disagree, disagree, or strongly disagree:

(a) The government should take responsibility for ensuring that everyone either has a job or is provided with adequate social welfare.
(b) We need a lot of government intervention in order to deal with today's economic problems.

D. Public Orientations Toward Globalization

Q 301: It is said we now live in an age when all sorts of things (e.g. products, money, people, and information) move around the world much more than they used to. Please tell me whether this kind of movement has any effect on your own life in each of the following areas, and whether the overall effect has been a good thing or a bad thing.

(a) What you can buy in the shops.
(b) The kind of food that is available.
(c) The kind of people who live in your neighborhood/community.
(d) Job security.
(e) More use of the English language and English expressions among people in (Japan).
(f) Your standard of living.
(g) The films and entertainment programs available on television in (Japan).
(h) The kind of things that are reported in the news on television.

ENDNOTES

1 The "developmental state" theories argue that the state shapes the market and intervenes in the economy in order to promote economic development. In his book *MITI and the Japanese Miracle*, Johnson (1982) outlined Japan as a state-dominated economy—what he referred to

as the developmental state—arguing that the actions of Japan's Ministry of Industrial Trade and Industry (MITI) lay behind that country's dramatic ascent in industry after industry. The concept of the developmental state subsequently produced a vast array of literature, focusing primarily on East Asian industrialization (Deyo 1987; Amsden 1989; Wade 1990; Leftwich 1995; Maxfield 1997; Chan, Clark, and Lam 1998; Woo-Cumings 2000). The developmental state model has its conceptual origin on the Gerschenkron's classical historical analysis of economic development among pre-World War I European nations. Gerschenkron (1962) argues that the backwardness of late developers necessitated banks and state institutions to afford financial and technical prerequisites for fast development. Gerschenkron's framework is taken, among the developmental theorists, as appropriate for the study of twentieth-century Asia as it was for nineteenth-century European economic development.

2 According to Taylor (1997), the Washington Consensus is an amalgam of "long-standing IMF macroeconomic stabilizing policies, the World Bank's adoption of the market deregulation and supply-side economics, ideas in vogue in Washington early in the Reagan period, and London's deal for privatization public enterprise which crossed the Atlantic a few years later".

3 In a sense, this crisis resembles those that swept Latin American countries such as Chile, Argentine, and Uruguay in the early 1980s. In each of these nations, under pressure from the IMF, the government ignited currency and debt crisis by deregulating the economy without establishing an appropriate regulatory framework (Banuri 1991; Khanna and Palepu 2000). Mexico and Brazil, which also pursed economic liberalization, experienced currency crisis in 1994 and 1999, respectively (Fernandez Jiberto and Mommem 1996; Baer and Love 2001). After years of import substitution development strategies that relied heavily on extensive government intervention, all these countries liberalized by removing various controls on prices, trade barriers, and constraints on capital flows and privatizing state-owned firms, including financial service firms.

4 The project, from which this data originated, was called "Globalization and Political Culture of Democracies: 18-Society Survey in Asia and Europe", led by Takashi Inoguchi (Blondel and Inoguchi 2002). The authors are grateful to Inoguchi for his permission and support of the use of the data. The sample sizes for the surveys are as follows: China (n = 1002), Indonesia (n = 1011), Japan (n = 1129), South Korea (n = 1010), Malaysia (n = 1000), Philippines (n = 1000), Singapore (n = 1006), Taiwan (n = 1002), and Thailand (n = 1000). The interviews were conducted either by telephone or face-to-face.

5 The correlation coefficients between the six items are presented in the following tables. They are all significant at the 0.01 level.

	Imports	Buying land	Competition	Freedom	Gov. resp
Imports	—				
Buying land	0.33	—			
Competition	0.13	0.20	—		
Freedom	0.15	0.18	0.39	—	
Gov. resp.	0.13	0.23	0.34	0.28	—
Gov. interv.	0.11	0.12	0.27	0.24	0.31

The responses were rescaled into three broader categories ranging from negative (−1) through neutral (0) to positive (+1) by collapsing "disagree" and "strongly disagree" into a score of −1, "neither agree nor disagree" into 0, and "strongly agree", and "agree" into 1. A score of −1 means the absence of support, and a score of 1 means support

6 To measure the level of overall support for market reform, positive responses to all three pairs of questions were summed into a seven-point index with scores ranging from a low of 0 (positive response to no questions, meaning no support for market reform) to a high of 6

(positive response to all six questions, meaning full support for market reform). Then, it was collapsed into a three-point index by trichotomizing the original scores (0, 1, 2=0; 3, 4=1; 5, 6, 7=2).

7 The Pew (2003: 71) survey asked about the effect of globalization on the nation. The percentage who thought that globalization had a good effect was: China 76 percent; Indonesia 79 percent; Japan 53 percent; Korea 84 percent; the Philippines 63 percent; and Vietnam 79 percent.

8 We created an index of the number of items in Table 9.4 that were seen as a benefit in each nation, and the mean scores follow: China 3.6; Japan 2.1; Korea 4.2; Indonesia 3.2; Malaysia 4.4; the Philippines 4.4; Singapore 3.9; Taiwan 4.0; and Thailand 4.4.

9 The globalization index is a count of the number of items in Table 9.4 that were seen as having a good effect. See endnote 8 for the national mean scores on this index.

10

Risk Avoidance and Economic Value Orientation: Functioning of Postmaterialist Values in the Pacific Rim Countries[1]

Ken'ichi Ikeda and Tetsuro Kobayashi

Ronald Inglehart (1990, 1997) coined the term "postmaterialists" to explain the value changes in postindustrial societies. Among its multiple effects, Inglehart argued that postmaterialism influenced orientations toward the economic system and economic policy. However, postmaterialism's influence on economic orientation needs to be reconsidered by analyzing the separate impact of risk avoidance, because risk avoidance is a potentially powerful source of resistance to taking risks in the market economy. In this chapter, we examine whether risk avoidance and postmaterialism have independent or interactive impacts on the support for the market economy, thereby shaping the developmental pattern in East Asia.

A number of recent studies have claimed that Japan and other East Asian societies are hesitant to take social or economic risks (Hofstede 1991, 2001; Suginoo 2001; Ochi 2003). These scholars suggest that these sentiments condition public support for market competition. These sentiments also potentially affect popular support for economic reforms, such as those debated following the East Asian financial crisis of the 1990s. Moreover, risk avoidance may attenuate the postmaterial value change that Inglehart demonstrated as occurring in Western democracies (Inglehart 1977, 1990; Inglehart and Welzel in this volume).

We test these theses by comparing public opinion across a set of Pacific Rim countries using the WVS data from 2000 to 2001. The results reveal an independent negative effect on having a market economy orientation from risk avoidance. Although we test for cultural difference throughout the analyses, there is no indication of a difference between East and West, suggesting the generalizabilty of the findings across the Pacific Ocean.

POSTMATERIALISM AND RISK AVOIDANCE

Postmaterialism now has an almost thirty year history of analysis. It started from an epistemological question on the transformation of social values in West European countries after World War II, and has provided an important perspective to explain value change as well as the impact of these new values on social life and political behavior. Inglehart (1977) first examined the relationship between economic development and equality of income in developing and advanced nations, and revealed that equality is emphasized more in advanced industrial nations. At the same time, Inglehart found that the motivations for income equality wither after achieving a certain level of parity. Leveling meant the weakening of the political priority for economic redistribution. In this situation, the new "postmaterialist values" overtake the older "materialist values" in societal importance.

As compared to materialists, postmaterialists are supposed to have a greater tendency to pursue self-actualization, which is the highest level in Maslow's stratification theory of human need. As the more basic needs, such as survival and security, are fulfilled, thanks to the fruits of economic development, postmaterialists have more say in politics and greater political participation. Although political participation is high, the decreased attention to economic equalization weakens the push for redistributive policies, and often makes it a negative correlation (e.g. Figure 1.9 in Inglehart (1990); Granato, Inglehart, and Leblang (1996)).

Although this stream of research was very influential and stimulating, it gradually became clear that social values are multifaceted. Advanced industrial societies do not necessarily change in a linear direction from materialist to postmaterialist. For example, in a debate by Inglehart (1987) and Flanagan (1987), the latter showed that authoritarian–libertarian values are an additional value dimension to the materialist–postmaterialist dimension. In addition, by analyzing survey data from Tokyo in late 1980s, other researchers discovered that postmaterialist values have two different orientations: private-oriented versus publicly-oriented postmaterialism (Shakai-keizai Kokumin-kaigi 1988). Self-actualization through publicly-oriented postmaterialism facilitates social participation, whereas privately-oriented postmaterialism seems to restrain civic engagement by creating a more private or consumer-centered life. Private self-actualization through, for instance, filling one's private life with consumer goods or consummatory experience, may make one feel lively, content, and that one is pursuing one's own goal, but will not inspire potentially dangerous political action. Thus, a private orientation in postmaterialist values may not facilitate participation or support for democratic attitudes. If a private or consumer-centered life has higher priority, citizens are less likely to be attentive to the political or public sphere.

Norris and Inglehart (2003) also studied this topic when they investigated—based on Huntington's clash of civilization arguments—whether Islamic values contradicted democratic or liberal social attitudes. They showed that democratic attitudes are similar as economic development increases, but the liberal social attitudes—such as approval of gender equality, homosexuality, abortion, and divorce—are different.

A second potential qualifying factor for postmaterialism is the impact of collectivism. Collectivistic cultures may limit postmaterialist values, as self-actualization implies individual freedom of value expression. This individualism versus collectivism dimension was one of several dimensions of cultural differentiation that emerged from Hofstede's cross-national study of values (1991, 2001). The dimension received a great deal of attention in cross-cultural psychology, and through a review by Marcus and Kitayama (1991), it became a typical logic in explaining East–West differences in orientations toward markets and the economy. While Western publics presumably are individualist, the Asian values thesis presumes collectivism in East Asia (also see chapter by Dalton and Ong in this volume).

However, to make matters more complicated, this East–West distinction in individualism/collectivism has not been empirically supported despite its perceived importance. An extensive meta-analysis showed that there is no systematic evidence of collectivism in Asia except in Chinese subjects (Oyserman, Coon, and Kemmelmeier 2002; see critical review in Matsumoto (1999)). In addition, Takano and Osaka (1999) clearly showed the lack of empirical evidence of Japanese "collectivism" except in sporadic observations and essays. Yamagishi also argued, and experimentally demonstrated through a prisoner's dilemma game, that both in Japan and the USA, collectivism does not reflect the mechanism of mind or mental tendency, but instead is the outcome created by institutional or group constraints (Yamagishi, Cook, and Watabe 1998; Yamagishi 1999).

Moreover, hybridization of cultures in many regions in the world should be more noticeable in terms of cultural differentiation, as the phenomenon refers to the values that infiltrate across national borders and ethnic differences (Herman and Kempen 1998). This hybridity promotes a cultural mixture as well as new cultural identities. More importantly, this process may undermine the basic assumptions of cross-cultural psychology that posits distinct national cultures. Successful experiences by Japanese-Western style education after World War II would be an earlier example of hybridization, which clearly attenuated the traditional values in Japan. In this Western-style education, its formal tenet publicly and effectively advocated an independent, nonauthoritarian, and democratic human being as a model civilized citizen, which had a far-reaching effect in socializing subsequent Japanese generations.

In opposition to this theory, some scholars argue that the Japanese educational system institutionally promoted "collectivistic features" by stressing rule and obedience even after the war. However, the formal signboard of education stressed quite the opposite, resulting in the slow but steady unsettling of the base of traditional culture. As far as the education of democracy concerns, Ikeda and Kohno (forthcoming) clearly showed this effect; there were unambiguous generational differences in support for democratic values. Japanese who were educated before World War II (over 70 years old) showed less support for democratic values than among younger generations. The old demonstrated less authoritarian regime rejection, lesser support for liberal democracy, and lesser inclination to conceptualize democracy in terms of social equality and justice.

Thus, in order to investigate the impact of postmaterialism on economic value orientation, we are naturally led to examine some other aspect of the cultural difference framework typical to collectivism versus individualism. Out of the value dimensions analyzed by Hofstede, we focus on uncertainty avoidance related to risk avoidance. The main reason comes from Japanese experiences. In Hofstede's dimension (1991) of uncertainty orientation, Japan was the seventh highest in uncertainty avoidance out of the fifty-three countries he studied. Considerable evidence endorses the high tendency of the Japanese (and possibly other Asians) to avoid uncertainty, including risk avoidance.

These sentiments have potential implications for marketization processes in East Asia. After the collapse of the so called "bubble economy" in the late 1980s, Japan experienced one of the worst and longest economic recessions in the late 1990s. Many people lost a positive image of Japan, and heated debates erupted over what type of societal model should be used for national reformation, as well as what kind of values should be emphasized, both of which have no conclusion as of 2005. This was not coincident with the realization of postmaterialist society. The same phenomenon did not happen in some other highly industrialized countries.

One of the well-received arguments was that Japan should move toward a more risk tolerant country (Human Studies 2001). The current delays in administrative reform, national financial renovation, and innovations in private sectors presumably demonstrated persistent risk avoidance tendencies. Indeed, much evidence shows that the Japanese are highly averse to risk. The Bank of Japan (Ochi 2003) compared the composition of individual monetary assets between Japan and the USA, and they discovered that the Japanese have a higher preference for safer assets, that is, Japanese are highly averse to risk. In addition, Suginoo (2001) analyzed comparative surveys among Japan, the USA, China, Korea, Thai, and Singapore, and found that preferences for a "salary based on ability and capability" are the lowest in Japan. He then showed that the option for having "hope of opening a shop by one's own" is least chosen in Japan, which further reveals that the Japanese emphasize safety.

Yet more evidence comes from an e-Bay auction study among Japan, Germany, and the USA (Vishwanath 2003). Generally, an online auction is a game with uncertain information, and this uncertainty is causally related to the amount of auction bidding. By comparing auctions for laptop computers, Vishwanath found that Japanese online bidding behavior is quite different between the conditions of when there is much information presented and when there is insufficient information (for instance, no photographs of the auctioned item). The Japanese were less likely to bid in the latter ambiguous situation compared to the situation when more information was given, and the difference is greater in Japan than in the USA or Germany.

These findings demonstrate a seemingly cultural factor that may explain behavioral differences in attitudes toward competition and other market economy orientations. At the same time, there is an apparent diversity in uncertainty avoidance across Asian nations. In the scores of uncertainty avoidance by Hofstede (1991), Japan comes 7th, Korea 16th, Canada 41st, the USA 43rd, the Philippines 44th, Hong Kong 49th, and Singapore 53rd (last in the 53 countries studied). Asian countries have clear diversity in terms of the rank. This enables us to take an alternative approach to studying Occidental versus Oriental differences, which may display variations of risk avoidance across nations in each region. For instance, Singapore has moved more aggressively than most of East Asia to become engaged in the international economy. In addition, when faced with an economic crisis in 1997, Korea dared to enforce far more fundamental reforms than Japan and accepted high risk and high uncertainty course of changes. Although this causes doubt in Hofstede's ranking because of Korea's high uncertainty avoidance rank, it still underscores the relevance of risk avoidance to marketization.

Considering this book's focus on cross-national values in Asia, this chapter examines the interplay of postmaterial values and risk avoidance tendencies. Of course, uncertainty avoidance and risk avoidance are conceptually different. However, as explained below, they are deeply intertwined. In addition, the measurement adopted below is more relevant to risk avoidance. As we have seen, previous research did not directly mention any relationship between risk avoidance and economic growth; nevertheless, it is worth analyzing because of the strong concern on the decelerating role of risk avoidance on development in postindustrial societies.

In addition, Inglehart (1977:55) suggested that risk-avoidance tendency may not be compatible with postmaterialism; the percentage of postmaterialists who avoid risks is less than among materialists. Hofstede (1991: 125) also pointed out that those who have high security needs have a higher uncertainty avoidant tendency; that is, risk avoidance and postmaterialism possibly have a negative correlation. However, risk/uncertainty avoidance is not necessarily inherent in materialist values, and there is no logical connection that having postmaterialist value weakens risk avoidance. Postmaterialists pursue self-actualization, which does not always motivate people to innovate by risking advocacy, such as trying to have one's say in politics. This was one of the implications from the discovery of private-oriented postmaterialism.

Risk avoidance, more or less, appears to be a cultural value that differs by nation. If so, an interaction between postmaterialism and risk avoidance is important because it may contradict the universality of postmaterialism's impact on politics and economic orientation, and has not been thoroughly investigated. Even if risk avoidance does not differ by nation, the possibility of interaction may reveal a conditional nature of postmaterialist value influence. Taking cultural hybridization into, consideration the dimension of risk avoidance itself could also be influenced by cultural transformation in the latter half of the twentieth century. Thus, the analyses in this chapter will not be on a country-by-country comparison (even though the Japanese are conspicuous in their high average of risk aversion). Instead, we will conduct multilevel analyses; that is, individual and national level comparisons simultaneously. We suppose that in each country there are two types of people: risk avoidant and risk tolerant; however, at the same time, we examine whether there is any systematic national difference. The present study differs from the previous Asian values study by focusing on risk avoidance, which is underinvestigated despite its importance being spotlighted in the early cross-cultural studies.[2] We test whether postmaterialist values interact with risk avoidance to influence economic orientation.

THE CONSEQUENCES OF POSTMATERIALISM

This chapter examines the relationship between postmaterialism and two dependent variables that are broadly linked to the postmaterial value change: economic value orientation and achievement motivation. In part, we want to examine the impact of postmaterialism across the nations of the Pacific Rim. More fundamentally, however, we want to test whether these widely postulated relationships are dependent on another cultural trait—risk avoidance—that would make the impact of postmaterialism conditional on other cultural factors.

Postmaterialism and Economic Values

According to the logic of postmaterialism, countries with a high percentage of postmaterialists should have relatively low priority on economic growth. In the last three decades, however, despite the increase of postmaterialism (Inglehart and Welzel 2005, and in this volume), countries in Western Europe, North America, and Oceania, as well as Japan, recorded continuing

GNP growth greater than the world average (Western Europe 155 percent, the USA and Oceania 162 percent, and Japan 178 percent as compared with the world average 139 percent between 1973 and 1998).[3] Although thirty years have passed since the central role of postmaterialist values was established in advanced industrialized societies, growth is not necessarily in gridlock.

The economic growth in the last decades of the twentieth century may be attributable to a late harvest from the previous materialistic endeavors before the 1970s. Perhaps an institutionalized built-in mechanism of economy established in the materialist era is still a powerful engine for growth? Alternatively, do some economic sectors with a high percentage of materialist-oriented people separately push growth as a whole? These possible explanations seem improbable. The IT economic sectors that currently accelerate growth—including the Internet and globalization—came well after the 1970s. In addition, if a decrease of materialism diminishes growth, the economic growth rate should decline as the population of postmaterialists increases. Actually, it seems not to be the case in many countries. In Japan, for example, despite the economic stagnation of the 1990s, the country still grew substantially between 1973 and 1998. However, the level of materialism in Japan seems not to have changed (it should have decreased), and this is not consistent with the postmaterialist argument.[4]

Moreover, it is improbable that postmaterialists did not contribute to the economic growth. Many postmaterialists are oriented toward an affluent consumer life and thus contribute to the development of consumer marketing. Although postmaterialist values deemphasized the movement towards income equality, the change did not logically nor necessarily decrease the level of economic achievement itself.

Therefore, we need to reconsider the relationship between postmaterialism, economic growth, and support for a market economy. Here, we examine the impact of postmaterialism and risk avoidance on economic value orientations.

RISK AVOIDANCE, POSTMATERIALISM, AND ECONOMIC ORIENTATIONS

In his early work, Inglehart (1977) suggests that postmaterialist values decrease economic orientations emphasizing market values and competition. Indeed, the definition of postmaterialism involves an emphasis on noneconomic and quality-of-life goals over economic growth, economic security, and many of the values of a market economy. However, given that postmaterialism and economic growth actually coexist, as was seen in the previous section, we need a theory that explains this relationship. We have two possible models.

The first hypothesis suggests that risk avoidance and postmaterialism independently influence economic value orientation (Model 1);

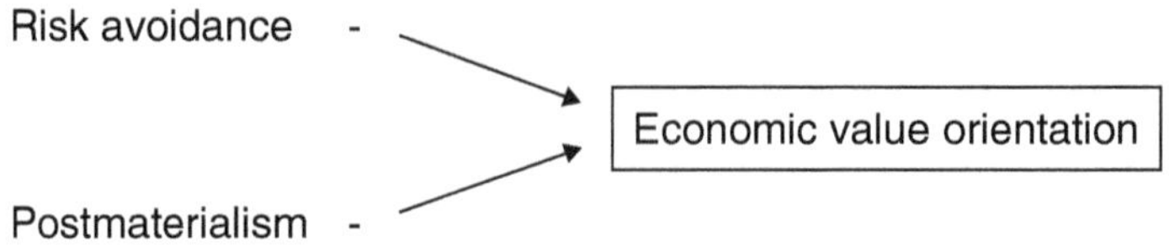

As for the effect of postmaterialism, we know that affluent postmaterialist societies do not emphasize economic achievement, thus producing a negative relationship. In addition, the more risk avoidant individuals are, the more they should resist a competitive economy. The economic value orientation is naturally a positive function of risk taking, that is, a reverse of the risk avoidance tendency, because the basic logic of the orientation implies risk-taking by emphasizing self-help, competitive free-market values. This logic is similar to the empirical criticism of the Japanese risk avoidance discussed above. We do not suppose an interaction of both of the independent variables, because postmaterialism is not always negatively related with risk avoidance.

This line of reasoning implies that where the tendency of risk avoidance is low enough (i.e. there is risk-taking), postmaterialism and economic growth can coexist. This relationship can be shown as in Figure 10.1, which depicts the Model 1; the point A where postmaterialist value (PM) is high and risk avoidance low is not lower in terms of economic value orientation as compared to point B, where the score is low in postmaterialism and high in risk avoidance. This may explain why the societies with high postmaterialist values still may maintain high economic value orientation. One possibility is that when the postmaterialists become dominant, at the same time the low risk-avoidant population increases, although all the people with high

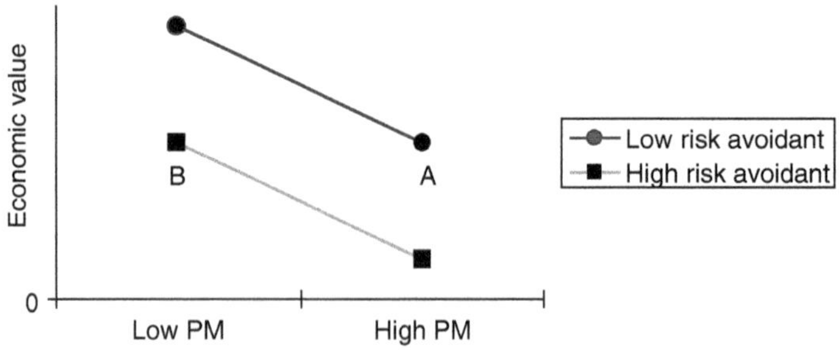

FIGURE 10.1. Hypothetical model of the impact of postmaterialism and risk avoidance on economic values

postmaterialist scores are not always at A, and all the people with low postmaterialist scores are not always at B.

The second model assumes a mediating role of achievement motivation on economic value orientations. It assumes an interaction of risk avoidance and postmaterialist values on the achievement motivation as outlined in Model 2:

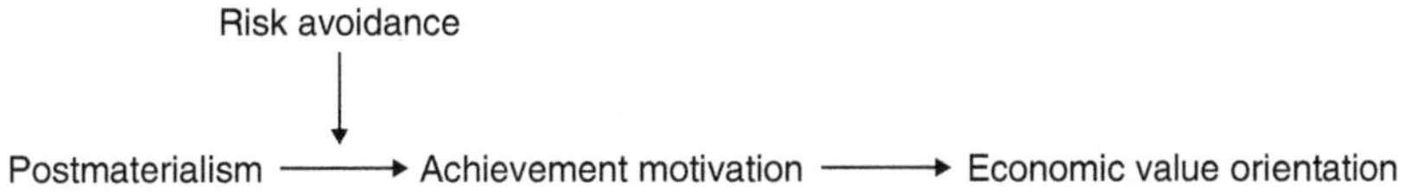

For instance, Granato, Inglehart, and Leblang's aggregate data analysis (1996) found a positive relationship between achievement motivation and economic growth. Based on this, the present model supposes that the same logical structure also applies to the individual.

The model also predicts an interaction effect of risk avoidance on achievement motivation. Respondents with postmaterialist values and low risk avoidance are more likely to have high achievement motivation than high risk avoiders. This model implies that although postmaterialist values presuppose higher achievement motivation to pursue self-actualization, this presumption itself may not be compatible with risk avoidance. High achievement motivation often requires extensive personal effort, as well as some risky choices, to pursue goals that have a higher possibility of failure or more unpredictable results. Consequently, those who have high risk avoidance would not pursue higher goals, and consequently escape chances for success. For those who have a high risk avoidance tendencies the positive relationship between postmaterialist values and high achievement motivation does not exist, and for those who have a low risk avoidance orientation, the relationship is positive.

ANALYTIC MODEL AND VARIABLES

Risk Avoidance

One of our first tasks is to measure risk avoidance with the data from the WVS (see Appendix A for information on the surveys in the project). Yamamoto (2001) contended that risk avoidance has two value elements. The first value relates to potential consequence with negative values such as loss or pain, and the second value relates to tolerance on uncertainty of the results. The latter is clearly equivalent to the major core of uncertainty avoidance. From this viewpoint, measuring risk avoidance approximates measuring uncertainty avoidance, which is a part of the concept. Hofstede (2001: 148) insisted on the distinction between uncertainty avoidance and risk avoidance, and wrote "more than toward an escape from risk, uncertainty avoidance leads to an escape from ambiguity". However, in his measurement of uncertainty avoidance and in many of his examples, there is a clear element of risk avoidance.

More concretely in this study, we partially adopt Hofstede's idea on uncertainty avoidance and try to create a measurement of risk avoidance items using stability of like career, which is a part of his measurement.[5] From the WVS 1999–2002, we identified a question that seemed appropriate as an *index of risk avoidance* (also see methodological appendix). The question asked respondents: "Now I would like to ask you something about the things which would seem to you, personally, most important if you were looking for a job. Here are some of the things many people take into account in relation to their work. Regardless of whether you're actually looking for a job, which one would you personally place first if you were looking for a job?" A follow-up probe asked: "(and) what would be your second choice?" In both of these questions, when the respondents chose either "a good income so that you do not have any worries about money" or "a safe job with no risk of closing down or unemployment", we defined these responses as indicating a preference for the stability of a job, and as a part of risk avoidance. This indicator is not only related to concerns over economic aspects of risk/uncertainty avoidance, but also to a more general aspect of risk/uncertainty avoidance, because the items are measured under a fictitious situation of career choice, which likely reflects value orientation free from real-life constraints.

Therefore, we suggest this criterion has both risk avoidance and uncertainty avoidance (at least a substantial part of it). We see no serious conceptual problem in the analyses below, as long as the dependent variables are economic orientations, because they are more closely tied to risks than uncertainty.

Postmaterialist Values

Our second major independent variable is *postmaterial values*. We used the twelve-item postmaterialist values scale. The respondents were presented with twelve different political goals and selected six items from this list. Half of these items are materialist goals, five are postmaterialist goals, and one has a mixed value meaning. The index counts the number of items selected from the five postmaterial choices in this list (Inglehart 1977; also see Appendix B of this volume).

In addition, as demographic control variables, we select gender, age, education, and income to control for possible spurious effects in these models.

Achievement Motivation

A measurement of *achievement motivation* comes from Granato, Inglehart, and Leblang (1996). It combines four variables: sum of thrift, determination, religious faith (reverse), and obedience (reverse) in response to a question on which values children should be encouraged to learn.

Economic Value Orientation

For the dependent variables, we have two measures of economic orientation (also see Appendix B; and Chapter 8). The *Economic Liberalism Index* is based on a pair of questions that underlie a market-oriented economy: private industry should be encouraged, and economic competition is a positive trait. The *Economic Individualism Index* combines a second pair of items: individual responsibility for one's welfare, and the acceptance of income inequality. We created an additive index of *Economic Value Orientation* from these two pairs in order to tap the broad value orientations that underlie a capitalist market economy, and thus, the marketization process in Asia.

The Analytic Model

For the analysis, we test two models. For Model 1, the dependent variable is the economic value orientation, and the independent variables are risk avoidance, postmaterialist values, and demographics. For Model 2, the dependent variable is the achievement motivation, and the independent variables are risk avoidance, postmaterialist values, interaction term of these two variables, and demographics. We used the WVS 1999–2002 data from the set of Pacific Rim nations that included all the relevant questions: the USA, Canada, Japan, Korea, China, the Philippines, Vietnam, and Singapore.

In order to estimate the effect of individual and cultural differences (here by national differences), our analytic approach uses hierarchical linear modeling (HLM).[6] HLM is useful in investigating data that have a hierarchical structure, especially when examining the interaction effects between the variables at the national and individual levels. For example, we can investigate whether the national factors, such as political and economic institutions, influence individual processes of behavior and psychology. We may find the relationships as in Model 1 or Model 2 at the individual level, but we may also observe large variations in these effects at the national level; for instance, the effect of postmaterialism differs from nation by nation, which can be explained by GNP or East–West dichotomy, etc. HLM is a statistical tool to differentially elucidate these two levels of effects. We analyze individual level data at the level 1, and at the same time, we estimate the level 2 effect of national differences. At level 2, we estimate any difference between the East and the West by introducing a dummy variable called West, which is mostly emphasized when focusing on the national comparisons.

Level 1 analysis At level 1, the dependent variables are economic value orientations and achievement motivation. The independent variables and control variables are postmaterialist values, risk avoidance, and demographic variables.

Level 2 analysis At level 2, HLM analyzes the national difference in the relationship found in the level 1 analyses. We also use an East–West variable, which may affect the variances in the slope of interaction term of postmaterialism and risk avoidance. That is, to analyze the determinant of coefficient of the interaction at level 2. This can be represented by the following equation:

$$B=G1+G2*(WEST)+U1$$

B;	coefficient of interaction term at level 1
G1;	intercept predicting B at level 1
WEST;	East versus West dummy; 1 representing West
G2;	coefficient for WEST
U1;	residual term in predicting B.

If we find a large U1 and no effect of G2, we conclude that the East versus West difference does not explain the difference between the nations. We may conclude that an other variable other than WEST could explain the national differences, which we will not try to identify in this chapter as it is beyond the current reach.

Basic Data Analysis

As a first step in the analyses, Figure 10.2 shows the mean score (and confidence intervals) for risk avoidance by nation. The result is somewhat inconsistent with Hofstede's data. According to Hofstede, Japan and Korea should have higher values of risk avoidance, whereas the Chinese should score lower. However, the WVS data show that the Japanese express unexpectedly low-risk avoidance tendencies, as low as Americans and Canadians. The Chinese come next, which was somewhat expected. Koreans show a high score, as was also expected from Hofstede's findings, but Filipinos and Singaporeans also scored unexpectedly high.[7]

Part of the reason of these irregularities may come from methodological differences; our index is composed of job choice-related questions, which can be strongly influenced by the current economic conditions or job market situations of the given country. Alternatively, patterns may have changed between Hofstede's analyses in the late 1960s and early 1970s, compared to the WVS data from 2000 to 2001. During this time, large economic and political upheavals, as well as huge value changes or hybridization of cultures, possibly occurred in East and Southeast Asia (e.g. China, Korea, Japan, and Vietnam).[8] In addition, Hofstede's respondents are IBM workers, whereas WVS respondents are a representative population sample of each

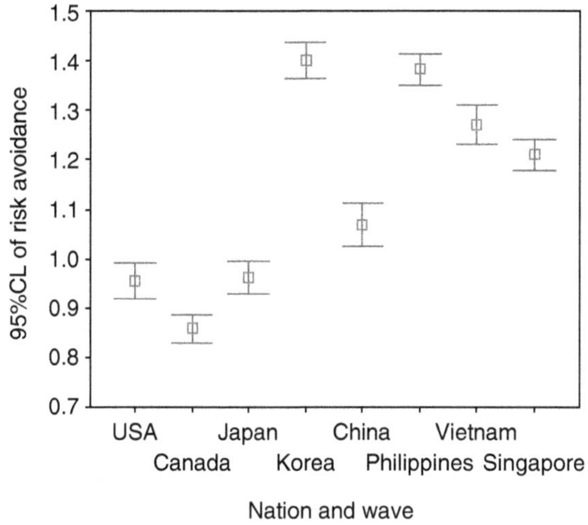

FIGURE 10.2. Risk avoidance by Pacific Rim nations

nation.[9] Lastly, the ranks of countries are not an essential part of analysis, since we focus on relationships within nations.

We detected a weak negative bivariate relationship between risk avoidance and postmaterialist values across the countries (values are around −0.11 with no large fluctuation). Hence, these variables are relatively independent; that is, those who are materialist are not necessarily those who score high regarding risk avoidance. This reflects our contention that risk-taking is not logically connected with postmaterialist values.[10]

Our other central variables are economic value orientations and achievement motivation (Table 10.1). The left half of Table 10.1 indicates that economic value orientations are relatively high in the USA, Canada, Japan, and Vietnam, while Korea is low (also see Chapter 8). This result somewhat contradicts the prediction theoretically derived from discussion of postmaterialism that highly developed countries like the USA, Canada, and Japan still favor the values underlying a materialist capitalist economy. This result is also inconsistent with the simple division of Eastern and Western culture. Japan and Korea are in the same East Asian culture, and have remarkably different tendencies in terms of their economic values.

From the right half of Table 10.1, Japan and Korea have relatively high mean scores on achievement motivation, while the USA, the Philippines, and Singapore have relatively low scores. This result does not correspond with the traditional notion that Japan is highly risk avoidant nation, if the motivation becomes high solely with a condition of high risk-taking. Perhaps the economic dislocation of the past decade has shifted these motivations.

TABLE 10.1. *Economic orientations by Pacific Rim countries*

	Economic value orientation		Achievement motivation	
	Mean	SD	Mean	SD
USA	26.451	5.905	−0.183	1.061
Canada	24.941	5.547	0.117	1.033
Japan	24.793	4.376	1.062	0.716
Korea	21.752	4.934	0.756	0.976
China	23.723	6.186	0.089	0.286
Philippines	22.702	5.225	−0.213	1.034
Vietnam	24.855	6.730	0.331	0.962
Singapore	24.157	5.117	−0.187	1.099

TABLE 10.2. *Bivariate correlations among the main variables*

		Postmaterialist value	Risk avoidance	Economic value orientation
	Risk avoidance	−0.18		
USA	Economic value orientation	−0.12	−0.09	
	Achievement motivation	0.10	−0.02	−0.08
	Risk avoidance	−0.16		
Canada	Economic value orientation	−0.13	−0.01	
	Achievement motivation	0.11	−0.01	0.02
	Risk avoidance	−0.18		
Japan	Economic value orientation	0.01	−0.04	
	Achievement motivation	−0.09	0.07	−0.02
	Risk avoidance	−0.19		
Korea	Economic value orientation	0.00	−0.03	
	Achievement motivation	−0.04	0.12	0.01
	Risk avoidance	−0.17		
China	Economic value orientation	0.06	−0.10	
	Achievement motivation	0.04	0.01	−0.08
	Risk avoidance	−0.08		
Philippines	Economic value orientation	−0.04	−0.01	
	Achievement motivation	−0.06	0.06	0.03
	Risk avoidance	−0.14		
Vietnam	Economic value orientation	−0.03	0.03	
	Achievement motivation	0.02	−0.01	0.02
	Risk avoidance	−0.21		
Singapore	Economic value orientation	0.07	−0.14	
	Achievement motivation	0.07	−0.09	0.10

The next step in our analysis examines the correlations of postmaterialist values, risk avoidance, economic value orientation, and achievement motivation for each country (Table 10.2). Postmaterialist values and economic value orientations are negatively correlated in the USA (−0.12) and Canada (−0.13). This indicates that postmaterialists are skeptical of market economy values in these nations, which is consistent with the postmaterialist critique of these economy systems. However, a consistent pattern is hard to observe across our set of East Asian nations. All these correlations are weak in East Asia, and the strongest relationships are in China (0.06) and Singapore (0.07), which suggests that postmaterialists are slightly more promarket in these nations. In addition, postmaterialist values and achievement motivation are positively correlated in the USA and Canada, but no systematic correlation is apparent across East Asia. Both of these results suggest that the nature or influence of postmaterial values is different outside the Western context.

In contrast, as was expected, risk avoidance and economic value orientations have weak negative correlations, except for a small positive correlation found in Vietnam. This means that people who hedge risky choices are less likely to accept economic competition and the values underlying a capitalist market economy. This reflects the very nature of a capitalist market economy with its Darwinian overtones. The correlations between risk avoidance and achievement motivation are less consistent than those with economic value orientation. Positive correlations in Japan and Korea are somewhat unexpected, and this may mean that even risk avoidant individuals are likely to have high achievement motivation, such as motivation to climb a fixed ladder of social stratification in these countries.

Finally, economic value orientation and achievement motivation are not correlated strongly. This point is not compatible with Inglehart's aggregate data mentioned above, although this is not an essential part of our model, which focuses on risk avoidance and postmaterialist values. Moreover, this is inconsistent with a Weberian image of the value bases of a market economy. These patterns suggest that the basis of economic values in East Asia lie elsewhere.

MULTIVARIATE ANALYSES OF ECONOMIC ORIENTATIONS

The final step in our research is a multivariate analysis predicting economic value orientations and achievement motivation. The HLM tests of Models 1 and 2 are shown in Table 10.3, which pools cases for all the nations in our set (the results for achievement motivation omits Chinese data because of missing variables).[11]

Our model of economic value orientations is shown in the left half of Table 10.3. Both postmaterialist values and risk avoidance have significant negative effects after controlling for the demographic variables—as posited by Model 1 above. Model 1 did not hypothesize an interaction between postmaterialism and risk avoidance. In order to verify that the interaction term does not have any effect on economic value orientations, we included an interaction term in the HLM analysis. The results show that the interaction terms were not significant (coefficient = 0.02). These results are consistent

TABLE 10.3. *HLM analyses of economic value orientation and achievement motivation*

Dependent		Economic value orientation		Achievement motivation	
Fixed effect					
For slope of		Coeff.	T ratio	Coeff.	T ratio
Intercept	Intercept	24.65	56.77 **	0.14	1.67 +
Sex(female)	Intercept	−0.87	−7.29**	−0.10	−4.20**
Age	Intercept	0.01	2.45*	0.00	−1.14
Education	Intercept	0.07	2.22 *	0.01	0.93
Income	Intercept	0.26	9.62 **	0.02	2.98**
Postmaterialist value	Intercept	−0.23	−2.31*	0.05	2.69**
Risk avoidance	Intercept	−0.91	−4.74**	0.06	1.66 +
Postmaterialist value* Risk avoidance	Intercept	0.02	0.16	0.02	0.25
	Eastern–Western (Western)	0.44	1.76	−0.10	−0.88
N		8556		8132	
Random effect					
		Variance component	χ^2	Variance component	χ^2
Postmaterialist value* Risk avoidance		0.09	184.87**	0.02	926.22**
Level 1		30.24		1.06	

with Model 1, which treats postmaterialism and risk avoidance as independent influences on the values underlying marketization.

The coefficients of HLM are difficult to interpret intuitively. Therefore, Figure 10.3 shows a graphical *post hoc* simulation of the relationship between postmaterialist values and economic value orientations for three different levels of risk avoidance. As was hypothesized in Model 1, there is no statistically significant interaction effect, since all three lines are roughly parallel (although the two predictors are somewhat interrelated). In addition, risk avoidance plays an independent role in determining economic value orientations. The less risk avoidant individuals are, the stronger their economic orientations. Moreover, these effects are considerably stronger than for postmaterialist values, which only slightly decrease economic value orientations.

Furthermore, as shown in Table 10.3, the East–West dummy variable does not have a significant effect in explaining the variation of coefficients of the interaction term.[12] In other words, there is not a significant East versus West divide in the effects of the interaction term on economic value orientations between postmaterialist values and risk avoidance, once other values and demographic characteristics are taken into account.

The second HLM model predicts achievement motivation, and this is displayed on the right side of Table 10.3. Postmaterialism has a positive

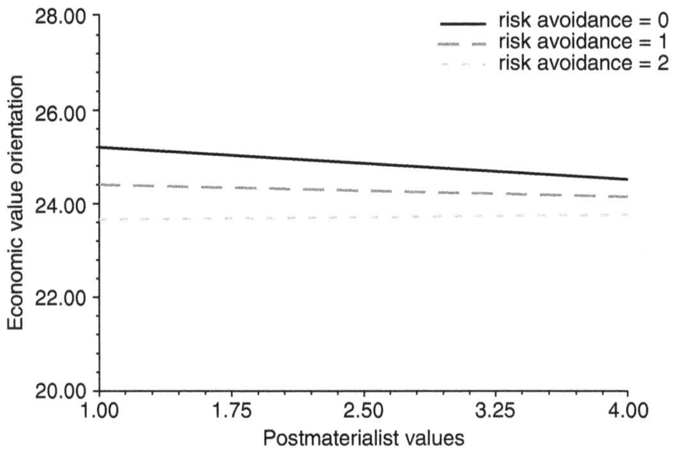

FIGURE 10.3. *Post hoc* simulation of economic value prediction
Note: Based on the HLM model of Table 10.3.

significant effect, and risk avoidance shows a marginal positive effect (at the 0.10 confidence level). The latter is contrary to our Model 2. The interaction term coefficient between postmaterialism and risk avoidance does not show a significant effect. Taking these results together, the analyses do not support the logic of Model 2 as presented above.

Again, the nature of the HLM makes it difficult to interpret the results in simple terms. Therefore, we again conducted a graphical *post hoc* simulation of the relationship between postmaterialist values and achievement motivation for different levels of risk avoidance (Figure 10.4). There is a positive correlation between postmaterialist values and achievement orientation. And, in this case, the impact of risk avoidance appears much weaker; the three levels of risk avoidance yield smaller differences than in Figure 10.2, and there is not a significant interaction with the postmaterialist values.

Table 10.3 also indicates that the East–West variable is not significant in this second model, but the random effect estimates show that there are significant variations in the slope of interaction term across countries.[13] Figure 10.5 shows the relationship between postmaterialist values and achievement motivation by nation, while controlling for risk avoidance. In some East Asian countries, such as Japan and Korea, postmaterialist values push people to have high-achievement motivations at high levels of risk avoidance. At the same time, in the two Western democracies—the USA and Canada—postmaterialist values erode feelings of achievement motivation, as Inglehart's theory would suggest. In addition, two East Asian countries (Singapore and the Philippines) follow this same pattern. Because of these varied patterns in East Asia, this made the East versus West variable insignificant.

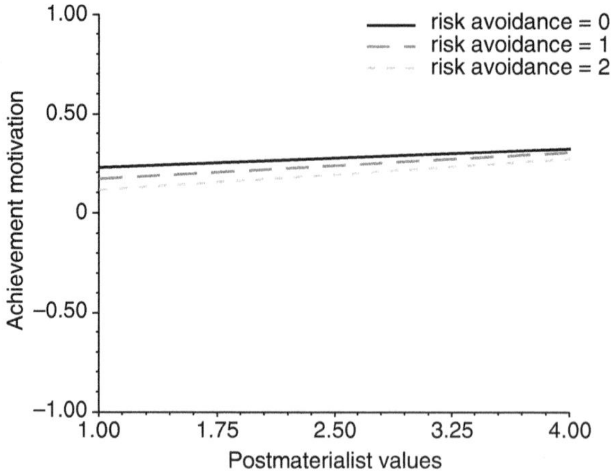

FIGURE 10.4. *Post hoc* simulation of achievement motivation prediction
Note: Based on the HLM model of Table 10.3.

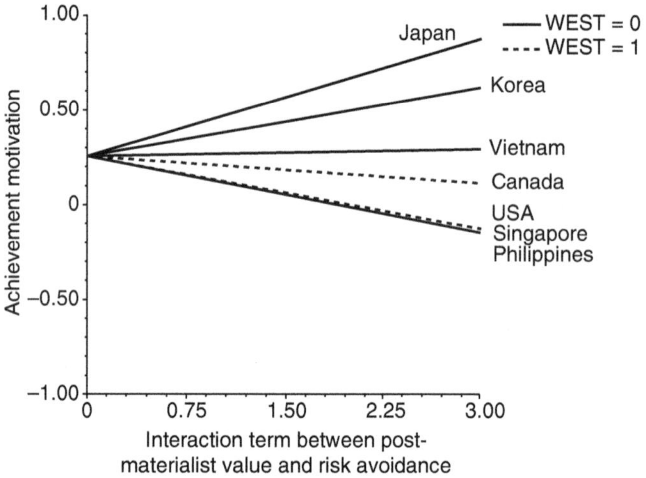

FIGURE 10.5. Effect of East versus West on achievement motivation

DISCUSSION

Our research has examined two major theories of value change that have been linked to the process of economic modernization and marketization in East Asia. On the one hand, we considered the universality of postmaterialist values as an influence on economic orientations (Inglehart 1990; Inglehart and Baker 2000). On the other hand, we introduced the concept of risk avoidance as a potential feature of East Asian cultural traditions, and a possible influence on economic orientations (Hofstede 1991, 2001). We do not disagree with the cross-cultural psychological approach that emphasizes human behavior as highly constrained by cultural factors. We do not deny the possibility of this approach, but we are interested in finding pan-cultural influences of human behavior by statistically controlling cultural (country) differences. As postmaterialist values may not be sufficient to explain the changes in human behavior, we also analyzed risk avoidance.

The results show that significant cultural (country) differences in risk avoidance do exist. However, these differences are not attributable to the familiar dichotomy of East versus West. In this sense, the results undercut the intuitive cultural explanation of differences in support for a capitalist market system between Western democracies and the nations of East Asia. Risk avoidance measured by the desire for job security seems lower in more affluent nations on both sides of the Pacific—the USA, Canada, and Japan—and risk avoidance is higher in Korea, Singapore, and the Philippines, with China in an intermediate position. After controlling possible cultural differences, risk avoidance has some effect as a pan-cultural influence on economic value orientations at the individual level possibly stronger than the impact of postmaterialism. These results imply that acceptance of risk—a trait independent of the East–West division—strongly influences the acceptance of a market economy by these publics.

Risk avoidance yields an unexpected result for achievement motivations. Risk avoidance encourages achievement motivation, once other causal factors are controlled. Perhaps this is a limit of the achievement motivation variable. Our four-variable measure might not be as highly relevant to risk-taking as was hypothesized. The same may be said for our recreating achievement motivation by other subsets of the four variables.[14] We may wonder if the relationships among postmaterialist values, achievement motivation, and risk avoidance are different in cultural contexts other than East and West.

Overall, postmaterialist values have a positive but shaky effect on market economy orientations through the achievement motivation. The theoretical literature may provide some clues to explain these results. In 1993, Hellevik (1993) claimed that the Norwegian value configuration is two dimensional: materialism versus idealism, and change (risk taking) versus stability. He argued that the shift from materialist to postmaterialist values does not just move from materialism to idealism, but from a pattern of materialism and stability to idealism and risk taking (it is almost like a movement from Point B to Point A in Figure 10.1). He further showed that younger generations emphasize both materialism and risk taking, which adds evidence that the value configuration is not one-dimensional.

This argument implies a systematic relationship between postmaterialist values and a risk taking orientation that stimulates ideas investigated in line with this chapter. A few questions come to mind: Do postmaterialist values have no impact on the desire for stability? For instance, self-actualization motivation seems compatible with a stability orientation; that is, seeking self-actualization has a consumer, without any risk taking via social participation or political commitment sounds plausible. We do not think this kind of self-actualization is socially desirable from the viewpoint that the ideal of democracy is attainable only through civic engagement. However, this type of self-actualization is still a plausible lifestyle model. In this sense, the mechanism of risk avoidance is the real social issue to be investigated in reference to social participation. Another question asks how a self-actualizing lifestyle is associated with economic value orientation; that is, whether nonrisk self-actualization in consumer life is attainable without risk taking in economic value.

Our findings contain a mix of lessons. On the one side, there are linkages between broad processes of social change of the sort that both Inglehart and Hofstede theorized, and the development of popular support for competitive market systems. On the other side, these relations are more complex and differentiated than prior theorizing has suggested. Thus, the nations of East Asia do not display a unifying characteristic regarding their social values, nor a single characteristic of their potential for developing popular support for a market economy linked to these values.

APPENDIX

We constructed scales for analyses as shown below. The variable names (such as v32 or v54) are from the WVS 2000–2001 questionnaire (Inglehart et al. 2004: 413–43).

Economic value orientation: See Chapter 8 and Appendix B of this volume.

Achievement motivation: additive index of four variables (v20, v21, v22, v24 with the reversal of v22 and v24). The higher the point, the higher the achievement motivation (MA, max 5 responses).

Postmaterialist value: See Appendix B of this volume.

Risk avoidance: additive index of two choices both in v84 and v85 (aforementioned). See more detail in the Appendix in this book.

ENDNOTES

1 The authors would like to thank the participants in the conference through which this book orignated, especially Russell Dalton and Doh Chull Shin. They also appreciate comments and cooperation given by Sean Richey, University of Tokyo.

2 Another possible East Asian value is authoritarianism, which Dalton and others (Dalton and Ong in this volume; Nevitte and Kanji 2003) investigate in the context of support for democracy.

3 These data are from the Global Policy Forum http://www.globalpolicy.org/globaliz/charts/percaptable.htm

4 The Japanese choice for "high economic growth" was:

1983	38% (JES)
1990	31% (WVS)
1993	32% (JES2)
1995	36% (WVS)
2000	36% (WVS)
2001	53% (JES3); The item used here was "stabilizing economy"
2003	52% (JES3); The item used here was "stabilizing economy"

[JES, JES2, and JES3 are "Japanese Election Studies" in 1983, 1993–7, and 2001–5 respectively]

5 Hosftede's measurement of uncertainty avoidance consisted of three sets of items:

Rule orientation: "company rules should not be broken—even when the employee thinks it is in the company's best interest".
Stability of job career: the extent to which a person thinks that he/she will continue working for the company which he/she is now working for.
Job stress: the extent to which a person feel nervous or tense at work.

Hofstede did not provide any statistically appropriate reasons to why these three lines of questions could create a single-dimensional scale on uncertainty avoidance (Hofstede 1991: 112). This is an obstacle to checking the validity of the measurement. Also, the WVS data does not have relevant questions on measuring rule orientation and job stress.

6 HLM is useful for cross-national comparison, as each individual is nested in each nation, that is, having hierarchical structure. Within each nation, intraclass correlations often violate the assumption of ordinary least square estimation of multiple regression models. For more about HLM, see Raudenbush and Bryk (2001).

7 From Figure 10.2, readers might think the national difference of risk avoidance is strongly affected by the level of economic development of each country. We conducted an analysis which included GDP per capita of each country in level 2. However, GDP per capita did not show statistically significant effect on the slope of interaction term between postmaterialist value and risk avoidance. In other words, the effect of the interaction term on economic value orientation and achievement motivation cannot be explained by the level of economic development of each country. Thus, in the following analysis we did not use this variable.

8 As for the Japanese low score on risk avoidance, we searched for whether there are any generational differences due to rapid value and cultural change in vain.

9 Hofstede's goal was to compare cultural differences in the context of people working in different countries for the same multinational company. However, he also noted that multinational corporations were likely to be atypical for each country's population as a whole.

10 When postmaterialist values and risk avoidance are regressed on demographic variables using pooled data of all countries, postmaterialist values are higher in the older, more educated people, and those with more income, while risk avoidance is higher in males, the older, the less educated and those with less income (table not shown).

11 The intercept of coefficients is the mean of coefficients of each independent variable at level 1 (individual level) which differs among countries. Therefore, a significant intercept value in

the table signifies that the average of the coefficients for the independent variable is statistically different from 0.

12 The random effect in the lower half of the table shows that the variance of coefficients of the interaction term among countries is still significantly large enough to be explained, that is, there could be other national-level explanatory factor(s) other than East versus West.

13 We also conducted analyses which did not include the East–West variable at level 2. The pattern of results did not differ from Table 10.3 and the intercept of coefficients of the interaction term between postmaterialist values and risk avoidance did not show significant effect, that is, the mean of coefficients of the interaction term is not statistically different from 0.

14 Although the results did not change by using newly created variables, we still doubt the approach of composite achievement motivation variables by adding and subtracting categorical variables. This causes additional errors in measurement.

11

Public Attitudes Toward a Market Economy in Vietnam

Pham Minh Hac and Pham Thanh Nghi

Democratization and economic development are two of the most important trends facing almost every nation in the developing world. Vietnam presents an economically and politically significant example of a nation that has consciously and systematically attempted to transform its economic system through a series of state-directed reforms over the past two decades. An essential point of the *doimoi* policy implemented in Vietnam since 1986 is to develop a market economy and democratize the society. These reforms have transformed the Vietnamese economy and affected the living standards and life conditions of the public in dramatic ways. Thus, Vietnam presents an example of the correlates of marketization in a developing nation. Even more so, Vietnam presents a unique opportunity to study a rapidly changing nation where marketization has stimulated dramatic economic growth, and this experience is potentially tranforming the political culture inherited from the nation's socialist past. This is a case where congruence between institutions and public values is in question in the midst of a major social transformation (see discussion in Chapter 1).

This chapter first describes Vietnam's experience with the *doimoi* reforms, and how these reforms have affected the economy. Over the past two decades, Vietnam has undergone a profound economic transformation, and this process continues. Then, the chapter examines public orientations toward the market and the values underlying market competition, drawing upon the WVS in Vietnam and additional survey evidence from the Institute of Human Studies. Are contemporary public values supportive of these reforms, and what are the social correlates of these attitudes? The results provide a picture of how economic change and public values are interrelated in the Vietnamese experience, and the implications of these relationships for the process of development.

VIETNAM'S HISTORY OF ECONOMIC REFORM

The *doimoi* reforms were stimulated by the broad recognition of Vietnam's severe economic problems the 1980s, and the need to restructure the economic system to address these problems (Turley and Selden 1992; Ha Huy Thanh 2000; Mai Ngoc Cuong 2001). At the start of the 1980s, Vietnam had a command-control economy directed by the state. The *domoi* policy can be briefly summarized by the following guidelines: (*a*) transformation of a central command, subsidized economy to a multisectoral economy with market mechanisms and state regulations; (*b*) economic development should be accompanied by social and cultural development and environmental protection; (*c*) democratization of social lives, building a legal state of people, for people, and by people; and (*d*) accomplishing an open policy in international cooperation with the spirit: "Vietnam wants to be a friend of all nations in the world for peace, independence and development" (CPV 1991).

For Vietnam, a country with backward economic and technological foundations and low social development, heavily damaged by long-lasting wars, and centrally controlled economic patterns, development of market economy is a major national goal. The reforms also represented a dramatic new economic experiment for the nation, to change the structure of the economy in a relatively short period. Entering the twenty-first century, Vietnam officially declared the goal of building the "market economy with socialist orientation" and followed this course as a coherent strategic direction (Nguyen Phu Trong 1994). At present, components of a market economy, such as a capital market, a real estate market, a labor market, and other structures, have been established. For instance, two stock centers opened recently in Hanoi and Ho Chi Minh City, through which more capital is invested for economic development. The real estate market is no longer dominated by the state, domestic and foreign investors have jumped in to do business; and consumers have more choices for their future apartments. The labor force, formerly forbidden in the market, is now a subject of trading. All these reforms have shown positive effects. The process of democratization in economic life has brought about dramatic change, both positive and negative.

Eighteen years after (1986–2004) the policy reforms, the country has changed and the lives of the people have been improved significantly. GDP per capita was $206 US in 1990, increasing to $423 US in 2004. In terms of purchasing price parity (PPP) measures, Vietnam's GDP per capita was approximately $2,500 in 2003, which represents a major advance in living conditions. The report "Millennium Goals: Closing the Millennium Gap" published on February 8, 2004 by the UNDP Office in Vietnam states that Vietnam has achieved impressive results in the process of implementation of the millennium development goals. Remarkably, the proportion of the public below poverty level decreased from 70 percent in the middle of the 1980s to 60 percent in 1990, and to 29 percent in 2002. From 1992 to 2003, 20 million people escaped famine and poverty.

Other social conditions followed the upward trajectory of the economy. For instance, the Gender Development Index (GDI) for Vietnam reached 0.687, ranking 89 among 144 countries. Democratization in education has been implemented successfully in Vietnam since 1945. These multiple achievements have brought about an increase in Vietnam's Human Development Index (HDI). In 1990, Vietnam's HDI was 0.608. By 2004, Vietnam's 0.691 HDI ranked it 112 among 177 countries (UNDP 2004).

Paralleling these developments, the literacy rate has increased from 5 percent in 1945 to 94 percent in 2000; the literacy rate among young people (aged 6–25) has increased to 96.7 percent. The universalization of primary education was completed in 2000, and compulsory education has been extended to the secondary education level. The total number of high school students (in age cohort 12–18 years old) is 55.1 percent (Pham Minh Hac 2001).

It can be said that the above-mentioned figures were achieved thanks to the *doimoi* renovation, the open door policy, and integration policy, in which democratization and marketization played a significant role. Without market reforms, many of the economic gains of the past two decades would not have been possible, and without economic gains, other government policies would not have been feasible. In the span of a single generation, the life conditions of the average Vietnamese have been transformed, and the nation has made dramatic progress in terms of its socioeconomic conditions.

Despite these achievements, Vietnam is facing challenges. For instance, the gap between the rich and the poor increased from 8 to 20 times over this same time span, as well as between different provinces and cities. The inequality in expenses indicated by Gini index gradually increased from 0.33 in 1993 to 0.35 in 1998 and 0.36 in 2002 (General Statistics Office 2002*b*: 25). The Gini index for income is 0.42, and for nonfood expenses it is 0.49 (Gini 0 indicating absolute equality, 1 absolute inequality). Together with the transition to the market economy, industrialization and urbanization have increased the population in the cities; after 13 years (1989–2002), the metropolitan population increase by 7.5 million and at the same time poverty has become a serious problem in cities. The human and social capital of the poor have a tendency to decrease (Nguyen Thu Sa and Nguyen Thi Mai Huong 2001; Nguyen Huu Minh and Nguyen Xuan Mai 2005).

In developing a market economy with a socialist orientation, the government has promulgated policies on diversification of ownership and has tried to keep the market regulated. Beside the state and collective forms of ownership, private ownership has been recognized, and capitalist economic elements are allowed to function in Vietnam. From the beginning of the twenty-first century, six types of production and business organizations were officially recognized by the state: (*a*) state-owned enterprises, (*b*) cooperatives, (*c*) household economy, (*d*) private capitalist enterprises, (*e*) state capitalist enterprises, and (*f*) foreign enterprises (CPV 2001). The state-owned enterprises play a leading role in producing goods and providing services, and contribute the largest part of GDP. The state sector contribution to the economy increased from 35 percent of GDP in 1990–5 to 40 percent in 1995–2000. The economic share of state-owned enterprises grew because of increased activities in areas such as electricity, telecommunications, and finance. Since then, however, the contribution of the state sector has declined due to growth of the nonstate sectors. The state sector contributed only 38.3 percent of GDP in 2003 (see Figure 11.1).

Household economic activity contributes the second largest part, with 31.4 percent of the GDP. This typically includes family agriculture and small-scale manufacturing and marketing. Income from personal production is the most important source of household economy. In fact, much of the initial market economy has functioned at the household or family level, with farmers and entrepreneurs selling their products in the cities.

Joint ventures and foreign companies—new kind of enterprises operating in Vietnam since the country opened up to the outside world, and growing with fastest rate compared to other sectors—contribute a significant part to Vietnamese economic development, with 13.9 percent of GDP. The private capitalist sector is growing and plays a more important role in economic development, but it still produces only 3.9 percent of GDP (General Statistics Office 2003). The relatively poor growth performance of Vietnam's private

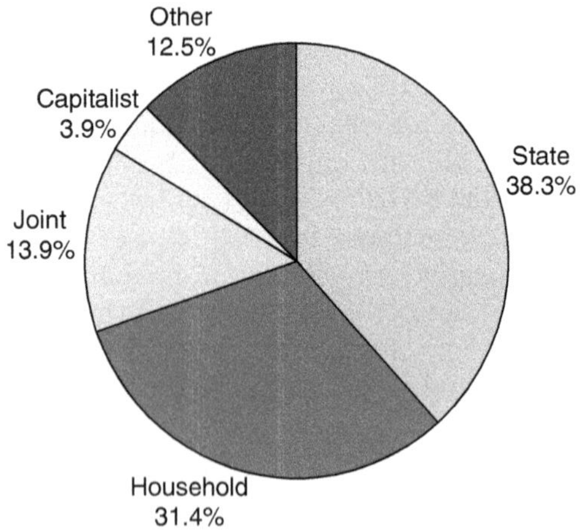

FIGURE 11.1. Sources of the Vietnamese gross domestic product in 2003
Source: General Statistical Office (2002).

firms in relation to private firms in other transition economies most likely reflects, in part, the constraints in entry and investment. The government required extensive paperwork and regulation of firms registering in the 1990s. Existing private firms had much less access to sources of formal credit than state-owned enterprises (Friedman 2004). State-owned enterprises are also allowed to control the most strategically important areas of economy, such as electricity, telecommunications, and mining. The state-owned enterprises, which produce common goods, are allowed to privatize, but this has occurred only to a limited degree. The government continues to reform policies and reorganize state-owned enterprises to allow free competition and efficiency improvement.

Since 1986, the state has recognized different types of markets. Commodity markets have developed in metropolitan and populated areas. Market mechanisms have been applied in the sphere of prices, exchange rates, and interest rates, which eliminates the determination of prices by the state. At present, the market determines almost all prices of goods and services in Vietnam. Imports and exports are undertaken based on market mechanisms.

Since the early 1990s, financial markets, including monetary and capital markets, have started operating. The revenue regime before renovation was extremely intricate, with numerous kinds of fees and taxes and at different rates. In the later 1990s, this regime underwent much renovation, particularly with the application of the value-added tax in 1998. The state issued treasury bills, at first with one-year maturity and then with five-year maturity. Stock markets were put into operation in August 2000, but the market volume has been small. A system of commercial banks has come into operation with 6 state-owned banks, 51 joint-stock banks, 23 affiliates of foreign banks, 4 joint ventures, and thousands of people's credit funds (Vo Dai Luoc 2004).

The real estate markets were not recognized until the early 1990s due to state ownership on land. Transferable land use rights promulgated in the 1993 Land Law, but as of 2001, the vast majority of titles in urban areas had still not been distributed by the State (Kim 2004). Despite the incomplete institution of legal property rights, people are offering real estate with various forms of property rights, and this has formed an illegal real estate market. In this situation, the claim to private property rights could be rejected due to incomplete legal papers. The formation of a legal real estate market in Vietnam still faces difficulties, even though the amended Land Law was put into effect on the first of July 2004.

Labor markets have been established on the basis that labor is considered as goods for exchange. However, there are many obstacles preventing laborers from accessing the labor market and moving from sector to sector, and/or within a sector. Information on the labor market is not collected regularly, and is not provided widely to facilitate labor mobility. The judicial environment is improving, but needs further development. Laws on competition and bankruptcy are expected to be passed by the Parliament in the near future.

Vietnam has consistently implemented policies on multilateralization, diversification of external economic relations, and active integration into the world economy. The law on foreign investment has been promulgated and has undergone several amendments to make it more liberal and favorable for foreign investors. The relations with foreign countries and international organizations have been expanded. Vietnam joined the Association of South East Asian Nations (ASEAN) in July 1995, has participated in Asia-Pacific Economic Cooperation (APEC) since November 1998, and it is now actively negotiating its entry into the World Trade Organization (WTO). The relations between Vietnam and the USA were normalized in 1995 and the two countries signed the Trade Agreement in July 2000. The three largest financial organizations (International Monetary Fund, World Bank, and Asian Development Bank) have come back to assist Vietnam since October 1994. The international trade has grown up dramatically. The value of exports has increased nearly sevenfold in twelve years, from $US 2,404,000 in 1990 to $US 15,029,000 in 2001. At the same period, the value of imports also increased almost six times, from $US 2,752,000 to $US 16,218,000 (General Statistics Office 2003).

After nearly two decades of transformation from a central command subsidized economy to a market economy, Vietnam has attained impressive achievements. The average growth rate was around 7 percent during the period of 1991–2000. There are positive changes in the economic structure. Agricultural production as a share of the GDP declined to 19 percent in 2003; industry and construction rose to 40.5 percent of the GDP; and service accounted for 40.5 percent. The World Bank, UNDP, and other international organizations and foreign countries have broadly recognized these achievements.

However, the market economy in Vietnam is not as developed as real life requires. Vietnamese goods and services have low competitive capacity compared to those of several neighboring countries. The labor market and the sciences and technology markets are still primitive; privatization is lagging behind the required level. In these situations, major inputs of production are more expensive than they should be. There are still heavily subsidized industries within the state-owned sector. In some areas, there is a shortage of regulations and judicial implementation, and corruption as a social evil is still rampant. Moreover, bureaucratic machinery and cumbersome administrative regulations create numerous obstacles for free competition and market development in Vietnam, as written in official documents.

Our goal in this chapter is to describe how the Vietnamese public has responded to these changes. While life conditions have generally improved, this has occurred with some dislocation and new economic demands. Many citizens who were raised under a different economic system are being asked to work in a new economic order. How have the Vietnamese responded to these economic changes?

SURVEY RESEARCH IN VIETNAM

Surveys of public values were undertaken for the first time in Vietnam in 1992 (Pham Minh Hac 2001). The State Research Program KX-07, entitled "Human development is the objective and driving force for social-economic development" (1991–5) conducted surveys on value systems, value scales, value measures, and value orientations.

In 2000–1, the Institute of Human Studies took part in the WVS carried out on a near global scale under unified forms and methodology (see appendix to this volume). The initial outcomes of the survey conducted in Vietnam were announced by Vietnamese and American researchers at the International Meeting on WVS, held in Stellenbosch, South Africa in October 2001, and subsequently published in Vietnamese and English (Pham Minh Hac and Pham Thanh Nghi 2002, 2003; Dalton et al. 2002).

Inheriting the success of the KX-07 and 2001 WVS, the State Research Program KX-05 (2001–4) conducted a survey on value orientations in 2003 in six groups of respondents.[1] The Institute of Human Studies was also selected as an agency to undertake a survey on openness and globalization in Vietnam for a study conducted at Glasgow University in Scotland, a part of this study was focused on integration into international markets.

The participation of Vietnamese scholars in the WVS in 2001 marked a turning point in the application of new ideas and methodology in values research and created a focus for Vietnamese social studies in recent years. This participation also presented a possibility for integration of Vietnamese social sciences into the international research community. Our concern here is to examine public attitudes toward a market economy that is considered one of the decisive bases for the country's development under impacts of the *doimoi* (renovation) policy. The WVS in Vietnam provides us with more information for understanding ourselves, and it also provides a database for international researchers to have a better understanding of Vietnamese situations (see other chapters in this book). This chapter provides information on market development and public attitudes toward an emerging market economy in Vietnam.

PUBLIC ATTITUDES TOWARD A MARKET ECONOMY IN VIETNAM

Our aim is to analyze Vietnamese public attitudes toward the market. In several cases, we compare Vietnam to two other nations from East Asia (China and Japan) and two from North America (the USA and Canada).

The evidence in this chapter is taken from the WVS conducted in Vietnam and statistics collected from other countries in the 2000–1 wave. In addition, we also analyze data collected by the State Research Program KX-05 in 2003 to support conclusions based on the WVS data.

The transition from an agricultural society into an industrial society has created profound changes in the people's material and spiritual lives. A 1993–4 survey showed that the people's economic life had registered considerable changes after a few years of renovation (Pham Minh Hac 2001). A full 39 percent of the interviewees said their material life had been remarkably improved, 24 percent said the material life had declined and 34 percent reported unsubstantial changes. The 2001 WVS reinforced this same image. A majority of the population (53 percent) stated that they were satisfied with their financial situation. We expect that this reflects the relative progress of the preceding decade rather than the absolute income levels in contemporary Vietnam. Similarly, 64 percent said they were satisfied with their life overall, which tends to reflect personal conditions and family life beyond economic conditions. Satisfaction levels in Vietnam are at or above the levels that one might predict, based on its overall level of economic development.[2]

With regards to the people's spiritual life, the research conducted within the State Research Program KX-07 recorded positive changes in the people's individual and social lives. Human potentials have been nurtured, and this has materialized into human resources. People highly appreciate such fundamental human values as peace, stability, friendship, integration, national independence, freedom, and other values, like blood relationship, family, community, education, employment, and traditional values. This study also shows examples of specific value changes that seem to reflect the consequence of the *doimoi* reforms: economic values are appreciated more than other values; personal and family interests are valued more than collective interests; immediate benefits are more urgent than long-term ones; there is a movement from an acceptance of passive waiting to an active confrontation with challenges, and from an acceptance of egalitarian distribution of wealth to a preference for income difference according to individual contributions (Pham Minh Hac 2001).

The economic reforms in Vietnam, on the one hand, have taken the country out of crisis and generated new impetus for development but on the other hand, they have widened the gap between the rich and the poor, and this has posed increasingly severe social problems. There exist two trends of attitudes: one advocates more thorough market development, and the other favors maintaining the state control over the economy. The results of values surveys conducted in Vietnam since 1993 show that the majority of the respondents supported the first trend. Support for a market economy with socialist orientations has grown stronger, not only among academics and administrators, but also among the general public.

These values surveys in Vietnam also show changes in value systems and value orientations of the Vietnamese people. There are transitional values emerging during the change from an agricultural society to an industrial society, and from a command subsidized economy to a market economy.

The WVS provides another opportunity to examine Vietnamese attitudes toward a market economy. The WVS questionnaire includes several items that characterize respondents' attitudes toward a market economy, which we examine in this section (also see Shin and Dalton, Chapter 8 in this volume).[3]

Attitudes Toward the Market Economy

One question used a 10-point scale to ask about private ownership of business and industry (point 10 on the scale) versus government ownership (point 1). Although market mechanisms have affected Vietnamese society only since 1986, we found that the Vietnamese are more positive toward the market (mean = 5.6) than the Chinese (mean = 4.2). A majority of the Vietnamese lean towards private ownership (57 percent). People in both these socialist states are more skeptical about the market than citizens in established market economies. However, the magnitude of these differences is surprisingly small. The attitudes of the Japanese, for instance, are closer to attitudes among the Vietnamese and Chinese, than to the American and Canadians.

Attitudes toward free competition are another characteristic of a market orientation. A second question measured attitudes toward competition. These attitudes may be different when people's economic interests are vested in different economic sectors. Again, however, Vietnamese support for competition (mean = 7.2) is roughly comparable to the Japanese, Americans, and Canadians, while the level of Chinese support is much higher (see Table 8.1).

These two items were combined to produce an index of support for a market economy (Figure 11.2). As Doh Shin and Russell Dalton noted in Chapter 8, these data suggest that support for the principles of private ownership is surprisingly common around the Pacific Rim. Moreover, despite Vietnam's mixed progress in developing a market system based on two decades of *doimoi* reforms, the Vietnamese appear quite positive toward market principles. These findings are also consistent with earlier research that found support for various market principles in Vietnam throughout the 1990s (Pham Minh Hac 2001). Even more striking are the data from the 2003 Pew Global Attitudes Survey. When asked if people are better off in a free market economy, 95 percent of the Vietnamese agreed—the highest in any of the forty-four nations included in this project.[4] Clearly, the progress of the past decade under the *doimoi* reforms has generated tremendous good will for a market economy in Vietnam.

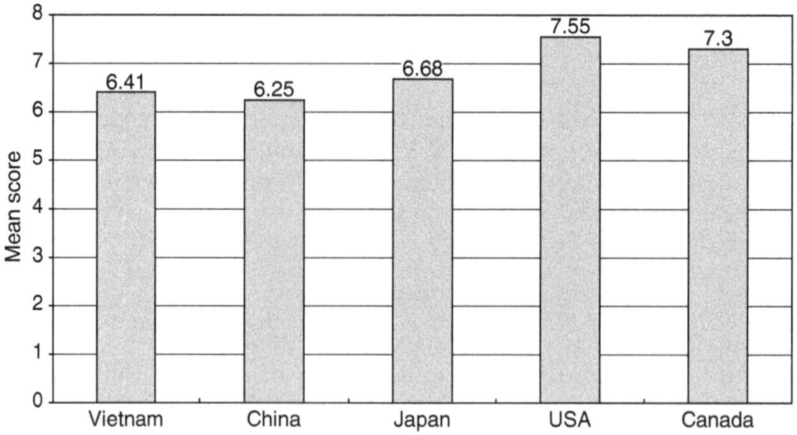

FIGURE 11.2. Cross-national differences in support for market economy index
Source: 1999–2002 WVS.

Note: Table entries are mean scores on the 10-point market economy index; the index combines the items on support for a private economy and acceptance of competition. A score of 10 indicates strong support for a private economy.

To describe these opinions in more depth, and to understand their implications for Vietnamese politics, we want to probe below the surface to look at the social correlates of these options. For instance, given the tremendous social changes that Vietnam has experienced in the last several decades, there are strong reasons to expect large age differences between those who support a market economy, and those who do not. Younger Vietnamese have grown up with the *doimoi* reforms and have seen their consequences; they are also more likely to have benefited directly from the new economic opportunities. In contrast, older citizens might be less willing to embrace the new system, and might have suffered disproportionately from some of the economic dislocations that accompanied the economic transition. Prior research has found such generational patterns in acceptance of a market economy in the postsocialist nations of Eastern Europe after the transition (Rose, Haerpfer, and Mishler 1998).

The first set of bars in Figure 11.3 demonstrates a clear relation between the market economy index and age (also see Table 11.1, $r = 0.10$). Younger Vietnamese are more positive toward private ownership and competition than their elders, even using a simple dichotomy of pre/post-1975 birthdate.[5] This is understandable as the young grew up during the time of renovation. As a reference point for these data, support for a market economy among younger Vietnamese is approximately the same as for the Japanese in Figure 11.2. These opinions among the young also imply that support for economic reforms will increase in the future as more young citizens come of age.

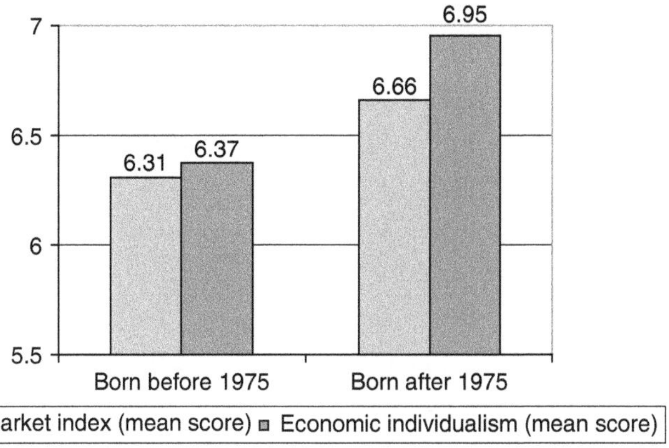

FIGURE 11.3. Age differences in support for a market economy and economic individualism

Source: 2001 WVS, Vietnam.

These patterns can also be seen in everyday Vietnamese life. Young people are more interested in the international economy, and more in tune with the style and norms of this international system. When one enters the office of an international firm in Vietnam, much of the staff is young. The Internet cafes in Hanoi or Ho Chi Minh City are filled with young people, and the young are attuned to international fashion. Some older Vietnamese decry these trends, but the orientations of young Vietnamese are clearly changing. In addition, with more than 60 percent of the Vietnamese population under the age of 30, they are the nation's future.

Region is another factor that may influence attitudes toward the market. The North and the South are culturally different. Southerners originally came from the North, but when conquering the new land, they changed their character and become more open-minded. Southerners also used to live with the market conditions in place before the reunification of the country in 1975.

TABLE 11.1. *The correlates of economic orientations in Vietnam*

Predictor	Market economy index	Economic individualism index
Age	0.10	0.13
Region	0.14	0.18
Education	0.17	0.17
Income status	0.13	0.19
Gender	0.07	0.15

Source: 2001 WVS, in Vietnam.

Note: Table entries are Pearson correlation coefficients.

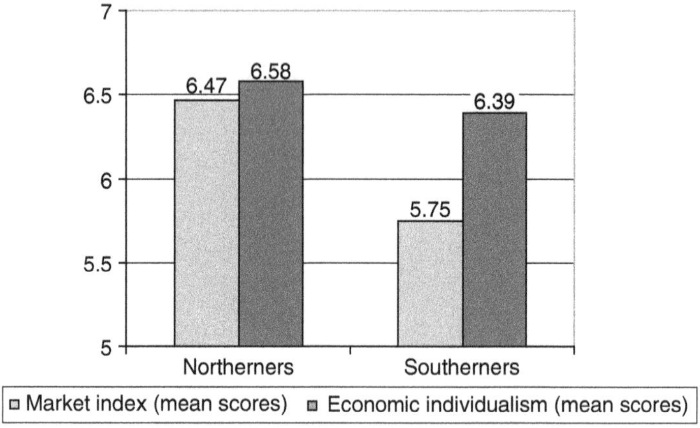

FIGURE 11.4. Region differences in support for a market economy and economic individualism

Source: 2001 WVS, Vietnam.

In addition, much of the foreign investment and activities of international firms have been focused in the South. According to the UN Development Program, Ho Chi Minh City alone accounts for 17 percent of national output, 30 percent of foreign investment, and 40 percent of Vietnam's exports. Foreign direct investment and exports per capita are several times higher in the four Southern provinces than in the Northern provinces around Hanoi. Yet even in Hanoi, one sees bustling economic activity from merchants and new private enterprises.

Figure 11.4 shows that respondents from the North are actually more positive toward a private market than respondents from the South. This may be due to the success of economic reforms introduced throughout the country that have affected people from the North more than people from the South. Southerners also may see less change as the result of the *doimoi* reforms, or be less willing to express support for what might be seen as the old ways.

Another potential predictor of support for a market economy is social status. The more affluent may disproportionately benefit from the *doimoi* reforms and rising living standards. They may have been more likely to be engaged in international or trade-related activities and thus exposed to other market systems. Surprisingly, we have not found any significant relation between economic status and attitudes toward market principles. The higher income group support for market (mean score = 6.35) is about the same as the lower income group (mean score = 6.39). It seems that most affluent people have not directly benefited from market principles or do not link their status to support for the market. They may take advantage of the transition to be rich when perfect market principles have not developed yet in Vietnam.

At the same time, education level provides another aspect of social status that might be related to support for markets and the *doimoi* reforms. On the one hand, those who are better educated are more aware of the potential of market reforms, and more exposed to political debates on the reforms and discussions of the impact of marketization. Better-educated Vietnamese are also more likely to hold occupations that involve them in international exchange, and more likely possess the skills to function better in a competitive market economy. The better educated are also more likely to live in a more cosmopolitan environment, in which there is more information about the processes of globalization and the activities of international agencies such as UNDP, ASEAN, and WTO. On the other hand, the better educated have typically benefited from the previous system that enabled them to receive additional education, and often may have been be employed by the state or state enterprises. Thus, we explored whether educational groups differ in their support for a market economy.

Education is related to support for a private market (Figure 11.5). Respondents with higher and secondary education support the market more strongly than respondents with primary education. These differences are modest (r = 0.17), but they suggest that Vietnam's expanding educational levels will reinforce the trend toward economic renovation and marketization.

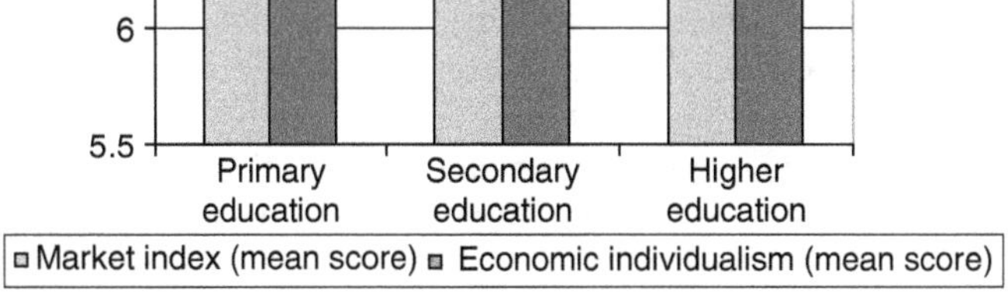

FIGURE 11.5. Education differences in support for a market economy and economic individualism

Source: 1999–2002 WVS.

Note: Table entries are mean scores on the 10-point market economy index; the index combines the items on support for a private economy and acceptance of competition. A score of 10 indicates strong support for a private economy.

Finally, we examined the relationship between gender and attitudes toward the market, as men and women typically have different positions in terms of employment and relationship to a market economy. Data suggests that gender has little effect on support for a market economy (r = 0.07). Vietnamese women are more skeptical about the market than men, though the gap is quite small. Vietnamese women are less active in business, especially in the countryside, where more than 70 percent of population live. This may explain their hesitancy toward economic change.

Together, these findings suggest that the *doimoi* reconstruction in Vietnam has gone hand in hand with changes in citizen orientations toward a market economy. Older generations and those at the periphery of the economy are less supportive of markets, and more in favor of the state-directed system of the past. However, as these reforms have improved economic conditions in Vietnam, they are endorsed by the young, the better-educated, and those who are more politically engaged. This is consistent with the broader processes of social modernization that Inglehart and Welzel described in their chapter in this volume. In addition, this suggests that continued economic improvements are likely to yield continuing popular support for these reforms.

Attitudes Toward Economic Individualism

Another dimension of values underlying a market economy is orientations toward income inequality and earning. In a market economy, income differences stimulate people to work hard and create new ideas. Similarly, the idea of competition is central to market principles. However, such values were antithetical to the socialist principles on which the prior Vietnamese command economy was constructed. Earlier Vietnamese governments stressed the need to provide basic social needs and the role of the state in providing these goods. Thus, we wanted to see how the contemporary Vietnamese public views these value choices in the context of two decades of *doimoi* reconstruction.

One question in the WVS asked if there should be more income differences to provide incentives for workers, or if there should be greater income equality.[6] Remember that we previously described high levels of income inequality in Vietnam, which is a dramatic change from the prior system. Still, most Vietnamese believe that there should be more income difference to create incentives (mean = 6.3). Moreover, as Doh Shin and Russell Dalton demonstrated in Chapter 8, Vietnamese acceptance of inequality is greater than in China, Japan, or the USA. This may be due to the long-standing system of equal income distribution in Vietnam, which leads people to favor more differences, or to the accomplishments of the reforms.

Another aspect of economic individualism involves the choice between a society with extensive social welfare benefits and high taxes, versus a society where taxes are low and individuals take responsibility for themselves.

This distinguishes between a welfare society versus competitive society. Vietnamese respondents again are very positive toward individual responsibility (mean = 6.52), while Chinese, Japanese, and Canadians are less positive (mean = 5.51, 4.33, and 6.10, respectively). Only the Americans score above Vietnam (mean = 6.71), depicting the strong individualistic tradition of American political culture (Lipset 1996).

As in the previous section, we combined these two questions into a single index measuring support for economic individualism (see Appendix B of this volume). This collective/individualism index does not display large differences across the five nations in our comparisons (Figure 11.6). Vietnam actually has a high index value (6.52), indicating strong support for a more competitive society. Japan has relatively low score (4.33), which fits Ikeda's emphasis on Japan as a risk adverse society (see Chapter 10 in this volume). The three other nations—China, the USA, and Canada—lie in between.

Similar findings are reported by the State Research Program KX-05 survey conducted in 2003. This survey found that 65.5 percent of 339 workers interviewed by the project supported greater income difference, the rest were for more equal income distribution. However, a full 70.5 percent considered that state ownership was the most important, 11 percent of them valued collective ownership, and only 18.5 percent of workers interviewed supported the private ownership. Compared with respondents in the WVS,

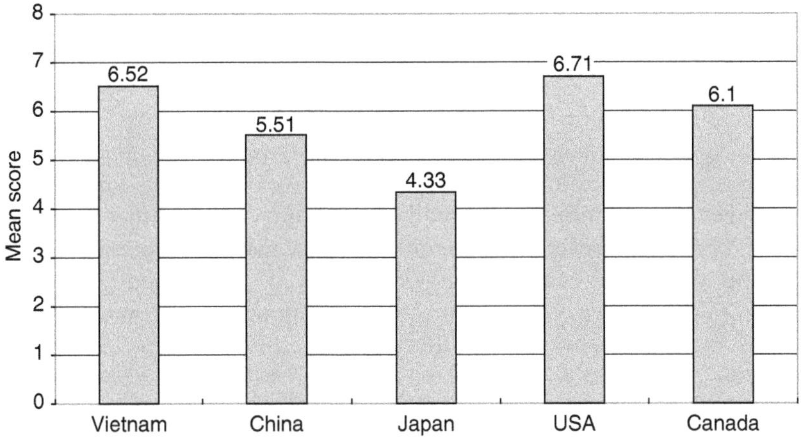

FIGURE 11.6. Cross-national differences on economic individualism index
Source: 1999–2002 WVS.

Note: Table entries are mean scores on the 10-point welfare question and acceptance of income inequality; 10 indicates strong support for a more individualist economy.

worker respondents are more supportive for government ownership even if they are positive toward different income distribution.

Given the socialist traditions of Vietnamese society, the acceptance of economic individualism is a striking finding. In part, we believe this reflects the endorsement of the principles underlying the government's *doimoi* reforms that make individuals responsible for the conditions of their lives. This is part of the movement toward choice that is also reflected in Inglehart and Welzel's human development model. In addition, despite the social disruption and economic difficulties that have resulted from the *doimoi* reforms, this marketization process has benefited many Vietnamese. For instance, the Pew study (2003) found that the Vietnamese are more likely than any other nation to say the availability of good-paying jobs has increased in the past five years (92 percent), and that working conditions have gotten better (85 percent). When marketization seems to be working, it is not surprising that public values endorse this system.

Again, we sought to go beyond the overall percentages to examine the social distribution of opinions toward economic individualism. The first factor we consider is age, which we expect to follow the same pattern as for the market index (the second set of bars in Figure 11.3). Indeed, there is a significant difference ($r = 0.13$) in the attitudes toward inequality; people born before 1975 are less supportive of inequality (mean = 6.37) than are those born after 1975 (mean = 6.95). Because the young grew up in the environment of a market economy, they have been treated differently according to their merit and contribution. Young people more easily accept working in a private company where their salary depends on their contribution to the firm. It is more common to see young, better-educated Vietnamese leave a bureaucratic governmental agency to work for a foreign company, where income is significantly higher but without a guarantee of lifetime work. These generational differences are even greater than for attitudes toward the market economy overall. The *doimoi* reforms are creating a generation of young entrepreneurs and individualists, scoring higher on economic individualism than any of the other nations in Figure 11.6, higher even than the individualist market economies of Canada and the USA. Many older Vietnamese are concerned about these trends and the turn toward consumerism among the young, but this reflects the sharp generational differences in economic values apparent in the figure.

We also considered whether region is correlated with these opinions. People from the North prefer income differences and individual responsibility more than people from the South (Figure 11.4). One can say that people from the South are used to living in a market economy; they may prefer individual responsibility and income differences more than people from the North. But in fact, *doimoi* policy is changing the lives of people in the North more than in the South. Consequently, it apparently changes the minds of Northerners much more than among Southerners.

Social status is another factor that should shape these economic values. For instance, one might plausibly assume that higher-income groups and the better-educated are those who have competed and benefitted most from their accomplishments. Thus, these groups should be more likely to endorse economic individualism. For example, prior research from the postsocialist societies of Eastern Europe found that upper status groups were more likely to embrace the new market system (Rose, Haerpfer, and Mishler 1998). At the same time, there is a potential tension between these present norms and the policies of the socialist past. Thus, social status—like generation—is a valuable marker of where the nation is headed.

We found a strong relationship between income and support for economic individualism (r = 0.19). Affluent people are more supportive for income inequality (mean = 6.86) compared with relatively poorer people (mean = 6.50). The Vietnamese have learned a lot from the past, when all citizens were treated equally without taking effort into consideration. Collective forms of economy showed their inefficiency during the decade years after the war. The practice of renovation in Vietnam has shown that affluent people experienced many more positive effects of slogan "working according to ability, gaining according to contribution" than those who are less affluent.

Similarly, education levels have a significant effect on attitudes of people toward economic inequality (Figure 11.5). People with higher and secondary education more strongly support inequality, while respondents with primary education is less supportive for economic inequality (r = 0.17). We believe that educated respondents have benefitted more from the economic growth and unequal distribution of the past decade, and they are more likely to understand the incentives of an unequal distribution system.

Gender might also influence these orientations, since we expect men to be more supportive of a competitive society. Indeed, Vietnamese men were likely to endorse a competitive society preferring income differences and individual responsibility much more than women. The difference in the mean scores was over a half point on the summary index (mean = 6.71 and 6.20 with r = 0.14). There is a tendency still existing in Vietnam that males should be the primary earner in the family and should take care the whole family. Therefore, men prefer to deal with challenges and to be responsible individually.

We have described popular attitudes toward the market and inequality of distribution and responsibility among the contemporary Vietnamese public. Two of these indices display the same general patterns across different ages, regions, education levels, and gender groups. While younger, more educated people are strongly supportive of a market orientation and of economic individualism, we can say that the market economy and a system of distribution according to contribution are seen as inevitable in Vietnam's future economic development. Gender and regional differences show cultural influence on people attitudes. Women, for instance, were previously considered as only homemakers, who practically cared for the family. This tradition held that she was not comfortable with inequality, but at the same time, she was not capable to compete with men. This situation still affects today's generation, albeit with probably weaker differences. Region is also a factor influencing public attitudes. In general, however, the Vietnamese people today are more aware of the importance of competition and private ownership as well as individual responsibility and income differences. The change in these attitudes might be derived from the change of the government policy that promoted marketization and democratization during two decades of renovation.

CONCLUSION

A key point of the *domoi* policy implemented since 1986 in Vietnam was to develop a market economy and democratize the society. During the *doimoi* process, there were different positions within the government and society on the degree to which the market should be transformed. The majority of people believed that it was necessary to abolish state protection for state-run enterprises and further reduce intervention by the government into business. These changes have produced positive economic results. Within the last generation, Vietnam has been transformed, and the social and economic conditions of the citizens have broadly improved. However, these gains have also come at the cost of social change, dislocation, and uncertainty as the public responds to a changing economic system. Thus, our research has focused on the question of how the Vietnamese public has responded to these reforms, and whether current economic values are congruent with the economic forces changing Vietnam today.

Our findings indicate that the contemporary Vietnamese public strongly supports the principles underlying a market economy, and they highly value the role of economic individualism and competition. The distribution of the fruits of labor, according to the average citizen, will be more encouraging if more difference in income is created to stimulate individual efforts. The WVS describes a strong tendency among the Vietnamese toward increasing individual responsibility and reducing the government's role in providing assistance. The market economy is a real way for releasing human potential and promoting socioeconomic development, and through this process human capacity can be improved sustainably. As we showed above, the Vietnamese public is overwhelmingly positive about the economic accomplishments of the past five years, and how their living conditions and job conditions have correspondingly improved (Pew 2002, 2003). And, undoubtedly, the values of the contemporary Vietnamese public represent a dramatic change from what would have been found before the *doimoi* reconstruction and the events of the subsequent two decades. The strong generational pattern in support for a market economy highlights this temporal change, and suggests that further change lies ahead, as younger citizens reflect the new realities.

At the same time, the strong apparent link to past economic performance and support for market reforms suggests that current values may be susceptible to future economic trends. Just as past economic gains have apparently generated support for marketization, economic downturns may erode this support. However, to the extent that these new economic values are internalized and encouraged by general processes of social modernization and globalization, these values may perhaps become more deeply embedded in the Vietnamese political culture.

Vietnam is being transformed to a market economy with socialist orientation; the leftovers of the centrally-controlled economy appear to be strong in the current economic structure. Achievements of economic development and growth of people's awareness of democratization create more space for political renovation. In a slogan from 2001 "prosperous people, strong nation, equal, democratic and civilized society", Vietnam included democratization of the society into the goal of the country's development. Marketization and democratization need to go hand in hand, and data collected in the surveys mentioned above, especially in the WVS, confirmed that the public strongly supports marketization and democratization in Vietnam.

ENDNOTES

1 KX-05 State Research Program Survey: The survey was undertaken by the KX-5 State Research Program in August 2003. It had 2,320 respondents, including 360 workers, 360 farmers, 150 business people, 400 school students, 700 university students, and 350 academics selected for interviewing using a quota method. The respondents were distributed proportionally to population in three regions of the country (North, Central, and South). In each region, there were two provinces selected for interviewing.

2 Additional evidence comes from the Pew Global Values Survey (2002). The 2002 survey found that 53 percent believed their lives had improved over the previous five years, compared to only 17 percent who said they had lost ground. In addition, a full 69 percent of Vietnamese are optimistic about their prospects for the future over the next five years. The positive responses about present life conditions are more common than in China (42 percent), Japan (21 percent), South Korea (38 percent), or the other East Asian nations in the Pew Survey, or even American (51 percent) and Canadian (48 percent) responses.

3 See Appendix B for the construction of the Market Economy Index. The two questions are as follows: "Now I'd like you to tell me your views on various issues. How would you place your views on this scale? 1 means you agree completely with the statement on the left; 10 means you agree completely with the statement on the right; and if your views fall somewhere in between, you can choose any number in between:"

(1) Private ownership of business and industry should be increased	10) Government ownership of business and industry should be increased
(1) Competition is good. It stimulates people to work hard and develop new ideas	10) Competition is harmful. It brings out the worst in people

4 By comparison, 70 percent of the Chinese agreed, but only 53 percent of the Japanese. In addition, 72 percent of Americans and 61 percent of Canadians were positive toward a free-market economy.

5 We used 1975 as the dividing point because this would allow us to distinguish between those who grew up under the *doimoi* reforms versus earlier generations.

6 See Appendix B for the construction of the Economic Individualism Index. The two questions are as follows: "Now I'd like you to tell me your views on various issues. How would you place your views on this scale? 1 means you agree completely with the statement on the left; 10 means you agree completely with the statement on the right; and if your views fall somewhere in between, you can choose any number in between:"

(1) Incomes should be made more equal	10) We need larger income differences as incentives for individual effort.
(1) The government should take more responsibility to ensure that everyone is provided for	10) People should take more responsibility to provide for themselves

Part IV

Democracy and Markets

12

The Parallel Development of Democracy and Markets

Doh Chull Shin and Russell J. Dalton

> Democracy is not necessarily better for development. Only when accompanied by the presence of competitive markets will democracy be able to shine. ... Democracy and markets are the twin pillars on which lasting development can thrive.
>
> —Jagdish N. Bhagwati, 2002

> If Korea had pursued a parallel development of democracy and a market economy from the start, it would have been possible to check the collusive relationship between government and big business that developed within the government-controlled financial sector. It would even have been possible to avoid the destructive storm of the currency crisis.
>
> —Kim Dae Jung, 2001

In East Asia, as in other regions of the world, democratic politics and free-market economy have emerged as the twin goals of national development. During the Third Wave of democratization, the number of countries promoting democracy and free markets in parallel has grown substantially (Kim 1996, 1999; Haggard 2000; Ravich 2000; Stiglitz 2002). This trend of building free markets while deepening democracy contrasts sharply with the slow and sequential pattern of capitalist democratic development in Western Europe and North America (Moore, Jr. 1966; Rueschemeyer, Stephens, and Stephens 1992; Collier 1999). Thus, the deliberate efforts of East Asian countries to implement democratic and market-oriented reforms simultaneously and rapidly have few historical precedents.

These two development trends also face a variety of challenges. Among the most crucial of these challenges is how the mass citizenry of each East Asian country reacts to the idea and practices of parallel development. Some analysts have argued that democratization and economic growth are contrasting goals, and developing nations must choose between them (Nelson 1994; Zakaria 2003). Other scholars have suggested that democratization in East Asia may unleash ethnic tensions, political forces that actually undermine democratic progress, and the institutionalization of civil liberties (Chua 2003).

In Chapters 4 and 8, we separately analyzed the attitudes of ordinary citizens to democracy and capitalism. Chapter 4 described the extent to which ordinary citizens in East Asia embrace democracy as the preferred political system and process, with comparisons to Western democracies. In Chapter 8, we examined the extent to which people endorse the structural principles and behavioral norms of market capitalism as the preferred economic system and process. These separate analyses determine citizens' reactions to democracy and capitalism as separate phenomena, but not how broadly and deeply these publics are committed to the globally-emerging movement of building capitalism and democracy in parallel (Bunce 2001). This chapter, therefore, examines public reactions to the dual or parallel transformation of authoritarian politics and crony capitalism into market democracy by considering jointly citizens' basic orientations toward democracy and capitalism.

Do the East Asian mass publics favor the building of political democracy and capitalist economy in parallel? Which subgroups are most and least supportive of the parallel development of democracy and capitalism? What factors motivate people to embrace capitalist democracy most and least powerfully? How does their embrace of capitalist democracy compare with their peers' in advanced capitalist democracies in the North American region of the Pacific Rim? The present chapter addresses these questions with further analyses of the WVS conducted in seven East Asian countries—China, Japan, Korea, Indonesia, the Philippines, Singapore, and Vietnam—and two North American countries—the USA and Canada.

The chapter is organized into six sections. First, we briefly review the theoretical literature on the relationship between capitalism and democracy, and discuss how the mass publics of Europe and other regions have reacted to the political and economic liberalization underway in their own countries. Second, we compare the mean levels of popular support for democracy and capitalism across the nine Pacific Rim countries, and determine whether political liberalization is more or less popular than economic liberalization in these countries. The third section identifies six different types of orientations to political economy on the basis of Charles Lindblom's (1977) classic typology of politico-economic systems. We compare the extent to which East Asians and North Americans favor the capitalist or market democracy and other systems of political economy. The fourth section profiles the demographic characteristics of the most and least supportive of capitalist democracy, and compares the profiles across these countries. The fifth section tests four alternative theories—socialization, modernization, culture, and social capital—of popular support for capitalist democratic development. The final section explores the prospects of parallel development in East Asia from the perspective of its citizenry.

SUPPORT FOR DEMOCRACY AND MARKETS IN OTHER REGIONS

How do democracy and capitalism relate to each other? Are democratization and market-oriented economic reforms mutually supportive processes, or are they in tension? To date, these questions have been examined mostly at the macrolevel of independent states (Almond 1991; Berger 1992; Elster 1993; Nelson 1994). Some scholars like Robert Dahl (1998), Barrington Moore Jr. (1966), and Joseph Schumpeter (1942), for example, contend that economic freedom is the foundation of political freedom, and thus, capitalism constitutes a historical precondition of democracy. More recently, advocates of democratic good governance and the Washington Consensus argue that economic and political liberalization complement each other (World Bank 1993; Williamson 1993; see also Chan 2002; Stiglitz 2002). This is also the logic of the human development model presented by Inglehart and Welzel in Chapter 2 in this volume.

Other scholars such as Jon Elster (1993) and Adam Przeworski (1991, 1993) hold that market reforms derail, rather than facilitate, the process of democratization because they inflict economic hardships on the mass public. In countries where ethnic minorities dominate markets, Amy Chua (2000, 2003) claims that the concurrent pursuit of free markets and democratic government based on universal suffrage often produces highly destructive ethnopolitical consequences such as in Indonesia, the Philippines, and some of the nations of Southeast Asia.

Other research suggests that the processes of democratization and economic liberalization affect each other differently across place and time. Valerie Bunce (2001) and Hyeok Yong Kwon (2004) recently compared the relationship between capitalist and democractic development across global regions. Their findings indicate that democratization has coexisted favorably with economic reforms in East and Central Europe, but not in Latin America or Southern Europe. Although economic reform has a positive impact on democratization in the former, its effects in the latter are negative. These studies, when considered together, suggest that the ethnic, historical, and regional contexts of independent states shape the form and strength of the relationship between capitalism and democracy.

These types of macroanalyses, however, do not reveal the nature of the relationship between capitalism and democracy in individual political beliefs. And, ultimately, the transformation of the political and economic cultures in East Asia will depend on how citizens view these two processes. In the minds of the citizens, how do capitalism and democracy interact with each other? Does their embrace of capitalism drive them toward democracy, or does their embrace of democracy drive them toward capitalism?

Over the past decade, an increasing number of survey-based studies have examined these questions. In East and Central Europe, for example, research has measured popular support for both political and economic liberalization (Rose, Haerpfer, and Mishler 1998; Mason et al. 2000). After the transition, democracy was more popular than capitalism (Duch 1995; Gibson 1996*a*). When democratic and economic attitudes are considered together, relatively small minorities of the East and Central European publics supported the building of democracy and capitalism in parallel (McIntosh et al. 1994; Hiller 2001; Zimmerman 2002). In these postcommunist nations, supporters of market democracy constitute relatively small minorities of less than one-third of the citizenry. Supporters are most often found among better-educated, male, younger, and urban people (McIntosh et al. 1994: 503; Zimmerman 2002: 64).

Other research has determined the nature of the relationship between attitudes toward democratic politics and free markets. Studies of postcommunist Eastern Europe found that democratic and capitalist attitudes were moderately interrelated, with democratic attitudes influencing economic attitudes more than economic attitudes do democratic ones (Gibson 1996*b*; Rose, Haerpfer, and Mishler 1998). Because these attitudes do not reinforce one another strongly, there are many democrats who oppose capitalism and many marketeers who oppose democracy. Over time, however, the democratic and economic attitudes of Eastern and Central Europeans have become more congruent as they gain more experience with democratic politics and market economics (Gibson 1996; Hiller 2001).

Recent surveys in Africa also find that more people welcome democracy than capitalism. Much more so than in Eastern and Central Europe; Africans' attitudes toward democratic and economic liberalization remain largely unrelated and incoherent. "On the one side, almost all sympathizers of free markets are firmly committed to democracy. On the other hand, less than one-third of all democrats favor the market" (Bratton, Mattes, and Gyimah-Boadi 2004: 350). In the minds of Africans, therefore, capitalism and democracy do not complement one another; they merely coexist because capitalism as a development process is viewed as secondary to democracy (Bratton and Mattes 2000). More surprising is the finding that support for democracy and markets is very weakly linked to demographic characteristics, including educational attainment. Comparing these findings from Africa and Eastern Europe reveals that public reactions to democracy and capitalism vary a great deal from one region to another.

How do the citizens of East Asian countries react to democratic and market reforms? How does their support for the development of capitalist democracy compare with what is noted in other regions? To date, no systematic effort has explored these questions. This chapter ascertains the patterns, distribution, and sources of East Asians' reactions to the parallel development of capitalism and democracy. We compare opinions in the East to the Western democracies included in the 2000–2 wave of the WVS.

COMPARING LEVELS OF PUBLIC SUPPORT FOR DEMOCRACY AND CAPITALISM

To address the question of East Asian support for democracy and markets, the WVS measured overall attitudes toward democracy and capitalism with separate opinion batteries. To measure support for democracy as a political regime, the WVS asked respondents to rate their approval of each of four different systems: (*a*) having a strong leader who does not bother with parliament and elections; (*b*) having experts, not government, make decisions according to what they think is best for the country; (*c*) having the army rule; and (*d*) having a democratic political system (also see Chapter 4).[1] These items tap the affective endorsement of democracy as a political system; the first three measure support for various autocratic regimes and the fourth a democratic system.[2]

To measure affinity for capitalism, the WVS asked respondents to rate the norms of market capitalism on a 10-point scale, which included: (*a*) the private ownership of business and industry, (*b*) competition in the marketplace, (*c*) the unequal distribution of income as an incentive for individual striving, and (*d*) individuals' responsibility for their own welfare (also see Chapter 8).[3]

Figure 12.1 shows the percentages of democrats and capitalists for each of the nine Pacific Rim countries surveyed in the 2000–2 WVS. In all of the East Asian and North American countries, democrats outnumber capitalists by substantial margins. This indicates that democracy is more popular than capitalism in both new and old democracies on the Pacific Rim, at least as measured in these surveys. The preponderance of democratic popularity, however, varies substantially across the countries within and between the two regions. In Indonesia and the Philippines, democracy is more popular than capitalism by a relatively small margin of 5 or 6 percent. In China, Japan, Korea, and Singapore, the margins are greater than 20 percentage points. Even in North America, there is relatively greater support for democracy among Americans (15 percent) and Canadians (23 percent). Comparing these figures between the two regions shows that the masses favor democracy and capitalism more unevenly in East Asia than in North America.

Across these nations, the Philippines is the only country where a minority (42 percent) supports democracy, as was shown in Chapter 4, as well as only minority support for market capitalism. The 2001 East Asian Barometer survey in the Philippines also found this pattern (Shin and Wells 2005).[4] Despite the imagery of the "people power" movement that restored democracy in this country nearly two decades ago, Filipinos are not strongly supportive of

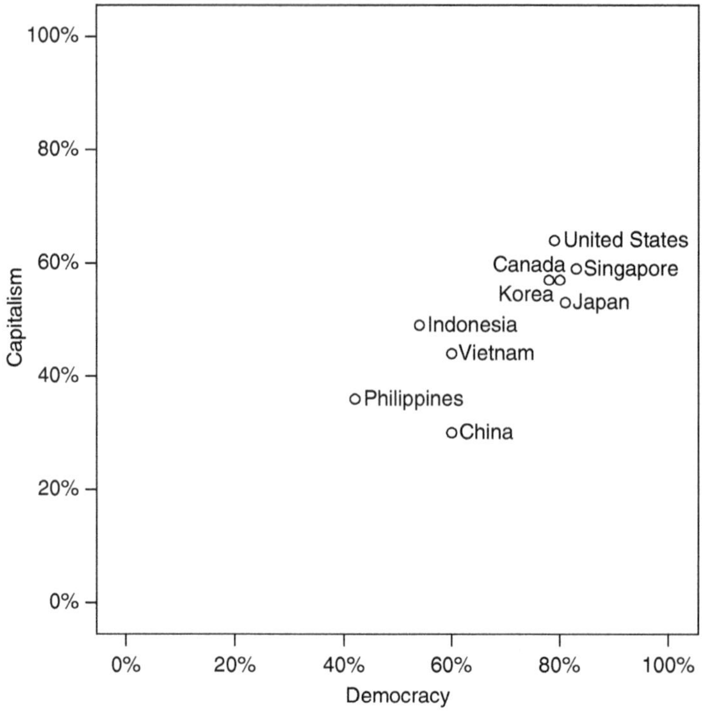

FIGURE 12.1. Levels of popular support for capitalism and democracy in comparison

Source: 2000–2 WVS.

democracy, which suggests that the cultural base of democracy in the Philippines remain uncertain.

By comparison with the two North American countries, where large majorities favor capitalism, there is only minority support for capitalism in four of the seven East Asian nations: China (30 percent), the Philippines (36 percent), Vietnam (44 percent), and Indonesia (49 percent). Clearly, East Asians, when considered as a whole, welcome capitalism much less than their North American peers who have lived all their lives in a free-market economy. This finding suggests that the more people experience in a capitalist economic system, the more strongly they support it. Among East Asians, however, popular support for such a system of economy is not always higher in the countries with longer and greater exposure to it. For example, support is significantly higher in socialist Vietnam than in the capitalist Philippines. Obviously, the cultural values of each country affect the performance of a capitalist system and popular reactions to the system.

Majorities in the two North American countries support both democracy and capitalism. In East Asia, however, this pattern of majority support for both democracy and capitalism exists in only three countries: Japan, Korea, and Singapore. In China, Indonesia, and Vietnam, majorities fail to support capitalism while supporting democracy. East Asia and North America are alike in that more people favor democracy than capitalism. Nonetheless, the two regions are significantly different in the patterns in which majorities favor or do not favor both democracy and/or capitalism.

SUPPORT FOR PARALLEL DEVELOPMENT

Why is it desirable to promote democracy and capitalism in parallel? Over the past decade, an increasing number of political scientists and economists have explored this question from a variety of theoretical and empirical perspectives (Bhalla 1997; LaPorta et al. 1998; Dethier et al. 1999; Olson 2000; Przeworski et al. 2000; Iqbal and You 2001; Chan 2002; Gwartney et al. 2004; Rivera-Batiz 2002). Specifically, these researchers have examined the reasons why, and the ways in which, democracy and capitalism form a symbiosis. According to their research findings, democracy and markets need each other to fulfill their own potentially favorable effects on human development.

As in India until recently, democracy without competitive markets cannot transform innovative ideas and new technologies into viable products. Consequently, it fails to achieve significant economic growth. Countries can grow faster when they expand the role of markets and introduce competition into the markets (Bhagwati 2002). Markets without the democratic institutions of the rule of law and checks and balances, on the other hand, cannot operate fully by laissez-faire principles. Only when authoritarian rule is transformed into a democracy and economic freedom comes to coexist with political freedom, can a genuine free-market economy be developed to foster sustained human development (Bhalla 1997). As the outbreak of the 1997 economic crisis in East Asia suggests, markets under authoritarian rule can, by themselves, produce the rapid growth of the economy. Rapid economic growth, however, cannot be sustained without the democratic political institutions that keep markets performing both efficiently and equitably (Iqbal and You 2001). As observed in postcommunist countries in Europe, moreover, democracy facilitates economic liberalization by legitimizing reform measures (Dethier et al. 1999).

In a nutshell, the literature displays general agreement that democracy and capitalism can and should form a symbiosis by acting as complementary forces in fostering and sustaining development. In the words of former South Korean President Kim Dae Jung (2001: 1): "Democracy and a market economy are like two wheels of a cart: both must move together, and each depends on the other for forward motion." In the words of economist Bhagwati (2002: 159): "Democracy and markets are the twin pillars on which lasting development can thrive." The fundamental solution to the economic problems of market authoritarianism, therefore, requires much more than the policies aiming to liberalize and restructure the economy alone. Such a solution requires the democratic transformation of an authoritarian political system that contributes to the malfunctioning of markets (Sen 2001; Stiglitz 2002). To build a nation of well-being, therefore, advocates of parallel development claim that the development of a democratic political system has to be pursued alongside the development of a free-market economy.[5]

To address the question of whether citizens around the Pacific Rim jointly endorse both market capitalism and liberal democracy, we identified basic mixes of opinions on both dimensions (see Table 12.1). The first four of these types of politico-economic orientations are built on the conceptual foundation that Charles Lindblom (1977) developed for his classic study of political economy (cf. Bhagwati 2002). *Market democrats* favor expanding both democratic rule and the role of markets simultaneously. This is the presumed modal pattern in the USA (Lipset 1994). *Social democrats* support further democratization, but are reluctant to reduce the involvement of the state in the economy. This category represents the long European tradition of social democracy such as represented in the Second International. Such orientations are identified with social democracy in Scandinavia or continental social democrats before their acceptance of market-based economies. *Market authoritarians* are the mirror images of social democrats; they support the reforms to expand markets while opposing the expansion of democracy. This orientation might be identified with Lee Kuan Yew's Singapore, Pinochet's Chile, or Deng Xiao Ping's China. *Social authoritarians* support neither democratization nor marketization. Zimmerman (2002) describes this orientation as ideological Leninists in the Soviet context, with strong commitments to state authority in both domains. The East Asian equivalent would be China under Mao, or Vietnam before its *doimoi* reforms. Indeed, it is a model widely seen in less-developed nations, and sometimes advocated as a course to government-directed development (Huntington and Nelson 1976).

TABLE 12.1. *Patterns of popular support for democracy and capitalism*

	Regime preferences		
Economic preference	Nondemocratic	Democratic	Other opinions
Market economy	Market authoritarians	Liberal democrats	Ambivalent
State-managed	Socialist	Social democrats	Uninformed

To this mix, we add two additional types. *The ambivalent* are neutral or evenly mixed in their overall orientations to either of these two changes. *The uninformed* are those who are either unable or unwilling to commit themselves to a viewpoint.

These four core types are also conceptually comparable to the ones that McIntosh et al. (1994) and Hiller (2001) used in their analyses of Eastern European reactions to the dual transformation of democratization and marketization. The last two types were used in Zimmerman's analysis of Russian public opinion (2002). Considering neutral or nonopinions is especially important in developing nations where attitudes might not yet be well-formed. Of all six types, only capitalist democrats are congruent with a system of political economy that promotes capitalism and democracy in parallel. Thus, the proportion of respondents falling into this particular type is considered an indicator of popular support for parallel development in each country.

Respondents of each country were placed into one of the six types by aggregating their overall democratic and capitalist support scores. Those whose overall scores on both the political and economic dimensions were higher than 0 were treated as capitalist democrats. Those who scored higher than 0 only on the democratic dimension were treated as social democrats. Those who scored higher than 0 only on the capitalist dimension were treated as capitalist authoritarians. Those who scored lower than 0 on the two dimensions were treated as social authoritarians. Those who scored 0 on either dimension were called the ambivalent, while those who did not answer most of questions in the two chosen sets of four questions were treated as the uninformed.

Table 12.2 presents the percentages falling into the six response types for each nation. What is most apparent is the high percentage of non-attitudes in the Asian nations, as well as in North America. In six of the seven East Asian countries, from one-third to more than one-half is either ambivalent or uninformed. Singapore is the only East Asian country where less than one-third falls into these two categories. In four of these East Asian countries, moreover, the uncommitted substantially outnumber the capitalist democrats, who support the parallel development of capitalism and democracy, by margins ranging from 18 percent (Vietnam) to 31 percentage points (China). Only in three countries—Japan, Korea, and Singapore—do capitalist democrats outnumber the uncommitted—a pattern observed in both Canada and the USA, where the uncommitted constitute much less than one-third of their populaces. These findings indicate two notable differences between the two regions of the Pacific Rim. First, East Asians, as compared to North Americans, are much less likely to express an opinion about the political economy.[6] Second and especially critical, the former are much less accepting of market capitalism than the latter.

TABLE 12.2. *Types of popular orientations toward the political economy*

	East Asia							North America	
	China	Japan	Korea	Singapore	Indonesia	Philippines	Vietnam	Canada	USA
Social authoritarian	4%	1%	1%	2%	4%	15%	3%	3%	3%
Capitalist authoritarian	2	2	5	4	10	15	3	5	7
Social democrat	23	17	16	15	10	14	12	18	12
Capitalist democrat	20	46	45	51	28	16	32	48	53
Uncommitted									
Ambivalent	28	21	27	27	40	39	30	23	24
Uninformed	23	13	6	1	9	0	20	3	1

Source: 2000–2 WVS.

In East Asia, the proportions of capitalist democrats vary a great deal across countries—from a small minority of 16 percent in the Philippines to a majority of 51 percent in Singapore. The adherence to both principles by the majority of Singaporeans underscores the public's lack of adherence to the separation of political and economic liberalism that the regime advocates. Respondents are most accepting of market capitalism in Japan, Korea, and Singapore, but even in these three countries, only four-ninths to a bare majority register as capitalist democrats in favor of both capitalism and democracy. In contrast, in the two North American countries, capitalist democrats constitute more than one-half or nearly half of the public. Evidently, support for the capitalist democratic system of political economy is much more narrowly based and more unevenly distributed in East Asia than in North America.

In terms of support for other types of political economy, however, the two Pacific Rim regions do not differ much from each other. In both regions, supporters of the social democratic system constitute less than one-quarter of the population. As in the two North American countries, moreover, supporters of the authoritarian system of either a socialist or capitalist nature constitute small minorities of less than one-tenth in five East Asian countries. Only in Indonesia and the Philippines are more than one out of seven attached to authoritarian rule. These findings indicate that the two regions are more alike in rejecting the authoritarian or socialist system of political economy than in embracing the capitalist democratic system.

Evidently, East Asians, like their peers in North America, do not subscribe to a political economy based on the principle of either authoritarianism or socialism. However, many of the East Asian opponents of the authoritarian or socialist political economy, unlike their North American peers, have yet to embrace the virtues of market capitalism. Only in the economically developed countries of Japan, Korea, and Singapore does a majority or a large plurality support market democracy as in Canada and the USA. In the other four East Asian countries, minorities from just one-fifth to nearly one-third support market democracy. Evidently, a positive relationship exists between levels of economic development and support for market democracy. This is not surprising. Interestingly, the people of Vietnam favor market democracy more strongly than the people of capitalistic Indonesia and the Philippines.

SUPPORTERS OF MARKET DEMOCRACY

Building on the themes of this volume, and the model of social modernization as a driving force for political and economic change, we examined a set of factors that might tap these modernization processes.[7] We focus on support for market democracy, since this represents the combined orientations toward both a market economy and a democratic political system.

Previous survey-based studies of democratic and economic reforms offer a variety of theories explaining popular reactions to democratic and market reforms. Several theories focus on individuals' attributes, such as predisposition toward risk and change, while others deal with the circumstances in which they lived in the past and in which they live at present. From the existing theories, we selected four general types to account for the reactions of the East Asian masses to market capitalism. They are: (*a*) modernization, (*b*) socialization, (*c*) culture, and (*d*) civil society.

The modernization theory emphasizes the emancipative and facilitative functions of economic and social development for the human lot (Inglehart and Welzel, in this volume). According to Lipset (1959*b*, 1994) and other modernization theorists (Inkeles and Smith 1974; Przeworski et al. 2000), socioeconomic development provides the resources that free people from the physical and cognitive constraints of poverty and illiteracy. In addition, growing socioeconomic resources enable individuals to pursue what they think improves the quality of their lives. Furthermore, individual citizens' acquisition of expanding intellectual resources available in their community affords them greater choices, opportunities, and possibilities. Formal education and economic wealth as core elements of socioeconomic development are, therefore, expected to orient ordinary East Asians toward the system of market democracy, which would allow them to make autonomous choices in their private and public lives.

Education represents the political sophistication of the individual and their likely employment in a higher status profession, exposure to the mass media, and greater awareness of global economic and political conditions. Income measures an individual's social status and their living conditions, and like education, may reflect exposure to broader information about the work. In addition, we combined education and income to create a summary measure of social status that might more broadly tap exposure to the influences of social modernization (also see multivariate analyses in Table 12.4 below).

Table 12.3 reports the percentages supporting market democracy for several social status variables. With increasing education, people become more supportive of market democracy in every nation. Those with little or no formal education are the least supportive of market democracy, while the college-educated are more supportive. Even so, the extent of such educational difference varies considerably within and between the two regions of the Pacific Rim.

In East Asia, educational differences are substantial in China, Japan, Korea, Singapore, and Vietnam, and these relationships are weaker in Indonesia and the Philippines. Educational differences are also substantial in the USA (25 percent) and Canada (19 percent). The existence of a marked educational pattern across political and economic systems suggests there is an individual element to this relationship, reflecting the social status of the individual and the improving life conditions that come with modernization. In addition, the stronger relationship in most East Asian nations implies that modernization effects are more clearly class stratified in these nations, since they have more recently experienced these social processes.

Income, like education, consistently has a positive association with support for market democracy. In all nine Pacific Rim countries, more household income means greater support for market democracy.

TABLE 12.3. *Supporters of market democracy by demographic characteristics*

Demographics	China	Japan	Korea	Singapore	Indonesia	Philippines	Vietnam	Canada	USA
Education									
<High school	14	42	29	44	22	11	24	38	34
High school	22	43	41	48	28	16	36	47	49
College	49	62	53	60	31	21	46	57	59
Income									
Low	15	41	31	44	23	15	30	40	47
Middle	19	46	49	56	28	15	31	50	51
High	27	57	54	73	30	24	51	61	64
Age									
<40	23	49	48	51	27	16	34	47	49
40–59	17	47	42	53	27	16	33	49	55
60+	13	41	39	43	30	17	21	49	58
Gender									
Male	24	54	50	57	28	16	37	55	53
Female	16	39	40	46	28	16	28	44	52

Source: 2000–2 WVS.
Note: Table entries are the percentage supporting market democracy.

Consequently, market democrats are most and least numerous among those people at the two extreme ends of the income scale. In East Asia, the social status differences again tend to be smaller in Indonesia and the Philippines compared to other nations in the region (the large gap is Singapore at 29 percent). Again, we appear to see the causal processes of social modernization at work in these relationships.

We next combined education and income into an index of socioeconomic resources. Figure 12.2 shows a striking parallel across most Pacific Rim nations. From one-half to two-thirds of the most modernized segments of the citizenry—high-income people with a college education—embrace market democracy as the preferred system of political economy. This pattern exists in the established democracies of North America, as well as in most East Asian nations. What differs most between East and West is not the level of support for market democracy across the better educated, but the percentage of the public that fit into this most modernized segment of the population.[8] Thus, further social modernization that increases educational levels, affluence and participation in modern economic sectors should stimulate even more support for market democracy in East Asia.

Another notable feature of Figure 12.2 is that Indonesia and the Philippines stand out from the rest of the Pacific Rim countries. In Indonesia and

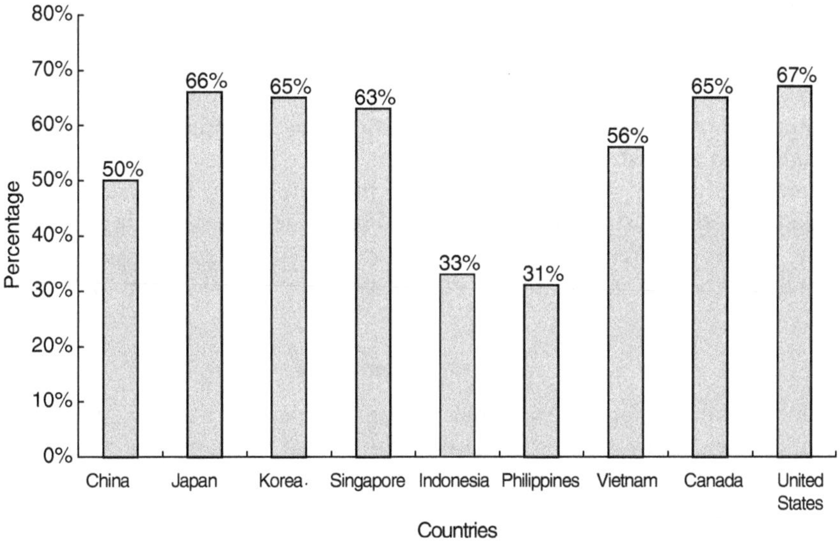

FIGURE 12.2. Supporters of market democracy among the college-educated/ high-income people

Source: 2000–2 WVS.

the Philippines, two countries that are relatively underdeveloped, both economically and politically, larger majorities of two-thirds of the most modernized segments refuse to embrace market democracy. This finding suggests that the two countries are likely to remain underdeveloped because their elites resist liberal economic and political reforms.

Socialization experiences are another potential influence on support for market democracy. We consider age as a predictor in order to tap the historical changes that might find their expression in the different opinions across generations. Gender also can be a marker of socialized values, with the expectation that women are more embedded in traditional cultural norms.

Table 12.3 indicates that in most East Asian countries—China, Japan, Korea, Singapore, and Vietnam—support for market democracy is greatest among the young. At least in part, these patterns probably reflect the substantial changes in the political economy of these nations over the past several decades, as either the economic or political systems (or both) have undergone fundamental transformations. As these societies have changed, younger generations have shifted their values to reflect the new realities as modernization theory would suggest.[9] In contrast, age differences are relatively small—or even reversed—in the two North American populations. On the one hand, since both capitalist markets and a democratic system have a long history in both of these nations, we would expect only small generational differences among Americans or Canadians. The slightly lower support for market democracy among American youth may reflect a growing alienation from the dominant order in this advanced industrial democracy (Inglehart 1990).

Support for market democracy is generally higher among males across both regions, although the magnitude of these differences is small. The gender gap is most pronounced in Japan, where females trail males by 15 percentage points. At the other end of the continuum, the gender gap is smallest in the USA, Indonesia, and the Philippines. These findings indicate that gender differences in support for market democracy are essentially unrelated to national wealth, the current type of political system, or region.

Multivariate Analyses

While social demographic variables help give a social location to support for market democracy, these orientations should also be shaped by other political attitudes. For example, cultural theory emphasizes the role that cultural values play in shaping human preferences and setting the relative priority of those preferences. According to Douglas and Wildavsky (1982), the culture that affirms the values of individualism and egalitarianism motivates people to choose political and economic systems that would maximize autonomous human choice. In contrast, the culture that stresses the values of collectivism and hierarchism, found in Confucianism, motivates people to opt for systems that would minimize autonomous human choice (Wildavsky 1987; see also Shin, Chey, and Kim 1989). The Confucian cultural values of communalism and hierarchism are, therefore, expected to deter East Asians from embracing market democracy.

However, cultural values cannot be considered the only force motivating people toward or away from market democracy. Even in the same culture, some people have been able to make autonomous choices in their private and public lives more often than others have. In this regard, the socialization theory maintains that the level of autonomy individuals have previously experienced affects their political and economic preferences (McClosky and Zaller 1984; Bahry 1987; Rose, Haerpfer, and Mishler 1988). The more often people have experienced the freedom of choice in the past, the more favorably they view a system that would allow them to steer their destinies in their own way. These cultural influences also interact with social position variables. Because East Asian males have generally experienced more freedom of choice than females, the former are expected to favor market democracy more than the latter. Young East Asians are also expected to be more supportive of market democracy than older East Asians, who lived most of their lives under oppressive rule.

In addition, the theory of civic society emphasizes membership in a network of voluntary associations and interpersonal trust as the social capital necessary for both democracy and capitalism to work effectively (Chapter 6 in this volume; Putnam 2000, 2002; Norris 2002). Engaging voluntarily in nonpolitical associations, people become less dependent on family or other closely knit groups, while simultaneously establishing connections with other diverse groups where they practice making autonomous choices that benefit others as well as themselves. Through the experience of such autonomous civic life, citizens come to appreciate the importance of institutional freedom for their public and private lives. They also come to appreciate the important role that interpersonal trust plays in sustaining the autonomy of their economic and political lives (Fukuyama 1995*a*). Civic engagement and interpersonal trust should, therefore, foster support for the system of market capitalism.

To test these alternative explanations for support for market democracy, we chose a set of variables from the 2000–2 WVS. For the modernization theory, we measured the command of socioeconomic resources in terms of formal education and family income that were previously displayed in Table 12.3. To test the socialization theory, we selected age and gender as indicators of authoritarian life experience. For the cultural theory, we selected adherence to the Confucian cultural values of hierarchical collectivism.[10] To test the civil society theory, we selected membership in voluntary associations and interpersonal trust as indicators of autonomous civic life.[11]

We used ordinary least squares techniques to estimate standardized regression coefficients (*betas*) for these predictors of support for market democracy. These coefficients estimate the impact of each variable while statistically controlling for the other variables in the model. According to the *betas* in Table 12.4, modernization, as measured by education and income, matters significantly in all seven East Asian countries. Socialization variables—either age or gender, or both—matter significantly in five of them. Social capital and the culture of hierarchical collectivism, in contrast, matter significantly in only four East Asian countries. In every East Asian country, moreover, indicators of socialization or modernization constitute one of the two most powerful predictors. These findings clearly indicate that support for market democracy among East Asians is, by and large, shaped by the level of freedom they enjoyed in the past and the extent to which they are currently exposed to the forces of modernization.

In the USA and Canada, as reference points, socialization and modernization also significantly influence support for market democracy. In addition, social capital matters significantly in both countries, although it is not one of the two most powerful influences. As the theory of civic community holds, social capital motivates North Americans to embrace democratic politics and a capitalist economy at the same time. The positive role it plays uniformly in North America contrasts sharply with the split roles it plays in East Asia.

Why does social capital drive people away rather than toward market capitalism in two East Asian countries, Singapore and the Philippines, contrary to what is expected from its theory? Perhaps social capital in these

TABLE 12.4. *Sources of support for market democracy*

Theories/ predictors	Countries								
	China	Japan	Korea	Singapore	Indonesia	Philippines	Vietnam	USA	Canada
Modernization									
Education	0.10*	0.14*	0.05	0.03	0.14*	0.09*	0.03	0.08*	0.12*
Income	0.09*	0.08*	0.13*	0.11*	0.05	0.01	0.10*	0.11	0.08*
Socialization									
Gender	−0.12*	−0.10*	−0.10*	−0.12*	0.03	0.00	−0.12*	−0.10*	0.00*
Age	−0.07*	0.05	0.05	0.05	0.05	0.00	−0.06	0.08*	0.08*
Civic society									
Trust	−0.03	0.06*	−0.02	−0.03	0.02	−0.11*	0.06*	0.09*	0.06*
Association	−0.01	0.00	0.06*	−0.07*	—	0.03	0.02	0.02	0.07*
Culture									
Familism	0.00	−0.05	−0.07*	0.01	−0.01	0.03	−0.05	−0.05	−0.02
Authority	0.01	−0.04	0.04	−0.14*	−0.03	−0.06*	0.17*	0.08*	0.02
R	0.22	0.25	0.24	0.24	0.15	0.17	0.27	0.25	0.27

Source: 2000–2 WVS.
Note: *= cofficients significant at the 0.05 level.

two countries is more of the bonding than bridging type. While bridging promotes interactions among people of diverse backgrounds, bonding merely strengthen ties among people with similar history (Putnam 1993), and therefore would not have the effects civil society theorists would expect.

Another regional difference concerns the impact of age and respect for authority. In the two East Asian countries where age matters significantly, China and Vietnam, old people are less likely than young people to embrace market capitalism. In the USA and Canada, on the other hand, old people are more likely to do so. This difference may be attributable to the fact that old people in the two different regions spent much of their lives experiencing two different realities, authoritarian life in the former and democratic life in the latter. In Singapore and the Philippines, greater respect for authority drives people away from market democracy, as the cultural theory of capitalist democratic development predicts. In Vietnam and the USA, however, adherence to this value drives them toward market democracy. The reason for this discrepancy remains a mystery.

DEMOCRACY, MARKETS, AND THE FUTURE

In East Asia, as in other regions of the world, democratization and market-oriented economic reforms have become dominant trends. These trends have become especially strong in the aftermath of the 1997 economic crisis. Whether these political and economic reforms will successfully transform the existing political economies of authoritarian and socialist natures into fully capitalist democracies depends considerably on the reactions of the masses to the systems and processes of capitalism and democracy.

The analyses presented above indicate that most of the East Asian countries have yet to build the solid popular foundations necessary for the development of a fully capitalist democracy—the system of political economy known as the most compatible with the current age of globalization. Only in three of the seven East Asian countries surveyed has a plurality or a majority of their ordinary citizens embraced capitalist democracy as the most preferred system of political economy, as citizens have done in both North American countries. In each of the four other East Asian countries, more than two-thirds of ordinary citizens are reluctant to embrace market democracy, mainly because these citizens are, by and large, uninformed or ambivalent about the virtues of capitalism.

In all of the East Asian countries, moreover, public opinions in favor of capitalism and democracy are not strongly interconnected in a complementary and reinforcing fashion, as imagined by advocates of the Washington Consensus and globalization. Consequently, there are many East Asians who refuse to embrace capitalism while welcoming democracy. There are also many East Asians who refuse to embrace democracy while welcoming capitalism. In all seven East Asian countries, however, those people who favor either democracy or capitalism constitute relatively small minorities. This finding provides little support for the theory that democratization and marketization should be treated as two contrasting or competing goals for human development.

At the same time, there is an optimistic element to our findings that a greater proportion of citizens comes to appreciate the virtues of capitalist democracy as education and standards of living improve. The higher the level of socioeconomic development among East Asians, the greater the level of their support for capitalist democracy. Indeed, individuals of roughly the same social status in East Asia and North America are almost identical in their support for market democracy!

By freeing the masses from the hardships of poverty and illiteracy, therefore, future advances in socioeconomic modernization in East Asian countries are likely to expand and solidify the popular foundations for capitalist democracy. Furthermore, there is a sharp generational gradient in support for market democracy in several East Asian nations, especially in China and Vietnam, where the economic and political reform processes are just beginning. Future generational shifts among the mass citizenry are likely to promote the expansion and solidification of the foundations. Contrary to the Asian values argument, Confucian cultural traditions are not likely to impede the building of capitalist democracy in East Asia.

ENDNOTES

1 The Vietnamese survey did not ask this set of questions. Instead, it asked a different set of questions tapping attitudes toward democracy as a process. We used this second set of questions to measure support for democracy in Vietnam (also see Chapter 4).

2 The ratings of these four systems were first rescaled to range from −2 (strongly antidemocratic) to +2 (strongly prodemocratic). Rescaled scores were then aggregated into an overall index of democratic support with scores ranging from a low of −4 to a high of +4. Those who scored higher than 0 on this index were considered supporters of democracy.

3 The original responses to each of these four items were first rescaled to range from −5 (most strongly anticapitalist) to +5 (most strongly procapitalist). We then aggregated the rescaled scores into an overall index of capitalist support with scores ranging from a low of −20 to +20. Those who scored higher than 0 were considered supporters of capitalism (also see Chapter 8).

4 The Filipinos who support democracy not only as a political system but also as a political process constitute a minority of 40 percent. Corresponding figures for other new East Asian democracies are 63 percent for South Korea, 61 percent for Taiwan, 38 percent for Thailand, and 22 percent for Mongolia.

5 A comprehensive and thoughtful review of the literature debating the democracy-economic development linkage can be found in Chan (2002).

6 In part, this may be a cultural tradition of East Asians, who when confronted by survey researchers are hesitant to express an opinion. Such patterns have been consistently noted in surveys in Japan, for example (Flanagan et al. 1979). In addition, several of our nations have nondemocratic governments where freedom of expression and the willingness to endorse

alternative economic or political systems might be restrained. Thus, Japanese and Korean nonresponses are not markedly different from Americans and Canadians, and the highest percentages of nonopinions are found in Vietnam, China, and Indonesia.

7 Respondents are divided into three age groups: (*a*) the young between the ages of 20 and 39, (*b*) the middle-aged between 40 and 59, and (*c*) the old aged 60 and older. Respondents are divided into three groups: (*i*) those with a primary school education or less, (*ii*) those with a secondary education, and (*iii*) those with a college education or more. To create income groups, the survey asked respondents to place themselves on a 10-point scale of household income where a score of 1 indicates the lowest level of income and a score of 10 correspondents to the highest level. The low-income group included those who rated their household income at a 1–3; the middle-income group included those who chose a rating of 4–7; and the high-income group included those who chose 8–10. Three-point scales measuring education and income were also combined into a 5-point index of socioeconomic resources.

8 In North America, about one-fifth (21 percent) falls into the most modernized segment of high-income people with a college education. In East Asia, however, this segment accounts for less than one-fifteenth (6 percent). Obviously, East Asians fall far behind their North American peers in modernizing the socioeconomic domains of their lives.

9 We also note that there are only modest age differences in the Philippines (1 percent) and Indonesia (3 percent).

10 The WVS asked four separate questions to determine whether respondents were willing: (*a*) to always love and respect their parents, (*b*) to do what is best for their children, (*c*) to instill obedience as a value in their children, and (*d*) to follow a superior's instructions even if they disagreed with them. Affirmative responses to the first two questions were considered indicators of familism and affirmative responses to the last two questions those of authoritarianism.

11 The WVS asked a set of fifteen questions to tap membership in a variety of voluntary associations and groups, including social welfare services for the elderly, religious organization, and sports clubs. Affirmative responses to these questions were summed up to measure the overall level of associational membership. The general level of interpersonal trust was measured by summing up affirmative responses to two questions asking, respectively, whether most people can be trusted, and if they are also fair.

13

Political Culture and Political Change

Russell J. Dalton and Doh Chull Shin

East Asia covers a vast territory endowed with few natural resources while being home to more than 2 billion people, nearly one-third of the world's population. Having always faced the problem of feeding too many people with too limited resources, East Asia was never expected to make rapid economic growth. During the 1950s, when this region and others were finally freed from colonial rule, resource-rich Africa was often favored as the place to experience high and steady economic growth. Contrary to these expectations in the scholarly community and policy circles, East Asia has achieved unprecedented economic growth and social development in the past three decades (World Bank 1993; Terry 2002).

In a single generation, East Asia's GDP per capita has quadrupled in real terms, which is the fastest regional growth rate ever recorded. As a result of such spectacular expansion of their economies, the percentage of East Asians living in poverty has fallen from more than half of the region's population to one quarter. In the places once known as little dragons or tigers—Hong Kong, Korea, Singapore, and Taiwan—many ordinary citizens became four times wealthier than the prior generation. East Asia has experienced a remarkable increase in its share of world trade, from 11 percent of world exports in 1970 to over 28 percent by 2003 (Aggarwal and Morrison 1998).

The rapid expansion of East Asian economies and their successful integration into the global economy have been accompanied by equally impressive improvements in other key dimensions of human development. During the 1970s, for example, average life expectancy was 48 years, and only 40 percent of the adult population was literate. Today, life expectancy has increased to 65 years, and about 70 percent of the adults are literate. Not only have the East Asian economies grown fast, but the quality of life among their citizens has improved significantly (United Nations Development Programme 2004; World Bank 2004).

Equal to the economic achievements has been the democratization process in East Asia. A generation ago, only a single nation in East Asia—Japan—

could claim to be democratic. The third wave of democratization steadily increased the number of democracies as the Philippines, South Korea, and Taiwan made their democratic transitions in the late 1980s. Democracy was introduced into Mongolia, Thailand, and Indonesia in the 1990s. Despite tremendous obstacles, such as the 1997–8 economic crisis, these new democracies have regularly held free and fair elections at all levels of government and carried a variety of institutional reforms to consolidate their nascent democratic rule (Shin and Wells 2005). Even in the remaining nondemocratic nations of the region, the pressure to move towards further democracy and human rights is clearly evident.

There is no doubt that East Asia has been far more successful than any other developing region in expanding its economies and enhancing the quality of people's lives. The region has grown more rapidly than what the West achieved during any comparable period of its long history of industrialization and modernization. To the non-Western world, East Asia offers the unforgettable lesson that poor countries, even with limited natural resources, can develop economically and politically with an appropriate mix of governmental policies and citizen commitment. The region's experiences also demonstrate that Western culture is not the only force promoting modernization, nor is it the most powerful force promoting it rapidly. To the whole world, therefore, East Asian developmental experiences, although deficient in human rights, are of enormous significance in both theory and practice. Those experiences not only discredit the once-dominant dependency theory of less-developed nations, but they offer an alternative model of achieving development (Balassa 1988; Haggard and Kaufman 1992).

Why did East Asia advance while other regions did not? There are a variety of contrasting explanations (Ito and Krueger 1995). One school of explanations argues that East Asia grew more rapidly than other regions because the state adopted the liberal policies that promoted free international trade and kept governmental spending at a minimal level (World Bank 1993). This neoliberal explanation focuses on the role of free markets, the developmental or statist explanation emphasizes the governmental effort to develop export industries through a variety of subsidies (Haggard 1990), and the cultural explanation emphasizes the role of Confucian values (Tai 1989).

In explaining the region's success in rapid modernization, contemporary scholarship has rarely taken into account the role of the ordinary East Asians who made a great deal of sacrifice to "enjoy fruits later". Consequently, little is known about how the socioeconomic and other processes of transforming East Asia have interacted with the attitudes, beliefs, and behavior of its people directly involved in these processes. To date, little systematic research examines how East Asian mass publics react to the parallel development of marketization and democratization in principle or in action—this volume's goal has been to provide this research.

CULTURAL CONGRUENCE

Like most regions in the world, previous descriptions of the political development of East Asia were frequently linked to the cultural and historical traditions of the region—in both social and political terms. With a new wave of public opinion surveys conducted as part of the WVS, we have been able to systematically study attitudes toward democracy and markets across the nations of East Asia and the Western democracies of the Pacific Rim.

We analyzed the political culture of East Asia by building on the theory of cultural congruence (see discussion in Chapter 1): *are the values and orientations of East Asian publics congruent with the development of democratic institutions and market economies in these societies?*

The Congruence of Social and Political Values

One aspect of congruence theory examines the link between broader patterns of authority relations in a society and political values (Eckstein 1966, 1998). Research on East Asia had often stressed the importance of hierarchic authority relations, paternalist family structures, and Asian values in shaping the political values of Asian publics, tracing these values to the Confucian heritage of many East Asian nations (see Chapter 5).

From the perspective of congruence theory, such authority relations would limit the potential for developing democratic values. Our findings from the WVS strongly challenge the Asian values thesis. We uncover broad support for democracy across the nations of East Asia, even in nations that still have authoritarian regimes. This is initial evidence that social relations and cultural traditions have not impeded the development of democratic political norms.

Even more directly, Dalton and Ong (Chapter 5) find little empirical evidence that East Asians support these values more than Western publics. Despite the continuing social traditions in many Asian nations that formalize the patterns of Confucian social relations, support for authority in the family, workplace, and other social relations is not distinctively different between the nations of East Asia and the Western democracies of the Pacific Rim. Moreover, even when such authority orientations exist, they are not strongly linked to democratic values. Dalton and Ong thus conclude that Confucian cultural traditions—to the extent that they do exist in contemporary East Asia—*are not necessarily an impediment for the formation of democratic norms among contemporary publics* in the region.

This does not mean that social norms are unrelated to political norms. Welzel and Inglehart (Chapter 2) demonstrate a strong link between levels of social modernization and the level of self-expressive values in a nation. Wang and Tan (Chapter 3) examine these same relationships in more detail within East Asia. Contemporary Asian publics broadly fit a model of human development that links social conditions to the development of self-expressive values. The good fit of the East Asian nations to this global model of human development argues against East Asian exceptionalism. In addition, these self-expressive values are, in turn, linked to democratic values. Similarly, Chapter 6 shows that civil society activity encourages political engagement; social groups are training grounds for political activism. Park and Shin (2004) also demonstrate that other social attitudes, such as social harmony and group primacy, are related to political attitudes. What is needed is a more comprehensive inventory of social values that are theoretically based in the Asian cultural and historical experience in order to see which values are linked to democratic values.

Our findings also suggest that the link between social norms and political norms is more complex than sometimes recognized. The earlier literature on East Asian political culture describes patterns that once may have applied to the region, but which have changed as a result of social modernization. Without empirical evidence to monitor these changes, descriptions of East Asian political culture have lagged behind the reality of opinions. In addition, the Asian values literature was probably always oversimplified. Just as there is no single European political culture, Asian nations vary greatly in their social, economic, and historical traditions. An Asian values thesis that was meant to span from Singapore to Beijing to Tokyo was probably always a poor fit to reality. Finally, even within Asian cultural traditions, such as Confucianism, there exists a variety of social norms from which one can draw political lessons. Elements of Confucianism—concern for the community and conflict management—are very congruent with democratic values. Thus, Dalton and Ong conclude that Confucian traditions are diverse and do not necessarily impede the development of democratic values among Asian publics.

The Congruence of Social and Market Values

A second aspect of congruence theory focuses on the link between social values and economic norms. Specifically, it evaluates the congruence of Confucian values with the preeconomic crisis model of the developmental state and the newly emerging model of market capitalism. In the 1960s, when East Asia remained a poor region, Confucianism was often blamed for its failure to modernize. Because it supposedly emphasized the values of stability and humanism over those of change and science, Confucianism was considered incompatible with modernization; Max Weber once associated Confucianism with economic stagnation. Ironically, when the region was making rapid economic growth in the 1980s, proponents of the Asian values thesis also attributed the region's economic success to Confucianism.

From the perspective of the Asian values thesis, Confucian values provide the preeconomic crisis model of developmental capitalism that contrasts sharply with Weber's model of market capitalism. By stressing the norms of promoting cooperation rather than competition among employers and employees, and their collective well-being rather than their own self-interest, Confucianism was cited as the cultural foundation of the precrisis model in which the state intervened actively in economic affairs. Obviously, these norms promoting a collectivist approach to economic development are not compatible with those of an individualist approach, which Weber characterized as important components of a capitalist ethic.

To what extent do the mass publics of East Asian countries adhere to the Confucian values of hierarchism and collectivism that are seen as congruent with the developmental state model? To what extent do they uphold the capitalist norms of hard work, thrift, independence, and responsibility? Shin and Dalton (Chapter 8) reveal that relatively small minorities of East Asian publics are attached to the two Confucian core values of hierarchism and collectivism, while smaller minorities support the four capitalist norms of hard work, thrift, independence, and responsibility. Shin and Dalton also reveal that, between the two regions of the Pacific Rim, attachment to the supposed Confucian values is more pervasive in North America, while attachment to the capitalist norms more pervasive in East Asia.

Contrary to the cultural facts presented in the Asian values thesis and the literature based on ethnographic and in-depth case studies, East Asians are not strongly attached to the values of hierarchy and familial authority. These values are no longer the dominant characteristics of East Asian cultures, nor is the attachment to these values an exclusively East Asian phenomenon. Equally notable is the finding that, even when individuals do adhere to the values of hierarchic collectivism, they are not strongly discouraged from embracing a capitalist market system.

In East Asian countries today, only small minorities are strongly attached to the social values of hierarchical collectivism linked to the precrisis model of the development state, in which the state stood above the rest of society on top of a hierarchical chain. Majorities are attached to behavioral norms compatible with the newly emerging model of market capitalism. More so than ever before, social values in East Asia are in the midst of dramatic change, and they are increasingly becoming more congruent with capitalist market values than corporatist economic values. As Kenichi and Kobayashi (Chapter 10) demonstrate, growing prosperity in the future should lead to the greater acceptance of risk, which, in turn, will contribute to the broader acceptance of a capitalist market economy.

The Congruence of Political and Economic Values

A third aspect of congruence theory involves the relationship between political and economic values: specifically, the relationship between attitudes toward democratic politics and free markets among Asian publics. Are their democratic and capitalist attitudes interconnected with each other in a positive and reinforcing way, as advocates of market capitalism assume? Or do they represent the distinct processes of dual transition that even contradict each other, as its opponents contend? We addressed these questions by analyzing jointly their basic orientations toward democracy and capitalism.

This analysis reveals that East Asians' support for democracy and capitalism does not strongly complement each other. As in other global regions, there is a positive relationship between support for democracy (democrats) and support for capitalism in most East Asian nations (capitalists). Yet democratic and capitalist attitudes are not always positively interrelated with each other, nor are they closely related with each other. In East Asian countries as a whole, therefore, orientations toward democratization and economic liberalization are not strongly connected. The Washington Consensus that advocates the complementarity of democracy and markets has yet to be mirrored in the subjective world in which many East Asian live.

Aggregate support for democracy and capitalism also varies across nations. In all East Asian countries, democrats outnumber capitalists by substantial margins; capitalists do not always support democracy. As discussed in Chapter 12, many East Asians support democracy while refusing to support capitalism. Many citizens also embrace capitalism while refusing to support democracy. As a result, those who support both democracy and capitalism do not constitute a large majority of East Asians. Only in Singapore do supporters of both democracy and capitalism constitute a majority of the population. In the other six countries, these supporters constitute small minorities or pluralities. These findings clearly indicate that most East Asian countries have yet to build the solid popular foundation for the building of a fully capitalist democracy.

Even in the East Asian countries where large majorities refuse to embrace market capitalism, however, socioeconomic modernization is a powerful force driving ordinary citizens toward it. As East Asians become more educated and experience higher standards of living, a greater proportion comes to appreciate the virtues of market capitalism and embrace this system of political economy known to be compatible with the current age of globalization. Therefore, future advances in economic prosperity and educational attainment are likely to broaden and solidify the popular foundation for the development of market capitalism in East Asia.

The Congruence between Citizen Values and Institutional Structures

The fourth aspect of congruence theory is the relationship between public opinion and institutions. Ultimately, congruence between the citizen values and institutional structures provides the rationale for political culture theory.

If values and institutions are congruent—regardless of their authoritarian or democratic content—then the political system is more likely to endure and function effectively. And although autocratic states may endure without popular support through the use of force and other authoritarian means, it is difficult to sustain a democracy without a population of democrats. Similarly, a successful market economy presumes that the participants of the system share the principles of liberal market competition.

From the perspective of congruence theory, our findings are perhaps most notable for the *lack of congruence between values and institutions* in several East Asian nations. On the one hand, democratic aspirations are widespread. The citizens of Japan, Korea, and Taiwan express their support for democracy, which provides a foundation for the democratic systems. In addition, support for democracy exists even in nations like China, Singapore, and Vietnam, which still function under an authoritarian system. In these cases, the evidence from the WVS and other recent public opinion surveys suggests that the popular basis for greater political reform exceeds the present development of the political system.

We admit we were initially surprised by these findings because of the critical description of East Asian political culture in previous research, and many Asian experts have questioned these results in conference presentations or lectures. Skepticism is healthy for research. These skeptics argue that these publics do not understand the meaning of democracy, so these are hollow responses. But other questions in the WVS show clear opposition to autocratic governments and authoritarian leaders, with which these publics are familiar. As Welzel and Inglehart argue in Chapter 3, it is not so difficult to believe that humans naturally seek to have more say in their lives, even if they do not live in Western democracies. Other evidence comes from survey questions that ask Asian publics about specific democratic principles, which also show prodemocratic sentiments (Shin and Wells 2005).

Certainly, we must accept that the democratic aspirations in the nondemocratic nations of East Asia are not as well-informed or robust as public opinion in the consolidated democracies of the region. A growing number of new surveys from China, for example, find clear support for a variety of democratic principles in different surveys of different samples using different questions (Chen 2004; Shi 2000*a*; Chu and Chang 2001; Zweig 2002; Tang 2005). Other skeptics claim that expressions of democracy really imply support for Western living standards, but survey evidence discounts this point as well (Albritton and Bureekul 2003). We believe that expressed support for democracy are real attitudes, and the breadth of these democratic aspirations signals the potential for further political development—if elites would allow it.

Vietnam provides an example. Even though Vietnam remains a relatively poor nation, the Vietnamese economy has made tremendous strides forward in the past two decades, dramatically improving living standards and the political resources of the public (Pham and Pham in this volume). Literacy rates (91 percent) and average life expectancy in Vietnam (71 years) lag only slightly behind the USA (97 percent and 77 years, respectively). The Vietnamese public, especially in urban areas, is increasingly exposed to the international economic system and international norms on politics and society. Thus, despite the dominant role still exercised by the Communist Party of Vietnam (CPV), three-quarters of the Vietnamese public say that democracy is the best form of government. From the perspective of our data, the question is not whether the Vietnamese public will support more democratic reform—the real question is whether government and CPV elites will allow the institutions to move closer to public preferences.

On the other hand, democratic values are weakly developed among the Philippine public. This also is surprising, given the people power image of the Philippines and the nation's reconstitution of democracy in 1987. But in terms of individual human resources, the Philippines remains one of the less-developed nations of East Asia, lagging far behind the consolidated democracies of Japan, Korea, and Taiwan (see Figure 2.4). Effective civil and political liberties lag behind the level of emancipative values. Consequently, many citizens in the Philippines express skepticism about democracy and criticism about the government. These two negative traits of the contemporary Philippine political culture are also apparent in the East Asian Barometer. Thus, the Philippines presents a case where many citizens lack faith in the democratic process, and unless this support is restored, this will weaken the democratic system.

In East Asia as a whole, there is also a considerable gap between capitalist economic values and institutions. In all East Asian countries, including the communist countries of China and Vietnam, those who fully embrace the capitalist principle of economic liberalism—private ownership and free competition—are more numerous than those who oppose economic liberalism (see Chapter 8). With the exception of China and the Philippines, two-fifths to more than half of the public endorse the capitalist institutions of both private ownership and free competition, which are widely regarded as the defining characteristic of capitalism. In China and the Philippines, pluralities are partially supportive of those characteristics.

Of the four East Asian countries where popular demand for a capitalist economic system is widespread, however, only Singapore is economically free with a score of less than 2.0 on the Economic Freedom Index (Chapter 1; Miles, Feulner, and O'Grady 2005). The other three countries—Japan, Korea, and Taiwan—are mostly free countries with scores higher than 2.00 but lower than 3.00. The Philippines and the two communist countries—China and Vietnam—are mostly unfree countries, with scores higher than 3.0. When popular demand for capitalism is compared with the Economic

Freedom Index scores measuring its supply, some levels of congruence or equilibrium between popular demand and institutional supply appear to exist only in three countries—Singapore, China, and the Philippines. In Singapore, there is an equilibrium between high levels of popular demand for and institutional supply of economic freedom. In China and the Philippines, in contrast, there is equilibrium between low levels of such demand and supply.

Ahn and Jang (Chapter 9) provide further evidence on the incongruent relationship between economic attitudes and institutions. They demonstrate that East Asians are more likely to reject the capitalist principle of economic individualism that emphasizes personal responsibility for own welfare and governmental nonintervention in economic affairs. Throughout East Asia, there is little support for the reduction of governmental involvement in the economy. This could be the reason why the restructuring of government agencies has been far more difficult to carry out than that of banking and other private enterprises. The prevailing anticapitalist values of economic collectivism, unlike the prevailing capitalist values of economic liberalism, trail behind the neoliberal structural reforms underway to reduce the economic role of government.

In the long run, we would expect congruence between the political culture and political structures and economic institutions—this is the logic of political culture research. But in the short term, there can be considerable discontinuity between the two, especially in societies that are undergoing profound socioeconomic change under autocratic leaders who resist the liberalizing effects of social modernization. Bueno de Mesquita and Downs (2005) have recently noted that authoritarian leaders are apparently becoming more sophisticated in avoiding the democratizing effects of social modernization. This is the condition of East Asia today, but the direction of change based on public attitudes is toward more democracy.

Because of the dynamic processes of change in contemporary East Asia, our findings also display an interaction between the political culture and institutional context. For instance, civil society activity encourages political engagement and the development of social trust across most Pacific Rim nations, but these effects are strongest where regime norms reinforce the democratic potential of these groups (see Chapter 6). Similarly, Wang, Dalton, and Shin (Chapter 7) show that the prodemocratic consequences of social modernization are greater in the consolidated democracies of East Asia that have already undergone a democratic transition. If broad processes of social modernization are driving the political development of nations in East Asia, the impact of these modernization forces will be stronger once regime change occurs, so the new regime will reinforce these new norms. This would further reinforce cultural and institutional congruence.

There are several examples of this process at work in East Asia. For instance, longitudinal studies of Taiwan and Korea point to the general deepening of democratic values with the continued democratic experience since their transitions (Shin 1999; Xu 1999). Indonesia provides an even clearer example. Its democratic transition is relatively recent, and somewhat unexpected. Despite Indonesia's earlier democratic history, the Suharto regime seemed relatively well entrenched, and in the mid-1990s, few experts would have selected it as the next Asian nation to make a democratic transition. Yet when the change came, public opinion responded. We found substantial support for democracy in our 1999 WVS. More extensive monitoring by the Asia Foundation has tracked a marked increase in understanding the democratic process in the years following the transition (Asia Foundation 2003). Knowledge of the electoral process and an understanding of democracy increased following the first democratic elections and the civic education campaigns that accompanied them.

In short, people cannot learn to be good democratic citizens unless they have the opportunity. Authoritarian leaders in East Asia have not given them this opportunity. Instead, they have used the rhetoric of Asian values and cultural traditions to justify their autocratic rule, and claimed the public is not ready for democracy, or democracy is inappropriate for Asia. But this rationale is not accepted by Asian publics.

CONCLUSION

Beyond the specific empirical lessons on the political culture of East Asia that have emerged from our project, there is a larger lesson about how we study political culture. We have described the political and economic values of citizens in East Asia and the Western democracies in broad terms. This is appropriate for a first systematic study of the region and the opinions of its citizens. We thus expect subsequent research will challenge some points in our findings, adding refinements—and sometimes contradictions—to the evidence presented here.

But we believe the most important development is the new ability to study public opinion and public values across East Asia in a systematic way. The insights from ethnographic and descriptive studies were useful when they were the only basis of knowledge. And this research methodology will continue to be useful in generating theory, tracing causal processes and generating new insights on political cultures. But such research typically observes the observable: what people do, rather than what people think and feel. Often societies generate a pattern of ritual conformity as "compliance without commitment" (Eckstein (1988: 797)). Such social rituals may persist even when the values that once may have supported these rituals no longer exist. Irish Catholics going to church on Sunday and Vietnamese engaging in ancestor worship are only imperfect indicators of what these individuals actually value in their lives and society. By systematically surveying publics, we can move beyond the externally observable behavior.

This new wave of survey research in East Asia—the AsiaBarometer, the East Asian Barometer, the WVS, the Comparative Study of Electoral Systems, and other surveys—also generate knowledge that goes beyond the personal experience and subjective judgments of the researcher. Again, we expect that there will be some disagreements among the findings from different projects as we gradually converge on a full description of political values in the nations of East Asia. But the value of this methodology is that it provides a systematic way to evaluate conflicting theories and interpretations by consulting the public themselves. If we have misspecified or mismeasured the content of Confucian traditions or democratic values, a new survey can demonstrate this. This leads to cumulative research, and eventually, a fuller understanding of political cultures in East Asia.

Indeed, we think the lack of such evidence has actually retarded the pace of political development in East Asia because academic research was slow to recognize the transformation of citizen values that was occurring in East Asia. Political elites such as Lee Kuan Yew, Mahathir Mohamad, and other autocratic leaders claimed that Asian values and public opinion supported their rule. However, when a survey shows that 78 percent of Singaporeans reject the idea of government by a strong leader and favor a democratic regime by an even larger margin, it is difficult for political elites to proclaim the legitimacy of an autocratic regime based on the popular will. Similarly, the breadth of democratic aspirations in the People's Republic of China and Vietnam will challenge past claims that these publics accept the current regimes and are critical of democracy. Giving voice to the public is one of the democratic consequences of public opinion surveys.

We quoted Amartya Sen earlier in this volume, and it is an observation that bears repeating (1999: 248): "to see Asian history in terms of a narrow category of authoritarian values does little justice to the rich varieties of thought in Asian intellectual traditions. Dubious history does nothing to vindicate dubious politics". We thus hope that the findings from this volume expand the dialogue on what is possible in East Asia, and what East Asians want for their political and economic future.

Appendix A: Methodology of the World Values Surveys

The WVS is a confederation of equal partners. An international network of social scientists carries out this project, coordinated by an international directorate.[1] An international board develops the questions to include in the survey, and these are translated into the national language by each research institute. Most surveys are funded from national sources, and conducted by leading survey research firms. The surveys are then assembled in a single data-set, and made available to the international research community.

The first wave of the project was a coordinated survey of twenty-one nations conducted in the early 1980s by the European Values Survey group and the WVS (Inglehart 1990). The second wave in the early 1990s expanded to forty-two nations, including many of the postcommunist states in Eastern Europe (Abramson and Inglehart 1995; Inglehart 1997). The third wave in the mid-1990s included fifty-four nations, and expanded the data collection to several nations in the developing world. The fourth wave of the WVS includes representative national surveys examining the basic values and beliefs of publics in more than seventy societies on all six inhabited continents, containing almost 80 percent of the world's population.

Table A.1 lists the nations included in our core analyses in this volume. An exceptional feature of the 1999–2002 WVS is the range of new nations included in the survey, and in combination with the prior 1995–8 wave, the project now includes eight East Asian nations: China, Japan, Indonesia, Philippines, Singapore, South Korea, Taiwan, and Vietnam. Partial data are also available from a 2005 Hong Kong Survey. This is one of the largest and most diverse range of East Asian nations that has ever been surveyed on political and social values. In addition, researchers conducted the same survey in Australia, Canada, New Zealand, and the USA, which provides reference points to compare to the opinions of East Asians to Western democratic publics.

As the range of nations has increased across the waves of the WVS, the sampling and fieldwork techniques also vary cross-nationally. The quality of the samples tends to be higher in advanced industrial societies that have been conducting representative national samples for several decades than in countries in which survey research is new. The logistical difficulties involved in interviewing a representative national sample of the population of such

TABLE A.1. *Number of respondents by country in each WVS wave*

Nation	1981	1990	1995	1999
China	—	1,000	1,500	1,000
Hong Kong	—	—	—	1,252
Indonesia	—	—	—	1,004
Japan	1,204	1,011	1,054	1,362
Philippines	—	—	1,200	1,200
Singapore	—	—	—	1,512
South Korea	970	1,251	1,249	1,200
Taiwan	—	—	1,452	—
Vietnam	—	—	—	1,000
Australia	1,228	—	2,048	—
Canada	1,254	1,730	—	1,931
New Zealand	—	—	1,201	—
USA	2,325	1,839	1,542	1,200

countries as China or Indonesia are far greater than they are in richer and more urbanized countries such as the USA or Japan. In many developing countries, a significant part of the population is illiterate and/or lives in inaccessible areas. The cost of carrying out random area probability samples in such cases may be prohibitive. In a number of the societies included in this project, survey research has only recently become possible, and in some cases, the WVS was the first representative national survey ever carried out in that country. The WVS has recruited some of best social scientists in each country to carry out the survey using the best available sampling techniques, rather than waiting until optimal conditions are present—which would mean limiting the project mainly to economically developed societies.

Another issue involves the reliablity of data collections and respondent openness across the range of political systems included in this project. While Americans are familiar with survey research, and few fear repercussions for expressing displeasure with the government and its policies, this is not the case in all the nations of the WVS. In such circumstances, we (and the reader) should approach some empirical findings with caution. However, our experience and empirical evidence reinforce the validity of surveys, even in non-democratic settings. First, other projects have attempted to systematically test whether worries about government responses are related to expressed support for the regime. These experiments find that these worries have an insignificant impact on opinions (Shi 2001: 405–7; Chen 2004: 35–6). Second, where possible, we have attempted to verify our findings with questions asked in other surveys and other researchers, such as the East Asia Barometer, the Asia–Europe Survey, and the Pew Global Values Surveys. Indeed, our personal experience is that the survey setting encourages answers from respondents that are more surprising for their frankness and openness to share opinions with the interviewer, even in less-than-ideal circumstances.

ORGANIZATION OF THE 1999–2001 SURVEYS

These data were assembled and integrated into a standardized SPSS cross-national data-set by Ronald Inglehart, at the Institute for Social Research of the University of Michigan. They were then sent to Madrid, where Juan Diez Nicolas of Complutense University and ASEP produced a CD-ROM version for distribution to the principal investigators in this project and to include in the published sourcebook from the project (Inglehart et al. 2004). Jaime Diez Medrano developed a software system for exploring the data that is included on the CD-ROM.

WAVE IV: SAMPLING INFORMATION

In most cases, the surveys used stratified multistage random sampling, with the samples being selected in two stages. First, a random selection of sampling locations was made ensuring that all types of location were represented in proportion to their population. Next, a random selection of individuals was drawn up. Most countries used multistage random sampling to select the household, with given individuals in the household being selected using a Kish grid to select the person to be interviewed from a listing of all those in the household. The survey organizations and fieldwork dates are presented in Table A.2; below, we describe the specific sampling process for the fourth wave surveys used in this study.

In many instances, one or more national weight variables must be used to generate representative national samples.

Canada

This was a nationally representative sample of Canadians 18 years of age and older. The sample points were distributed across the provinces of Canada except for The Yukon, Northwest Territories, Labrador, all native reservations and households in primary sampling units located in remote areas of the country. (These excluded groups account for about 3 percent of Canadians aged 18 year or older.) The sample points were proportionately distributed according to community size, categorized into six population size strata. Households were randomly selected from 313 primary sampling units (EAs) throughout Canada. The project selected a total of 4,201 households and achieved a response rate of 56 percent (excluding households without eligible respondents), yielding a total of 1,931 completed personal in-home interviews. The interviews were done between August and September 2000.

Two weight schemes are applied for estimates of Canadians aged 18 years and older. (*a*) Household weighting: corrects for the disproportionate area

Table A.2. *Survey organizations and fieldwork periods*

Wave IV Surveys	
Canada	Canadian Facts, August 3–September 24, 2000 Principal investigator: Neil Nevitte
China	The Research Center for Contemporary China, Peking University, March–June 2001 Principal investigator: Shen Ming Ming
Hong Kong	Policy 21, University of Hong Kong; March–May 2005 Principal investigators: Ng Chun Hung and Tsang Gar Yin
Indonesia	Institute of Quranic Studies; March 1–September 30, 2001 Principal investigator: Nadra Muhamad Hosen
Japan	Nippon Research Center, Ltd (Tokyo), July 2000 Principal investigators: Seiko Yamazaki and Toru Takahashi
Philippines	Social Weather Station/Trends-MBL, July 9–27, 2001 Principal investigators: Linda Luz Guerrero and Felipe Miranda
South Korea	Ewah Women's University (Seoul), November 10–21, 2001 Principal investigator: Soo Young Auh
Singapore	National University of Singapore/Joshua Research Consultants, March 14–August 7, 2002 Principal investigator: Tan Ern Ser
USA	MORI-USA, University of Michigan, November–December 1999 and August–September 2000 Principal investigators: Virginia Hodgkinson, Ronald Inglehart, and Miguel Basáñez.
Vietnam	The Institute for Human Studies of Viet Nam (Hanoi), August 28–September 30, 2001 Principal investigators: Pham Minh Hac and Pham Thanh Nghi
Wave III Surveys	
Australia	Roy Morgan Research Center (Melbourne), Fall 1995 Principal investigator: Alan Black, Edith Cowan University
China	Gallup-China (Beijing), Fall 1995
Japan	Nippon Research Center, Ltd (Tokyo), Fall 1995
New Zealand	Massey University Department of Marketing (Palmerston North), September 1998
Philippines	Social Weather Stations (Quezon City), March–April 1996
South Korea	Ewah Women's University (Seoul) and Seoul National University, Spring 1996
Taiwan	Survey Research Center, Academia Sinica (Taipei), Summer 1994 and Summer 1995
USA	The Gallup Organization (Princeton), Fall 1995

sampling. The regional/area groupings are: Atlantic, Quebec, Ontario, and the West. This also includes an adjustment weight correcting for different response rates achieved by household size. Individual weighting corrects for different chances of selection depending on the number of people 18 years or older in the household. The weight also adjusts for regional, community size, age, and gender variations in response rates.

China

The survey was conducted between March and June 2001 by the research team at The Research Center for Contemporary China of Peking University, under the direction of survey expert Shen Ming Ming. It was carried out on a stratified national probability sample of adults aged 18 and over that covers half of the provinces and about 60 counties in China. The sample reflects the national demographic characteristics of China, such as urban residency (about 30 percent) versus rural residency (about 70 percent), educational levels, gender, age structure, and large geographic regions. A total of 1,000 respondents were interviewed face-to-face.

Hong Kong

The sample for the survey was selected from the Frame of Quarters maintained by the Census & Statistics Department. In the first stage, a random sample of 2,000 living quarters was selected from the Frame of Quarters. For the second stage, a person aged 18 and above was randomly selected from each household using a modified Kish grid. Data collection was carried out during the period from March to May 2005. A total of 1,252 respondents aged 18 and above were interviewed face-to-face, and the response rate in the survey was 71 percent.

Indonesia

The sample was designed to be representative of the entire national population aged 18 or older. A stratified multistage area probability process was used to select districts (Kabupaten/Kota), subdistricts (Kacamatan), and then clusters within districts. Within each cluster, quota controls were used to select respondents based on a matrix of age and gender. The survey was conducted from March to September in 2001.

Japan

The survey was conducted using a stratified area probability sample. The population census from regions and cities were used to stratify the sample at the first stage, starting with 2,000 names and addresses. Selected respondents were at least 17 years of age or older. The response rate was 68 percent. The interviews were collected in July 2000.

Philippines

The survey was conducted in July 2001 using a stratified area probability sample with a random-walk procedure at the last stage. Four study areas were designated, and 300 adults were interviewed per study area. Sampling units were electoral precincts (for urban areas) and barangays or villages (for rural areas).

For the National Capital Region (NCR)'s first stage, 60 precincts were distributed among the 17 NCR cities and municipalities so that each city/municipality was assigned a number of precincts in rough proportion to its population size. An additional provision was that each municipality must receive at least one precinct. Precincts were then randomly selected from within each municipality with probability proportional to population size. In each sample precinct, interval sampling was used to draw five sample households: a starting street corner in the precinct map was drawn at random. The first sample household was selected randomly from the households nearest to the starting street corner. Subsequent sample households were chosen using a fixed interval of six households in between the sampled ones. In each selected household, a respondent was randomly chosen among the household members who were 18 years of age and older, using a probability selection table.

For the rest of the Philippines, provinces were picked using probability proportional to population size. Sample municipalities were then randomly selected from within each sample province. Then, sixty spots for each of the major areas were allocated among the sample municipalities. Using the quota set for spots in each region, the spots were distributed so that each municipality was assigned a number of spots roughly proportional to its population size. After that, the selection scheme was similar to that of the NCR population. The interviews were done in July 2001.

Singapore

The WVS Singapore is based on a stratified random sample of 1,512 Singapore citizens aged 15 and above. The Chinese majority was undersampled, while the minorities were oversampled. The final data-set is therefore weighted on ethnicity. The respondents were interviewed face-to-face. The response rate was 79 percent. The interviews were completed in August 2002.

South Korea

The survey was conducted in November 2001 using a stratified area probability sample of adults who were 20 years and older, living in private dwelling units, excluding those living on islands. First, 120 clusters (towns or villages) were obtained through Probabilities Proportional to Size measure (PPS). Then, two smaller blocks were selected from each cluster. Five households were selected within one smaller block by an appointed procedure. Finally, the interviewers called at selected households and interviewed the person whose birthday was earliest among the family members who were 20 years and older. The interviews were conducted in November 2001.

United States

The sample was drawn in two waves. The first wave used 100 randomly generated sampling points (zip codes) from around the USA. Interviewing facilities within a reasonable distance of each sampling point were identified and lists of residential telephone numbers within a 15-mile radius of the facility were randomly generated. In five cases, due to geographic obstacles, the radius was reduced to 5 miles to facilitate recruiting. A birthday screen was utilized to select the adult in the household who had the most recent birthday. A minimum of three call-back attempts were made on each number. In the first wave, which took place in November–December 1999, 120 telephone numbers were supplied for each sampling point. When the sample was exhausted, the last digit of each phone number was replaced with a randomized digit to generate more telephone numbers. Telephone prerecruits were invited to a central location for in-person interview, approximately forty-five minutes in duration. Twelve interviews were required for each of the 100 sampling points for a total of 1,200 completed interviews.

In the second wave, which took place in August–September 2000, a minimum of 240 telephone numbers were supplied for each sampling point, provided in batches of 120. Each batch was worked in its entirety before the next batch was released. No more than seven males or females were permitted for each sampling point during the second wave.

Vietnam

The survey used a multistage area probability sample. In the first stage, provinces were stratified by the eight census regions and twenty provinces were selected on a basis proportional to population. Within these provinces, ninety-nine districts were randomly selected, and two villages or towns were selected from each district. In the final stage, there were 200 primary sampling units; within each sampling unit, the interviewer conducted a designated random walk to select five households. Within each household, the interviewer selected the adult with the nearest birthday. The response rate was approximately 83 percent. The survey was conducted in August–September 2001.

ENDNOTE

1 Ronald Inglehart is the coordinator of the WVS and an international executive committee oversees the project. The European data are collected by the European Values Group

headquartered at the University of Tilburg. More information on the project is available at the website: http://www.worldvaluessurvey.org. The data from the surveys are available from the Interuniversity Consortium for Political and Social Research at the University of Michigan and other national social science data archives.

Appendix B: Survey Questions and Indices

This appendix describes several of the indices and scales that are used across multiple chapters.

Attachment to the Capitalist Norms
Here is a list of qualities that children can be encouraged to learn at home. Which, if any, do you consider to be especially important? Please choose up to five.

	Important	Not mentioned
Independence	1	2
Hard work	1	2
Feeling of responsibility	1	2
Thrift, saving money and things	1	2

The index counted whether these items were listed as important: 0) none listed to 4) all listed.

Attachment to Confucian Values
Here is a list of qualities that children can be encouraged to learn at home. Which, if any, do you consider to be especially important? Please choose up to five.

	Important	Not mentioned
Independence	1	2
Hard work	1	2

The index counted whether these items were listed as important: 0) none listed, 1) 1 listed, or 2) both listed.

Authority Orientations
The authority orientations index consists of six items:

(1) Regardless of what the qualities and faults of one's parents are, one must always love and respect them,
(2) Parents' duty is to do their best for their children, even at the expense of their own well-being,

(3) One of my main goals in life has been to make my parents proud,
(4) Here is a list of qualities that children can be encouraged to learn at home: obedience is important,
(5) Some say that one should follow one's superior's instructions even when one does not fully agree with them, and
(6) Greater respect for authority is a good thing.

The scale was computed as the simple sum of the approval of authority option on each of the six items. The scale thus runs from 0 to 6 in each nation, except in New Zealand where one item was not available.

Democratic Process Index

The index combines four questions:

'I am going to read off some things that people sometimes say about a democratic political system. Could you please tell me if you agree strongly, agree, disagree, or disagree strongly, after I read each one of them?

- In a democracy, the economic system runs badly
- Democracies are indecisive and have too much quibbling
- Democracies are not good at maintaining order
- Democracy may have problems but it is better than any other form of government'

The items were rescaled to all run in a prodemocratic direction. The four variables were added together to produce an additive scale, and then divided by four. The resulting scale is scored: 1) critical of the democratic process, 4) supportive of democratic process.

Democratic Regime Index

The index combines four questions:

'I am going to describe various types of political systems and ask what you think about each as a way of governing this country. For each one, would you say it is a very good, fairly good, fairly bad, or very bad way of governing this country?

- Having a strong leader who does not have to bother with parliament and elections
- Having experts, not government, make decisions according to what they think is best for the country
- Having the army rule
- Having a democratic political system'

The items were rescaled to all run in a prodemocratic direction. The four variables were added together to produce an additive scale, and then divided by four. The resulting scale is scored: 1) critical of the democratic process, 4) supportive of democratic process.

Economic Individualism
Economic individualism is based on two questions:

'Now I would like you to tell me your views on various issues. How would you place your views on this scale? 1 means you agree completely with the statement on the left; 10 means you agree completely with the statement on the right; and if your views fall somewhere in between, you can choose any number in between. SHOW CARD R'

Incomes should be made more equal — We need larger income differences as incentives for individual effort

1 2 3 4 5 6 7 8 9 10

The government should take more responsibility to ensure that everyone is provided for — People should take more responsibility to provide for themselves

1 2 3 4 5 6 7 8 9 10

These two questions were added together, and then divided by 2 to produce a 1–10 scale. 10 represents greater support for economic individualism.

Economic Liberalism
Economic liberalism is based on two questions:

'Now I would like you to tell me your views on various issues. How would you place your views on this scale? 1 means you agree completely with the statement on the left; 10 means you agree completely with the statement on the right; and if your views fall somewhere in between, you can choose any number in between. SHOW CARD R'

Private ownership of business and industry should be increased — Government ownership of business and industry should be increased

1 2 3 4 5 6 7 8 9 10

Competition is good. It stimulates people to work hard and develop new ideas — Competition is harmful. It brings out the worst in people

1 2 3 4 5 6 7 8 9 10

These two questions were added together, and then divided by 2 to produce a 1–10 scale. The scale was reversed so that 10 represents greater support for economic liberalism.

Personal Satisfaction
This index combined two questions on personal financial satisfaction and life satisfaction:

'How satisfied are you with the financial situation of your household? If '1' means you are completely dissatisfied on this scale, and '10' means you are completely satisfied, where would you put your satisfaction with your household's financial situation?'

'All things considered, how satisfied are you with your life as a whole these days? Please use this card to help with your answer.'

We averaged the individual's overall financial satisfaction and overall life satisfaction, both of which were measured on a 1) dissatisfied to 10) satisfied scale. This averaging results in a variable that ranges from 1 to 10.

Postmaterial Values
The four item index asks respondents to rank four goals: Maintaining order in the nation; giving people more say in important government decisions; fighting rising prices; and protecting freedom of speech. Those who chose the first and third are coded as materialists; the second and fourth as post-materialists. See Inglehart (1990).

Risk Avoidance Index
'Now I would like to ask you something about the things which would seem to you, personally, most important if you were looking for a job. Here are some of the things many people take into account in relation to their work. Regardless of whether you are actually looking for a job, which one would you personally place first if you were looking for a job?'

'(And) what would be your second choice?'

In both of these questions, when the respondents chose either "a good income so that you do not have any worries about money" or "a safe job with no risk of closing down or unemployment", we defined these responses as indicating a preference for the stability of a job, a part of risk avoidance. The resulting scale ranges from 0) low risk avoidance to 2) high risk avoidance.

Self-Expressive Values
See the explanation in Welzel and Inglehart (Chapter 2). Also see Inglehart and Welzel (2005).

References

Abramson, Paul, and Ronald Inglehart (1995). *Value Change in Global Perspective*. Ann Arbor, MI: University of Michigan Press.

Adorno, Theodore, et al. (1950). *The Authoritarian Personality*. New York: Harper.

Aggarwal, V. K. and C. E. Morrison (eds.) (1998). *Asia-Pacific Crossroads: Regime Creation and the Future of APEC*. New York: St. Martin's Press.

Ahn, Chung-Si, and Won-Taek Kang (2002). Trust and confidence in government in transitional democracies: South Korea in comparative perspective, *Journal of Korean Politics* 11: 3–40.

—— —— (2003). South Korea's Political Culture at the Dawn of the New Millennium: Undoing or Reinventing a Developmental State? Discussion Paper No. 5, Institute of Oriental Culture, The University of Tokyo.

Alagappa, Muthiah (1995). *Political Legitimacy in Southeast Asia: The Quest for Moral Authority*. Stanford, CA: Stanford University Press.

—— (ed.) (2004). *Civil Society and Political Change in Asia: Expanding and Contracting Democratic Space*. Stanford, CA: Stanford University Press.

Albritton, Robert, and Thawilwadee Bureekul (2003). The Meaning of Democracy in a Developing Nation. Paper presented at the annual meetings of the Midwest Political Science Association, Chicago.

—— —— (2004). Impact of Asian Values on Support for Democracy in Thailand. Paper presented at the annual meetings of the Association for Asian Studies, San Diego, March 3–6.

—— —— and Gang Guo (2005). Social Contexts of Asian Democracy: A Cross-National, Within-Nation Analysis of Eight Asian Nations. Center for the Study of Democracy, Paper 03-05. http://repositories.cdlib.org/csd/05–14

Albrow, Martin (1996). *The Global Age: State and Society Beyond Modernity*. Stanford, CA: Stanford University Press.

Almond, Gabriel (1991). Capitalism and democracy, *Political Science and Politics* 24: 467–74.

—— and Sidney Verba (1963). *The Civic Culture*. Princeton, NJ: Princeton University Press.

—— —— (eds.) (1980). *The Civic Culture Revisited*. Boston, MA: Little Brown.

Ames, Roger (1999). *The Analects of Confucius: A Philosophical Translation*. New York: Ballantine Books.

Amsden, Alice (1989). *Asia's Next Giant: South Korea and Late Industrialization*. New York: Oxford University Press.

Apinall, Edward (2004). Indonesia: Transformation of civil society and democratic breakthrough, in M. Alagappa (ed.), *Civil Society and Political Change in Asia*. Palo Alto, CA: Stanford University Press.

Asia Foundation (2003). *Democracy in Indonesia: A Survey of the Indonesian Electorate in 2003.* Washington, DC: The Asia Foundation.

—— —— and Joshep Love (2001). *Liberalization and Its Consequences.* Cheltenham, UK: Edward Elgar.

Bahry, Donna (1987). Politics, generations, and change in the USSR, in J. Miller (ed.), *Politics, Work, and Daily Life in the USSR: A Survey of Former Soviet Citizens.* Cambridge: Cambridge University Press.

Baker, Kendall, Russell Dalton, and Kai Hildebrant (1981). *Germany Transformed.* Cambridge: Harvard University Press.

Balassa, Bela (1988). The lessons of East Asian development: An overview, *Economic Development and Cultural Change* 36(3): 273–90.

Ball, Richard (2001). Individualism, collectivism, and economic development, *Annuls of the American Academy of Political and Social Science* 573: 56–84.

Banuri, Tariq (1991). *Economic Liberalization: No Panacea.* New York: Oxford University Press.

Bardhan, Pranab (1997). Corruption and development: A review of issues, *Journal of Economic Literature* 35: 1320–46.

Beck, Ulrich (2002). Losing the traditional: Individualization and "precarious freedoms", in U. Beck and E. Beck-Gernsheim (eds.), *Individualization.* London: Sage.

Beeson, Mark (2000). *The Political Economy of East Asia at a Time of Crisis.* University of Queensland.

—— (2002). Theorizing institutional change in East Asia, in M. Beeson (ed.), *Reconfiguring East Asia: Regional Institutions and Organisations After the Crisis.* London: Curzon Press.

Bell, Daniel A. (2000). *East Meets West: Human Rights and Democracy in Asia.* Princeton, NJ: Princeton University Press.

—— and Chaibong Ham (2003). *Confucianism for the Modern World.* New York: Cambridge University Press.

Bellah, Robert N. (1968). Reflections on the Protestant ethic analogy in Asia, in S. N. Eisenstadt (ed.), *The Protestant Ethic and Modernization: A Comparative View.* New York: Basic Books.

Berger, Peter (1988). An East Asian development, in P. Berger and H. Hsia (eds.), *In Search of an East Asian Development Model.* New Brunswick, NJ: Transactions Books.

—— (1992). The uncertain triumph of democratic capitalism, *Journal of Democracy* 3: 7–16.

Bermeo, Nancy (1992). *Liberalization and Democratization: Change in the Soviet Union and Eastern Europe.* Baltimore, MD: Johns Hopkins University Press.

—— (2003). *Ordinary People in Extraordinary Times: The Citizenry and the Breakdown of Democracy.* Princeton, NJ: Princeton University Press.

Bhagwati, Jagdish N. (2002). Democracy and development: Cruel dilemma or symbiotic relationship? *Review of Development Economics* 6(2): 151–62.

Bhalla, Surjit (1997). Freedom and Economic Growth: A Virtuous Cycle? in Jon Elster, Partha Dasgupta, Axel Hadenius, and Daniel Tarschys, eds., *Democracy's Victory and Crisis.* Cambridge: Cambridge University Press.

Blinder, Alan S. (1997). Is government too political? *Foreign Affairs* 76: 115–26.
Blondel, Jean, and Takashi Inoguchi (2002). Political cultures do matter: Citizens and politics in Western Europe and Southeast Asia, *Japanese Journal of Political Science* 3(2): 151–71.
Booth, John, and Patricia Richard (1996). Repression, participation and democratic norms in urban Central America, *American Journal of Political Science* 40: 1205–32.
Bratton, Michael, and Robert Mattes (2000). Democratic and Market Reforms in Africa: What the People Say, Presented at a workshop on Democracy and Development in Africa convened by the Calouste Gulbenkian Foundation in Lisbon, Portugal, June 22–24.
—— —— and E. Gyimah-Boadi (2004). *Public Opinion, Democracy, and Market Reform in Africa.* Cambridge: Cambridge University Press.
Brook, Timothy, and B. Michael Frolic (eds.) (1997). *Civil Society in China.* Armonk, NY: ME Sharpe.
—— and Hay Long (eds.) (1997). *Culture and Economy: The Shaping of Capitalism in Eastern Asia.* Ann Arbor, MI: University of Michigan Press.
Bueno de Mesquita, Bruce, and George Downs (2005). Development and democracy, *Foreign Affairs* 84: 77–86.
Bunce, Valerie (2001). Democratization and economic reform, *Annual Review of Political Science* 4: 43–65.
Cain, Bruce, Russell Dalton, and Susan Scarrow (eds.) (2004). *Democracy Transformed? Expanding Political Opportunities in Advanced Industrial Democracies.* Oxford: Oxford University Press.
Canache, Damarys, Jeffrey Mondak, and Mitchell Seligson (2001). Meaning and measurement in cross-national research on satisfaction with democracy, *Public Opinion Quarterly* 65: 506–28.
Chan, Adrian (1996). Confucianism and development in East Asia, *Journal of Contemporary Asia* 26(1): 28–45.
Chan, J. (1998). Asian values and human rights: An alternative view, in L. J. Diamond and M. F. Plattner (eds.), *Democracy in East Asia.* Baltimore, MD: Johns Hopkins University Press.
Chan, Steve, Cal Clark, and Danny Lam (1998). *Beyond the Developmental State: East Asia's Political Economies Reconsidered.* New York: St Martin's Press.
Chan, Sylvia (2002). *Liberalism, Democracy, and Development.* New York: Cambridge University Press.
Chang, Ha-Joon (1999). The economic theory of the developmental state, in M. Woo-Chumings (ed.), *The Developmental State.* Ithaca, NY: Cornell University Press.
Chen, Jie (2004). *Popular Support in Urban China.* Stanford, CA: Stanford University Press.
—— and Yang Zhong (1998). Defining the political system of post-Deng China: Emerging public support for a democratic political system, *Problems of Post-Communism* 45: 30–42.
Chen, X. and Tianjin Shi (2001). Media effects on political confidence and trust in the People's Republic of China in the post-Tiananmen period, *East Asia* 19(3): 84–118.

Chirkov, V. I., R. M. Ryan, Y. Kim, and U. Kaplan (2003). Differentiating autonomy from individualism and independence: A self-determination theory perspective on internalization of cultural orientations and well-being, *Journal of Personality and Social Psychology* 84: 97–110.

Chow, Peter (2002). Financial Reform and Corporate Governance in Asia after the 1997 Financial Crisis, http://www.aoef.org/papers/2002/chow.doc

Chu, Yun-han (1992). *Crafting Democracy in Taiwan*. Taipei: Institute for National Policy Research.

Chu, Yun-han (2003). Paper presented at the conference on "*How People View Democracy: Public Opinion in New Democracies*", at the Center for Democracy, Development and the Rule of Law, Stanford University, July 2003.

—— (2005). Taiwan's year of stress, *Journal of Democracy* 16(2): 43–57.

—— and Yu-tzung Chang (2001). Culture shift and regime legitimacy: Comparing mainland China, Taiwan, and Hong Kong, in S. Hua (ed.), *Chinese Political Culture, 1989–2000*. Armonk, NY: ME Sharpe.

—— Larry Diamond, and Doh Chull Shin (2001). Halting progress in Korea and Taiwan, *Journal of Democracy* 12(1): 122–36.

—— and Yu-tzung Chang, and Fu Hu (2003). Regime performance, value change and authoritarian detachment in East Asia. Paper presented at the conference on "*How East Asians View Democracy*". Taipei, December.

—— Alfred Hu, Yu-tzung Chang (2004). Sources for the Uneven Development of Democratic Culture in East Asia: Regime Performance and Authoritarian Detachment. Paper presented at the East Asian Barometer conference, Taipei.

Chua, Amy (2000). The paradox of free market democracy: Rethinking development policy, *Harvard International Law Journal* 40(2).

—— (2003). *World on Fire: How Exporting Free Market Democracy Breeds Ethnic Hatred and Global Instability*. New York: Doubleday.

Collier, Ruth (1999). *Paths Toward Democracy: Working Class and Elites in Western Europe and South America*. Cambridge: Cambridge University Press.

Communist Party of Vietnam (CPV) (1991). *Materials of VII Congress*. Hanoi: Su that Publishing House.

—— (2001). *Materials of IX Congress*. Hanoi: National Political Publishing House.

Conradt, David (1980). The changing political culture, in G. Almond and S. Verba (eds.), *The Civic Culture Revisited*. Boston, MA: Little Brown.

Converse, Philip (1970). Attitudes and non-attitudes, in E. Tufte (ed.), *The Quantitative Analysis of Social Problems*. Reading, MA: Addison-Wesley.

Dahl, Robert (1971). *Polyarchy: Participation and Opposition*. New Haven, CT: Yale University Press.

—— (1982). *Dilemmas of Pluralist Democracy*. New Haven, CT: Yale University Press.

—— (1989). *Democracy and Its Critics*. New Haven, CT: Yale University Press.

—— (1998). *On Democracy*. New Haven, CT: Yale University Press.

Dahrendorf, Ralf (1967). *Society and Democracy in Germany*. Garden City, NY: Doubleday.

Dalton, Russell (1977). Was there a revolution?: A note on generational versus life cycle explanations of value differences, *Comparative Political Studies* 9(4): 459–73.

—— (1988). Politics and culture in West Germany, in S. H. Barnes (ed.), *Politics and Culture Series*. Ann Arbor, MI: University of Michigan Press.

—— (1994). Communists and democrats: Democratic attitudes in the two Germanies, *British Journal of Political Science* 24: 469–93.

—— (2004). *Democratic Challenges, Democratic Choices: The Erosion of Political Support in Advanced Industrial Democracies*. Oxford: Oxford University Press.

Dalton, Russell, and Alix van Sickle (2005). The resource, structural, and cultural bases of protest. Center for the Study of Democracy research series (http://repositories.cdlib.org/csd/05-11/).

—— and Nhu-Ngoc Ong (2005). Civil society and social capital in Vietnam, in G. Mutz and R. Klump (eds.), *Modernisation and Social Transformation in Vietnam*. Hamburg: Institut für Asienkunde (IFA).

—— Pham Minh Hac, Pham Thanh Nghi, and Nhu-Ngoc Ong (2002). Social relations and social capital in Vietnam: The 2001 World Values Survey, *Comparative Sociology* 1: 369–86.

Davis, Michael C (1998). The price of rights: Constitutionalism and East Asian economic development, *Human Rights Quarterly* 20: 303–37.

Davis, Winston (1987). Religion and development: Weber and the East Asian experience, in M. Weiner and S. Huntington (eds.), *Understanding Political Development*. Boston, MA: Little Brown.

Dean, Garry (1999). East Asia and the root of the economic crisis, http://okusi/garydean/works/asiacrisis.html

DeBary, William (1998). *Asian Values and Human Rights: A Confucian Communitarian Perspective*. Cambridge: Harvard University Press.

Deci, Edward. L. and Richard M. Ryan (2000). The what and why of goal pursuits: Human needs and the self-determination of behavior, *Psychological Inquiry* 11: 227–68.

Dethier, Jean-Jacques, Hafez Ghanem, and Edda Zoli (1999). Does democracy facilitate the economic transition? An empirical study of Central and Eastern Europe and the former Soviet Union. Washington, DC: World Bank.

Deutsch, Karl (1961). Social mobilization and political development, *American Political Science Review* 55: 493–514.

Deyo, Frederick (ed.) (1987). *The Political Economy of New Asian Industrialism*. Ithaca, NY: Cornell University Press.

Diamond, Larry (1988). Introduction, in L. Diamond, J. Linz, and S. M. Lipset (eds.), *Democracy in Developing Countries: Asia*. Boulder, CO: Lynne Reiner Press.

—— (1993). The globalization of democracy, in R. Slater, B. Schutz, and S. Dorr (eds.), *Global Transformation and the Third World*. Boulder, CO: Lynne Rienner.

—— (1994). Toward democratic consolidation, *Journal of Democracy* 5: 4–17.

—— (1999). *Developing Democracy: Toward Consolidation*. Baltimore, MD: Johns Hopkins University Press.

—— (2002). Elections without democracy: Thinking about hybrid regimes, *Journal of Democracy* 13: 28–9.

—— (2003). Can the whole world become democratic? Democracy, development, and international policies. Center for the Study of Democracy. Paper 03-05, http://repositories.cdlib.org/csd/03-05

Dore, Ronald (1998). Asian crisis and the future of Japanese model, *Cambridge Journal of Economics* 22: 773–87.

Douglas, Marry, and Aaron Wildavsky (1982). *Risk and Culture*. Berkeley, CA: University of California Press.

Drysdale, P. (ed.) (2001). *Reform and Recovery in East Asia: The Role of the State and Economic Enterprise*. London: Routledge.

Duch, Raymond M. (1993). Tolerating economic reform: Popular support for transition to a free market in the former Soviet Union, *American Political Science Review* 87: 590–608.

—— (1995). Economic chaos and the fragility of democratic transition in former communist regimes, *Journal of Politics* 57(1): 121–58.

Easton, David (1965). *A Systems Analysis of Political Life*. New York: Wiley.

Easton, David (1975). A reassessment of the concept of political support. *British Journal of Political Science*, 5: 435–57.

Economist, The (1998). Asian values revisited: What would Confucius say now? (July 25–31).

Eckstein, Harry (1966). *Division and Cohesion in Democracy*. Princeton, NJ: Princeton University Press.

Eckstein, Harry (1988). A culturalist theory of political change, *American Political Science Review* 82: 789–804.

—— (1998). Congruence theory explained, in W. Reisinger et al. (eds.), *Can Democracy Take Root in Post-Soviet Russia?: Explorations in State-Society Relations*. Lanham, MD: Rowman and Littlefield.

Edwards, Bob, Michael Foley, and Mario Diani (eds.) (2001). *Beyond Tocqueville: Civil Society and the Social Capital Debate in Comparative Perspective*. University of New England Press.

Eisenstadt, Samuel N. (eds.) (1968). *The Protestant Ethic and Modernization: A Comparative View*. New York: Basic Books.

Elster, Jon (1993). The necessity and impossibility of simultaneous economic and political reform, in D. Greenberg, S. Katz, M. Oliviero, and S. Wheatley (eds.), *Constitutionalism and Democracy: Transitions in the Contemporary World*. Oxford: Oxford University Press.

Ember, Melvin, Carol R. Ember, and Bruce M. Russett (1997). Inequality and democracy in the anthropological record, in M. Midlarski (ed.), *Inequality, Democracy and Economic Development*. Cambridge: Cambridge University Press.

Emmerson, Donald (1995). Singapore and the "Asian Values" debate, *Journal of Democracy* 6: 95–105.

Evans, Jeoffrey, and Stephen Whitefield (1995). The politics and economics of democratic commitment: Support for democracy in transition societies, *British Journal of Political Science* 25: 485–514.

Evans, Peter E. (1995). *Embedded Autonomy: States and Industrial Transformation*. Princeton, NJ: Princeton University Press.

Fernandez Jilberto, Alex, and Andre Mommem (1996). *Liberalization in the Developing World*. London: Routledge.

Finer, Samuel E. (1999). *The History of Government*, vol. 1. Oxford: Oxford University Press.

Finkle, J. L. and R. W. Gable (eds.) (1971). *Political Development and Social Change*, 2nd ed. New York: Wiley.

Flanagan, Scott (1982). Changing values in advanced industrial society, *Comparative Political Studies* 14: 403–44.

—— (1987). Value change in industrial societies, *American Political Science Review* 81: 1303–1319.

—— and Aie-Rie Lee (1991). Modernization and the emergence of the authoritarian libertarian value cleavage. Paper presented at the annual meeting at the Southern Political Science Association, Tampa, Florida.

—— —— (2000). Value change and democratic reform in Japan and Korea, *Comparative Political Studies* 33: 626–59.

—— —— (2003). The new politics, culture wars, and the authoritarian-libertarian value change in advanced industrial democracies, *Comparative Political Studies* 36(3): 235–70.

Flanagan, Scott, et al. (1979). *The Japanese Voter*. New Haven, CT: Yale University Press.

Franco, Jennifer (2004). The Philippines: Fractious civil society and competing visions of democracy, in M. Alagappa (ed.), *Civil Society and Political Change in Asia*. Palo Alto, CA: Stanford University Press.

Freedom House (2000). *Democracy's Century: A Survey of Global Political Change in the 20th Century*. Washington, DC: Freedom House.

—— (2002). *Freedom in the World Today*. Washington, DC: Freedom House.

—— (2003). *Freedom in the World 2003: The Annual Survey of Political Rights and Civil Liberties*. Lanham, MD: Rowman and Littlefield.

Friedman, E. (ed.) (1994*a*). *The Politics of Democratization: Generalizing East Asian Experiences*. Boulder, CO: Westview.

—— (1994*b*). Democratization: Generalizing the East Asian experience, in E. Friedman (ed.), *The Politics of Democratization: Generalizing East Asian Experiences*. Boulder, CO: Westview.

—— (2004). Firm Ownership and Internal Labor Practices in a Transition Economy: An Exploration of Worker Skill Acquisition in Vietnam. Paper read at the International Policy Conference on Transition Economies, 31 May–1 June, Hanoi.

Frolic, B. Michael (1997). State-led civil society, in T. Brook and B. Frolic (eds.), *Civil Society in China*. Armonk, NY: ME Sharpe.

Fuchs, Dieter, Giovanna Guidorossi, and Palle Svensson (1995). Support for the democratic system, in H. Klingemann and D. Fuchs (eds.), *Citizens and the State*. New York: Oxford University Press.

Fukuyama, Francis (1992). *The End of History*. New York: Free Press.

—— (1995*a*). *Trust: The Social Virtues and the Creation of Prosperity*. New York: Free Press.

—— (1995*b*). Confucianism and democracy, *Journal of Democracy* 6: 20–33.

—— (1998). *Asian Values and Civilization*, Institute for Korean-American Studies Symposium, Philadelphia, PA.

—— (2003). Asian values in the wake of the Asian crisis, Available at: http://idep.kdi.re.kr/conference/program/

Furman, Jason, and Joseph E. Stiglitz (1998). Economic crises: Evidence and insights from East Asia, *Brookings Paper on Economic Activity* 2: 1–135.

Gallup International (2005). Voice of the People 2005: Trends in democracy global summary, http://extranet.gallup-international.com/uploads/internet/VOP2005_Democracy%20FINAL.pdf

Garron, Robert (1998). *Tigers Tamed: The End of the Asian Miracle*. Honolulu: University of Hawaii Press.

General Statistics Office (2002*a*). *Vietnam Economy in the Years of Reform*. Hanoi: Statistical Publishing. House.

—— (2002*b*). *Results of Family Life Level Inquiry*. Hanoi: Statistical Publishing House.

—— (2003). *Statistical Yearbook 2002*. Hanoi: Statistical Publishing House.

Gerschenkron, Alexander (1962). *Economic Backwardness in Historical Perspective*. Cambridge: Harvard University Press.

Gibbins, J. R. (ed.) (1989). *Contemporary Political Culture: Politics in a Postmodern Age*. Newbury Park, CA: Sage.

Gibson, James (1996*a*). Political and economic markets: Changes in the connections between attitudes toward political democracy and a market economy within the mass cultures of Russia and Ukraine, *Journal of Politics* 58(4): 954–84.

—— (1996*b*). *Putting up with Fellow Russians: Political Tolerance in a fledging Democracy*. Glasgow, Scotland: Centre for the Study of Public Policy, University of Strathclyde.

Gibson, James L. (2000). Changes in Russian Attitudes Toward Democratic and Economic Reform: Results from a 1996–2000 Panel Survey, Presented at the Annual Meeting of the American Political Science Association, Chicago, August 31–September 3.

Gilley, Bruce (2003). *China's Democratic Future: How It Will Happen and Where It Will Lead*. New York: Columbia University Press.

Gilley, Bruce (2006). The determinants of state legitimacy: Results for 72 countries. *International Political Science Review* 27: 47–71.

Goldman, M. and R. MacFarquhar (1999). Dynamic economy, declining party-state, in M. Goldman and R. MacFarquhar (eds.), *The Paradox of China's Post-Mao Reforms*. Cambridge: Harvard University Press.

Gong, Yunshik, and Wonho Jang (1998). Culture and development: Reassessing cultural explanations on Asian economic development, *Development and Society* 27: 77–97.

Granato, Jim, Ronald Inglehart, and David Leblang (1996). The effect of culture on economic development: Theory, hypotheses and some empirical tests, *American Journal of Political Science* 40: 607–31.

Granovetter, Mark S. (1973). The strength of weak ties, *American Journal of Sociology* 78: 1360–80.

Guillen, Mauro F. (2001). Is globalization civilizing, destructive or feeble?: A critique of five key debates in the social science literature, *Annual Review of Sociology* 27: 235–60.

Gwartney, James D., Randall G. Holcombe, and Robert A. Lawson (2004). Economic freedom, institutional quality, and cross-country differences in income and growth, *Cato Journal* 24: 205–233.

Ha Huy Thanh (2000). *Nhung tac dong tieu cuc cua co che thi truong ow Viet Nam (Negative Impacts of Market Mechanisms in Vietnam)*. Hanoi: Social Sciences Publishing.

Haggard, Stephen (1990). *Pathways from the Periphery: The Politics of Growth in the Newly Industrializing Countries*. Ithaca, NY: Cornell University Press.

—— (2000). *The Political Economy of the Asian Financial Crisis*. Washington, DC: Institute for International Economics.

—— and R. R. Kaufman (eds.) (1992). *The Politics of Economic Adjustment*. Princeton, NJ: Princeton University Press.

Halman, Loek (2002). *The European Values Study: A Third Wave*. Tilburg Netherlands: Tilburg University.

Harding, Harry (1998). The halting advance of pluralism, *Journal of Democracy* 9: 11–17.

Harris, Bruce, and Caroline M. Robb (1998). Social impacts of the crisis on households and communities: Preliminary findings in Indonesia, *World Bank draft paper*.

Harrison, Lawrence (1992). *Who Prospers? How Cultural Values Shape Economic and Political Success*. New York: Basic Books.

Hefner, Robert (1998). *Market Cultures: Society and Morality in the New Asian Capitalism*. Boulder, CO: Westview Press.

Hellevik, Ottar (1993). Post-materialism as a dimension of cultural change, *International Journal of Public Opinion Research* 5: 211–33.

Heritage Foundation (2001). *Index of Economic Freedom*. Washington, DC: Heritage Foundation.

Herman, Hubert J. M. and Harry J. Kempen (1998). Moving cultures: The perilous problems of cultural dichotomies in a globalizing society, *American Psychologist* 53: 1111–20.

Hickey, Gerald Cannon (1964). *Village in Vietnam*. Cambridge, MA: Yale University Press.

Hiller, Darby L. (2001). The Honeymoon Is Over: Crystalization of Public Opinion in Central and East European Countries, Presented at the annual meeting of the Midwest Political Science Association, Chicago, April 19–22.

Hobsbawm, E. J. (1962). *The Age of Revolution, 1789–1848*. New York: New American Library.

Hofheinz, R. and K. Calder (1982). *The East-Asian Edge*. New York: Basic Books.

Hofstede, Geert (1991). *Cultures and Organizations: Software of the Mind*. London: McGraw-Hill.

Hofstede, Geert (2001). *Culture's Consequences: Comparing Values, Behaviors, Institutions, and Organization Across Nations*, 2nd ed. (1st edition was published in 1980). Thousand Oaks, CA: Sage

—— and Michael Harris Bond (1988). The Confucius connection: From cultural roots to economic growth, *Organizational Dynamics* 16(4): 4–21.

Howard, Marc Morjé (2003). *The Weakness of Civil Society in Post-Communist Europe*. New York: Cambridge University Press.

Human Studies Journal (2001). *Special Issue: Challenging Japan*, No. 27. Dentsu Institute for Human Studies (DIHS) (in Japanese).

Huntington, Samuel (1991). *The Third Wave: Democratization in the Late Twentieth Century*. Norman, OK: University of Oklahoma Press.

—— (1996). *The Clash of Civilizations and the Remaking of World Order*. New York: Simon & Schuster.

—— and Joan Nelson (1976). *No Easy Choice: Political Participation in Developing Countries*. Cambridge: Harvard University Press.

Ike, N. (1973). Economic growth and intergenerational change in Japan, *American Political Science Review* 67(4): 1194–1203.

Ikeda, Ken'ichi, and Masaru Kohno (forthcoming). Japanese attitudes and values toward democracy, in F. Hu, H. Kuan, and A. Nathan (eds.), *East Asia Barometer: Comparative Survey of Democratization and Value Changes, vol. 1. Democratization and Value Change in East Asia Project*.

Inglehart, Ronald (1977). *The Silent Revolution: Changing Values and Political Styles Among Western Publics*. Princeton, NJ: Princeton University Press.

—— (1987). Value change in industrial societies, *American Political Science Review* 81: 1289–1303.

—— (1990). *Culture Shift in Advanced Industrial Society*. Princeton, NJ: Princeton University Press.

—— (1997). *Modernization and Postmodernization*. Princeton, NJ: Princeton University Press.

—— (1999). Postmodernization erodes respect for authority, but increases support for democracy, in P. Norris (ed.), *Critical Citizens*. Oxford: Oxford University Press.

—— (2000). Culture and democracy, in L. Harrison and S. Huntington (eds.), *Culture Matters*. New York: Basic Books.

—— (ed.) (2003). *Human Values and Social Change: Findings from the World Value Surveys*. Brill.

—— and W. Baker (2000). Modernization, cultural change, and the persistence of traditional values, *American Sociological Review* 65: 19–51.

Inglehart, Ronald and Pippa Norris (2003). *Rising Tide: Gender Equality and Cultural Change Around the World*. Cambridge, UK: Cambridge University Press.

—— —— (2004). *Sacred and Secular: Religion and Politics Worldwide*. Cambridge, UK: Cambridge University Press.

—— and Christian Welzel (2003). Political culture and democracy: Analyzing the cross-level linkages, *Comparative Politics* 36: 61–79.

—— —— (2005). *Modernization, Cultural Change and Democracy: The Human Development Sequence*. New York: Cambridge University Press.

Inglehart, Ronald, et al. (2004). *Human Values and Beliefs : A Cross-Cultural Sourcebook*. Siglo XXI Editores.

Inkeles, Alex (1966). The modernization of man, in M. Weiner (ed.), *Modernization*. New York: Basic Books.

—— (2000). Measuring social capital and its consequences. *Policy Sciences* 33: 245–268.

—— and David Smith (1974). *Becoming Modern: Individual Change in Six Developing Nations*. Cambridge MA: Harvard University Press.

Inoguchi, Takashi (2000). Can the Asian Values Be the Basis of Democratic Governance in the Asia-Pacific Region? Paper presented at the conference on *Changing Values and Challenges of Democratic Governance in Asia*, Seoul National University, Seoul, Korea.

—— (2002). Broadening the basis of social capital in Japan, in R. Putnam (ed.), *Democracies in Flux*. Oxford: Oxford University Press.

Inoguchi, Takashi, et al. (2005). *Values and Life Styles in Urban Asia: A Cross-Cultural Analysis and Sourcebook Based on the Asia Barometer Survey of 2003*. Tokyo: Institute of Oriental Culture, University of Tokyo.

Iqubal and Jong-il You, eds. (2001). *Democracy, Market Economics, and Development: an Asian Perspective*. Washington, DC: World Bank.

Ito, Takatoshi, and Anne O. Krueger (1995). *Growth Theories in Light of the Asian Economic Experience*. Chicago, IL: University of Chicago Press.

Jennings, M. Kent, and Richard Niemi (1974). *The Political Character of Adolescence: The Influence of Families and Schools*. Princeton, NJ: Princeton University Press.

—— —— (1981). *Generations and Politics*. Princeton, NJ: Princeton University Press.

Jochim, Christian (1992). Confucius and capitalism: Views of Confucianism in works on Confucianism and economic development, *Journal of Chinese Religions* 20: 135–69.

Johnson, Chalmers (1982). *MITI and the Japanese Miracle: The Growth of Industrial Policy, 1925–1975*. Stanford, CA: Stanford University Press.

Joppke, Christian (1994). Revisionism, dissidence, nationalism: Opposition in Leninist regimes. *British Journal of Sociology* 45: 543–61.

Kaminsky, Graciela L. and Carmen M. Reinhart (1998). Financial crisis in Asia and Latin America: Then & now, *The American Economic Review* 88(2): 44–8.

Kadir, Suzaina (2004). Singapore: Engagement and autonomy within the political status quo. In Muthiah Alagappa, ed. *Civil Society and Political Change in Asia*. Palo Alto: CA: Stanford University Press.

Kang, David (2002). *Crony Capitalism: Corruption and Development in South Korea and the Philippines*. Cambridge: Cambridge University Press.

Kerkvliet, Benedict J. T. (2001). An approach for analysing state-society relations in Vietnam, *Sojourn* 16: 238–78.

Khanna, Tarun, and Krishna Palepu (2000). The future of business groups in emerging markets: Long-run evidence from Chile, *Academy of Management Journal* 43(3): 268–85.

Kim A. M. (2004). A market without the 'Right' Property Rights: Ho Chi Minh City, Vietnam's newly emerged private real estate market, Paper read at the *International Policy Conference on Transition Economies*, 31 May–1 June 2004, Hanoi.

Kim, Choong Nam (1978). *Political Socialization in a Dependent System: A Rational Choice Perspective, The Case of Korea*. Ph.D. thesis. Minneapolis, MN: University of Minnesota.

Kim, Dae Jung (1994). Is culture destiny? The myth of Asia's anti-democratic values, *Foreign Affairs* (Nov./Dec.).

—— (1996). *Mass Participatory Democracy: Korea's Road to World Economic Power*. Washington, DC: University Press of America.

Kim, Dae Jung (1999). *Djnomics: A New Foundation for the Korean Economy*. Seoul: The Republic of Korea Ministry of Finance and Economy.

Kim, Dae Jung (2001). Democracy and the market economy: Two wheels of a cart. In Farrukh Iqubal and Jong-Il You, eds., *Democracy, Market Economics* and Development: An Asian Perspective. Washington, DC: World Bank.

Kim, Sunhyuk (2000). *The Politics of Democratization in Korea: The Role of Civil Society*. Pittsburgh: University of Pittsburgh Press.

—— and Doh Chull Shin (2004). *Economic Crisis and Dual Transition in Korea*. Seoul: Seoul National University Press.

Kim, Yung-Myung (1997). Asian-style democracy: A critique from East Asia, *Asian Survey* 37.

Klingemann, Hans-Dieter (1999). Mapping political support in the 1990s: A global analysis, in P. Norris (ed.), *Critical Citizens*. New York: Oxford University Press.

—— (2004). Support of democracy and confidence in government: On the ability of citizens to make distinctions. Paper presented at the conference on *Citizens, Democracy and Markets around the Pacific Rim*, March 19–20, East-West Center, Honolulu, Hawai.

Koh, Gillian, and Ooi Giok Ling (ed.) (2000). *State-Society Relations in Singapore*. Oxford: Oxford University Press.

—— —— (2004). The relationship between state and civil society in Singapore: Clarifying concepts, assessing the ground, in L. Guan (ed.), *Civil Society in Southeast Asia*. Singapore: Institute of Southeast Asian Studies.

Koh, Tommy TB. (1995). *The United States and East Asia: Conflict and Cooperation*. Singapore: Institute of Policy Studies, Times Academic Press.

Konrad, Gyorgy and Ivan Szelenyi (1991). Intellectuals and domination in post-communist societies. In Pierre Bourdieu and James S. Coleman, eds., *Social Theory for a Changing Society*. Boulder, CO: Westview Press.

Krugman, Paul (1998). Asia: What went wrong?, http://MIT.hedu/krugman/www/DISINTERI/

Kwon, Hyok Yong (2004). Economic reform and democratization: Evidence from Latin America and post-socialist countries, *British Journal of Political Science* 34(2): 357–68.

La Porta, Rafael, Florencio Lopez-de Silanes, Andrei Shleifer, and Robert Visny (1998). The quality of government, *Journal of Law, Economics and Organization* 15: 222–79.

Lau, Siu-kai, and Shin-chi Kuan (1988). *The Ethos of the Hong Kong Chinese*. Hong Kong: The Chinese University Press.

Laurence, Henny (1999). Financial system reform and the currency crisis in East Asia, *Asian Survey* 39(1): 348–73.

Lee, Chung H. (2002). *Financial Liberalization and the Economic Crisis in Asia*. London: Routledge.

Lee, Felicia R. (2004). Faith can enrich more than the soul: Research around the world links religion to economic development, *New York Times* (January 31).

Lee, Yew Kuan (1994). Culture is destiny, an interview with Fareed Zakaria, *Foreign Affairs* 73(2): 109–126.

Leftwich, Adrian (1995). Bringing politics back in: Toward a model of the developmental state, *Journal of Development Studies* 31(3): 400–27.
Lerner, Daniel (1958). *The Passing of Traditional Society: Modernization in the Middle East*. New York: Simon & Schuster.
Lessnoff, Michael H. (1994). *The Spirit of Capitalism and the Protestant Ethic: An Enquiry into the Weber Thesis*. Aldershot, UK: Edward Elgar.
Levy, Jr. Marion J. (1992). Confucianism and modernization, *Society* 29: 15–18.
Li, L. (2004). Political trust in rural China. *Modern China* 30(2): 228–58.
Lim, Linda (1998). Whose model failed? Implications of the Asian economic crisis *Washington Quarterly* 21(3): 25–36.
Lindblom, Charles (1977). *Politics and Markets: The World's Political Economic Systems*. New York: Basic Books.
—— (1988). *Democracy and Market System*. New York: Oxford University Press.
Lingle, Christopher (1998). *The Rise and Decline of the Asian Century: False Starts on the Path to the Global Millennium*. Seattle, WA: University of Washington Press.
Linz, Juan, and A. Stepan (eds.) (1996). *Problems of Democratic Transition and Consolidation: Southern Europe, South America, and Post-Communist Europe*. Baltimore, MD: Johns Hopkins University Press.
Lipset, Seymour M. (1959*a*). Democracy and working-class authoritarianism, *American Sociological Review* 24: 482–501.
—— (1959*b*). Some social requisites of democracy: Economic development and political legitimacy, *American Political Science Review* 53: 69–105.
—— (1960). *Political Man*. New York: Doubleday.
—— (1994). The social requisites of democracy revisited, *American Sociological Review* 59: 1–22.
—— (1996). *American Exceptionalism: A Double-Edged Sword*. New York: W.W. Norton.
Lockart, Greg (1997). Mass mobilization in contemporary Vietnam, *Asian Studies Review* 21: pgno.
Lynch, D. (1999). *After the Propaganda State: Media,Politics, and "Thought Work" in Reformed China*. Stanford, CA: Stanford University Press.
Mai Ngoc Cuong (2001). *Kinh te thi truong dinh huong xa hoi chu nghia o Viet Nam* (*Market Economy with Socialist Orientations in Vietnam*). Hanoi: Political Publishing.
Mannheim, Karl (1952). The problem of generations, in P. Kecskemeti (ed.), *Essays on the Sociology of Knowledge*. London: Routledge and Kegan Paul.
Maravall, Jose Maria (1997). *Regimes, Politics and Markets: Democratization and Economic Change in Southern and Eastern Europe*. Oxford: Oxford University Press.
MacFaquhar, Roderick (1980). The post-Confucian challenge, *The Economist* 9: 67–72.
Markus, Hazel R. and Shinobu Kitayama (1991). Culture and the self: Implications for cognition, emotion, and motivation, *Psychological Review* 98: 224–53.
Markus, H. R., S. Kitayama, and R. J. Heiman (1996). Culture and basic psychological principles, in E. T. Higgins and A. W. Kruglanski (eds.), *Social Psychology: Handbook of Basic Principles*. New York: Guilford.

Mason, David, et al. (2000). *Marketing Democracy: Changing Opinion about Inequality and Political in East Central Europe*. Lantham, MD: Rowman & Littlefield.

Matsumoto, David (1999). Culture and self: An empirical assessment of Markus and Kitayama's theory of independent and interdependent self-construals, and some speculations about new directions, *Asian Journal of Social Psychology* 2: 289–310.

Maxfield, Sylvia (1997). *Gatekeepers of Growth: The International Political Economy of Central Banking in Developing Countries*. Princeton, NJ: Princeton University Press.

McClosky, Herbert, and John Zaller (1984). *The American Ethos: Public Attitudes Toward Capitalism and Democracy*. Cambridge: Harvard University Press.

McDonough, Peter, Doh Shull Shin, and José Álvaro Moisés (1998). Democratization and participation: Comparing Spain, Brazil, and Korea, *Journal of Politics* 60: 919–53.

McIntosh, Mary E., Martha Abele Mac Iver, Daniel G. Abele, and Diana Smeltz (1994). Public meets market democracy in Central and East Europe, 1991–1993, *Slavic Review* 53(2): 483–512.

McNeill, William (1990). *The Rise of the West: A History of the Human Community*. Chicago, IL: University of Chicago Press.

Miles, M., E. Feulner, M. O'Grady (eds.) (2005). *2005 Index of Economic Freedom*. Washington, DC: Heritage Foundation.

Milgram, Stanley (1974). *Obedience to Authority: An Experimental View*. New York: Harper & Row.

Miller, Arthur (1974). Political issues and trust in government, *American Political Science Review* 68: 951–72, 989–1001.

—— E. Goldenberg, and Lutz Erbring (1979). Type-set politics: Impact of newspapers on public confidence, *American Political Science Review* 73(1): 67–84.

Mittelman, James H. (2000). *The Globalization Syndrome: Transformation and Resistance*. Princeton, NJ: Princeton University Press.

Moore, Barrington Jr. (1966). *Social Origins of Democracy and Dictatorship: Lord a And Peasant in the Making of the Modern World.* Boston: Beacon Press.

Morishima, Michio (1982). *Why Has Japan "Succeeded"? Western Technology and the Japanese Ethos*. Cambridge: Cambridge University Press.

Muller, Edward, and Thomas Jukam (1977). On the meaning of political support, *American Political Science Review*, 71: 1561–95.

Nathan, Andrew (2003*a*). Patterns of traditionalism in East Asia. Paper presented at the conference on *How East Asians View Democracy*, Taipei, December.

—— and Tianjin Shi (1993). Cultural requisites for democracy in China, *Daedalus* 122: 95–124.

Nathan, John (2004). *Japan Unbound: A Volatile Nation's Quest for Pride and Purpose*. New York: Houghton Mifflin.

National Education Development Center (2003). *Green Book of Chinese Education*. Beijing: People's Education Press.

Neher, C. and R. Marlay (1995). *Democracy and Development in Southeast Asia: The Winds of Change*. Boulder, CO: Westview.

Nelson, Joan (1994). How market reforms and democratic consolidation affect each other, in J. Nelson, et al. (ed.), *Intricate Link: Democratization and Market Reforms in Latin America and Eastern Europe*. New Brunswick, NJ: Transaction Publishers.

Nevitte, Neil (1996). *The Decline of Deference: Canadian Value Change in Cross-national Perspective*. Orchard Park, NY: Broadview Press.

—— and Meba Kanji (2003). Authority orientations and political support: A cross-national analysis of satisfaction with governments and democracy, in R. Inglehart (ed.), *Human Values and Social Change: Findings from the Value Surveys*. Leiden: Brill.

Newton, Kenneth (1999). Social and political trust in established democracies, in P. Norris (ed.), *Critical Citizens*. Oxford: Oxford University Press.

—— (2001). Trust, social capital, civil society, and democracy, *International Political Science Review* 22: 201–14.

Nolan, Patrick, and Gerhard Lenski (1999). *Human Societies: An Introduction to Macrosociology*, 8th ed. New York: McGraw-Hill.

Nguyen, Huu Minh, and Nguyen Xuan Mai (2005). Do thi hoa va ngheo kho do thi o Viet Nam: Mot so dac diem co ban (Urbanization and Poverty in Vietnam: Basic Charateristics), in N. Nghia, M. Duong, N. Vinh (eds.), *Do thi hoa va van de giam ngheo o Thanh pho Ho Chi Minh: Ly luan va thuc tien* (*Urbanization and Problem of Poverty Reduction in Ho Chi Minh City: Theory and Practice*). Hanoi: Publishing House of Social Sciences.

Nguyen, Phu Trong (1994). Kinh te thi truong dinh huong xa hoi chu nghia o Viet Nam: Quan diem va giai phap phat trien, in *Chu nghia Xa hoi va Kinh te thi truong: Kinh nghiem cua Trung Quoc, Kinh nghiem cua Viet Nam. Ha Noi: NXB Chinh tri Quoc gia* (*Market Economy with Socialist Orientation in Vietnam: Positions and Measures for Development*, in *Socialism and Market Economy: Chinese and Vietnamese Experience*). Hanoi: National Political Publishing House .

Nguyen, Thu Sa, and Nguyen Thi Mai Huong (2001). Ve kha nang cai thien muc song cua tang lop co thu nhap thap (Possibility of improving living standard for people with low income), in N. Nghia, M. Dong, N. Vinh (eds.), *Van de giam ngheo trong qua trinh do thi hoa o thanh pho Ho Chi Minh* (*Problem of poverty reduction in the process of urbanization*). Hanoi: Publishing House of Social Sciences.

Norris, P. (ed.) (1999*a*). *Critical Citizens: Global Support for Democratic Government*. New York: Oxford University Press.

—— (1999*b*). Introduction: The growth of critical citizens?, in P. Norris (ed.), *Critical Citizens*. Oxford: Oxford University Press.

—— (2002). *The Democratic Phoenix*. New York: Cambridge University Press.

—— and Ronald Inglehart (2003). Islamic culture and democracy: Testing the "Clash of civilizations" thesis, in R. Inglehart (ed.) *Human Values and Social Change: Findings from the Value Surveys*. Leiden: Brill.

Ochi, Makoto (2003). International comparison: Japanese financial resource (in Japanese). [online] http://www.boj.or.jp/wakaru/keiki/whikaku.htm (originally from *Nichigin Quarterly*, Spring).

O'Donnell, Guillermo (1994). Delegative democracy, *Journal of Democracy* 5: 55–69.

O'Dwyer, S. (2003). Democracy and Confucian values, *Philosophy East and West* 53(1): 39–63.

Olson, Mancur. (2000). *Power and Prosperity: Outgrowing Communist and Capitalist Dictatorships*. New York: Basic Books.

Oyserman, Daphna, Heather M. Coon, and Markus Kemmelmeier (2002). Rethinking individualism and collectivism: Evaluation of theoretical assumptions and meta-analyses, *Psychological Bulletin* 128: 3–72.

Pagano, Michael S. (2002). Crises, cronyism, and credit, *Financial Review* 37(2): 227–56.

Page, Benjamin, and Robert Shapiro (1992). *The Rational Public. Fifty Years of Trends in Americans' Policy Preferences.* Chicago, IL: Chicago University Press.

Park, Chong-Min, and Doh Chull Shin (2004). Do Asian Values Deter Popular Support for Democracy? The Case of South Korea. Paper presented to 2004 annual meeting of Association for Asian Studies, San Diego, CA.

Pei, M. (2002). China's governance crisis, *Foreign Affairs* 81(5): 96–119.

Pew Center (2002). *What the World Thinks in 2002: The Pew Global Attitudes Project.* Washington, DC: Pew Center for People and the Press.

—— (2003). *Views of a Changing World 2003: War with Iraq Further Divides Global Publics.* Washington, DC: Pew Center for People and the Press.

Pham Minh Hac (2001). *Nghien cuu Con nguoi va Nguon Nhan luc di vao Cong nghiep hoa, Hien dai hoa* (*Human Studies and Human Resource in the Process of Industrialization and Modernization*). Hanoi: Political Publishing House.

—— and Pham Thanh Nghi (2002). Values orientation in socio-economic transition from the centrally controlled economy to the market economy in Vietnam, *Nghien cuu Con nguoi* (*Human Studies*) 1(1): 47–53.

—— —— (2003). Citizen's attitudes toward democracy and market through World Values Survey 2001, *Nghien cuu Con nguoi* (*Human Studies*) 1(4): 38–45.

Pharr, Susan (2000). Officials' misconduct and public distrust: Japan and the trilateral democracies, in S. Pharr and R. Putnam (eds.), *Disaffected Democracies: What's Troubling the Trilateral Countries?* Princeton, NJ: Princeton University Press.

—— and Robert Putnam (2000). *Disaffected Democracies: What's Troubling the Trilateral Countries?* Princeton, NJ: Princeton University Press.

—— and Russell Dalton (2000). Trouble in the advanced democracies? A quarter century of declining confidence, *Journal of Democracy* 11(2): 5–25.

Porter, Gareth (1993). *The Politics of Bureaucratic Socialism.* Ithaca, NY: Cornell University Press.

Putnam, Robert (1993). *Making Democracy Work.* Princeton, NJ: Princeton University Press.

—— (2000). *Bowing Alone: The Collapse and Revival of American Community.* New York: Simon & Schuster.

—— (ed.) (2002). *Democracies in Flux: The Evolution of Social Capital in Contemporary Society.* Oxford: Oxford University Press.

Przeworski, Adam (1991). *Democracy and the Market: Political and Economic Reform in Eastern Europe and Latin America.* New York: Cambridge University Press.

—— (1993). The neoliberal fallacy, in L. Diamond and M. Plattner (eds.), *Capitalism, Socialism, and Democracy Revisited.* Baltimore, MD: Johns Hopkins University Press.

Przeworski, Adam, et al. (2000). *Democracy and Development: Political Institutions and Well-Being in the World 1950–1990.* New York: Cambridge University Press.

Pye, Lucian (1985). *Asian Power and Politics*. Cambridge: Harvard University Press.

—— (1997). Political science and the crisis of authoritarianism, *American Political Science Review* 84: 3–20.

—— (1999). Civility, social capital and civil society: Three powerful concepts for explaining Asia, *Journal of Interdisciplinary History* 29: 763–82.

—— and S. Verba (eds.) (1965). *Political Culture and Political Development*. Princeton, NJ: Princeton University Press.

Raudenbush, Stephen W. and Anthony S. Bryk (2001). *Hierarchical Linear Models: Applications and Data Analysis Methods* (Advanced Quantitative Techniques in the Social Sciences). Thousand Oaks, CA: Sage Publications.

Ravich, Samantha F. (2000). *Marketization and Democracy: East Asian Experiences*. New York: Cambridge University Press.

Remmer, Karen L. (1991). The political impact of economic crisis in Latin America in the 1980s, *American Political Science Review* 85(3): 777–800.

Reisinger, William (1995). The renaissance of a rubric: Political culture as concept and theory, *International Journal of Public Opinion Research* 7: 328–352.

Richardson, Bradley (1974). *The Political Culture of Japan*. Berkeley: University of California Press.

Richardson, Bradley (1978). *The Political Culture of Japan*. Berkeley, CA: University of California Press.

Rivera-Batiz, Francisco L. (2002). Democracy, governance, and economic growth: Theory and evidence, *Review of Development Economics* 6: 225–247.

Robb, Caroline M. (1998). Social aspects of the East Asian financial crisis: Perceptions of poor communities. Paper presented at a World Bank seminar on the implications of the East Asian crisis for poverty elimination.

Roberts, Kenneth M. (1995). Neoliberalism and the transformation of populism in Latin America: The Peruvian case, *World Politics* 47(2): 82–116.

Robinson, Michael (1976). Public affairs television and the growth of political malaise: The case of "The Selling of the Pentagon", *American Political Science Review* 70(2): 409–32.

Rohrschneider, Robert (1999). *Learning Democracy: Democratic and Economic Values in Unified Germany*. Oxford: Oxford University Press.

Rose, Richard (1995). Freedom as a fundamental value, *International Social Science Journal* 145: 457–71.

—— (1998). *Trends in Democracies and Markets: New Democracies Barometer 1991–1998*, Studies in Public Policy 308. Center for the Study of Public Policy, University of Strathclyde: Glasgow, Scotland.

—— (2001). A divergent Europe, *Journal of Democracy* 12(1): 93–106.

—— Christian Haerpfer, and William Mishler (1998). *Democracy and Its Alternatives: Understanding Post-communist Societies*. Baltimore, MD: Johns Hopkins University Press.

Rozman, G. (ed.) (1991). *The East Asian Region: Confucian Heritage and Its Modern Adaptation*. Princeton, NJ: Princeton University Press.

Rueschemeyer, Dietrich, Evelyn Huber Stephens, and John D. Stephens (1992). *Capitalist Development and Democracy*. Chicago, IL: University of Chicago Press.

—— M. Rueschemeyer, and B. Wittrock (eds.) (1998). *Participation and Democracy, East And West: Comparisons and Interpretations*. New York: ME Sharpe.

Ryan, Richard M. and Edward L. Deci (2000). Self-determination theory and the facilitation of intrinsic motivation, social development, and well-being, *American Psychologist* 55: 68–78.

Saich, Tony (2000). Negotiating the state: The development of social organizations in China, *China Quarterly* 161: 124–41.

Sandholtz, Wayne, and Mark Gray (2003). International integration and national corruption, *International Organization* 57(4): 761–800.

Scalapino, Robert (1989). *The Politics of Development: Perspectives on Twentieth Century Asia*. Cambridge: Harvard University Press.

Schumpeter, Joseph (1942). *Capitalism, Socialism and Democracy*. New York: Harper & Row.

Schwartz, Frank (2003). Civil society in Japan reconsidered, *Japanese Journal of Political Science* 3: 195–215.

Schwartz, Shalom H. (2003). Mapping and interpreting cultural differences around the world, in H. Vinken, J. Soeters, and P. Ester (eds.), *Comparing Cultures, Dimensions of Culture in a Comparative Perspective*. Leiden, Netherlands: Brill.

Seligson, Mitchell (2002). The renaissance of political culture or the renaissance of the ecological fallacy, *Comparative Politics* 34(April): 273–92.

Sen, Amartya (1999). *Development as Freedom*. New York: Knopf.

—— (2001). Culture and economic development: Asian values and economic growth, www.unesco.org/culture/world report/html-eng/wcrb12.shtml

Shakai-keizai Kokumin-kaigi (Okano, Kahoru) (ed.) (1988). *Value and Behavioral Changes in Post-war Generations: Political Implications of Post-industrial Values in Japan*. Japan: NIRA (National Institute for Research Advancement).

Shi, Tianjian (2000*a*). Cultural values and democracy in Mainland China, *China Quarterly* 62: 540–59.

—— (2000*b*). Village committee elections in China, *World Politics* 51: 385–412.

—— (2001). Cultural values and political trust: A comparison of Mainland China and Taiwan, *Comparative Politics* 33(4): 401–20.

—— (2003). Does it matter or not? That is the question. Cultural impacts on the political process. Paper presented at the conference on *How East Asians View Democracy*. Taipei, December.

Shin, Doh Chull (1999). *Mass Politics and Culture in Democratizing Korea*. Cambridge: Cambridge University Press.

—— (2000*a*). The Dynamics of Democratization in Korea: The Korea Democracy Barometer. Honolulu, HI: East-West Center.

—— (2000*b*). The Economic Crisis and Popular Support for Democracy in Korea. Honolulu, HI: East-West Center.

—— (2001). Democratic consolidation in Korea: A trend analysis of public opinion surveys, 1997–2001, *Japanese Journal of Political Science* 2: 177–209.

—— (2003). The democratization of mass political orientations in South Korea. *International Journal of Public Opinion Research* 15(3): 265–84.

—— and Jason Wells (2005). Is democracy the only game in town? *Journal of Democracy* 16: 89–101.

—— Myung Chey, and Kwang-Woong Kim (1989). Cultural origins of public support for democracy in Korea, *Comparative Political Studies* 22(2): 217–38.

—— and Chong-min Park, and Jiho Jang (2005). Assessing the shifting qualities of democratic citizenship: The case of South Korea, *Democratization* 12: 202–22.

Sidel, Mark (1995). The emergence of a nonprofit sector and philanthropy in the Socialist Republic of Vietnam, in T. Yamamoto (ed.), *Integrative Report. Emerging Civil Society in the Asia Pacific Community*. Institute of Southeast Asian Studies, Singapore, and Japan Center for International Exchange, Japan.

Song, Y.-b. (2002). Crisis of cultural identity in East Asia: On the meaning of Confucian ethics in the age of globalization. Paper presented at the University of Michigan Center for Chinese Studies Lecture Series, Ann Arbor, MI.

Stallings, Barbara (1995). *Global Change, Regional Response: The New International Context of Development*. New York: Cambridge University Press.

Steinberg, David (1997). Civil society and human rights in Korea: On contemporary and classical orthodoxy and ideology, *Korea Journal* 37: 144–65.

Stiglitz, Joseph (1999). Wither Reform? Ten Years of the Transition, Presented at the World Bank Annual Conference on Development Economics Washington DC, April 28–30.

—— and S. Yusuf (eds.) (2001). *Rethinking the East Asian Miracle*. New York: Oxford University Press.

Stigliz, Joseph E. (2002). *Globalization and Its Discontents*. New York: W. W. Norton.

Stokes, Susan (1996). Economic reform and public opinion in Peru, *Comparative Political Studies* 29: 544–665.

Stokes, S. (ed.) (2001). *Public Support for Market Reforms in New Democracies*. New York: Cambridge University Press.

Stolle, Dietlind (2003). The sources of social capital, in M. Hooghe and D. Stolle (eds.), *Generating Social Capital: Civil Society and Institutions in Comparative Perspective*. New York: Palgrave Macmillan.

Stolle, Dietlind and Thomas Rochon (1998). Are all associations alike? Member diversity, associational type and the creation of social capital, *American Behavioral Scientist* 42(1): 47–65.

Suginoo, Takeshi (2001). Low risk challenging Japan (in Japanese), *Human Studies* 27: 35–7.

Sundhaussen, Ulf (1988). Indonesia: Past and present encounters with democracy, in L. Diamond, J. Linz, and S. M. Lipset (eds.), *Democracy in Developing Countries: Asia*. Boulder, CO: Lynne Rienner.

Tai, Hung-Chao (ed.) (1989). *Confucianism and Economic Development: An Oriental Alternative*. Washington, DC: Washington Institute Press.

Takano, Yohtaro, and Eiko Osaka (1999). An unsupported common view: Comparing Japan and U.S. on individualism/collectivism, *Asian Journal of Social Psychology* 2: 311–42.

Takao, Yasuo (2001). The rise of the third sector in Japan, *Asian Survey* 41: 290–309.

Tanaka, Ajii (2001). *Does Social Capital Generate System Support in Japan?* Paper presented at the annual meeting of the American Political Science Association, San Francisco.

Tang, Wengfang (2005). *Public Opinion and Political Change in China*. Stanford, CA: Stanford University Press.

Taylor, Charles, and David Jodice (1983). *World Handbook of Political and Social Indicators III*. New Haven: Yale University Press.

Taylor, Lance (1997). Editorial: The revival of the liberal creed-the IMF and the World Bank in a globalized economy, *World Development* 25(2): 145–52.

Terry, Edith (2002). *How Asia Got Rich*. Armonk, NY: ME Sharpe.

Thayer, Carlyle (1995). Mono-organizational Socialism, in B. Kerkvleit and D. Porter (eds.), *Vietnam's Rural Transformation*. Boulder, CO: Westview Press.

Thurston, Anne (1998). *Muddling Toward Democracy: Political Change in Grassroots China*. Washington, DC: US Institute of Peace.

Tocqueville, Alexis de. (1945). *Democracy in America* New York: Knopf.

Triandis, Harry C. (1995). *Individualism and Collectivism*. Boulder, CO: Westview Press.

Tu, Wei-ming (ed.) (1991). *The Triadic Chord: Confucian Ethics, Industrial East Asia and Max Weber*. Singapore: Institute of East Asian Philosophies.

—— (2000*a*). Implications of the rise of "Confucian" East Asia. *Daedalus* 129(1): 195–218.

—— (2000*b*). Multiple modernities: A preliminary inquiry into the implications of East Asian modernity, in L. E. Harrison and S. P. Huntington (eds.), *Culture Matters: How Values Shape Human Progress*. New York: Basic Books.

Turley, William, and M. Selden (eds.) (1992). *Reinventing Vietnamese Socialism: Doi Moi in Comparative Perspective*. Boulder, CO: Westview Press.

United Nations Development Programme (2004). *Human Development Report 2004*. New York: UNDP.

Vanhanen, Tatu (1990). *The Process of Democratization: A Comparative Study of 147 States, 1980-88*. New York: Crane, Russak.

Vanhanen, Tatu (1997). *Prospects of Democracy: A Study of 172 Countries*. New York: Routledge.

Verba, Sidney (1965). Germany, in L. Pye and S. Verba (ed.), *Political Culture and Political Development*. Princeton, NJ: Princeton University Press.

—— Norman Nie, and Jae-on Kim (1978). *Participation and Political Equality*. New York: Cambridge University Press.

Vishwanath, Arun (2003). Comparison online information effects: A cross-cultural comparison of online information and uncertainty avoidance, *Communication Research* 30: 579–98.

Vo Dai Luoc (2004). Vietnam's Economic Renovation Along Socialist-Oriented Market Economy. Paper read at the International Policy Conference on Transition Economies, 31 May–1 June 2004, Hanoi.

Vogel, Ezra (1991). *The Four Little Dragons*. Cambridge: Harvard University Press.

Wade, Richard (1990). *Governing the Market: Economic Theory and the Role of Government in East Asian Industrialization*. Princeton, NJ: Princeton University Press.

Wang, Z.-X. (2005*a*). Before the emergence of critical citizens: Economic development and political trust in China, *International Review of Sociology* 15 (1): 155–71.

—— (2005*b*). *Changing Social Values and Democratization in China and East Asia: The Self-Expression Phenomenon and Citizen Politics in Six Confucian Societies, 1981–2001*. Ann Arbor, MI: University of Michigan Press.

Warren, Mark (ed.) (1999). *Democracy and Trust*. New York: Cambridge University Press.

—— (2000). *Democracy and Association*. Princeton, NJ: Princeton University Press.

Weber, Maria (2002). *Reforming Economic Systems in Asia*. Cheltenham, UK: Edward Elgar.

Weber, Max [1904–5] (1976). *The Protestant Ethic and the Spirit of Capitalism*. Talcott Parsons (trans.). New York: Scribner's Press.

—— (1951). *Religion of China: Confucianism and Taoism*. New York: Free Press.

Wei, Shang-Jin (1999). Corruption in economic development: Beneficial grease, minor annoyance, or major obstacle? Working paper No.2048, the World Bank.

Weiner, M. (ed.) (1966). *Modernization*. New York: Basic Books.

Weiss, Linda (1999). State power and the Asian crisis, *New Political Economy* 4: 317–42.

Weller, Robert (2001). *Alternate Civilities: Democracy and Culture in China and Taiwan*. Boulder, CO: Westview Press.

Welzel, Christian (2002). *Fluchtpunkt Humanentwicklung: Über die Grundlagen der Demokratie und die Ursachen ihrer Ausbreitung* (Focal Point Human Development: On the Foundations of Democracy and the Causes of Its Expansion). Opladen, Germany: Westdeutscher Verlag.

—— Ronald Inglehart, and Hans-Dieter Klingemann (2003). The theory of human development: A cross-cultural analysis, *European Journal of Political Research* 42(2): 341–79.

—— —— and Franziska Deutsch (2005). Social capital, voluntary associations, and collective action: Which aspects of social capital have the greatest "civic" payoff?, *Journal of Civil Society* 1: 121–146.

Weyland, Kurt (1998). Swallowing the bitter pill: Sources of popular support for neoliberal reform in Latin America, *Comparative Political Studies* 31(5): 539–68.

White, Gordon, J. Howell, and Z. Shang (eds.) (1996). *In Search of Civil Society: Market Reform and Social Change in Contemporary China*. Oxford: Oxford University Press.

Whitehead, L. (ed.) (2002). *Emerging Market Democracies*. Baltimore, MD: Johns Hopkins University Press.

Widner, J. (ed.) (1994). *Economic Change and Political Liberalization in Sub-Saharan Africa*. Baltimore, MD: Johns Hopkins University Press.

Wildavsky, Aaron (1987). Choosing preferences by constructing institutions: Culture theory of preferences formation, *American Political Science Review* 81: 3–21.

Williamson, John (1993). Democracy and the "Washington Consensus," *World Development* 21(8): 1329–36.

—— (1994). *The Political Economy of Reform*. Washington, DC: Institute for International Economics.

Woo-Cumings, Meredith (2000). *Economic Crisis and Corporate Reform in East Asia*. New York: Council on Foreign Affairs.

World Bank (1992). *Governance and Development*. Washington, DC: World Bank.

World Bank, the (1993). *The East Asian Miracle: Economic Growth and Public Policy.* Oxford: Oxford University Press.

World Bank (2002). *World Development Report 2003.* New York: Oxford University Press.

—— (2004). *World Development Report 1978–2004 with Selected World Development Indicators 2004.* Washington, DC: World Bank.

Xu Huoyan (1999). Taiwan de xuanju yu shehui fenzhi jigou, in Y. Chu, et al. (eds.), *Liang'an jiceng zuanju yu zhengzhi shehui bianqian.* Taipei: Yuedan chuban gufen yousian gongsi.

Yamagishi, Toshio (1999). Collectivistic culture as a bundle of expectations of generalized reciprocity (in Japanese), *Organizational Science* 33: 24–34.

—— Karen Cook, and Motoki Watabe (1998). Uncertainty, trust, and commitment: Formation in the United States and Japan, *American Journal of Sociology* 104: 165–94.

Yamamoto, Koichi (2001). Is it possible to change Japanese risk orientation? (in Japanese), *Human Studies* 27: 21–6.

Yang, Kuo-shu (1988). Chinese personality and its change, in M. H. Bond (ed.), *The Psychology of the Chinese People.* Hong Kong: Oxford University Press.

Yongnian, Zheg (1994). Development and democracy: Are they compatible in China? *Political Science Quarterly* 109: 235–59.

Yutaka, Tsujinaka (2003). Japan's civil society organizations in comparative perspective, in F. Schwartz and S. Pharr (eds.), *The State of Civil Society in Japan.* New York: Cambridge University Press.

Zakaria, Fareed (1994). A conversation with Lee Kuan Yew, *Foreign Affairs* 73(2).

—— (2003). *The Future of Freedom: Illiberal Democracy at Home and Abroad.* New York: Norton.

Zha, J. (1995). *China Pop: How Soap Operas, Tabloids, and Bestsellers Are Transforming a Culture.* New York: New Press, distributed by W.W. Norton.

Zimmerman, William (2002). *The Russian People and Foreign Policy: Russian Elite and Mass Perspectives, 1993–2000.* Princeton, NJ: Princeton University Press.

Zweig, David (2002). *Democratic Values, Political Structures and Alternative Politics in Greater China.* Washington, DC: US Institute of Peace.

Index

Ingram Content Group UK Ltd.
Milton Keynes UK
UKHW020222100323
418355UK00004B/102

9 780199 297252